SAN DIEGO

An Introduction to the Region
FOURTH EDITION

Philip R. Pryde

A Historical Geography of the Natural Environments
and Human Development of San Diego County

PEARSON
Custom
Publishing

Sunbelt Publications
San Diego, California

San Diego: An Introduction to the Region (Fourth Edition)
Sunbelt Publications, Inc./Pearson Custom Publishing
Copyright © 2004 by Philip R. Pryde
Previously published by Kendall/Hunt Publishing Company
All rights reserved. Fourth edition 2004
First edition 1976

Printed in the United States of America

Sunbelt Publications, Inc.
P.O. Box 191126
San Diego, CA 92159-1126
(619) 258-4911, fax: (619) 258-4916
www.sunbeltbooks.com

08 07 06 05 04   5 4 3 2 1

Library of Congress Cataloging-in-Publications Data

San Diego: an introduction to the region / [edited by] Philip R. Pryde.— 4th ed.
    p. cm.
Includes bibliographical references and index.
ISBN 0-916251-68-3
1. San Diego County (Calif.)—History. 2. San Diego County (Calif.)—Geography. 3. San Diego County (Calif.)—Environmental conditions. 4. Natural history—California—San Diego County. I. Pryde, Philip R.
F868.S15S16 2005
979.4'98—dc22

                                        2004001988

Please visit our web site at *www.pearsoncustom.com*

PEARSON CUSTOM PUBLISHING
75 Arlington Street, Suite 300, Boston, MA 02116
A Pearson Education Company

SUNBELT PUBLICATIONS, INC.

Contents

Preface to the Fourth Edition

The arrival of a new century is always a momentous occasion, and certainly marks an opportune time to prepare a revised and updated edition of *San Diego: An Introduction to the Region*.

The mystique and lures of California have brought large numbers of new residents to the San Diego region over the last several decades. Not only have these recent arrivals found themselves in a new environment, but for many of them it represents an environment quite different in landscape and history from that with which they were previously familiar.

If they wished to acquaint themselves with their new environs, they could find numerous works available about the San Diego region. While these provide excellent advice on shops, attractions, tours, restaurants, trails, etc., there has been a lack of a convenient one-volume introduction to the history and geography of this dynamic and diverse region.

This book endeavors to fill that gap.

The goal of this volume is to give the reader a wide variety of descriptive and explanatory information concerning San Diego County's natural environment, history, economy, urbanization, and contemporary challenges, without being overly technical or requiring any prior knowledge of the topics being discussed. It is hoped that the book will be equally useful to both the many new arrivals to our region, as well as longer established San Diegans.

Since the preparation of the first edition of *San Diego: An Introduction to the Region* twenty-seven years ago, vast changes have taken place across the face of the county. It has been the recipient of well over a million new residents, five new cities, a light-rail trolley system, an almost entirely new face for downtown, and far too many new roads, businesses, homes, freeways, schools, and other amenities to enumerate. The 2000 census alone would have been adequate reason for this new Fourth Edition, but the rapid pace of change in the region makes it essential.

All of the chapters were originally written especially for this book, and all have been completely re-written and updated for the 4th edition. We welcome some new chapter authors to the project as part of the current update. John Weeks has prepared the new version of Chapter Five, Lowell Lindsay has done the same for Chapter Six, and Alan Rice is a new co-author for Chapter Eighteen. The editor has prepared the new text, and contributed some new photos, for several of the chapters.

The new edition continues the historical geography format of the previous editions, as well as their tradition of extensive cross-referencing, concise bibliographic lists, and inclusion of historical photos. With regard to the latter, we are pleased to include some mid-20th century photographs taken by the late Prof. Lauren Post. In addition, internet addresses have been included with the bibliographies, many new illustrations were added, and a new chapter was prepared on preserving San Diego's natural environment.

In addition to the chapter authors, the 4th edition has benefited from the assistance of a great many persons throughout the community. The editor would like to acknowledge and thank the following persons and institutions for their assistance in the preparation of the new edition. Appreciation is extended to Richard Carrico, Jerry Schad, the County Water Authority, SANDAG, the Unified Port District, the San Diego Historical Society, and the City and County of San Diego for making available various maps, photos, and diagrams used in this edition. A similar acknowledgement is extended to the various cartographic specialists within the Department of Geography at San Diego State University who assisted with previous editions, and whose maps appear in updated form in the 4th edition.

Others whose contributions to the Fourth Edition are gratefully acknowledged include Kathryn Bacon of the U.S. Forest Service, Jim Bowersox of the City of Poway, Steve Bouchard, Paul Hardwick, Michael Hix, John Hofmockel, Mark Polinsky, and Anne Steinberger at SANDAG, Richard Carrico at Mooney and Associates, Linda Fisk at the Museum of Man, Dale Frost and Melissa Mailander at the Unified Port District, Marcus Chiu, Karen Hennequin, Harry Johnson, Dave McKinsey, and Serge Rey in the Department of Geography at San Diego State University, Brian Kelley and Jimmy Smith at the Regional Water Quality Control Board, Barbara Kus of the U.S. Geological Survey, Tom Oberbauer at the County Department of Planning and Land Use, Jeff Stephenson at the County Water Authority, Phil Unitt at the San Diego Natural History Museum, and all the staff at the San Diego Historical Society's photographic archives. Additionally, appreciation is again extended to those who helped with the previous three editions and who are thanked individually therein. While the input of all these individuals has been of immeasurable help in preparing this work, the editor assumes responsibility for any lapses in accuracy that might be encountered.

The editorial and institutional help provided by Pearson Custom Publishing Company and its field editors, and by Sunbelt Publications, the book's distributor, are also most sincerely acknowledged.

Philip R. Pryde, San Diego, May 2003

Chapter One

Philip R. Pryde

Introduction
The Uniqueness of the Region

In the last twenty years about a million new residents have come to San Diego County. Because it is a large county, and because so many of its residents have lived here a relatively short while, many San Diegans would acknowledge only a passing familiarity with the area. This is unfortunate, for San Diego County possesses a richness of history and geography matched by few other areas in the country, and partly for this reason many observers perceive of the county as being a distinct and attractive region. The goal of this book is to provide in a single volume a concise introduction to the natural and manmade environments of the San Diego region, a

Philip R. Pryde is professor emeritus of environmental studies in the Department of Geography at San Diego State University.

basic reference work for the county resident, new or old, who would like to better understand this unique and historic corner of America.

The County in Overview

San Diego County is most easily and immediately identified as one of the major metropolitan areas of the United States. San Diego itself is now the seventh largest city in the country in population (totaling 1,223,000 in 2000), and the county ranks sixth in population among all United States counties. San Diego's importance as a metropolitan center is not widely recognized because it tends to be overshadowed by Los Angeles to the north, the nation's largest county in population. Few things annoy San Diegans more than the Easterner's mental image of the city as a suburb of Los Angeles ("like Burbank or Santa Monica," or "isn't it somewhere around Long Beach?"). Instead, natives here understand that if there were no Los Angeles, San Diego would be the largest city in the most populous state in the nation. In fact, San Diego County is larger in population than 21 of the 50 states. To some residents this is a desirable feature and to others not, depending on their views on regional growth. This controversial topic will be discussed in several of the chapters that follow.

San Diego County, with 4,261 square miles (an area larger than the states of Delaware and Rhode Island combined—see Figure 1.1), at first impresses itself upon the newcomer as a very large political entity. Yet, it used to be considerably larger than it is now. When California first became a state in 1850 and began carving out counties, San Diego was one of the twenty-seven counties that were formed immediately (February 18, 1850). At that time, there were no Riverside, Imperial, or San Bernardino counties; San Diego took in all these areas. Fledgling San Diego County stretched from the Mexican border to Death Valley, and included about 39,400 square miles (Figure 1.2). It may have been the largest county in the United States at that time. Slowly, it was reduced in size, losing what is now San Bernardino County in 1851, Riverside in 1893, and Imperial in 1907. Nor does it include any major off-shore islands; Los Coronados, the most visible, are south of the border in Mexico, and San Clemente, sixty miles due west, is actually part of Los Angeles County. Nevertheless, even at its present reduced size, it is still in the largest five percent of all United States counties in land area.

Equally distinctive, and of much greater practical importance, is San Diego's diversity of natural regions. In few other counties might residents have a choice, on a single March day, of surfing in the ocean, enjoying snow in the

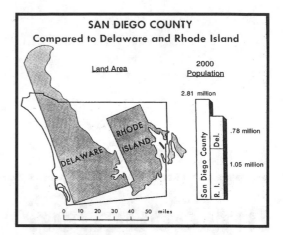

Figure 1.1. Relative size of San Diego County.

mountains, or studying spring wildflowers in the desert. This variety of environments is largely the effect of the Peninsular Ranges, those mountains we know by such names as Palomar, Volcan, Cuyamaca, and Laguna, which straddle the center of the county in a northwest to southeast direction. They divide the county into a number of natural zones (the exact number depends on the phenomenon being studied), and these zones will be looked at in more detail in the next two chapters.

Of lesser familiarity to most San Diegans is the complex nature of the county administratively. In most places the county government has jurisdiction over the whole of the county's area (except for incorporated cities), but in San Diego County a wide array of agencies own or otherwise control large portions of the land (Table 1.1).

The eighteen incorporated cities of the county take in about 16 percent of its land area; the other 84 percent is unincorporated rural or semi-urbanized land. Of this other 84 percent, much is administered by agencies other than the county government. For example, about 22 percent of the county is administered by agencies of the state of California, mainly because we are

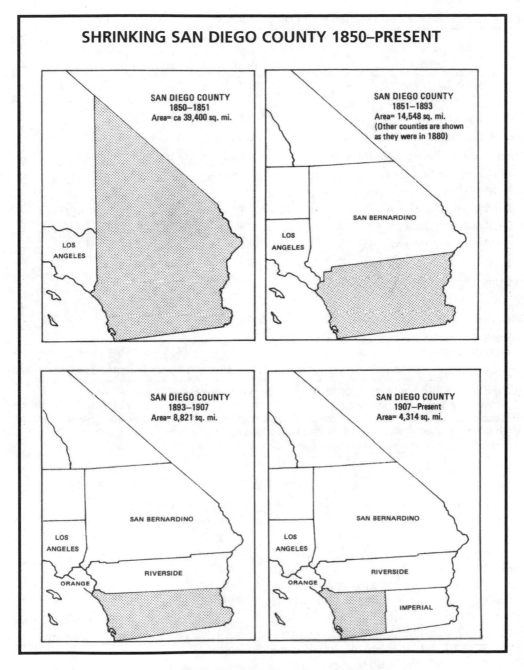

Figure 1.2. Relative size of San Diego County 1850–present.

TABLE 1.1. Who Owns and Manages San Diego County?

Agency	Land Administer (sq. miles)	Land Owned (sq. miles)	Population in Indicated Area (2000)	Percent of County Population
Cities: City of San Diego	342	146	1,223,400	43.5
Other 17 incorporated cities	346	[a]	1,147,514	40.8
County owned	46	46		
Special districts	122	122		
Roads (local, excluding CALTRANS)	116	116		
State owned: CA Dept of Parks and Recreation	857	857		
Other state owned land	112	112		
Federally owned: U.S. Forest Service	449	449		
Department of Defense	255	255	[b]	
Bureau of Land Management	277	277		
Other federal agencies	18	18		
Indian reservations	197	197	[c]	
Total of all unincorporated areas	3,572			
Privately owned land under county administration		1665	442,919	15.7
TOTAL COUNTY:	[d] 4,261	4,261	2,813,833	100.0

[a] Land owned by other cities included in the 146 sq. mi. figure above.
[b] Active duty personnel stationed anywhere in the county are included in the population figure for cities.
[c] Included in the population of the unincorporated portion of the county (see also Chapter 4).
[d] Equals total of cities and unincorporated land. Areas of land in all other local, state and federal ownership categories is included in either the "Cities" or "Unincorporated" entries.

fortunate enough to have the largest state park in the country (Anza-Borrego Desert State Park) within our borders (see Chapter 15).

Among federal agencies, the largest land-holder is Cleveland National Forest, which owns about 11 percent of the county. As is the case with the state parks, there is a great deal of privately owned land within the boundaries of the national forest. The Department of Defense, the Bureau of Land Management, and the various Indian reservations each take in from 4 to 7 percent of the county's area. While this diver-sity of ownership provides a variety of life styles, land uses, and recreation potentials, it also makes integrated planning for the future of the county more complex.

San Diego County as a Region

A region is defined as a portion of the earth's surface having certain cohesive, unifying, or homo-geneous properties and characteristics. To what extent is San Diego County a cohesive region?

From the physical point of view, only the western boundary of the county is a logical one, for it is the only one clearly defined by a significant natural feature. The southern boundary, of course, was pre-determined by events of international scale, done at a time when straight lines and rivers were thought to make good boundaries. International boundaries are sometimes described as "only lines on maps," but a glance at Figure 2.1 shows the diagonal trace of the Mexican border clearly and easily visible from the air, reflecting differing land use patterns.

The northern boundary is in a reasonably logical position (given that there are no east-west trending mountain ranges), although it would have been better located about five miles further north so that all of Temecula Creek would have lain south of it. Most county residents, however, have a good mental image of where the county's northern limits are. This is not so true for the eastern boundary.

The most obvious eastern boundary would be the Laguna Mountains, separating the Pacific Ocean and the Salton Sea drainage basins; but because the Lagunas are often of gentle slope near their summits, rather than pointed, they are an imperfect political boundary. Since the thought in 1907, when Imperial County was split off, was probably to create two counties of approximately equal size, the present eastern boundary is probably as good as any that could have been devised east of the Laguna crest, even though it's hard to mentally envisage just where it lies. Most San Diegans are delighted to have the eastern boundary where it is, so as to include Anza-Borrego Desert State Park as part of their county.

The above considerations notwithstanding, San Diego is considered as having fairly logical boundaries, and as forming a rather defensible region. This can be seen from the number of environment-oriented state agencies that have accorded San Diego a separate planning region status (e.g., coastal commission, air quality), while other counties are often bunched together.

A region will be more strongly defined if some homogeneous, or distinctive, characteristic exists within it. Physically, San Diego is neither homogeneous nor distinctive. It is not confined within one major watershed, and it boasts three quite different landscapes—coastal terraces, inland valleys and mountains, and deserts. Basically, except for maximum elevations, the natural environment differs little from any other southern California county.

Yet, many would argue that the human landscape that has been created in San Diego County, and the people that created it, are somehow different from those in any of the surrounding counties. Certainly San Diegans think of themselves and their region as different and, by implication, a bit better than the areas to the north. Perhaps the most common comparative phrase locally is "we don't want to become like Los Angeles." Riverside, Orange, and San Bernardino are not viewed as much better. The Marine Corps' Camp Pendleton is perceived by many San Diegans as kind of an open-space Maginot Line, holding off the march of subdivisions from the north. While the foregoing may be slightly overstated, and we've certainly marched our own army of sub-divisions towards Camp Pendleton from the south, the feeling definitely exists that the San Diego environment has somehow survived urbanization better than any of the four counties to the north, and a strong desire exists to keep it that way. This may be thought of as a "regional consciousness," and is an extremely important factor in the formation and identification of a geographic region.

Periods of San Diego's History

San Diego considers itself the "birthplace of California." It was the first part of what is now the state of California to be explored by Europeans, and the first to be colonized. Although San Diego was not settled by Europeans as early as were many East Coast areas, its history is at least as rich. Home to four major cultures (Indian, Spanish, Mexican, American), a succession of explorers, missionaries, governors, overland traders, and land promoters all arrived here early and left their marks, threatening to eliminate in the process the native Americans who had known the land for centuries before. Famous western personages who either visited or lived in San Diego in the nineteenth century included Richard Henry Dana, Kit Carson, "Judge" Roy Bean, Jedediah Smith, and Wyatt Earp.

For convenience, San Diego County's history may be divided into several distinct periods. The earlier periods are well defined, the later ones somewhat more arbitrary.

All human history in San Diego County prior to 1769 may be termed the Native American period, for they were its sole residents for many thousands of years. Only twice, in 1542 and 1602, do historical records indicate that the native peoples were surprised by the arrival of strange ships from out of the ocean. In 1542 the Spanish explorer Juan Rodriguez Cabrillo sailed into San Diego Bay while looking for the elusive shortcut to China, and named it San Miguel Bay.[1] He was followed sixty years later by Sebastian Vizcaino. Vizcaino sailed into the bay on the feast day of Saint Didacus, known in Spanish as San Diego de Alcala, and felt that this was an appropriate manner in which to rename the bay. Vizcaino's designation prevailed, and a bay, river, city, and county received their names.

[1]Although it is often stated that Cabrillo was the first European to view Alta California, at least one and possibly two overland parties had ascended the Colorado River to what is now the Yuma-Winterhaven area two years earlier.

There followed a 167-year void in European exploration. Then, in 1769, the Franciscan missionary Father Junipero Serra arrived in San Diego from Mexico City, anxious to continue the northward expansion of the string of missions that had begun in Loreto, B.C., in 1697. The years from 1769 to 1821 represent the Spanish period. Other noteworthy events in this period were the first overland explorations of the county by Portola in 1769 and de Anza in 1774 (see Figure 11.1), the founding of a second mission in the region (San Luis Rey in 1798), and the construction of Mission (Padre) Dam during the period 1807–1816.

In 1821, Mexico achieved independence from Spanish rule, and gained control over what is now the state of California until 1848. This was the Mexican period. It was a time of secularization and stagnation of the missions, and of the granting of many vast areas, or ranchos, to friends of the various Mexican governors (Figure 1.3). Many contemporary place names and area configurations, such as Cuyamaca Rancho State Park, Rancho de las Peñasquitos, Camp Pendleton (Rancho Santa Margarita y las flores), and Rancho Guejito, can be traced to these early land grants (Figure 9.1).

Mexican control ended in 1846, an eventful year in San Diego history, which saw United States warships secure the harbor, General Kearny's arrival (after his "long march" from Independence, Mo.) and subsequent defeat at the Battle of San Pasqual (in which Kit Carson participated), and the massacre of Mexican residents near the Pala Mission.

The years from 1848 to about 1880 may be called the early United States period. This period saw California become a state and San Diego become a city (1850), the establishment of San Diego as the new state's first county (also 1850), the arrival of the first overland stages in 1857, the start of New Town in 1867, the short-lived

Figure 1.3. The San Miguel Chapel near Warner Springs, originally built in 1830, is one of the few remaining vestiges of San Diego's Mexican period. Photo by P. R. Pryde.

but spirited Julian gold rush which began in 1870, and the establishment of the first of San Diego County's Indian reservations (1875). The city looked considerably different at that time, not just the community but the physical features as well (Figure 1.4). Note the different appearance of North Island and San Diego and Mission ("False") Bays, and that the San Diego River emptied into San Diego Bay.

The last two decades of the nineteenth century are usually referred to as San Diego's Victorian period, but it is convenient to extend this period until around 1907. It was during this period that the region began to "boom"; the first railroads arrived, and with the construction of several large dams irrigated agriculture began to prosper. The "Boom of the Eighties" was one of San Diego's more colorful periods, although it was followed by the "bust" of the 1890s. Fortunately, many flamboyant Victorian houses and buildings still remain from that era (Chapter 12). During this period, the county was greatly

reduced in size with the splitting off of both Riverside and Imperial counties.

The years between 1908 and 1945 may be called San Diego's Air and Sea period, for air and water navigation, both military and commercial expanded greatly. This era begins with the arrival of the Great White Fleet in San Diego in 1908. The two world wars were, of course, the major catalysts, and many of our naval bases were created in 1917. Probably the best known symbol of this era was a shy young civilian aviator named Charles Lindbergh, whose "Spirit of St. Louis" was built in San Diego. He was not the only air pioneer, however, for during the 1920s San Diego gained fame as the terminus of the first nonstop cross-continental flight, and as a terminus of the first regularly scheduled commercial passenger flights (by Ryan Airlines to Los Angeles).

The current era, which begins with the end of the Second World War, can only be termed the Contemporary Boom period. The last sixty

Figure 1.4. Subdivision map of the city of San Diego, about 1872. Courtesy of the San Diego Historical Society. See also Figure 17.4.

years have been ones of spectacular growth in the county, with San Diego mushrooming from the thirty-first to the seventh largest city in the country. It is an era of high-rise and suburbs, of freeways and smog, of civic revitalization and still newer urban problems. Many of the ensuing chapters will discuss the results, promises, and implications of this rapid urban growth.

This, then, is a book about the entire San Diego County metropolitan region, including the rural backcountry. It will take a look at what nature provided, what human transformations have occurred, what is desirable about the region and what problems exist, and, perhaps most important of all, what questions we should be asking about our future. The chapters that follow will examine a variety of aspects of the county, often from a historical perspective, in order to discover where we've been and how we got to be where we are at the turn of the new century. First, if we are to know the San Diego region, we must begin with what nature provided us. The initial chapters will examine the natural environment of the county.

Appendix 1.1. San Diego County Chronology

1540   Alarcon probably visits Alta California via the Colorado River
1542   Cabrillo discovers a bay he names San Miguel (now San Diego Bay)
1602   Vizcaino arrives at San Miguel Bay; renames it San Diego Bay
1769   Fra Junipero Serra arrives; camp at Presidio established
1774   Mission is moved six miles up San Diego River valley
1774   Anza expedition crosses Borrego Desert
1784   Mission San Diego de Alcala completed
1797   Fort Guijarros built at Ballast Point to guard San Diego Bay
1798   San Luis Rey mission established
1800   First United States ship visits San Diego
1816   Padre Dam completed
1816   Asistencia (outlying mission) established at Pala
1818   Asistencia established at Santa Ysabel
1821   San Diego becomes part of Mexico
1823   First private rancho (Los Peñasquitos) granted
1826   Jedediah Smith is first overland American visitor to San Diego
1833   Missions secularized by Mexico
1835   Vicinity of present San Diego City is made a rancho. Richard Henry Dana visits San Diego.
1844   Don Juan Warner establishes Warner's Ranch
1846   Gen. Kearny defeated at Battle of San Pasqual
1847   Mormon Battalion opens first wagon road to San Diego from the east
1848   San Diego (and California) become part of the United States
1848   Overland mail route Yuma-San Diego opened through Mexican territory
1849   San Diego hosts commission to delineate U.S.-Mexico border
1850   California becomes a state; San Diego County created

1850   City of San Diego incorporated
1851   Garra Indian uprising at Warner's Ranch
1854   Original Point Loma lighthouse completed
1857   First overland mail route across United States territory to San Diego
1862   Largest flood in recorded San Diego history occurs
1867   New Town founded by Alonzo Horton
1868   Land for Balboa Park set aside
1870   Gold discovered in Julian
1872   Fire destroys Old Town
1875   First San Diego County Indian reservations established
1885   San Diego connected to the east via railroads
1887   National City incorporated as the second city in the county
1888   Escondido and Oceanside incorporated; Hotel del Coronado opened
1889   End of first "boom" period
1891   Coronado splits off from the city of San Diego and incorporates
1893   Riverside County is split off from San Diego County
1893   Cleveland National Forest created (then known as the Trabuco Reserve)
1896   Work began on harbor fortifications at Point Loma
1900   John Spreckels opens Coronado "Tent City." County population is 35,000.
1905   Dike failure on Colorado River re-creates the Salton Sea
1907   Imperial County is split off from San Diego County
1908   Great White Fleet visits San Diego
1911   First seaplane is launched from a navy ship, San Diego Bay; Chula Vista incorporates
1912   El Cajon and La Mesa incorporate
1913   Cabrillo National Monument created
1915   Panama-California Exposition opens
1916   Worst recorded floods in county history occur in January; San Diego Zoo opens
1917   Camp Kearny and North Island Air Station established
1919   Completion of San Diego and Arizona Railroad
1922   County population reaches 100,000
1923   First nonstop transcontinental flight, New York-San Diego
1925   First regular airline service in United States, Los Angeles-San Diego
1927   Charles Lindbergh welcomed by 60,000 on return to San Diego
1928   First paved highway out of the county (to Los Angeles) completed
1930   County population reaches 200,000
1933   Cuyamaca Rancho and Anza-Borrego Desert State Parks established
1935   California-Pacific International Exposition opens
1941   World War II greatly expands military activity in the county
1942   Camp Pendleton established as a Marine Corps base. Japanese residents relocated.
1944   San Diego County Water Authority organized
1946   County population reaches 500,000
1947   First water from the Colorado River reaches San Diego

1948 200-inch Hale telescope completed on Palomar Mountain
1948 First San Diego County freeway completed through Balboa Park
1952 Carlsbad incorporates as a city
1956 Torrey Pines city park becomes a California State Park Preserve
1956 Imperial Beach incorporates
1959 Del Mar incorporates
1959 Population of San Diego County reaches 1,000,000
1962 First of the modern high-rise office buildings built in downtown San Diego
1963 Vista and San Marcos incorporate
1969 San Diego celebrates its 200th anniversary
1969 Coronado Bay Bridge opens
1970 Great Laguna fire burns 180,000 acres
1971 Amtrak takes over passenger rail service to Los Angeles
1974 Population of San Diego County reaches 1,500,000
1976 Tropical storm Kathleen destroys SD&AE railroad and severs 1–8
1977 Lemon Grove incorporates
1980 Poway and Santee incorporate
1980 Largest floods in 53 years inundate Mission Valley
1981 San Diego trolley opens rail transit link to Tijuana
1981 Olympic equestrian competition held in San Diego county
1985 County population reaches 2,000,000
1986 Encinitas and Solana Beach incorporate
1986 City of San Diego's population reaches 1,000,000
1990 County population reaches 2,500,000
1992 San Diego hosts the world America's Cup yacht races
1993 Fifth rainiest year in San Diego history; flooding on local rivers
1999 Miramar Air Station changes hands from Navy to Marine Corps
2002 Driest year in San Diego history; 63,000 acre "Pines" fire
2003 "Cedar", "Otay", and "Paradise" fires burn 345,000 acres, destroy 2,300 homes

---

Appendix 1.2. English Meaning of San Diego County Placenames (1)

Agua Caliente	Hot water
Agua Hedionda	Stinking water
Bataquitos	Uncertain; three different translations exist (S,10)
Bonita	Pretty
Borrego	Lamb (S); Big horn sheep
Campo	Field
Carrizo	Reed grass, or Cane (S)

Chula Vista	Good view (P); Pretty or magnificent view (S)
Coronado	Possibly after Francisco de Coronado, explorer (P); after four early Roman martyrs (S)
Cuyamaca	Rain above (P); from Indian ekui-amak; 'Place beyond the rain' (S)
Del Mar	Of the sea, or By the sea
Descanso	Rest, or Resting place
El Cajon	The box (P), or Box-like canyon (S)
Encinitas	Little live oaks (P); Place of little oaks (S)
Escondido	Secluded, Hidden
Guatay	From Diegueño Indian word meaning 'large' (P), or 'large rock' (S)
In-Ko-Pah	Indian: 'Place of the mountain people' (S)
Jacumba	Diegueño: 'water' (P), or 'hut by the water' (S)
Jamacha	Either Gourd, or Small squash vine
Jamul	Slimy water (P); (S) offer two other possibilities
La Jolla	The jewel (P); from Spanish 'hoya' or 'joya,' or corruption of Indian word (S)
La Mesa	The plateau (P); Table land (S)
Leucadia	Greek for 'Sheltered place' (S)
Los Peñasquitos	The little cliffs (P); (S) also suggests 'Small round rocks'
Miramar	View of the Sea
Olivenhain	Olive grove (P); Home of the olive (S)
Otay	Brushy (P); (S) suggests also 'Wide and level place'
Pala	Shovel, trowel, scoop (P); Place of water (S)
Palomar	Dovecote or pigeon coop (P); Place of the pigeon (S)
Pauma	Indian: 'I bring water' (P); Place of little water (S)
Potrero	Cattle ranch, Stock farm (P); Meadow, Pasturing place (S)
Poway	Indian: 'Place where the valley ends' (S)
Ramona	From the heroine of a novel of the same name
Rancho Santa Fe	Holy Faith ranch
San Diego	Saint Didacus
San Dieguito	Probably 'little San Diego'
San Luis Rey	St. Louis, King
Solana	Sunny place (P); Sunshine (S)
Tijuana	Aunt Jane or Joanne (P), or Indian word of similar sound (see Chapter 18)
Vallecito	Little or small valley
Viejas	Old Women (S)

(1) Sources: R. F. Pourade (ed.), *Historic Ranchos of San Diego,* San Diego: Union-Tribune Publishing Co., 1969, pp. 114–115 (P); and L. Stein, *San Diego County Placenames,* San Diego: Tofua Press, 1975 (S). The interested reader is referred to these two sources, particularly the latter, for a more complete list.

References

County Supervisors Association of California. *California County Fact Book 1991–92*. Sacramento: C.S.A.C., 1992.

Crosby, H. W. *Gateway to Alta California: The Expedition to San Diego, 1769*. San Diego: Sunbelt Publications, 2003.

Crumpler. Hugh, "Heroism and Tragedy: The Battle of San Pasqual", *San Diego Union-Tribune*, December 6, 1996, pp. B-1 and B-4.

Engstrand, I. *San Diego: California's Cornerstone*. Tulsa: Continental Heritage Press, 1980.

Heilbron, C. H., ed. *History of San Diego County*. San Diego: The San Diego Press Club, 1936.

Hornbeck, David. *California Patterns: A Geographical Historical Atlas*. Mayfield, 1983.

Journal of San Diego History. San Diego: San Diego Historical Society (quarterly).

Kooperman, E. L. *San Diego Trivia*. San Diego: Silver Gate Publications, 1989.

Kurillo, Max. *California's El Camino Real and Its Historic Bells*. San Diego: Sunbelt Publications, 2000.

McPhail, Elizabeth. *The Story of New San Diego and of Its Founder Alonzo E. Horton*. San Diego: San Diego Historical Society, 1979.

Mills, J. R. *San Diego: Where California Began*. San Diego: San Diego Historical Society, 1976. (Available on-line: see below)

Pourade, R. F. *History of San Diego,* 7 vols. San Diego: Union-Tribune Publishing Co., 1960–1967.

Showley, R. M. *San Diego : Perfecting Paradise*. Carlsbad, CA: Heritage Media Corp., 1999.

Smythe, W.E. *History of San Diego, 1542–1907*. San Diego: The History Company, 1907.

Starr, R. G. *San Diego: A Pictorial History*. Norfolk: The Donning Co., 1986.

State of California. *California Statistical Abstract*. Sacramento: California Department of Finance, 2001.

Stein, L. *San Diego County Placenames*. San Diego: Tofua Press, 1975.

Internet Connections:

San Diego Historical Society: *www.sandiegohistory.org*

Mills book on line: *www.sandiegohistory.org/books/wcb/wcb.htm*

Chapter Two

David S. McArthur

Building the Region
The Geologic Forces that Shape San Diego County

In order to understand any region, the best place to start is with the geologic processes that produced its surface forms and vertical relief. The term given to these processes is *geomorphology*.

One of the most striking aspects of San Diego County's surface relief is its diversity. A high-altitude easterly view across the county, such as the one shown in Figure 2.1, typically will show a foreground of canyon-dissected mesas, backed by broken plateaus which may rise eastward into mountain ranges over 6,000 feet high. Broad basins and steep-sided valleys occur within and between the ranges, which then descend

David S. McArthur is a professor of geomorphology in the Department of Geography at San Diego State University.

abruptly on their eastern flanks to the valleys of the Anza-Borrego desert and the Salton Trough. These diverse components of county relief are further illustrated in Figure 2.2.

The first section of this chapter will introduce the relief forming ("geomorphic") controls that have shaped the region. This will be followed by a brief description of the county's three main geomorphological regions. Finally, some of the environmental problems that stem from contemporary geomorphic processes will be reviewed.

Geomorphic Processes

For simplicity, geomorphic processes can be placed into two broad categories, depending on

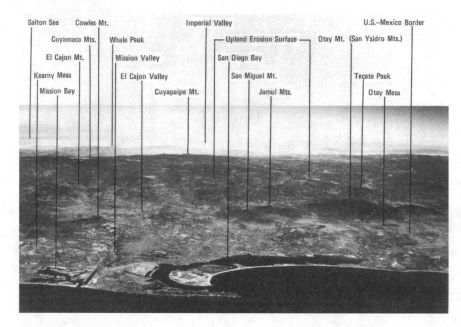

Salton Sea   Cowles Mt.   Imperial Valley   U.S.–Mexico Border
Cuyamaca Mts.   Whale Peak   Upland Erosion Surface   Otay Mt. (San Ysidro Mts.)
El Cajon Mt.   Mission Valley   San Diego Bay
Kearny Mesa   El Cajon Valley   San Miguel Mt.   Tecate Peak
Mission Bay   Cuyapaipe Mt.   Jamul Mts.   Otay Mesa

Figure 2.1. Aerial oblique eastward view across southern San Diego County. Photograph courtesy of United States Navy.

whether the energy that transforms the landscape originates beneath or above the earth's surface. Types of processes that originate within the earth include *faulting*, the rupturing and displacement of earth materials, *folding*, the bending of earth materials into folds, and *volcanism*, the extrusion of molten rock and other materials at the earth's surface.

The other category takes in the processses of *rock weathering* and *erosion*, by which the earth's surface is modified by energy originating at or above the surface. All types of erosion are fostered by rock weathering, which is the weakening, disintegration, and chemical decomposition of surface rocks due to their exposure to air, water, and biological agents. The weathering processes are vital in producing soil, on which most plant life depends.

In San Diego County, the more important erosional processes are landslides, creep, slope wash, and abrasion. Landsliding and creep describe the downslope movement of surface materials in response to gravity forces. Although landsliding, the rapid downhill movement of slope materials, is a spectacular and at times disastrous erosional process, *creep,* the imperceptibly slow mass wasting of slope materials, generally is considered to be more important because it operates continuously over both time and space.

During storms, rainwater received at the surface that neither evaporates back to the atmosphere nor infiltrates into surface rocks and soil will move downslope as surface runoff. Prior to entering major stream channels, this overland flow is instrumental in washing surface rock

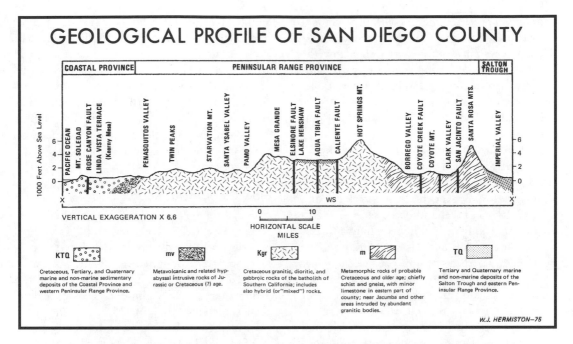

Figure 2.2. Simplified geological cross section between La Jolla, Warner Springs, and the northeast corner of San Diego County. Profile location is shown in Figures 2.3 and 2.5. Sources: Relief compiled from the USGS Santa Ana and San Diego 1:250,000 topographical sheets; geology compiled from Jahns (1954) and Weber (1961).

debris and soil particles downslope. This process of *slope wash* assists in eroding valley sides, and supplies sediment to valley floors.

A third erosional process that has played a major role in the development of San Diego County relief is *abrasion*. Abrasion is the process by which the land surface is scoured by rock particles in motion. Valley deepening and widening by rivers, sea-cliff erosion by waves, and rock etching by wind are all accomplished largely by abrasion.

All these processes operate in unison to shape the landscape. For example, the pace of erosion is directly proportional to the elevation of the land surface above sea level. That elevation is in turn due to a prior raising of the land surface by faulting, folding, or volcanism. As soon as a por-

tion of the earth's surface is raised above sea level, its modification by erosion will begin, and erosion ultimately will reduce the surface to a general elevation near sea level. A large proportion of San Diego County has a high elevation because the process of faulting has recently (in geologic terms) been dominant in shaping the land surface. The resistance to erosion of the surface rocks has contributed to maintaining high elevations above sea level.

Types of Rocks in the County

Surface rocks are classified according to the processes that formed them. Many rocks and minerals are produced by crystallization of molten elements as they rise through the earth's crust towards the surface. Minerals so produced form *igneous* rocks. If the crystallization occurs at the earth's surface, the result is termed a *volcanic* rock. If crystallization occurs well below the earth's surface, the resulting igneous rock is called a *plutonic* rock. Granite and basalt are examples of plutonic and volcanic rocks, respectively. Diorite and gabbro are other examples of plutonic rock.

When surface materials are eroded, rock particles are transported downslope and eventually are deposited to form a *sediment*. Sediments generally are found over the lowest surfaces of a region. River gravel and beach sand are sediments. If a body of sediments remains undisturbed for a substantial period of time, the sedimentary particles become cemented together to produce a *sedimentary rock*. Because sediments characteristically are deposited in layers, or strata, sedimentary rocks usually exhibit stratification. Cemented river gravel and beach sand are given the names conglomerate and sandstone, respectively. Shale and limestone are other examples of sedimentary rocks.

Rock-forming minerals sometimes are changed into new minerals by their exposure to some combination of heat, pressure, and chemical solutions. New rocks produced in this fashion are known as *metamorphic rocks*. Limestone and siltstone can be metamorphosed to form marble and slate, respectively.

The simplified geological map of San Diego County (Figure 2.3) shows the distribution of surface rocks and faults in the region. Note that the coastal lowland belt and parts of the Salton Trough are underlain by sediments and sedimentary rocks, whereas the intervening upland area is underlain mostly by plutonic rocks. The sedimentary rocks are comprised of materials that originally were supplied by upland erosion. Sedimentary cover also occurs on the floors of inland basins, such as the area around Lake Henshaw (southwest of Warner Springs), and

in the intermontane valleys, such as San Felipe and Earthquake valleys (east of Julian). Volcanic rocks occur at the surface only in a small area of the southern Borrego Desert, just west of the Imperial County line. The *metavolcanic* rocks mapped along the western boundary of the plutonic rocks (in the vicinity of San Miguel Mountain, for example) are just what the term suggests: transformed or metamorphosed volcanic rocks.

How Old Are Our Rocks?

Some of the terms in the geological map key, such as Cretaceous, Tertiary, and Quaternary, describe rock age: the time at which crystallization occurred for igneous and metamorphic rocks, and the time of sediment deposition for sedimentary rocks. A simplified geological time scale is presented in Table 2.1.

A brief geological history of the county might be of interest. During the Mesozoic Era (the "age of reptiles") volcanoes were active in what today is western San Diego County, while farther to the east, granitic and other plutonic rocks were crystallizing beneath the surface to provide the core of a developing mountain range. Subsequently, erosional processes became dominant, and by early Tertiary time, they had largely consumed the Mesozoic uplands. In so doing they had exposed the plutonic rocks that once had comprised the mountain core. The large amounts of sediment yielded by erosion were transported westward by rivers and deposited on the ocean side of the older Mesozoic volcanic belt. In these, dinosaur fossils from the Cretaceous period have been found in the county.

It was not until the latter half of the Tertiary Period that most of the broad outline of contemporary county relief began to be established. At that time, the Pacific Ocean floor and part of California began to slide northwestward as the great San Andreas Fault came into being. In

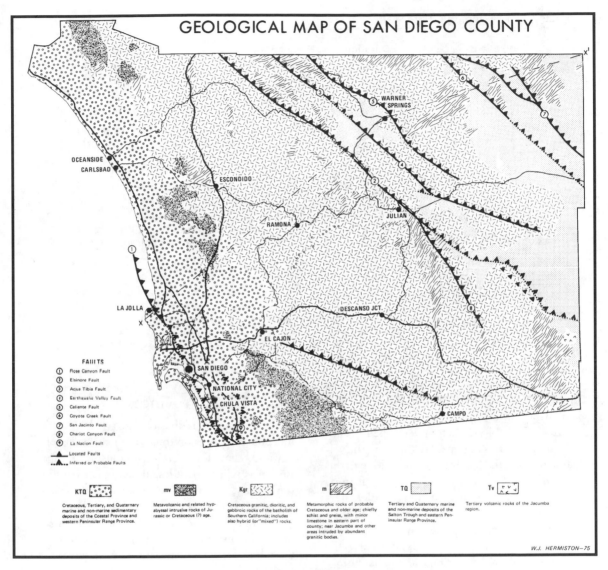

GEOLOGICAL MAP OF SAN DIEGO COUNTY

FAULTS

① Rose Canyon Fault
② Elsinore Fault
③ Aqua Tibia Fault
④ Earthquake Valley Fault
⑤ Caliente Fault
⑥ Coyote Creek Fault
⑦ San Jacinto Fault
⑧ Chariot Canyon Fault
⑨ La Nacion Fault

▲▲▲ Located Faults
···▲··· Inferred or Probable Faults

KTQ Cretaceous, Tertiary, and Quaternary marine and non-marine sedimentary deposits of the Coastal Province and western Peninsular Range Province.

mv Metavolcanic and related hypabyssal intrusive rocks of Jurassic or Cretaceous (?) age.

Kgr Cretaceous granitic, dioritic, and gabbroic rocks of the batholith of Southern California; includes also hybrid (or "mixed") rocks.

m Metamorphic rocks of probable Cretaceous and older age; chiefly schist and gneiss, with minor limestone in eastern part of county; near Jacumba and other areas intruded by abundant granitic bodies.

TQ Tertiary and Quaternary marine and non-marine deposits of the Salton Trough and eastern Peninsular Range Province.

Tv Tertiary volcanic rocks of the Jacumba region.

W.J. HERMISTON–75

Figure 2.3. Simplified geological map of San Diego County. XX′ locates the cross section of Figure 2.2. Sources: Weber (1961); faults based on Seismic Safety Element, San Diego Co. General Plan (1975).

conjunction with this motion, a giant rift developed between the areas which today are northwestern mainland Mexico and southwestern California, and the land surface to the west of

the rift was thrown up on its eastern margin. The rift today finds expression in the Gulf of California and Salton Trough, while the tilted block to the west provides the broad outline of

TABLE 2.1. The Geologic Time Scale

Eras/Periods		Millions of Years Duration	Age of Rocks	Events in San Diego County
Cenozoic				
Quaternary:	Recent	25		Further uplift and erosion of mountains
	Pleistocene			Linda Vista formation deposited
Tertiary:	Pliocene	62.5		San Diego formation deposited
	Miocene		65	Peninsular Ranges, Sea of Cortez formed
	Eocene			La Jolla formation and Poway conglomerate deposited
Mesozoic				
Cretaceous		71		Batholith exposed
Jurassic		54		So. California batholith implanted
Triassic		35	225	Black Mountain volcanics deposited
Paleozoic		345		
Oldest Paleozoic rocks			570	
Precambrian = oldest dated rocks on Earth:			3,300	
(Proterozoid) origin of the earth:		4,000–5,000		

Source: Compiled from Remeika and Lindsay (1992) and the San Diego Museum of Natural History.

the Peninsular Ranges of southern California and Baja California.

Localized volcanic action developed in conjunction with this regional faulting, and the volcanic rocks in the Jacumba region belong to this episode. As erosion of the newly-formed Peninsular Ranges continued into the Quaternary (most recent) Period, corresponding sediments of that age, supplied by erosion, were deposited in the low-lying areas adjacent to the uplands: in the Salton Trough and its extensions into the Peninsular Ranges (such as Borrego Valley), in the western coastal region, and in the intermontane basins and valleys. In some areas of North County, recent Quaternary sedimentary rocks contain fossil remains of mammoths and other prehistoric animals.

Geomorphic Provinces

San Diego County is divisible into two large geomorphic provinces on the basis of surface geology and relief. These are the Peninsular Range Province, which includes all the higher land in the county, and the Coastal Province, which essentially corresponds to the western region of sedimentary surface rocks. A smaller third province consists of the westernmost portions of the Salton Trough in Anza-Borrego Desert State Park.

The Coastal Province

The dominant relief element of the coastal Province is a series of marine terraces, geographically known as "mesas". Within the metropolitan San Diego region, for example, three terraces are recognized. In order of increasing age, elevation, and distance from the coastline, these are designated as the La Jolla Terrace, which lies between 50 and 70 feet above sea level, the Linda Vista Terrace, which occurs between 300 and 500 feet above sea level, and the Poway Terrace, which is located between 800 and 1,200 feet above sea level.

The La Jolla Terrace is best developed around the seaward flanks of Mount Soledad and in the vicinity of Mission Bay. The Linda Vista is the most apparent and extensive of the three terraces, although its surface has been considerably altered by canyon formation. It includes most of the familiar mesas of the San Diego metropolitan area. Only remnants of the Poway Terrace remain, the once continuous ter-

race surface having been substantially consumed by erosion. Similar terraces occur throughout the coastal Province, as for example in the southwestern corner of the county (Figure 2.4).

The history of a marine terrace begins with the cutting of an underwater marine platform by abrasion associated with coastal wave and current action. Ocean waves are present not only on the ocean surface, they also extend beneath the surface to a water depth known as the wave base. In shallower areas near the coast, subsurface wave action erodes the ocean floor and produces a platform. Marine platforms often are exposed at low tide. Over time, a lowering of mean sea level or a raising of the coastal sea floor will elevate the platform, at which time it becomes a marine terrace.

Figure 2.4. Aerial oblique southeastward view across Otay Mesa. It has been proposed that Avondale Terrace and Otay Mesa once were a continuous surface, but have become separated due to vertical movement along the La Nacion Fault. Photograph courtesy of Bill Waldrop.

Worldwide sea level fluctuations have occurred over geologic history mainly by the addition or subtraction of water from the ocean basins. It is well known that during the last 2.5 million years before present, a time known as the Quaternary Period (Table 2.1), there were several spans of time during which large quantities of ice accumulated on the land. The water contained in these ice caps was drawn from the oceans and so during these glacial times sea level was lower than at present. The estimated lowering is in the vicinity of 450 feet below the present level. Alternatively, during times of ice melting, water was returned to the oceans and the sea level rose, reaching maximum elevations during interglacial periods. Current sea-level change is in an upward direction, in response to deglaciation caused by global warming.

Marine terraces may have been produced by the several high sea level events that occurred during the Quaternary Period. This explanation, however, can't explain the higher marine terraces of San Diego County. If all the ice presently on the land (most of it existing in the ice caps of Greenland and Antarctica) were to melt, sea level would rise to only about 180 feet above its present elevation. This elevation is insufficient to account for the Linda Vista and Poway terraces at their present elevations. Research into the history of these two terraces, and of the other higher terraces in the Coastal Province, suggests that they have been raised since they were cut.

Marine terraces today exhibit considerable surface relief. All of the local terraces are dissected by canyon systems, the degree of dissection increasing with the age of the terrace. Canyon cutting by stream erosion is a consequence both of terrace elevation relative to sea level, and of the general weakness of the rocks through which the terrace canyons were cut. Mission Valley and its tributary valleys are good examples of canyons that have been cut into the Linda Vista Terrace. Many of the canyons were originally cut much deeper than their present floors, when sea level was depressed below its present elevation. Subsequently, they were filled in as sea level rose in response to deglaciation. This explains why thick deposits of river sand and gravel underlie many valley floors in the Coastal Province.

The terraces have been altered since their emergence from the ocean by events other than canyon cutting. Prominent examples are old beach ridges such as those located on the Linda Vista Terrace in the Clairemont Mesa area, north of Sharp Hospital. These north-south trending ridges, which attain elevations of 25–50 feet above the local terrace surface, consist of old beach and dune sediments. Beach ridges on the Linda Vista Terrace mark the positions of several shorelines that existed during the time that the terrace was near sea level.

The Peninsular Range Province

Major relief features of the Peninsular Range Province are shown in Figure 2.5. Features of note include the general northwest-southeast trend of the mountain ranges, the location of the highest peaks (listed in Table 2.2), the steep eastern slopes of most mountain ranges, and the near sea-level elevations along the San Diego-Imperial County line. All of these features are related to the geological structure of the province.

The broad structure of the Peninsular Range Province is often described as a giant westerly-tilted fault block. The upthrusted eastern boundary of the block is more pronounced north of San Diego County where, in the vicinity of Palm Springs, San Jacinto Peak abruptly rises to an elevation in excess of 10,000 feet above the floor of the Coachella Valley. Nevertheless, the results of block faulting are also reflected in the relief pattern of eastern San Diego County and are easily seen by driving along Highway S-2.

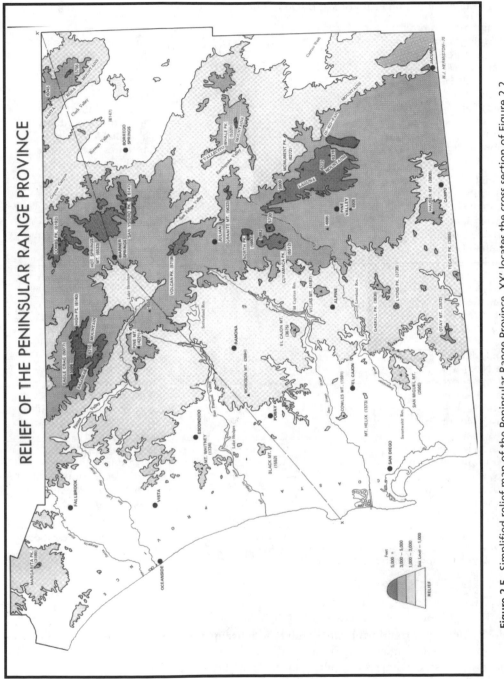

Figure 2.5. Simplified relief map of the Peninsular Range Province. XX' locates the cross section of Figure 2.2. Source: Compiled from the USGS Santa Ana and San Diego 1:250,000 topographic sheets.

TABLE 2.2. Major Mountain Peaks of San Diego County. (Locations are given in Figure 2.5)

The ten highest mountains:

1.	Hot Springs Mountain	6,533'	San Ysidro Mountains*
2.	Cuyamaca Peak	6,512'	Cuyamaca Mountains
3.	Cuyapaipe Mountain	6,378'	Laguna Mountains
4.	Monument Peak	6,272'	Laguna Mountains
5.	Wooded Hill	6,223'	Laguna Mountains
6.	Combs Peak	6,193'	Bucksnort Mountain
7.	San Ysidro Peak	6.147'	San Ysidro Mountains*
8.	High Point	6,140'	Palomar Mountain
9.	Rabbit Peak (arm)	6,045'	Santa Rosa Mountains
10.	North Peak	5,993'	Cuyamaca Mountains

Other well-known county mountains:

Garnet Peak	5,909'	Laguna Mountains
Middle Peak	5,883'	Cuyamaca Mountains
Villager Peak	5,756'	Santa Rosa Mountains
Stonewell Peak	5,730'	Cuyamaca Mountains
Volcan Peak	5,719'	Volcan Mountains
Birch Hill	5,710'	Palomar Mountain
Granite Mountain	5,633'	east of Julian
Morgan Hill	5,596'	Palomar Mountain
Whale Peak	5,320'	Vallecito Mountains
Eagle Crag	5,077'	Agua Tibia Wilderness
Long Valley Peak	4,906'	south of Pine Valley
Guatay Mountain	4,885'	northwest of Pine Valley
Angel Mountain	4,555'	west of Lake Henshaw
Pine Mountain	4,221'	west of Lake Henshaw
Viejas Mountain	4,187'	northeast of Alpine
Tecate Peak	3,885'	west of Tecate
Gaskill Peak	3,836'	east of Jamul
Hauser Mountain	3,808'	northwest of Campo
Lyons Peak	3,738'	east of Jamul
El Cajon Mountain	3,675'	east of Lakeside
Otay Mountain	3,572'	San Ysidro Mountains*
Margarita Peak	3,189'	northwest county
Woodson Mountain	2,894'	northeast of Poway
San Miguel Mountain	2,565'	east of Chula Vista
Cowles Mountain	1,591'	north of La Mesa

*There are two San Ysidro ranges in the county. The lower and better known is near the Mexican border east of Otay Mesa. The higher range of that name takes in the high mountains on the watershed devide between Warner Springs and the Borrego Valley.

This province, however, has a much greater structural complexity than that of a single tilted fault block. Most importantly, the tilted fault block has been greatly fragmented by internal faulting. Traces of several important fault zones are shown in Figure 2.3 (although many smaller ones exist in the province). Major movement along most county faults has been sidewise, but vertical rock displacement can also be found in the upland province. The

Santa Rosa Mts.
Borrego Valley
Coyote Mt.
Clark Valley
Coyote Creek Fault
San Jacinto Fault

Figure 2.6. Northeastward view across Borrego Valley, showing fault-controlled relief.

northwest-southeast orientation of ranges such as the Laguna, Palomar, Vallecito, and Santa Rosa mountains and of lowlands such as Borrego, Clark, San Felipe, and Earthquake valleys obviously is related to the orientation of the major faults, and identifies faulting as a dominant process involved in shaping the surface of the eastern region of the Peninsular Range Province (Figure 2.6).

Much of the contemporary upland relief is due to a process called differential erosion. Faulting displaces rocks and so it is characteristic to find on adjacent sides of a fault plane rocks which have different compositions and therefore different resistances to erosion. Thus, erosion will proceed at different rates on either side of many fault traces with one side eroding faster than the other. This has probably happened, for example, on the east side of the Elsinore Fault in the Laguna Mountains. In general, many examples of abrupt elevation changes in the vicinity of fault traces probably are due as much to differential erosion as to vertical rock displacements.

West of the Elsinore Fault, the predominant relief features of the Peninsular Range Province are extensive upland erosion surfaces that have been deeply dissected by stream action. These are arranged in step-like fashion between elevations around 1,400 feet above sea level near the western boundary of the province and elevations as high as 6,000 feet above sea level in the Lagunas. Relief between the Coastal Province and the Elsinore Fault, which includes the Laguna Mountains, thus is characterized for the most part not by rugged mountainous configurations but rather by broad, reasonably flat, plateau surfaces. The Laguna and McCain plateaus and the Ranchita area are good examples of these surfaces. Isolated summits, such as Viejas Mountain and Cuyamaca Peak, because of their greater resistance to erosion, rise appreciably above the surrounding plateau surfaces.

Unlike the terraces of the Coastal Province, which were cut during the Quaternary Period by marine erosion, these upland erosion surfaces were produced earlier, during the Tertiary Period, by the combined action of terrestrial weathering and erosion processes.

A striking feature of the old upland erosion surface is the deep valleys cut into it by rivers, such as the Sweetwater and San Diego, which drain the western slopes of the Peninsular Range Province. The upland erosion surfaces have been fragmented by stream dissection in much the same way, and for the same basic reasons, that the higher coastal terraces have been dissected. Coastal terrace fragmentation is more severe than fragmentation of the upland surface because sedimentary rocks, which underlie the coastal terraces, are much more susceptible to erosion than are the plutonic rocks of the Peninsular Range Province.

River valleys that have been cut into the upland erosion surface fall into two distinct categories: low valleys, such as the El Cajon and

Poway valleys, and high valleys, such as the Santa Ysabel, San Vicente, and Ramona valleys. Floors of valleys in the former group characteristically are found at elevations between 350 and 600 feet above sea level, while floors of valleys in the latter group generally are in excess of 1,200 feet above sea level, and increase eastwards in conjunction with the easterly increase in elevation of the erosion surface.

It can be seen that floor elevations of low and high valleys near the western boundary of the Peninsular Range Province correspond reasonably well with elevations of the Linda Vista and Poway terrace surfaces, respectively. The implication is that higher and lower valleys were cut by streams graded to the same earlier sea levels, which controlled the marine cutting of the Poway and Linda Vista terraces. However tenuous this correlation, it emphasizes that land surface form evolves over a spatial continuum. The separate treatment here of the Coastal and Peninsular Range provinces in no way implies that the landforms of one province evolved in isolation from the surface development of the other province.

To the immediate east of San Diego County, the Salton Trough, which is an extension of the Gulf of California, has also been produced by block faulting. Coachella and Imperial valleys, and the Salton Sea, are located within the downfaulted trough, while Clark and Borrego valleys as well as Carrizo Wash (Figure 2.5) are extensions of the Salton Trough westward into San Diego County.

Contemporary Geomorphic Hazards and Environmental Problems

Although the processes that have produced the relief of San Diego County have fluctuated in intensity through time, those processes have nevertheless operated continuously since the Ter-

tiary period, and are still operating today. This brief survey of county geomorphology will conclude with a consideration of how several of these processes affect, and are affected by, human activities. Some of the environmental problems that arise from these interactions will be emphasized.

Earthquakes

The continued strain accumulation in rocks along the county fault zones finds its most spectacular expression in occasional seismic events we call earthquakes. Earthquakes result from shock waves which are generated when a large quantity of strain accumulation in rocks suddenly is released, in association with rock rupture. The location of strain release characteristically occurs along fault zones, and its projection on the earth's surface is referred to as an earthquake epicenter.

Seismicity studies in the San Diego area reveal that within a radius of eleven miles of downtown San Diego, twelve earthquake epicenters were recorded during a sixty-six year period. Although earthquakes corresponding to these epicenters have registered an average magnitude of less than 4 on the Richter scale (which produces light to moderate shaking), experts have recommended that a major earthquake of 7.3 magnitude, having an epicenter located along the Elsinore Fault (Figure 2.3), and having an average repeat interval of sixty years, should be considered the "maximum probable" earthquake for purposes of local risk assessment. But there is also high earthquake risk near the coast, with the Rose Canyon fault believed capable of a 6 to 7 magnitude tremor. The risk was demonstrated in the Borrego Desert area, where in 1968 an earthquake of 6.5 was recorded in the area north of Ocotillo Wells. Consideration of seismic risk is especially important when building on unconsolidated sediments, such as those underlying Mission and San Diego Bays.

Landslides

Landslides sometimes occur during earthquake activity, but rarely are earthquakes their primary cause. Earthquake shocks may function as a triggering mechanism in releasing earth materials that already have been prepared for rapid downslope movement by other processes.

Slope materials generally are weakened by water accumulation within them, which is often increased by the removal of valley-side vegetation. On a vegetated slope, some rainfall never runs off the ground due to its uptake by, and evaporation from, plant foliage. Ground cover also permits water to soak into the soil layers at a slower pace. Vegetation removal also directly weakens slope materials by depriving them of the coherence afforded by plant-root branchworks.

The most common cause of landslides in the San Diego region is slope oversteepening, which may be produced either by natural processes or by human activities. Undercutting of a valley wall by stream erosion or of a sea cliff by wave erosion are ways in which slopes may be naturally oversteepened. Preparation of land for highway or building construction frequently calls for slope grading, and in some instances the newly formed slope angle will approach the critical value for slope failure.

Actual slope failure will occur when the strength of slope materials can no longer withstand the pull of gravity. The exact form of the resulting landslide will depend on the structure and water content of the materials involved. Slope materials that are highly saturated with water characteristically flow downslope on failure.

However, if the arrangement of slope materials is such that a layer of permeable material overlies a layer of impermeable material, then water draining through the upper layer, not being able to move through the lower layer, will move along the contact plane between them, literally lubricating that contact. Under these circumstances, failure frequently will occur along this contact plane, and the upper layer will move downslope as a unit. The unit is called a slump block (Figure 2.7), and the process is known as "slumping." Flowing and slumping often occur when heavy rainfall follows vegetation burning. The Fletcher Hills landslide of 1974 and the several San Carlos landslides of 1977–1983 are all examples of slumping.

Slope Wash and Sedimentation

Many environmental problems in San Diego County result from its arid and semiarid climates. Not the least of these is the intensity of slope wash, the erosion of slopes by surface water

Figure 2.7. Mount Soledad landslide (slump) of December 14, 1961. Slope failure was due principally to oversteepening associated with slope grading for housing construction. Photograph courtesy of Union-Tribune Publishing Company.

runoff. Severe slope wash gives rise to topsoil depletion and to gullying, which finds extreme expression in a "badlands" surface. These types of erosion have a marked negative impact on the agricultural and pastoral potential of rural areas.

The soils of arid and semiarid climates, having a sparse vegetation cover, are more susceptible to erosion by surface runoff than is the case for soils of humid regions.

Surface runoff also is greatly increased in urban and suburban areas due to the presence of surfaces such as road pavements, parking lots, tennis courts, buildings and the like, which have zero infiltration capacities. If this runoff is not adequately accommodated by artificial drainage systems, then slope wash and bank cutting problems will develop.

For every erosion problem there will usually exists a corresponding sedimentation problem. In urban areas, sediment transported downslope by slope wash often will clog storm drains, which in turn will aggravate the erosion problem by further increasing the adverse effects of surface runoff. Generally, excessive sediment yield often will be deposited in floodplain river channels, thus decreasing their water-storage capacity. As a result, serious flooding will occur at smaller rates of stream discharge. If rivers have been dammed, excessive sediment yield will accelerate the rate of reservoir silting, which decreases reservoir capacity.

In San Diego County, an additional problem arising from accelerated surface erosion develops in the coastal lagoons and estuaries. Silting of lagoon channels significantly decreases lagoon capacity, which in turn substantially decreases the tidal flow into and out of an estuary or lagoon. In San Diego County, an appreciable tidal flow is required to maintain an inlet between the ocean and a lagoon. An inadequate flow closes county lagoon inlets, an event that has far-reaching ecological ramifications, to say nothing of the sensory unpleasantness of stagnant water. San Elijo, Bataquitos, and San Dieguito lagoons in particular have suffered from excessive siltation.

Coastal Erosion

Notwithstanding the accelerated rates of erosion and sedimentation within the county as a result of human activities, the basic erosion-sedimentation sequence is a natural one. Dam construction on the major rivers of San Diego County has broken this natural chain of events, causing sediments, which under natural conditions would reach the coastal lagoons and beaches to instead become trapped behind the dams. Deprived of a major sand supply, the county beaches are becoming increasingly undernourished due to an annual loss of sand into offshore submarine canyons (see Chapter 7). In other words, dam construction has led to an unbalanced budget of county beach sand: more sand is lost each year to offshore submarine canyons than is being added to the beaches by rivers and by coastal erosion.

Not only does this budget deficit contribute to the depletion of a valuable county recreational resource, but also, by exposing sea cliffs to the unchecked attack of storm waves, it is a primary cause of accelerated sea-cliff erosion at several coastal locations (Figure 2.8). It helped produce widespread damage along the coast in the winters of 1980 and 1983.

Landsliding, topsoil depletion, aggravated river flooding, reductions in river reservoir capacities, lagoon stagnation, and accelerated coastal erosion in San Diego County are all related to poorly thought out interactions between people and nature. It should be clear that an understanding of geomorphic processes, those natural processes that shape the land surface, is a necessary part of finding satisfactory solutions to these recurring environmental problems.

Figure 2.8. Bluff collapse ("debris slide") on an unstable coastal bluff in Leucadia, 1989. Photograph by D. S. McArthur.

References

Abbott, P. *The Rise and Fall of San Diego: 150 Million Years of History Recorded in Sedimentary Rocks.* San Diego: Sunbelt Publications, 1999.

Abbott, P. and W. Elliott, eds. *Environmental Perils, San Diego Region.* San Diego: San Diego Association of Geologists, 1991.

Abbott, P. and J. Victoria, eds. *Geologic Hazards in San Diego.* San Diego Society of Natural History, 1977.

California Division of Mines and Geology. *Character and Recency of Faulting, San Diego Metropolitan Area, California* (Special Report 123). Sacramento: C.D.M.G., 1975.

Clifford, H., F. Bergen, and S. Spear. *Geology of San Diego County.* San Diego: Sunbelt Publications, 1997.

Heller, J. and B. Lieberman, "Earthquake Fault Zones Increase on Latest Maps", *San Diego Union-Tribune,* November 25, 2002, pp. B1–B2.

Jahns, R. H., ed. *Geology of Southern California* (Division of Mines Bulletin 170). Sacramento: State Department of Natural Resources, 1954.

Kern, Philip. *Earthquakes and Faults in San Diego County.* San Diego: The Pickle Press, 1993.

Kuhn, G. and F. Shepard. *Sea Cliffs, Beaches, and Coastal Valleys of San Diego County.* Berkeley: University of California Press, 1984.

Lindsay, L., ed. *Geology of San Diego County: Journey Through Time.* San Diego: Sunbelt Publications, 2001.

Niiler, Eric, "Well-Preserved Tusk of Mammoth Brings Insight on Prehistory", *San Diego Union-Tribune,* February 27, 1999, p. B2.

Remeika, P. and L. Lindsay. *Geology of Anza-Borrego: Edge of Creation.* Dubuque: Kendall-Hunt, 1992.

Remeika, P. and A. Sturz. *Paleontology and Geology of the Anza-Borrego Desert State Park, California.* San Diego: San Diego Associaion of Geologists, 1995.

Roquemore, G., ed. *Proceedings, Workshop on "The Seismic Risk in the San Diego Region: Special Focus on the Rose Canyon Fault System.* San Diego: Southern California Earthquake Preparedness Project, 1989.

San Diego County. *San Diego County General Plan: Seismic Safety Element.* San Diego County Environmental Development Agency, 1982.

Weber, F. H. Jr., "Economic Geology of the San Diego Region, California—1961", in *Guidebook for Field Trips,* edited by B. Thomas, pp. 66-70. Geological Society of America, annual meeting, 1961.

Internet Connections:
California Geological Survey: *www.consrv.ca.gov/CGS/index.htm*
County of San Diego: *www.co.san-diego.ca.us/*
San Diego Association of Geologists: *www.sandiegogeologists.org/index.html*

Chapter Three

Philip R. Pryde

The Nature of the County
San Diego's Climate, Soils, Vegetation, and Wildlife

The climate, soils, vegetation and wildlife of a region are closely related. Of these, climate usually provides the most popular concern and interest. It also tends to govern the other three, which are directly determined by climate. For example, natural vegetation is dependent upon the soils, rainfall, and average temperatures of any given locale, but at the same time vegetation helps to prevent soil erosion and modifies the local climate. Wildlife is highly dependent on local vegetation communities, but at the same time wild animals act both to transform and to

Philip R. Pryde is a professor emeritus of environmental studies in the Department of Geography at San Diego State University.

propagate the plant life within these communities. Smaller organisms are an important part of the process of creating soils. These interdependencies are termed ecological relationships, and need to be well understood before any of their components are significantly or irreversibly disturbed.

The Climate of the County

If most county residents were asked to describe the local climate they would probably say, succinctly, that it is "very nice." By very nice they would mean that it is usually warm and sunny, and indeed the metropolitan area enjoys about 3,200 hours of sunshine a year, or about 73 percent of the maximum possible. Why is it that sunshine and dry weather dominate in San Diego County?

The reason is that our local climate is influenced most of the year by the proximity of the subtropical high pressure systems. Although these systems occasionally weaken or strengthen or shift location, they are generally found somewhere near southern California, usually displaced a little to the north in summer and to the south in winter. In high pressure systems such as this, dry air moves earthward from higher altitudes and spreads out in a mild, clockwise wind pattern when it reaches the surface. This dry, subsiding air is what keeps southern California in sunshine most of the time.

From time to time, the high pressure is centered farther inland, perhaps over Nevada. This produces periods of two or three days of very dry, subsiding winds from the east, which are locally known as a *Santa Ana*. Santa Ana wind conditions often produce the coastal cities' annual high temperatures in August or September (over 100°)[1], and can spread wildfire through the dry brush very rapidly.

Our climate is generally described as warm, of course, because of our relatively low latitude location. Yet areas of the county inland from the coast (El Cajon, Ramona, Escondido, Fallbrook) have warmer summers and cooler winters than does the city of San Diego, because they lack the moderating effects of breezes off the ocean (caused by the water warming and cooling more slowly than the land). This moderating effect of the ocean is easily seen on a typical August day, when the high temperature for the day may be 70° at Ocean Beach, 80° in East San Diego and 90° in the El Cajon Valley (Figure 3.1). The

reverse effect occurs with regard to low temperatures in winter, but the difference is not as great, and is dependent on other variables such as wind speed and local topography (Figure 3.2).

The proximity of the ocean has two other effects. One is a frequent afternoon "sea breeze," a gentle wind off the ocean that has the beneficial effect of cleansing the downtown air. It is most pronounced during the summer months. The other effect is a frequent occurrence of coastal "fog", especially in late spring and summer. The relatively cool ocean waters cause a low, thin layer of stratus clouds (sometimes called a "fog bank") to form offshore, which extends inland at night almost every day during spring and summer, and generally "burns off" the next day sometime between 9 A.M. and noon, as the land heats up. Sometimes, though, it may linger all day, especially near the coastal areas. Indeed, some coastal communities receive more hours of sunshine in the winter than they do in the summer.

San Diego's infrequent and highly seasonal rainstorms generally occur between the months of October and April. During these winter months the high pressure system occasionally weakens or moves further south, thus allowing major storms from the Pacific to reach southern California. Some of these originate in the Gulf of Alaska, while others (often the wettest ones) originate in the warmer tropical waters near Hawaii. On the average, between ten and twenty such storms reach San Diego County each winter, with the heaviest ones dropping one to two inches of rain in the metropolitan area. Once in a great while a major tropical cyclone may reach us from the south but this is quite rare (although two occurred in the consecutive years of 1976 and 1977).

In the summer, the sparse rainfall in coastal areas usually comes from an occasional thunderstorm, but some summers are completely

[1]All temperature figures are expressed in degrees Fahrenheit.

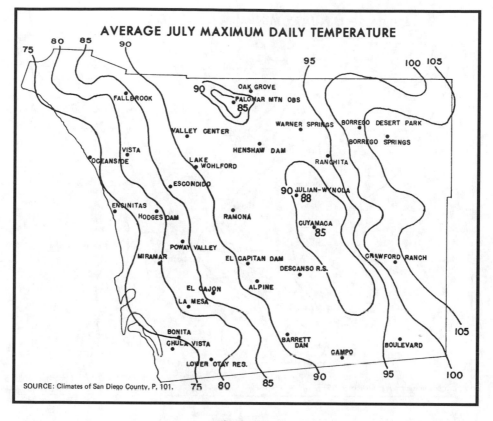

Figure 3.1.

without measurable precipitation. The key terms to describe the county's rainfall are "highly seasonal" and "highly variable." A further discussion of San Diego's rainfall characteristics can be found in Chapter 8.

Mountains are another important control on climate. As you gain elevation by driving eastward into the mountains of San Diego County, average temperatures decrease and average annual precipitation increases. This creates differing vegetation belts on mountains as one increases in elevation, a phenomenon known as *vertical zonation*. Although there can be excep-

tions, on an average annual basis, the higher you go into the hills the cooler and wetter it becomes. Thus Palomar Mountain is the wettest location in the county, receiving over forty inches of precipitation a year, and usually the most snow in winter; the Laguna and Cuyamaca mountains are the next coolest and wettest areas (Figure 3.3). The mountainous areas are more apt to get beneficial thundershowers in the summer than are low-lying areas, and one huge thunderstorm in 1891 reportedly dropped 11.5 inches of rain on Campo in just 80 minutes. Palomar Mountain is also the coolest spot in the county,

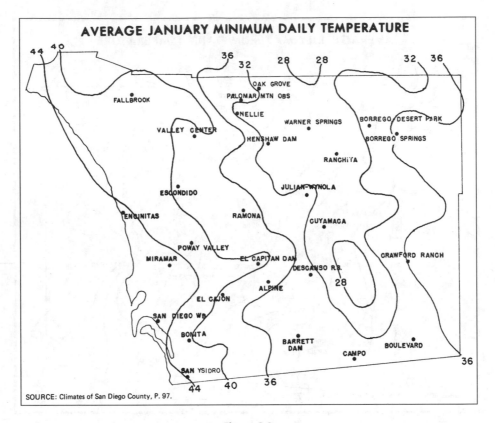

AVERAGE JANUARY MINIMUM DAILY TEMPERATURE

SOURCE: Climates of San Diego County, P. 97.

Figure 3.2.

with an average annual temperature of about 53°. Mountain areas tend to experience a greater range of temperatures, both daily and annual, than do coastal areas. The only subzero temperatures ever recorded in the county were a –4 and –1 at Cuyamaca State Park (Table 3.1).

Another common consequence of mountain ranges is to produce what is termed a *rain shadow* on the downwind side of the range. Thus, east of the Laguna crest, the average annual precipitation drops off very rapidly, and the community of Borrego Springs averages less than four inches of rain a year. The valley areas of Anza-Borrego Desert State Park form the west-

ernmost portion of the great Sonoran Desert, and are one of the driest parts of the United States. In summer, they are also one of the hottest, with the daily high temperature from mid-June to mid-September averaging between 105° and 115°. Yet in winter, near-freezing temperatures are not uncommon. This great range in temperatures in inland locations is termed *continentality,* and illustrates how completely the mountains of the county block off the moderating influence of the ocean (Table 3.2). The average range of temperature for any one day in downtown San Diego is only about 16°, but in Borrego Springs it is over 30°.

Figure 3.3. Heavy snow in the Cuyamaca Mountains, illustrating decreased temperatures at higher elevations. Photo by P. R. Pryde.

The desert is not always the hottest part of the county, however. Under the influence of subsiding Santa Ana winds, Spring Valley or Fallbrook (or even Point Loma!) may record the highest temperature in the county, and all stations in the county have registered temperatures of over 100°. Except under Santa Ana conditions, though, the daily high temperature in Borrego Springs will be anywhere from 10° to 30° higher than in San Diego.

It is clear that the coastal belt, the mountains, and the deserts all have significantly different climates. Based on considerations of average temperatures and precipitation, the world can be divided into several different natural climatic zones, and four or five of these can

be found in San Diego County. The four most common locally are (1) cool Mediterranean, (2) warm Mediterranean, (3) semiarid (or steppe), and (4) arid (or desert). The semiarid classification is sometimes divided into cool and hot subcategories, but the hot steppe region of San Diego county is found only in a relatively narrow belt as one descends the steep east face of the Laguna, Volcan, and San Ysidro (Hot Springs) mountain ranges, and thus is of lesser importance (Figure 3.4).

If almost any Californian were asked what climatic zone the city of San Diego lies in, they would probably respond "Mediterranean." But in fact, it does not! The entire coastal area of the county is properly classified as a semiarid

TABLE 3.1. Temperature and Precipitation Summary, Selected Stations

Weather Station	Elevation (feet)	Average Annual Precipitation (inches) (1971–2000)	Average Annual Temp. (F) (1971–2000)	Average July or August (a) High T (F)	Average January Low T (F)	Difference between All-time High and All-time Low T (F)
Alpine	1,700	18.7	63.8	90.3	38.0	94 (112:18)
Borrego Springs	625	6.9	72.8	106.0	36.5	106 (121:15)
Campo	2,630"	15.4	58.7	94.3	32.4	96 (108:12)
Cuyamaca	4,650	35.7	53.1	85.2	28.1	104 (100:-4)
El Cajon	525	12.8	65.1	88.2	36.7	93 (113:20)
Escondido	660	15.7	62.5	87.9	36.7	91 (108:17)
Julian/Wynola	3,655	27.5	57.4	88.4	32.5	95 (105:10)
Oceanside	60	11.2	60.6	72.9	42.6	78 (103:25)
Palomar Mtn./ Observatory	5,350	29.8	55.7	83.9	31.0	91 (100:9)
Ramona	848	17.1	61.7	91.4	36.5	85 (106:21)
San Diego/Lindbergh	13	9.9	63.2	78.0	45.4	77 (106:29)
Warner Springs	3,180	12.9	56.5	93.4	30.0	98 (109:11)

(a) Whichever is higher.

Sources: U.S. Weather Bureau, NOAA.

steppe climate. The reason for this is that the coastal strip, which receives only about ten inches of rain a year on the average, is too dry to be termed a Mediterranean climate. Most of the Mediterranean-type vegetation with which we have landscaped the metropolitan area could not survive the dry climate here if it were not regularly watered, as the average homeowner well knows. The sparse, brown vegetation seen on undeveloped mesas, such as the area around Miramar N.A.S., gives a hint as to our true climate. Only when one has gone inland far enough to receive about fourteen inches of rain a year (Alpine, Escondido) can the climate be accurately termed Mediterranean. In most inland valley and foothill areas, where the average temperature of the warmest month is above 71.6°, the climate is termed warm-summer Mediterranean, and in the higher elevations (Julian, etc.) it is a cool-summer Mediterranean. East of Julian, as noted above, the traveler quickly passes through a hot steppe transition belt, and then drops into the arid or desert zone as soon as they are below about 3,000 feet elevation (Table 3.2).

These natural zones are useful ways of viewing the county, because of their close relationship to soils and vegetation belts. For example, the cool Mediterranean climate zone of the mountains corresponds quite closely to the areas of coniferous forests in the county. The rest of the chapter will examine the principal features of the soils and vegetation zones that are most common in San Diego County, and the wildlife found within them.

TABLE 3.2. Climatic Data for Representative San Diego County Locations

Station		J	F	M	A	M	J	J	A	S	O	N	D	Year
San Diego	High T[a]	64.6	65.4	67.7	69.2	70.9	72.6	76.8	78.0	77.6	74.4	72.1	67.0	71.4
	Low T[b]	45.4	46.9	50.2	53.8	57.0	59.8	63.4	65.5	62.2	57.8	51.4	47.2	55.1
	Average P[c]	2.01	2.15	1.57	.79	.15	.05	.01	.08	.15	.49	.90	2.05	10.40
	Most P[d]	6.26	5.31	5.89	3.58	.88	.28	.16	.87	2.58	2.90	5.82	7.60	24.93
El Cajon	High T[a]	67.0	68.0	70.2	73.5	76.7	81.0	88.0	88.2	87.5	81.4	76.5	70.5	77.4
	Low T[b]	36.7	38.8	40.9	46.1	49.9	53.6	57.6	58.4	55.6	48.9	40.2	37.5	47.0
	Average P[c]	2.41	2.57	2.23	1.19	.46	.07	.04	.15	.23	.58	.93	2.22	13.08
	Most P[d]	7.13	7.68	8.08	6.10	3.69	.88	.20	1.92	5.03	3.13	4.02	7.59	28.14
Palomar Mountain (West slopes)	High T[a]	47.0	48.8	51.7	59.2	65.2	80.4	83.8	83.9	77.5	66.9	57.6	49.5	64.3
	Low T[b]	31.0	31.5	34.9	37.6	40.6	51.3	57.4	57.3	51.4	44.7	37.8	32.0	42.3
	Average P[c]	10.83	8.65	10.67	2.57	2.24	.18	.55	.60	.53	1.91	3.30	5.94	47.97
	Most P[d]	44.41	16.78	36.88	9.94	7.21	1.14	3.75	1.70	4.40	6.79	9.99	26.90	82.21
Borrego Springs (airport)	High T[a]	68.8	73.7	76.8	85.6	91.7	100.6	106.0	104.3	100.8	90.5	77.3	70.4	87.2
	Low T[b]	36.5	40.6	44.6	51.4	56.0	62.6	70.3	69.4	63.6	54.2	42.9	37.4	52.5
	Average P[c]	.51	.27	.34	.14	.01	.01	.12	.58	.16	.29	.38	.56	3.37
	Most P[d]	2.17	1.44	1.35	.74	.13	.22	.46	5.51	1.10	2.64	2.56	3.05	10.75

[a] Average daily high temperature during the month.
[b] Average daily low temperature during the month.
[c] Average precipitation for the month, in inches.
[d] Greatest monthly precipitation ever recorded for that month, or (last column) for one year.

Source: Climates of San Diego County: Agricultural Relationships, pp. 38–42 and 60–65.

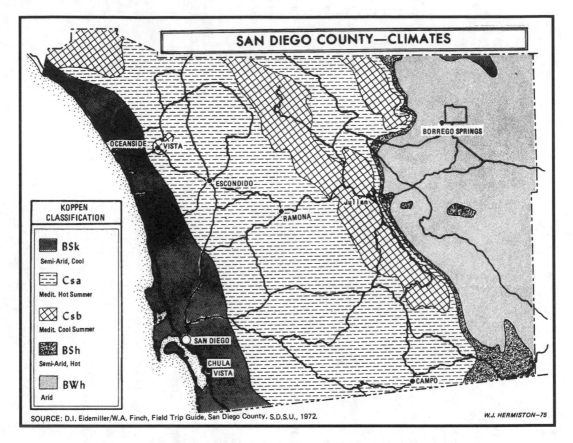

Figure 3.4. San Diego County's five main climate zones.

San Diego County Soils

Soils are an easily overlooked but extremely important component of the physical environment of any region. They not only support the area's natural vegetation, as well as the agriculture with which we replace this vegetation, but they are also the foundation for our homes and all the other structures of our neighborhoods and cities. Used with care, they provide the physical foundation of our civilization; abused, they can become an agent of its destruction, as the preceding chapter pointed out.

All soils contain varying amounts of organic and inorganic (mineral) matter, as well as water and air. They are a product of the weathered bedrock beneath them, and the decomposed organic (plant and animal) material on top of them. Climate and surface waters together with the various living agents of decomposition (worms, etc.) slowly transform these parent materials into soils. Depending on the area's climate and bedrock, thousands or even millions of years may be required for this process.

The majority of San Diego County, except for Anza-Borrego and Cuyamaca State Parks, has been well mapped in terms of its soils (see the "Soil Survey" reference at the end of the chapter). Soils that are similar are grouped together into what is known as a *soil series*. There are 53 of these series in San Diego County. Each has been studied to determine its suitability or limitations for certain types of uses, such as agriculture or construction. The Soil Survey rates their suitability for these uses as good, fair, or poor; their limitations (such as erodibility) are designated as slight, moderate or severe.

As an example, a commonly occurring soil in San Diego County is Diablo clay. Diablo clays have high shrink-swell characteristics, which means that moisture causes them to expand. Thus, they can cause cracks in buildings, and must be dealt with carefully in the course of urban construction. Further, these clays can precipitate landslides under adverse developmental conditions, as was observed in Chapter 2. On the other hand, Diablo clays are moderately fertile, and are a very good soil for growing certain truck crops, such as tomatoes.

Thus, it is a wise policy to learn about local soil characteristics before buying land for any purpose. It is particularly important to understand basic soil properties, and to hire a soils engineer, before committing land to any economic use involving significant capital expenditures or permanent structures.

On the coastal terraces, most of the soil series are comprised of sandy loams, clay loams, and clays. These range from poor to good for agriculture, depending on their depth and permeability. As noted above, clay soils pose problems for urban development, and are also underlain by an iron-silica hardpan, making either gardening or landscaping difficult. They are frequently poorly drained, causing numerous back-yard ponds during the wet season. On the other hand, some of the best soils in the region are found in the coastal river floodplains, and

unless waterlogged or salinized are generally quite fertile.

In the foothills on the western slopes of the mountains, the soils are generally well-drained sandy loams or silt loams over decomposed granitic or metavolcanic rock. They are fairly fertile though often rocky, and support much of the county's extensive avocado acreage. As in the coastal province, the most fertile soils are generally found in the valley areas, such as around Lakeside, Ramona, and the San Pasqual and San Luis Rey valleys. Conversely, other areas are mostly rocky outcrops having almost no soil at all.

The higher mountain areas are characterized for the most part by usually well drained sandy loams over granitic bedrock. Due to rocky outcrops and generally steep slopes, these have limited agricultural potential, with the famous orchards around Julian representing a notable exception. Other agriculture in the mountains occurs mainly on relatively flat alluvial sandy loams, such as around Campo and Warner Springs, or on natural meadows as occur in the Laguna Mountains.

In the desert, the soils range from virtually none on the steep mountain slopes, to coarse sandy alluvial soils on the gentler slopes. If these latter are irrigated, as they are in the area north of Borrego Springs, they can support a variety of agricultural activities. Since in this area evaporation exceeds precipitation, these desert soils are often alkaline, and in low lying areas saline basins can develop, such as Borrego Sink and Clark Dry Lake. In easily erodible areas of moderate local relief, steep mazelike canyons called badlands may form, such as the scenic Borrego Badlands at Font's Point.

Vegetation Communities

Probably most San Diegans are unaware that California contains more plant and animal species—6,717 according to The Nature Conservancy—than any other state. Even fewer may realize that San Diego is the most biologically diverse county in the state, and quite possibly in the country. This is because we have such a variety of natural climatic regions within the county.

Plant species are closely related to the type of climatic zone in which they are found, and animal life in turn corresponds to the plant composition. There are five major vegetation communities (also called biotic zones) within San Diego County: coastal sage scrub, chaparral, oak-pine woodlands, pinyon-juniper, and desert scrub. The areal expanse of these biotic zones exhibits a high correlation with the five basic climatic zones illustrated in Figure 3.4, and this correlation is further illustrated in the schematic cross-section of the county depicted in Figure 3.5. Within most of these five basic vegetation communities may be found two or three distinct types of subzones, or localized biotic communities, some of which are fairly limited in size though not necessarily in importance (Table 3.3).

The placing of the county's vegetation into five broad biotic zones necessarily involves a certain amount of generalization. There is no visible line in the natural world that precisely delimits these zones. Rather, their boundaries are usually wide transition zones. Neighboring plant communities tend to mutually "invade" one another, since similar soils and microclimates usually exist for some distance on either side of the generalized biotic zone boundary.

Coastal Sage Scrub

The Coastal Sage Scrub zone extends from the ocean inland to approximately the 1,500 foot elevation contour. The eastern boundary is necessarily very general, as chaparral species widely invade into the coastal zone, especially in canyons and on cooler north-facing slopes.

The Coastal Sage Scrub zone is characterized by a semi-open appearance, with most of the typical vegetation species not exceeding 3–4 feet in height. The dominant species include California sagebrush *(Artemisia californica),* flat-top (or California) buckwheat *(Eriogonum fasciculatum),* laurel sumac *(Rhus laurina),* and white and black sage *(Salvia apiana* and *S. mellifera)*. This zone is also characterized by a large number of forbs (forbs are broad-leafed herbaceous plants, and include most small spring wildflowers), as well as many woody-stemmed flowering plants such as the attractive mimulus, also known as monkey-flowers. The zone also contains a large variety of both natural and introduced grasses, introduced varieties of mustard, and certain species of cacti such as prickly pear *(Opuntia littoralis)*.

Within the coastal province, two other very familiar natural zones occur, the intertidal and coastal marsh-lagoon communities. Both of these are very fragile, and their intricate ecological relationships are easily disturbed (see Chapter Seven). The lagoons in particular are repeatedly threatened by development proposals and siltation, and for this reason, much effort has gone into their preservation.

Much of San Diego county's original Coastal Sage Scrub zone (over 70%) has been transformed by urban development (Table 3.4). Locations where it may still be found include undisturbed areas near Lake Hodges and the Otay lakes, Miramar Marine Air Station, and Point Loma. Two convenient places to study Coastal Sage vegetation are the nature trails in Florida Canyon in Balboa Park, and in the Bernardo Bay area of the San Dieguito River Park.

Chaparral

The Chaparral plant community is characteristic of inland hillsides, most commonly within

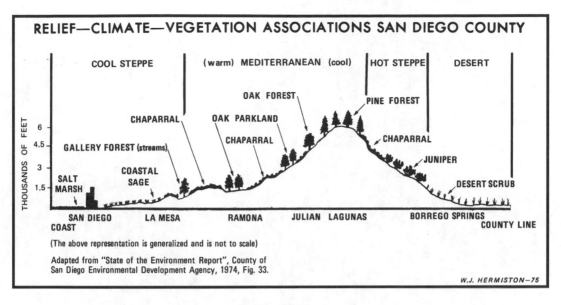

RELIEF—CLIMATE—VEGETATION ASSOCIATIONS SAN DIEGO COUNTY

(The above representation is generalized and is not to scale)

Adapted from "State of the Environment Report", County of
San Diego Environmental Development Agency, 1974, Fig. 33.

W.J. HERMISTON—75

Figure 3.5.

an elevation range of from 1,000 to 5,000 feet. In terms of acreage, it is the most extensive biotic zone in the county (Table 3.4). On its western margins, it mixes freely with the coastal sage scrub, with several species, such as the laurel sumac and black sage, found in both zones. Here, the plants rarely exceed 5–10 feet in height. Further inland, at the zone's eastern margins where it mixes with pine-oak woodlands, typical mountain chaparral species such as manzanita *(Arctostaphylos spp.)*, redshank *(Adenostoma sparsifolium)*, and various oaks *(Quercus spp.)*, may grow to fifteen feet or more. Other common chaparral species include chamise *(Adenostoma fasciculatum)* and several varieties of California lilac *(Ceanothus spp.)*.

Chaparral is a remarkable plant community. First, chaparral plants must be able to survive the prolonged summer drought season. To do this, they have adapted both their root structure, which is extensive and deep, and their leaves, which are often waxy and curl easily to minimize evaporation losses. Second, they have developed the ability to recover readily from wildfire, which is a natural part of chaparral ecology and which is rapidly spread by these dense, tinder-dry woody plants in the summer and fall dry season.

Spring is a particularly attractive season in the chaparral, with the ceanothus and other shrubs and forbs displaying a profusion of wildflowers. Resident mammals, which generally prefer the more open edges and margins to the dense interior of the chaparral, include mule deer, fox, racoon, coyote, bobcat, skunks, and rabbits. Most of these common species, as well as others less often seen such as ringtail cat and mountain lion, are nocturnal, using the cover of darkness both for protection and to avoid the summer heat. Many species of birds and rodents have adapted themselves to the denser interior of the chaparral zone.

TABLE 3.3. Correspondency Table of Climatic and Biotic Zones in San Diego County

Biotic Zone/Subzone	Climatic Zone	Elevation Range	Some Typical Species of the Zone
1. Coastal Sage Scrub	Cool Steppe (BSK)	0–1500*	Flattop buckwheat, Calif. sage, Laurel sumac
1a. Intertidal		–5– +5	Mollusks, Anemones, Crustaceans, loose kelp
1b. Coastal Marsh/Lagoon		0– 20	Salicornia, Saltbush, Sea fig, grasses
2. Chaparral	Warm Mediterranean (Csa)	1000*–5500	Scrub Oak, Chamise, Ceanothus, Manzanita
2a. Riparian Woodland		50–5000	Cottonwood, Sycamore, Willow
2b. Oak Parkland ("Savanna")		3000–4500	California live oak, grasses
3. Oak and Pine/Oak Woodlands	Cool Mediterranean (Csb)	3500–6500	Black oak, Var, pines, Live Oak, Incense Cedar
3a. Southern Oak Woodland		3500–6000	Black oak, Coulter pine, chaparral sp.
3b. Coniferous Forest		4500a–6500	Jeffrey pine, Incense cedar, other pines
3c. Mountain Grassland		3500–6000	Grasses, Forbs
4. Pinyon/Juniper association (Chaparral is common in this zone, in which the main indicator species tend to be very very intermittent)	Hot Steppe (BSh)	5000–2000	Juniper, Yucca, Pinyon, Cacti, chaparral
5. Desert (or Creosote Bush) Scrub	Desert (BW)	3000– 0	Cresote Bush, Brittlebush, Ocotillo, Cacti
5a. Desert Riparian		2000–500	Mesquite, Ironwood, Smoke tree
5b. Palm Oasis		2000–500	Fan Palm

*The boundary between the Coastal sage scrub and chaparral communities is very imprecise as the two blend together over a wide elevation range. Chaparral can be found on north-facing canyon slopes at any elevation in the coastal province.
a3500 feet in Pine Valley

Two other major biotic communities can be identified within the chaparral zone. These are the riparian woodland and the oak parkland (or "savanna"). The riparian woodland is the familiar canopy of cottonwood *(Populus fremontii)*, willows *(Salix spp.)* and sycamores *(Platanus racemosa)* that are found along most of the larger streams in the county. This community has high aesthetic and wildlife habitat values, but is also highly depleted (Table 3.4). The oak parkland consists of widely spaced California live oaks *(Quercus agrifolia)* growing in natural grasslands, usually with various chaparral species attempting to invade from the edges. Easily seen oak parklands exist along I-8 and Highway 94 in the Boulder Oaks and Potrero areas, and around Ramona.

An excellent natural area in which to study chaparral vegetation is the Silverwood Wildlife Sanctuary on Wildcat Canyon Road. Although heavily burned in the 2003 "Cedar" fire, the chaparral here will recover.

Oak and Pine-Oak Woodlands

The oak and pine-oak woodlands are characteristic of the higher mountain areas, and are generally encountered above about 3,500 feet, corresponding to the cool mediterranean climatic belt. The dominant community in this biotic zone is the southern oak woodland, in which black and live oak *(Quercus kelloggii* and *Q. agrifolia)* dominate. There are commonly many chaparral species mixed in, especially on the margins and in recently burned areas. Above 5,000 feet, pines and oaks often occur in about equal proportion.

At elevations above 6,000 feet, the forest may become predominantly, or totally, coniferous. In

TABLE 3.4. Vegetation Communities in San Diego County

Community Type	Original Acreage	1990 Acreage	Percent Change
Chaparral (all types)	1,120,970	937,192	−16.4
Creosote bush and mesquite scrub	536,900	504,429	−6.1
Coastal sage scrub	480,260	135,370	−71.8
Desert transition	143,680	143,680	0
Native grassland and mountain meadow	142,160	23,730	−83.3
Oak woodland	109,400	105,680	−3.4
Coniferous forest (a)	79,010	79,010	0
Riparian woodland	34,580	13,570	−60.8
Desert wash and desert wash complex	26,080	26,080	0
Pinyon—juniper woodland	20,420	20,420	0
Coastal salt marsh	6,530	810	−87.6
Cypress woodland (a)	4,440	4,229	−4.8
Coastal strand	1,940	0	−100
Dry lake sink	1,580	1,580	0
Freshwater marsh	1,090	100	−90.8
Torrey pine woodland	310	250	−19.4
Urban-agricultural complex	0	339,030	
Disturbed grassland	0	203,760	
Agriculture	0	159,640	
Lakes and reservoirs	0	10,800	

Source: Adapted from T. Oberbauer, "Rare Plants and Habitats in San Diego County", 1990.
(a) The area of conifer forests was probably permanently reduced by the 2003 fires.

addition to Jeffrey and Coulter pine, incense cedar *(Libocedrus decurrens)* and white fir *(Abies concolor)* are locally common. In the more open areas, spring wildflowers, such as various species of penstamon and lupine, can be spectacular. Good examples of both the southern oak woodland and coniferous forests can be found in Palomar State Park, and along the Sunrise Highway (S-1) in the Laguna recreation area in Cleveland National Forest.

The third zone within the mountain province comprises areas of grasslands, the smaller of which are often called meadows. By far the largest mountain grassland in the county is around Lake Henshaw and Warner Ranch, which has long been used for cattle grazing. Unfortunately, most natural grasslands in the county have been taken over by introduced species (Table 3.4). Some, such as the Laguna meadows, may contain seasonal lakes.

Pinyon-Juniper Associations

The pinyon-juniper communities are found within the hot (arid) steppe belt on the eastern slopes of the county's Peninsular Ranges, but are not completely conterminous with it (Figure 3.6). Due to fires, topography, and unsuitable soils, these communities are localized to just a few regions within, or near, the hot steppe belt.

The community is named for two of the larger tree species found within it, California juniper *(Juniperus californica)* and pinyon pine *(Pinus monophylla)*. Also common within this community are several species of cacti and yucca, various chaparral plants, as well as a few desert species that can tolerate rocky slopes and slightly moister conditions.

The pinyon pine is now uncommon within the county. It was formerly more widespread, but was burned out in many areas due to a wildfire-inducing build-up of chaparral species within the pinyon-juniper community. This build-up was in part abetted by the policy of attempting to suppress all fires, which resulted eventually in such a fuel accumulation that the larger and hotter wildfires were able to decimate the community. Today, the policy of the Forest Service and other similar agencies is to manage undergrowth in conifer forests by various techniques, including deliberate controlled burns. Controlled burns, if done properly, can produce the combined results of protecting developed property, preventing dangerous levels of fuel build-up, and preserving the natural values of the conifer forests.

Because it is relatively small, there are no major sub-zones within the pinyon-juniper community. A good place to study this biotic association is along Highway 78 east of the base of the Banner Grade, and in the Box Canyon area along S-2. A huge pinyon pine, slightly out of place, is at the top of the hill on the Wooded Hill nature trail.

Desert (or Creosote Bush) Scrub

The desert scrub plant community is generally conterminous with the Sonoran desert climatic zone within the county. It is also sometimes referred to as the creosote bush scrub community after its dominant (or "indicator") species *(Larrea tridentata)*, also called (improperly) greasewood. Other common plants in this sparse but highly diverse community include ocotillo *(Fouquiera splendens)*, bursage *(Franseria dumosa)*, a large number of cacti *(Opuntia, Echinocereus,* and *Mammillaria spp.)*, and an even larger number of perennial and seasonal forbs and annual grasses.

The Sonoran desert is famous for its annual profusion of wildflowers. Their magnitude depends on the particular year's rainfall characteristics, but in wet years the blooming season usually extends from January to mid May, with the peak generally in March or early April.

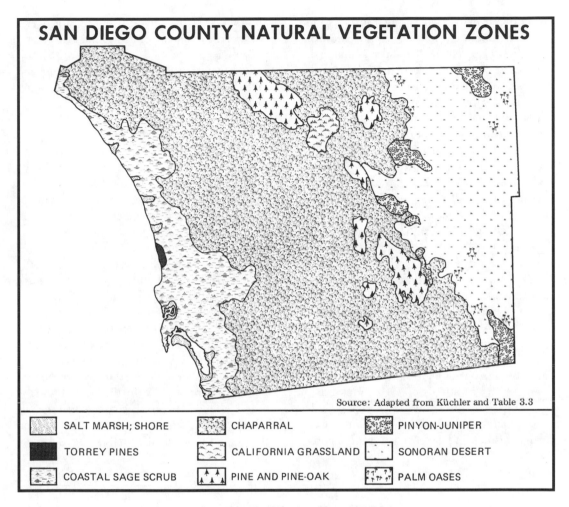

Figure 3.6. The major natural vegetation zones of the county.

In addition to the ocotillo and cacti, other colorful blooms include chuparosa *(Beloperone californica)*, brittle-bush *(Encelia farinosa)*, desert lavender *(Hyptis emoryi)*, desert primrose *(Oenothera deltoides)*, and sand verbena *(Abronia villosa)*. There are dozens of other less common flowers, one of the most looked-for being the desert lily *(Hesperocallis undulata)*, which usually blossoms right around Easter. The nature

trail at the end of the road in Borrego Palm Canyon provides a good introduction to the profusion of desert species.

Within the desert zone are two important sub-communities, the desert riparian and the palm oasis. The desert riparian, like its chaparral counterpart, occurs along stream courses where somewhat more abundant sub-surface moisture allows larger and different types of vegetation to exist. Two common species found here are mesquite *(Prosopis juliffora)* and ironwood. *(Olneya tesota)*. The spectacular palm oasis, most likely remnants of much larger palm forests that existed in an earlier and wetter era, are generally found near streams or springs that can supply their greater moisture requirements. They are comprised of the only native California palm, the fan palm *(Washingtonia filifera)*. The half-mile hike to the first grove in Borrego Palm Canyon is well worth the effort, especially during the winter and spring wildflower season.

In all of the county's biotic zones except the desert, wildfire is a significant annual threat. Summer and fall are the major fire seasons, but devastating brush fires can occur in any month (Table 3.5). Fire is a naturally occurring phenomenon in many semi-arid regions such as San Diego County, and the seeds of many plants in such biomes as chaparral and oak woodland will germinate only following wildfires. Under dry, Santa Ana wind conditions, brush fires can occasionally rage out of control and consume vast acreages and hundreds or even thousands of dwellings. The disastrous, fast-moving Cedar fire of October, 2003 was the largest in California's history, and destroyed over 2,200 homes

and took at least 14 lives. It burned for over a week and extended from Miramar Air Station in San Diego to beyond Julian (Figure 3.7). It is incumbent upon those who live near canyons and in the backcountry to take all necessary measures to protect their property from wildfires.

Rare and Unusual Vegetation

There are many rare, endangered, unique, and introduced species of vegetation in San Diego County. The California Native Plant Society lists a total of 154 rare or endangered species of flora in the region, many of which are not found in any other county or state.

One of the best known is the familiar Torrey pine *(Pinus torreyana),* restricted within the county to the coastal bluffs immediately north and south of Peñasquitos Lagoon. These trees depend on the frequent coastal fog for much of their moisture. Many of these trees are preserved in Torrey Pines State Reserve. Besides San Diego County, the only other place in the world they occur is on Santa Rosa Island in the Santa Barbara channel. Also in the coastal zone is found the endangered coast barrel cactus *(Ferocactus viridescens),* as well as the unusual flora found in seasonal vernal pools.

TABLE 3.5. Some Major San Diego County Wildfires

Year	Name	Significance
1913, September	Barone	65,470 acres burned
1928, September	Witch Creek	33,240 acres burned
1956, November	Inaja (Santa Ysabel)	11 firefighters perished
1970, September	Kitchen Creek (Laguna)	180,000 acres burned
1985, July	Normal Heights (San Diego)	76 homes destroyed
1987, October	Palomar Mountain	16,100 acres burned
1989, August	Vail (Agua-Tibia area)	15,600 acres burned
1993, October	Guejito	20,720 acres burned
1996, July	Harmony Grove	8,600 acres and 110 homes burned
2001, January	Viejas (Alpine)	10,350 acres burned
2002, July	Pines (Banner, Ranchita)	62,000 acres and 37 homes burned
2003, July	Coyote (Chihuahua Valley)	19,000 acres burned
2003, October	Paradise (Valley Center)	56,700 acres and 221 homes burned
2003, October	Cedar (I-15 east to Julian)	273,000 acres and 2,230 homes burned

Unusual chaparral plants include the coast spice bush *(Cneoridium dumosum),* which is actually in the citrus family, and a native species of orchid, the rein orchid *(Habenaria unalascensis).* Also in the chaparral zone is the rare Tecate cypress *(Cupressus forbesii),* found primarily on Otay Mountain where it is frequently subjected to fire losses, as it was in 2003.

The desert region is predictably rich in unusual vegetation. In addition to the fan palm and numerous annual flowers, another species of interest is the elephant tree *(Bursera microphylla).* Elephant trees are common in Mexico, but in the United States occur only in Anza-Borrego Desert State Park.

In the foothill and mountain provinces there occur occasional small meadows called *cienegas,* These usually form in low-lying areas where the soil is sufficiently wet to prevent the development of chaparral species. They are comprised of a rich variety of grasses and forbs that are a favorite food of foraging animals.

Among what is now our county flora are almost 200 species of plants that were introduced from other parts of the United States or the world. Many of the grasses and forbs that are found in the coastal sage and chaparral zones may have been brought in by the early Spaniards, mixed in with hay or crop seeds. Numerous others have been more recently introduced into the urban areas. The most visible and best known non-native species are the many groves of towering eucalyptus trees, brought here from climatically analogous parts of Australia. In urban areas, practically all decorative plants, flowers, and trees have been introduced. This makes the naturally rich flora of San Diego County even more varied.

With the advent of the twenty-first century, one of the most insidious environmental threats most everywhere on earth are introduced ("alien") plant and animal species that disperse rapidly and overrun beneficial native species. This is most definitely true in San Diego County, especially as regards plants. Among the worst of the local invasive plants are various tamarisk species, giant reed *(Arundo donax),* castor bean *(Ricinus communis),* pampas grass *(Cortaderia jubata),* fennel *(Foeniculum vulgare),* star thistle *(Centaurea solstitialis),* perennial peppergrass *(Lepidium latifolium),* and a large selection of other introduced plants. Various public agencies in the county must spend millions of dollars annually, and enlist countless volunteer citizens to provide manual labor, in order to try to control these non-native invasives. Unfortunately, the task is only expected to get worse in the future.

Wildlife Resources

Although the wildlife resources of San Diego County are rich enough to merit a detailed treatment, it will be possible only to summarize them here. There are probably three main points that should be made concerning our native wildlife. First, the wildlife resources of the county are richer and more varied than the average urban dweller may realize. Second, urbanization has made significant changes in the composition and numbers of our wildlife. And third, many unusual or endangered species may be found in the county, and deserve our special consideration.

Many of the mammals of San Diego County, as elsewhere, are secretive and try to avoid contact with people, and many are nocturnal in their habits. The fact that we seldom see them, however, does not mean that they are not around. Mule deer are still plentiful in the county, as are the easily seen cottontails, jackrabbits, skunks, and a large variety of rodents. Less often seen, but nevertheless widespread, are opossum, raccoons, and twenty-one species of bats. Carnivores include bobcat, coyotes, ringtails, two kinds of foxes, and an increasing number of

Figure 3.7. Remains of one of the residences as San Diego Audubon's Silverwood Wildlife Sanctuary following the vast 2003 "Cedar" fire. Photo taken by Pete Nelson on October 27, 2003.

mountain lions. The California grizzly bear has been extinct in the county since about 1901, although a mother black bear with cub was reported at Camp Pendleton in 1973, and several sightings were reported in 1999.

Reptiles include the common fence lizard, alligator lizard, and others; also several species of snakes, most of which are beneficial, including the three poisonous species. Among marine mammals, the sea lion, harbor seal, and of course the California grey whale are the most often seen. Other species of whales and dolphins may be encountered further offshore.

It is in terms of bird life that the county is truly outstanding. The annual Audubon Society Christmas bird census regularly turns up one of the highest counts recorded anywhere in the nation. The reasons for this outstanding selection of bird life are, first, the wide variety of natural zones and habitats in the county (Table 3.3), and second, our strategic location on the Pacific Flyway (the spring-fall migration route). The county is also an important wintering area for many species of birds, especially waterfowl and shorebirds which use our coastal lagoons and estuaries. In all, about 490 species of birds have been recorded in the county, of which about 170 breed here.

Urbanization inevitably brings changes to the wildlife populations that formerly inhabited an area. Some species, such as deer, quail, rodents, and some species of songbirds and waterfowl are capable of adapting to the human presence, perhaps even thriving because of the increased water and vegetation. Others, however, are less adaptable, and are usually eliminated as land is converted from a rural to an urban status. We have tried to compensate for the inevitable changes by protecting or improving the habitat of some of the remaining species. Numerous wildlife preserves have been established, artificial feeding and watering stations have been installed, and important breeding areas are posted and protected.

Many species have been so reduced in numbers that they have been given "endangered" or "threatened" status. Indeed, because of the uniqueness of San Diego's natural environment and the extent of local urbanization, San Diego County has more endangered species than any other county in the United States. Habitat destruction has been the most common cause of this.

The county's best known endangered mammal is probably the desert bighorn sheep. Several endangered or threatened species of birds nest in the county, of which the brown pelican, Bell's vireo, and least tern are probably the most famil-

iar. Several others (including the symbol of our country, the bald eagle) are regularly seen here. There are also several endangered species of amphibians and invertebrates (butterflies, etc.) in the county. A complete list is given in Table 3.6.

Local governments are working to identify the most important wildlife habitats in the county, as a first step towards preserving the wildlife that utilize them. It is desirable to do this not just for aesthetic and educational reasons, but also to reap psychological and even economic benefits. The natural environment, like the built environment, is an important part of San Diego's heritage, and neither should be thoughtlessly destroyed.

To this end an extensive network of preserved lands and open space reserves has been created in the county (see Chapter 17). These are owned and managed by a variety of public and private entities, and virtually all are accessible to the public. Numerous excellent nature centers exist in the county, from the Tijuana Estuary Visitors Center in Imperial Beach to the unique underground state park visitors' center in Borrego Springs. These present marvelous opportunities for families and individuals to further acquaint themselves with San Diego's impressive natural environment.

TABLE 3.6. San Diego County: Endangered and Threatened Fauna

	Extir-pated?	Federal Endan.	Federal Threat.	Calif. Endan.	Calif. Threat.
Invertabrates					
Riverside fairy shrimp		X			
San Diego fairy shrimp		X			
Laguna Mountain skipper		X			
Quino checkerspot butterfly		X			
Fish					
Desert pupfish (introduced in ABDSP)		X		X	
Tidewater goby		X			
Unarmored three-spine stickleback (introduced)		X		X	
Southern steelhead trout		X			
Amphibians and Reptiles					
Desert slender salamander	?	X		X	
Arroyo toad		X			
California red-legged frog (extirpated)	X		X		
Mountain yellow legged frog	?	X			
Barefoot banded gecko			X		
Mammals					
Pacific pocket mouse		X			
Stephen's kangaroo rat		X			X
Peninsular bighorn sheep					X
Birds					
California brown pelican		X		X	
California condor (extirpated)	X	X		X	
Bald eagle (winter migrant)		X		X	
Swainson's hawk (winter migrant)					X
American peregrine falcon		X		X	
California black rail (extirpated)	X				X
Light-footed clapper rail		X		X	
Western snowy plover			X		
California least tern		X		X	
Marbled murrelet (only found offshore)			X	X	
California spotted owl					X
Yellow-billed cuckoo (extirpated)	X				X
Southwestern willow flycatcher		X		X	
Least Bell's vireo		X		X	
California gnatcatcher			X		
Bank swallow (formerly bred)	?				X
Belding's savannah sparrow		X			

* Species that are listed have some protection at the Federal or State level. Other species of concern that are not yet listed include: White abalone, Orange-throated whiptail, Flat-tailed horned lizard, Southwestern pond turtle, Golden eagle, Burrowing owl, San Diego cactus wren, Grasshopper sparrow, and many others.
There are also 32 species of plants on the federal or state lists.

Sources: San Diego County DPLU and San Diego Museum of Natural History.

References

Bailey, H. P. *The Climate of Southern California.* Berkeley: Univ. of California Press, 1966.

Beauchamp, R. M. *A Flora of San Diego County, California.* National City: Sweetwater River Press, 1986.

California Native Plant Society. *Inventory of Rare and Endangered Plants of California* (6th ed.). Berkeley: C.N.P.S., 2001.

Clarke, C. *Edible and Other Useful Plants of California,* Berkeley: Univ. of California Press, 1977.

Hickman, James C. *The Jepson Manual: Higher Plants of California.* Berkeley: UC Press, 1993.

Küchler, A. W., *Map of the Natural Vegetation of California* (Map and text). Lawrence, KA: University of Kansas, 1977.

LaFee, Scott, "Burned Beyond Recognition", *San Diego Union-Tribune,* Dec. 31, 2003, pp. E-1 and E-4.

LaRue, Steve, "Seeds of Destruction: Exotic Invaders Crowd Out Native Plant Species," *San Diego Union-Tribune,* Oct. 16, 1996, pp. E-1 ff.

Munz, Philip A. *A Flora of Southern California.* Berkeley: Univ. of California Press, 1974.

Munz, P. A. *California Spring Wildflowers.* Berkeley: Univ. of California Press, 1961 (see also the companion volume *California Desert Wildflowers).*

Oberbauer, Thomas. *Rare Plants and Habitats in San Diego County. San Diego: County Department of Planning and Land Use, April 1990.*

Parisi, Monica, ed. *Atlas of the Biodiversity of California.* Sacramento: California Department of Fish and Game, 2003.

San Diego Association of Governments. *INFO: Vegetation in the San Diego Region.* San Diego: SANDAG, Jan.–Feb. 1998.

Soule, M.E. "Land Use Planning and Wildlife Maintenance: Guidelines for Conserving Wildlife in an Urban Landscape", *Journal of the American Planning Association,* Vol. 57 (199 1), No. 3, pp. 313–323.

U.S. Dep't of Agriculture. *Soil Survey, San Diego Area, California.* USDA, Soil Conservation Service, 1971.

Unitt, Philip. *Breeding Bird Atlas of San Diego County.* San Diego: Natural History Museum, 2004.

Univ. of California (in cooperation with U.S. Weather Bureau). *Climates of San Diego County: Agricultural Relationships.* Univ. of California Agricultural Extension Service, 1970.

Internet Connections:

California Native Plant Society: *www.cnps.org*

San Diego Audubon Society: *www.sandiegoaudubon.org*

San Diego Natural History Museum: *www.sdnhm.org*

U.S. Weather Bureau: *www.nws.noaa.gov*

Chapter Four Clifford E. Trafzer

American Indians
The County's First Residents

In May 1989, a concerned group of Native Americans from San Diego County met at San Diego State University to discuss desecration of a sacred site. The parish at the Mission San Diego planned to build a recreation hall on top of the ruins of the old church and a cemetery encircling the site. Most of the people buried in the cemetery were local Indians, and the church

Clifford E. Trafzer is Professor of History and Director of American Indian Studies at the University of California, Riverside. He wrote the first version of this essay while he was Professor of American Indian Studies at San Diego State University with the assistance of Richard Carrico. Trafzer is of mixed Wyandot Indian ancestry, and is the author of *Exterminate Them*! He is currently completing research on a book dealing with the health of Indian people of Southern California living within the Mission Indian Agency.

had ordered the removal of several skeletons from the graveyard. Indian delegates at this meeting began to organize, and by July they convinced the church to abandon their construction project and permit the Indian people to rebury their dead.

Details of the unfortunate event are mired in controversy, but the episode was significant for many reasons. The Indian people joined forces to ward off the destruction of holy ground, and the various bands of Kumeyaay Indians formed a cultural heritage committee which functions to protect the remains, material culture, and sacred sites of their ancestors. The event also brought together local Indian people with the California Native American Heritage Commission. Most important, the controversy at Mission San Diego illustrates the presence, prominence, and power of contemporary Native Americans in southern California. These Indians did not "vanish" with the nineteenth century. They survived and are ever-present in matters concerning Indian people.

Native American Beliefs, Values, and Ceremonies

Native Americans believe that the creative forces placed them in California at the time when the earth was young and that life emerged as a series of creations in a process. According to the elders, life originated from the depths of the water where the creative beings generally worked together to shape land, rivers, plants, and animals. At this time, the various forms of life communicated with each other orally, forming the basis of the first history and literature of this land. Indians of southern California have a rich oral literature that carefully chronicles the positive and negative forces so important in understanding human relations with the earth, animals, plants, and the invisible forces.

Within the current county boundaries, there are four Indian groups, which include the Kumeyaay (erroneously called Diegueño by the Spaniards), Luiseños, Cupeños, and Cahuillas. The Indians generally lived in small villages (Figure 4.1). Prior to 1907, San Diego County extended eastward to the Colorado River, the traditional home of Quechan Indians.

Like the other Indians of the region, Quechans have many creation stories. Lee Emerson, a long-time tribal historian, once confided that while *Kwikumat* created living things, his cohort, a being known as Old Blind Man, dove deep into the water in opposition to the creation. "When Old Blind Man went underwater," Emerson said, "a great mist went around the earth." He explained that this was a negative force, one that affected everything. "That's why we have positive and negative today," he explained. The dualism of life is a common

theme with the Indians of southern California, and their literature reflects the belief.

Archaeologists argue that all of the Indians now living in the San Diego area moved here after making the lengthy and arduous trek across the Bering Strait. Most scholars argue that the first Indian people settled in the region 15–20,000 years ago. While scientists maintain that the evidence suggests such dating, many Indian elders scoff at such notions. In general their view is that Native Americans emerged from the earth and water of their native lands. The older Indians and traditional teachers say that the life, culture, literature, religion, and history of the Indians emerged in the Americas.

Of course, there is no "generic" Indian belief system, history, or culture in southern California. The native people of the larger San Diego area—including the Kumeyaay (Ipai, Tipai, Pai Pai), Luiseño, Cupeño, Cahuilla, Chemehuevi, Quechan, and Cocopa—each enjoy a unique and varied past. Still, they have some things in common with each other. Most important, all of these people are tied in a spiritual way to the mountains, ocean, rivers, springs, plants, animals, and fish.

Creative powers molded the people and their natural environment together as one. Indians did not place themselves "above" nature or consider it something to be controlled. Indians did not feel they had dominion over the plants, animals, or fishes. Instead, they believed themselves to be on an equal basis with the creatures of the earth and with the earth itself. All of the Indians in the region had sacred places, sites where they sang, danced, and prayed. They had special places where they conducted ceremonies. Religion was the heart of the Indian communities, and they worshiped in different ways at sacred sites throughout the county.

The Kumeyaay and Luiseño both revere a site near present-day Rancho Bernardo. A large village once extended along a gentle valley

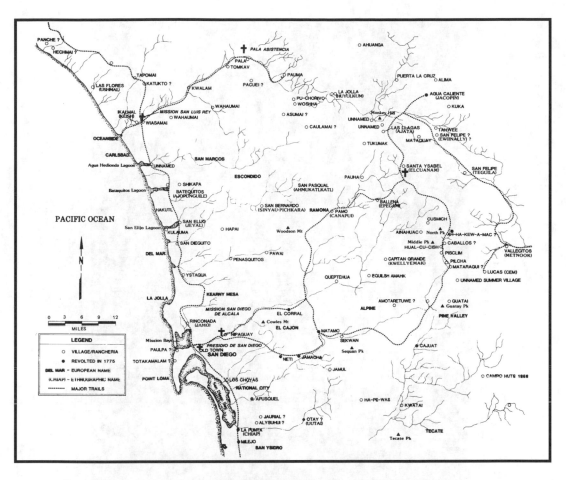

Figure 4.1. San Diego County native villages, during the period 1769–1820. Map courtesy of Richard Carrico.

where a creek flowed year around. A large outcropping of rocks stood near the creek, where the waters tumbled over a few small falls. The rocks are marked with pictographs and petroglyphs, and some of the signs were likely made during female puberty ceremonies (Figure 4.2). The Kumeyaay and Luiseño feel that this area of San Diego County was the birthplace to deities, spirits whose forces still influence the

people. The site is considered sacred to the Indian people, and some of them continue to use the place for prayer. It now has a protected status, and is off-limits to general public visitation.

San Diego County is dotted with such sacred Indian sites, places that are known to the native peoples. Over the years many of the sites have been damaged due to roads, highways, bridges, businesses, and homes. Indian leaders share a

Figure 4.2. Kumeyaay pictographs at the Piedras Pintadas site near Rancho Bernardo. Photograph by P. R. Pryde.

concern about all of these sites, including those used for puberty ceremonies for boys and girls. When young people reached the age of eleven or twelve, their elders took them aside and taught them the truths of adulthood. This time of change in their lives was marked by ritual and ceremony.

The puberty ceremony among Indians of San Diego differed from tribe to tribe, but each group considered their teachings, procedures, and rites holy. Among the Kumeyaay, ceremonies for boys and girls differed but both ended with the creation of a sand painting. The paintings are well known and consisted of a drawing done in colored sands constructed of and on the earth. Sand paintings were round, representing a circle with no beginning and no ending. Various sands represented the cosmos, including the Milky Way, home of spirits. With sand an elder made a mountain lion, cactus, and rattlesnake. White sage and salt were placed in a hole in the center of the painting. The ceremony ended when an elder collected the sand painting and removed it to a site where nothing could disturb it.

The Luiseño also employed sand paintings as well as paintings drawn on rocks. During the female puberty ceremony, girls formed a sisterhood that was symbolically united by a painting of diamonds. Each girl placed paint on her finger and with it retraced a diamond that had been previously pecked into the face of a rock. Elders today say that this act tied young women together with each other and with all past females who had undergone the ceremony. The bond between the girls was made holy through this action, and young females entered the world of adults as a result of the teachings, rituals, and ceremony.

The Kumeyaay and Luiseño conducted a special dance known as *Tathuila* or Whirling Dance. A medicine man conducted this ceremony, using feathers and a wooden wand inlaid with abalone shells. He wore a skirt woven with eagle feathers, which rose and moved upward and outward as he twirled, representing an eagle in flight. During the dance, Indians provided music using gourd and turtle shell rattles. The Whirling Dancer skillfully performed the ceremony, taking care not to trip, a sign of ill to come.

Another important ceremony among the four major county groups (Kumeyaay, Luiseño, Cupeño, and Cahuilla) was cremation. Generally, the Indians did not bury their dead without the cremation ceremony until after 1769 with the arrival of Christians. Prior to this date, most Indians cremated their loved ones, although the more ancient people before 2,000 years ago practiced inhumation. Among the Kumeyaay, Quechan, Mojave, and Cocopa, when a person died their family and friends burned their home and their belongings. Elders argue that this was done to keep the spirit from returning and so that the person would have their goods in the next life. According to Lee Emerson, a Quechan elder, it also prevented families, friends, and foes from fighting over a person's property. Indians placed the cremated remains in an olla made of earthen pottery, burying it in the bosom of Mother Earth. The Indians still conduct a reverent burial ceremony regardless of whether the person is inhumed or cremated.

The Indian people mourned the death of friends and family. They believed that the dead moved on to another life. The Kumeyaay, Quechan, and Cocopa believe that death did not completely separate the people of this earth from those of the "next world." These Indians conducted a sacred ceremony known as *Keru* or *Karuk*, a mourning celebration of all who had passed away. Once thought by anthropologists to be a forgotten ceremony, this rite has persisted within Indian communities. In 1989 Anna Sandoval of the Sycuan Reservation hosted a *Karuk* Ceremony. Indians throughout the region, including the Cocopa and Quechan from the lower Colorado River, participated in this sacred event.

Karuk Ceremonies last all night, and during the course of the evening singers sang their ancient songs accompanied by their gourd rattles. The Hyde family from Somerton, Arizona attended the Sycuan ceremony, and an elderly man of this family served as a singer. When asked if he knew a Cocopa named Ronnie Soto, he replied: "He passed on a long time ago, but don't be sad. He'll be here tonight, he'll be glad we're doing this tonight." The spirit returns to earth during the ceremony, renewing their bonds with the people.

All of the Indians of the area have their own particular songs, ceremonies, and dances. These cultural elements did not die with the passing of older generations but have survived today. Katherine Saubel, a Cahuilla elder born on the Los Coyotes Reservation in 1920, has spent her life preserving Cahuilla culture. Her family includes Cahuilla Indian singers, who know the old "Bird Songs." This is also true of the Christman family who resides on the Viejas Reservation. Ron, Virginia, and their children sing Kumeyaay Bird Songs. They perform the ancient songs and dance at special events. The Christmans are often joined by Jane Dumas, another Kumeyaay elder and preservationist.

Lee Dixon, a Luiseño Indian from the Pauma Reservation, was leader of a unique dance group, which sang the old songs. In 1990 Dixon sang one at an event honoring Sycuan tribal officers. Other Luiseño Indians, including Henry Rodriquez, Lorena Dixon, Patricia Dixon, and James Luna, have also spent their lives preserving and teaching the old ways. They have their counterparts among all of the tribes and bands in southern California, where the Indians have sparked their own cultural rebirth. Fern Southcott, former Chair of the Mesa Grande Reservation and former Co-Chair of the Kumeyaay Cultural Committee, represents those Indians who treasure the old cultures and use them to cope with the rapidly changing world today.

The End of Isolation

Indian elders point out that cultures are dynamic, not static, and that they change with time. The life of Indians had evolved over time, and it continued to change after the arrival of the first Spaniards into California. Hernando de Alarcon reached Alta California in 1540 by way of the Colorado River and was followed by the overland expedition of Melchoir Diaz the same year. The Cocopa and Quechans of California met these Spaniards in the deserts of the lower Colorado River. In 1542 the Kumeyaay met Juan Rodriguez de Cabrillo near Point Loma.

These meetings ultimately affected the lives of the Indians in southern California for one important reason. The Europeans believed in the "Right of Discovery," a concept created by non-Indians, which justified the invasion, conquest, and resettlement of non-Christian lands. Everywhere the Spaniards traveled, they claimed land for themselves. Thus, Alarcon, Diaz, and Cabrillo claimed California for Spain, which provided Europeans with an assumed right under European tradition to return one day in the name of their king and religion. The result of this "Right of Discovery" would be very costly to all Indians of California.

On foot, Father Junipero Serra traveled up the coast of Baja California, while Gaspar de Portola sailed up the coast commanding three ships. On July 2, 1769, the Spanish inaugurated the displacement of the native population and Spanish resettlement of the region. On July 16, Serra founded Mission San Diego de Alcala. Within a matter of days, the Kumeyaay watched the newcomers establish two institutions of the Spanish empire—a mission (or *reduccione*) and a presidio. The ceremonious actions of the Spaniards did not immediately threaten the Indians, since the white men suffered severely from scurvy and starvation. Yet from this inauspicious beginning came a social, cultural, and military invasion that forever changed Indians in southern California.

In 1774 Father Luis Jayme received permission from Serra to move Mission San Diego from what is now Presidio Park to the Kumeyaay village of Nipaguay, at the present site of Mission San Diego de Alcala. By 1797, over 1400 Indians were associated with the mission. The Kumeyaay helped build the first church in the heart of their village, and they endured the changes that came with the Spanish invasion of their home until November 1774, when they rose in a major rebellion against the church and military. Indians living in at least eighteen villages south of the San Diego River joined in the revolt, which was led by Indian religious leaders opposed to Christianity.

Ultimately, the soldiers snuffed the revolution, and missionaries ordered the Indians to rebuild the mission. Mission Indians contributed much to the mission system, serving as brick and tile makers, carpenters, cowboys, farmers, and freighters. The Kumeyaay managed the cattle herds and slaughtered, dressed, and preserved the meat. They cured the hides and hauled the leather to ships bound for foreign markets, earning profits for the mission.

While the Kumeyaay worked at Mission San Diego, the Luiseño did the same at Mission San Luis Rey. In 1820, over 1500 Indians lived at the San Diego mission and 2600 at San Luis Rey. Indians had little freedom at these missions, and the priests often treated them like slaves or, at best, as children. Some Indians chose the life of Mission Indians, but many fled the *reducciones* whenever possible. If the soldiers caught these "runaways," they severely punished them. Punishment at Indian missions was common throughout Latin America at the time. Father Serra—presidente of California's missions—and

the priests sanctioned the use of whips on men, women, and children for a variety of offenses. The missionaries kept records of the punishments, and Indians remember the beatings and ill treatment in their oral traditions.

Indian elders whose families lived at the missions of San Diego, San Luis Rey, Concepcion (near present-day Winterhaven, California), Santa Ysabel, Pala, San Juan Capistrano, San Gabriel, and others argue that life at the missions was disagreeable and deadly. Priests overworked Indians, punished them severely, and prevented them from openly worshipping in their traditional way. Often Indians starved or were undernourished, and they died from European diseases such as measles, influenza, and smallpox. The priests locked up unmarried women in enclosed adobe structures. Some Cahuilla scholars have argued that these unsanitary dwellings killed large numbers of women and babies.

These conditions led many Indians of southern California to escape the mission system. According to historian George Phillips, some fled inland to villages not tainted by the Spanish. Others moved onto ranches where men, women, and children worked as *vaqueros*. Still others joined bands of hostile Indians who stole horses and cattle from the missions and ranches, selling them to eager New Mexican buyers. As a result, the *reducciones* declined before the Mexican government secularized the missions in 1833. Indians chose not to remain within the missions before and after secularization, and many moved away from white communities to live an altered but "traditional" life of hunting, gathering, farming, and fishing (Figure 4.3).

The Indians of San Diego County hunted a variety of animals with bows, arrows, and throwing sticks. They hunted deer, rabbit, bighorn sheep, antelope, quail, geese, squirrel, and other small game. They fished for lobster,

Figure 4.3. A simulated native village on display in downtown San Diego, a part of the Cabrillo Celebration of September 1892. The original photo indicates the women are probably Luiseno, with the woman on the left reportedly over 100 years old. Photograph courtesy of the San Diego Historical Society.

crab, octopus, grunion, scallops, abalone, and clams. Most important, they ate acorns from the different oak trees in southern California—Live, Black, White, Scrub, and Jack. However, the favorite acorn came from the Black Oak found in the mountains. After the Indians hulled the nuts, they pounded them with mortar and pestle before ingeniously leaching the poisonous tannin from the acorns. The people either poured hot water over the meal or buried the acorns in the earth for a period of time. The meal made a nutritious mush, the staple for all Indians in the region.

Women provided for their families by gathering many kinds of natural foods. They were master ethno-botanists, and knowledge of native plants is still treasured by such women as Cahuilla elder Katherine Saubel and Kumeyaay elder Jane Dumas. Women collected such edible foods as mesquite beans, screw beans, chia, peony, prickly pear cactus fruit, pansy, watercress, miner's lettuce, wild mustard, lamb's quarters, manzanita berries, strawberries, blackberries, cherries, grapes, cattails, tule potatoes, mushrooms, clover, and many others (see Appendix 4.2, Edible Plants). The Indians collected a variety of foods from cactus, preserving them in intricate baskets and utilitarian pottery.

In the late nineteenth century Indians faced many problems. Most important was the invasion of non-Indians onto their lands. Following the United States-Mexican War, 1846–1848, the United States established political, economic, and military control of the region. When California became a state in 1850, American Indian policy reached the Pacific Coast and all of the Indians became "wards" of the federal government. Federal agents made a whirlwind tour of California in 1850–1851, negotiating several Indian treaties, including two with Indians in the greater San Diego region (Temecula and Santa Ysabel). However, the Senate of the United States rejected all 18 treaties negotiated with California's first nations.

Because the Senate failed to ratify the treaties, non-Indians in California refused to honor the natural right of Indians to own their own lands. In fact, as early as 1850 the California legislature passed Statutes Chapter 133, "An Act for the Government and Protection of Indians." This act contained several provisions, including: custody and control of Indian children could be assumed by whites; non-Indians could not be convicted of offenses based on the testimony of Indians; Native Americans could be forced to work off fines and court costs through bondage to whites; Indians could be lashed for stealing livestock; Indian vagrants could be hired out.

Indians had to contend with several forms of racial, legal, and economic discrimination. After years of neglect, the federal government established two reservations in San Diego County in 1870, only to rescind them within a year. Opposition by local ranchers, businessmen, and

the *San Diego Union* ensured the closure of the reservations. Finally, in 1875 President Ulysses S. Grant signed executive orders establishing ten reservations in the country. Collectively, the Indians secured slightly more than three-fourths of the land proposed in 1870. Over one hundred years has passed in which land has been added and subtracted, resulting in a patchwork of Indian lands throughout San Diego County (Figure 4.4).

With only a limited land base, the Indians had a hard time surviving due to the changes to their former environment. White people settled along the coast and controlled areas where former villages once stood. Miners overran Indian lands, pushing aside the original owners and tearing apart the earth in search of gold. Ranchers and farmers claimed large areas where Indians once hunted and gathered. Humans, horses, cattle, sheep, and other European animals altered and destroyed native plant and animal populations. The result proved devastating for Indians.

Indian people sometimes starved, not because they were not industrious but because whites took their land and destroyed their natural environment. This caused Indians to move from place to place in search of work. Indians throughout San Diego County found work wherever they could, particularly on ranches. Many had learned to handle cattle and horses at the missions and *asistencias*, and they continued this livelihood into the twentieth century. Indian men, women, and children worked on the ranches and farms. Some Indians owned their own livestock, using their animals to eke out a meager living. A few Indian ranchers became successful and independent.

In 1904, the noted author and Indian activist Charles F. Lummis wrote that "the condition of these Indians, peaceful, and industrious, but left by the government to starve for want of proper

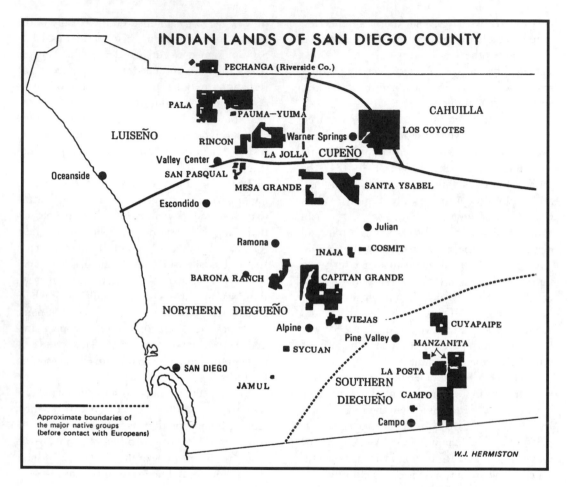

Figure 4.4.

lands, was a disgrace to the state and the nation." Indians suffered economically, and found few ways to benefit themselves through education. Whites did not permit Indians to attend public schools, and the Bureau of Indian Affairs established only a few Indian day schools. Agents sent Indian students to Sherman Indian Institute and other educational institutions located miles from San Diego.

Formal education for Indians centered on vocational tasks: girls learned to cook, clean, sew, and boys learned to garden, milk, and construct in iron and wood. This limited education system did little to alleviate poverty. Indian children sometimes died at Indian schools from exposure to tuberculosis, influenza, and measles. Sometimes they returned home with these maladies, spreading disease among their people. Deaths from disease affected the Indian populations of San Diego County, and births declined in the early twentieth century. Some observers at that time felt that the Indians would "vanish," but this was not to be; they persisted and survived.

The Current Status of County Indians

Locally, Indian people settled into two societies based on land tenure: an urban group that gradually acculturated but retained vestiges of their own culture, and a reservation group that fought to continue their way of life in rural settings. Urban Indians initially formed a large segment of the labor force, working as fishermen, dockworkers, and domestics. Reservation people ranched and farmed their own land. They also worked as cowboys, wranglers, and field hands for non-Indian ranchers. However, the migration of Chinese, Filipino, and other Asian workers led to the displacement of Indian workers.

Like others in the region, Indians lived through World War I and World War II, sending their men and women to fight for the United States. Later, young men and women fought in Korea, Vietnam, and the Persian Gulf, where they served with distinction. Local Indians participated in all the major events of the twentieth century and, far from vanishing, they continue to be a unique group of people within the ethnic fabric of San Diego County. In the 1950s and 1960s, Indians asserted themselves through the Indian Claims Commission. Many people represented the Indian claims, including Florence Shipek, a scholar known nationally for her work with Indians of the region. Local Indians received minimal cash payment for their claims, but the government did not return their land. Poverty continued with little educational opportunity.

During and after the Great Depression, many Indians from Oklahoma, Arizona, New Mexico, Montana, South Dakota, and other states moved to San Diego County. These "urban" Indians sought new opportunities in California, and they brought different religions, cultures, and experiences. By 1980 California became the state with the largest Indian population in the United States. According to the 1990 census, 242,000 Indians lived in California (over 80% being urban), of which over 18,000 lived in San Diego County. In the 2000 Census, 15,253 people in San Diego County indicated that they were American Indian or Alaskan Native, and over 27,000 people in the county stated they were of mixed race, including Native American.

However, native California Indians are the only Native Americans with tribal land bases in the state. Eighteen reservations, including the tribal lands of the Jamul band of Kumeyaay, are located in San Diego County, the largest number of reservations found in any county in the country (Table 4.1). On November 1, 1988, the Indian Land Transfer Act, Public Law 101-581, passed into law whereby the Bureau of Land Management transferred hundreds of acres to eight Indian reservations in San Diego County. Lands which prior to white settlement had been the sole domain of the county's Indians legally became tribal land.

The decades of the 1980s and 1990s proved pivotal for Indian people in San Diego County in large part because of the growth and development of high stakes gaming among some of the tribes.

For hundreds of years after the founding of Mission San Diego, Indian people of San Diego County struggled to survive because of famine, disease, land theft, and the destruction of resources. During the nineteenth and twentieth

TABLE 4.1. Reservations in San Diego County

Reservation	Tribal Group	Established	Acres	Tribal Enrollment	Enrolled Members on Reservation	Total Population on Reservation	Operating a Casino?(b)
Barona	Kumeyaay (a)	1931	6,000 (unallotted)	453	350	500	yes
Campo	Kumeyaay (a)	1893	15,480 (tribal)	203	?	120	yes
Capitan Grande	Kumeyaay (a)	1875	15,753 (tribal)	0	0	0	no
Cuyapaipe (Ewiiaapaayp)	Kumeyaay (a)	1893	4,102 (tribal)	8	?	?	planning
Inaja-Cosmit	Kumeyaay (a)	1875	846 (unallotted)	18	?	?	no
Jamul	Kumeyaay (a)	1975	6	56	18	86	planning
La Jolla	Luiseño	1892	7,957 (part allotted)	652	?	300	slots only
La Posta	Kumeyaay (a)	1893	3,556 (unallotted)	25	19	26	considering
Los Coyotes	Cahuilla and Cupeño	1889	26,000 (unallotted)	280	?	>200	considering
Manzanita	Kumeyaay (a)	1893	4,580 (unallotted)	97	?	45	planning
Mesa Grande	Kumeyaay (a)	1875	920 (tribal)	632	?	175	no
Pala	Luiseño and Cupeño	1875	12,117 (part allotted)	893	650	1,480	yes
Pauma-Yuima	Luiseño	1891	5,877	ca. 200	87	168	yes
Rincon	Luiseño	1875	4,200 (allotted)	552	ca.280	ca.1,800	yes
San Pasqual	Kumeyaay (a)	1910	1,380 (unallotted)	335	86	500	yes
Santa Ysabel	Kumeyaay (a)	1893	15,527 (unallotted)	1,011	?	499	considering
Sycuan	Kumeyaay (a)	1875	729 (part allotted)	129	?	122	yes
Viejas	Kumeyaay (a)	1931	1,609 (tribal)	289	?	800	yes

(a) Previously referred to as Southern and Northern Diegueño.
(b) As of January 1, 2003.

Source: County of San Diego, Impacts of Tribal Economic Development Projects in San Diego County, July 2002, pp. 1386.

centuries, the Indians of San Diego had to shift for themselves by finding wage labor to make ends meet, supplementing their diets with some traditional foods. But as the twentieth century progressed and the governments confined Indians more and more to reservations, tribal members had little economic opportunity except through wage labor and small gardens. During the 1960s and 1970s, tribes in San Diego tried to enter the market economy primarily through agricultural developments. Without sufficient capital, water, fertile land, or other economic advantages, the tribes did not prosper. Disease, death, malnutrition, and ill health haunted them during the twentieth century, in large part because they had little opportunity.

But in the 1980s, tribes in San Diego used their tribal sovereignty to benefit their people by beginning bingo and other gaming businesses. Gaming proved to be a remarkable opportunity for the tribes, one that has changed the geography of Indian country. The tribes have used gaming money to create more economic opportunity by buying land, businesses, and banks. San Diego's gaming tribes employ thousands of people and add to the economy by buying food, beverages, electricity, gas, and a host of services. They hire engineers, designers, consultants, construction workers, and many others who benefit from gaming money. Tribes pay thousands, sometimes millions, of dollars in taxes to county, state, and federal governments, significantly benefiting all of society. Some casinos are the largest employers in their areas of the county.

Those tribes that have reservations in fairly close proximity to the large population concentrations of San Diego County decided to launch gaming enterprises. Other Indian tribes with reservations some distance from population centers chose not to enter into gaming. However, the decision by certain tribes to enter into gaming involved more than the tribe's proximity to non-native populations with financial resources. Cultural, historical, and spiritual decisions were also factors.

After the Pauma Band of Mission Indians decided to enter the gaming business a reporter, Edward Sifuentes of the *North County Times*, asked Luiseño elder Henry Rodriguez "if he wished his tribe could have a casino." He responded, "No, I like my mountain the way it is." Rodriguez presented one view of casinos, but other Indians felt that the economic benefits of having a casino far outweighed arguments against the enterprise. Sycuan and Barona were the first tribes in San Diego County to engage in bingo and other forms of gaming. Others soon followed. Since 1990, a number of tribes have launched gaming businesses, including Viejas, Pala, Pauma, and Rincon. In addition to gaming, some operations include golf courses, factory outlets, hotels, and other attractions (Figure 4.5).

Gaming tribes often provide their people per capita payments for being a tribal member, but tribes without casinos rarely offer per capita payments, unless the tribe redistributes money earned from land, water, wood, minerals, or land leases. Many tribes reinvest their earnings into economic, social, and health interests of the people. Some tribes offer their students educational opportunities that never existed in the past. Since the 1930s, the Bureau of Indian Affairs (BIA) had allowed Indian students to apply for competitive grants, but the BIA guaranteed no native student educational opportunities. As a result of gaming, some tribes can afford to send their students to any university in the world. They can also afford to provide their people quality housing.

In years past, Indian people residing on reservations lived in hovels made of sticks, mud, rocks, clapboard, plywood, and cardboard. Mobile homes provided Indians with the best

Figure 4.5. Kumeyaay art work ("The Greeters") at a San Diego area casino, an effort to include traditional values in the midst of commercial development.

housing until the 1990s when gaming tribes built modern homes for their people with electricity, central heating and cooling, running water, sewers, and paved streets. Per capita payments provided tribal members with sufficient money to buy nutritional food for their families and health insurance. In the past, the Indian Health Service (IHS) offered some medical care for Indians in northern and southern parts of San Diego County, but the IHS limited its health care to native people and maintained only five central clinics located a considerable distance from some of their clients. Gaming money allows some tribal members to enjoy first-rate health care, a luxury still lacking on most Indian reservations in the county.

Although Indian tribes in San Diego County have always been politically active, funds from gaming have greatly increased the political power of the tribes and Indian people. The state witnessed this power during the campaign to pass Propositions 5 and 1A, two initiatives that allowed tribes to operate big stakes gaming, including slot machines. Both measures passed with the support of over 60% of the voters, an overwhelming mandate in support of the tribes. Indians have used this momentum to their advantage, tapping into the political structures of the county, state, and nation to encourage elected officials to support bills advantageous to Indian people.

In 2002, Kumeyaay people of the Barona, Viejas, and Sycuan reservations supported a bill creating an American Indian commission to implement the Native American Graves and Repatriation Act on a state level. Additionally, with the support of many tribes, the state supported a commemorative seal honoring California Indians on the steps of the state capitol. Indeed, Robert Freeman, a Luiseño man from the county, designed the artistic seal that represents all California Indians and will always be part of the Capitol Building in Sacramento. Gaming money and tribal officials have offered a new day for Native Americans in San Diego, and this political influence will grow in the future.

Although Indian gaming has significantly changed some of the tribes in San Diego County, other Indian tribes and people still suffer from poverty, ill health, poor housing, and little educational opportunities. The Cahuilla of Los Coyotes, Kumeyaay of Mesa Grande, Campo, Jamul, and others still struggle to make ends meet. Most Indians of non-gaming tribes find work through day labor, but others are unemployed. The very young and tribal elders suffer the most, with some depending on Social Security and other government assistance to help them survive.

Nevertheless, gaming and non-gaming tribes in San Diego County often join hands on spiritual and cultural matters, sharing bird songs, mourning ceremonies, and memorial celebrations. The people are united in a desire to repatriate the remains of the dead and protect Indian cemeteries and burials from destruction. They are united in an on-going effort to preserve their languages, cultures, and spiritual beliefs.

The Native peoples of San Diego County—Kumeyaay, Luiseño, Cupeño, and Cahuilla—all cling to their traditions. The Malki Museum on the Morongo Reservation in Riverside County and the Pala Cultural Center are just two institutions designed to preserve Indian history. In addition, the people of the Barona Reservation, and others, have made major strides in historical and cultural preservation.

The Pauma Indian Education Center, in cooperation with Palomar College, also preserves the Native heritage of Southern California Indians. The Viejas Indian School, under the direction of Robert Brown, made great strides in educating Kumeyaay children about their heritage. In addition, the economic development of the reservation has accelerated the efforts of the tribe, and individual members, toward further cultural preservation. Similar successes are found at the Pala Mission School and Campo Indian School, often supported by the Departments of American Indian Studies at San Diego State University and Palomar College. The urban Indian Education Program, Museum of Man, and San Diego American Indian Health Clinics also contribute to the preservation of Native California Indian heritage, sponsoring programs, including a week-long California Indian Days Celebration in Balboa Park.

Each year, the Indians of San Diego County celebrate their "Indianness" at Pow Wows. The Pow Wow originated on the Great Plains and Great Lakes, but with the arrival of American Indians from many parts of the country after World War II, Native people congregated in urban areas like San Diego and began offering Pow Wows. For many years, the Barona Reservation sponsored a Pow Wow over Labor Day Weekend, and each spring since 1970, San Diego State University hosted one of the largest Pow Wows in the state. Since the 1990s, and the growth of the Native economy, many reservations in Southern California sponsor Pow

Figure 4.6. Kumeyaay women exhibiting basketry and other traditional utensils at a 1994 Native American display in the Laguna Mountains.

Wows, drawing thousands of people to share in Native American culture through song, dance, music, food, and art. Pow Wows draw dancers and singers from Oklahoma, the Dakotas, Montana, Wyoming, Canada, and a host of other places. Pow Wows are always open to the public so that all people may share in the color, traditions, and movement that are the Pow Wow (Figure 4.6). In addition, several reservations now host cultural programs unique to California Indians, including bird singing, peon games, and memorial services, some of which last all night long.

While there is no denying that health, education, employment, and other problems still exist on some of the reservations of San Diego County, as well as in urban areas, Indian people can now point to many successes that have been supported by tribal initiatives. Tribes have exerted their sovereignty and developed their own health care systems, a community college at Sycuan, housing, water and sewer systems, and other improvements. The federal government has helped tribes with some of these initiatives, but for the most part, Indians themselves have made these changes. Challenges remain, and both Indians and non-Indians seek answers to the problems still facing Indian people, but a Native renaissance has taken hold in San Diego County. Further, Indian tribes have become politically astute and active, working directly with governmental officials to fulfill political and economic agendas created by the tribes themselves.

The Indian people of San Diego County are committed to extending and preserving their own self-determination, and they are fulfilling their destiny to take more control over their own well being. In many different ways, the Indian people are protecting their tribal sovereignty, working to maintain and preserve their cultures within an ever-changing world. In this way, the Indians of San Diego County will survive the twenty-first century and look to a bright future as sovereign native people.

Appendix 4.1. Indian Medicinal Plants

Most medicinal plants (parts or whole) were boiled to make a liquid that was either drunk as a tea or used to bathe or wash the afflicted part of the body. The principal sources for this appendix are the referenced works by Hedges and Almstedt. When available, the Latin name is given for the first time that the plant is named.

    I. *Aches, pains, bruises, wounds*

       A. *Pains in bones, muscles, and members*

Turpentine Bush *(Haplopappus larlioifolius)*; juniper *(Juniperous californica)*; Saltbush *(Atriplex canescens)*; Creosote Bush, Greasewood *(Larrea tridentata, divaricata)*; Wild Cherry *(Prunus Emarginata)*; Tobacco Tree *(Niceiniana glauca)*; Wild Peony *(Paeonica californica)*; Clematis; White sage *(Salvia apiana)*; Stinging Nettle *(Urtica holosericea)*

       B. *Inflamed eyes*

Chia Sage *(Salvia columbariae)*; Elderberry *(Sambucus species)*; Wild Buckwheat *(Eriogonum fasciculatam)*; Tomentillo *(Physalis ixocarpa)*; Squawbush *(Rhus trilobata)*; Scrub Oak Galls

       C. *Headache*

Romero *(Trichostema species)*; Wild Buckwheat; Yerba Santa *(Eriodictyon trichocalyx)*

       D. *Toothache*

Winter Current *(Ribes indecorum)* or *(Malvaceum)*; Yarrow *(Achillea millefolium)*; Live Oak *(Quercus agrifolia)*

       E. *Sore throat*

Tobacco Tree; Lizardtail

       F. *Earache*

Yarrow; apply heat

       G. *Stiff neck*

White Sage

       H. *Broken bones*

Elm *(Ulmus pubescens)* bark used for splints; Cottonwood *(Papulus fremanti)*

I. *Bruises and wounds*

Turpentine Bush; Honeysuckle *(Lonicera species);* Cottonwood; Yerba Mansa *(Aremopsis californica);* burns; Chia Sage; Yellow Monkey Flower *(Minulus guttatus);* Prickly Poppy *(Argemone Playceras);* Honeysuckle or Pipe stem; Wild Cherry; Greasewood or Chamise *(Adenostoma sparitolium);* Western Goldenrod *(Solidago nemoralis);* Swamp Root *(Anemopsis californica);* Gum Plant *(Grindelia squarrosa);* Cactus Pear *(Opuntia);* Plantain *(Plantago major)*

II. *Bites*

A. *Snake Bites*

Fairy Mats *(Euphorbia polycarpa);* Squaw Purge or Golondrina *(Emphorbia melanadenia);* Jimsonweed *(Datura meteloides);* Wild Field Garlic *(Allium canadense* or *Allium vineale)* used for protection against bites by grinding into pulp and rubbing over bare legs

B. *Insect bites*

Dodder *(Custa californica)* picked from buckwheat plant, used for black widow spider bites; snake bite medicine listed above is also good for insect bites

III. *Alimentary disturbances*

A. *Stomach ache and vomiting*

Sage, Rosemary, and Nettle plant inhaled smoke; Wild Buckwheat twigs; Blue Star Flower Grass *(Sigrinchium angustifolium);* Field Camomile *(Anthemis nobilis);* Wild Peony

B. *Diarrhea and dysentery*

Monkey Flower; Shepherd's Purse *(Capsella bursa-pastoris);* Penny royal *(Hedeoma pulegioides);* Buckwheat; Wild Strawberry *(Frageria californica);* Wild Blackberry *(Rubus ursinus);* Cascara *(Rhamnus californica)*

C. *Indigestion*

Wild Cucumber or Chilicothe *(Echinocystis macrocarpal);* Blue Eyed Grass *(Sisyrinchium bellum);* Creoste Bush; California Wild Rose *(Rosa californica);* Peony; Palmita, Peppergrass *(Lepidium nitidum)*

D. *Constipation*

Cascara, Coffee Berry; Greasewood, Chamise

IV. *Respiratory illnesses*

A. *Coughs and colds*

Yerba Santa; Canatilla, Mormon Tea or Desert Tea *(Ephedra californica);* Holly Leaf Cherry *(Prunus ilicifolia);* Wild Cherry; White Sage; Creosote Bush; Saltbush; Yerba Mansa; Turpentine Bush; Horehound *(Marrubium vulgare)* naturalized from Europe; Romero; Elder *(Sambucus coerulea);* Mountain Mahogany *(Cercocarpus betuloides);* Wild Buckwheat; Honeysuckle or Pipe Stem; Juniper *(Juniperus californica);* Sumac *(Rhus orata)*

B. *Asthma*

Coyote Tobacco *(Nicotiniana attenuata);* Deer's Tongue, Chalk Lettuce *(Dudleya pulverulenta);* Sycamore *(Platanus racemosa)*

C. *Damaged lungs*

Mountain Mahogany; Gum Weed *(Grindelia robusta);* Wild Peony

V. *Internal conditions*
   A. *Frio*
      Yerba Mansa; Turpentine Bush; Manzanilla *(Matricaria matricariodes);* Romero; Creosote
      Bush
   B. *Influenza*
      Coyote Tobacco
   C. *Urinary and kidney disorders*
      Spurge *(Croton corymbosus);* Ephedra; Sand Verbena; Wild Peony; Lupine *(Lupinus
      species);* Cana Tea or Desert Tea; Manzanita *(Arctostaphylos)*
   D. *Fever*
      Juniper Berry; Wild Peony; Elder; Bee Plant; Clematis *(Clematis pauciflora);* Malva *(Malva
      parriflora)* native to Eurasia; Wild Rose; Mansanilla, Pineapple Weed *(Matricaria matri-
      carioides)*
   E. *Tonics*
      Squaw Weed; Canatilla, Desert Tea or Cana Tea
   F. *Narcotic*
      Jimsonweed

VI. *Veneral diseases*
    Mahogany Shrub *(Cercocarpus betulaefolius);* Canatilla or Desert Tea

VII. *Skin eruptions*
    A. *Dandruff and scalp care*
       Mistletoe *(Phoradendron species);* White Sage; Creosote Bush
    B. *Poison oak*
       Cascara; White Sage; salt mixed with water
    C. *Other skin ailments*
       Fairy Mats or Golondrina; Encina, Live Oak *(Quercus agrifolia)*; Deer's Tongue or Chalk
       Lettuce; Wild Lilac *(Ceanothus leucodermis);* Wild Fuchsia *(Penstemon cordifolius)*; Saltbush;
       Wild Cherry; Creosote Bush; Gum Plant; Cotton Weed *(Antennaria margaritacea);* Thorny
       Cucumber *(Micrapelis micracarpa);* Castor Bean *(Ricinus communis)* for acne and pimples

VIII. *Menstrual difficulties and birth*
    A. *Menstrual difficulties*
       Desert Mallow; Coffer or Rock Fern *(Pellaea andromedaefolia);* Manzanilla or Pineapple
       Weed; Creosote Bush; Agave; Romero
    B. *Birth*
       White Salvia *(Ramona polystachya);* Wormwood *(Artemisia californica);* Elder Tea; White
       Sage; Yerba Mansa; Sumac; Romero; Manzanilla or Pineapple Weed; Desert Mallow, tea
       made from root used for birth control
    C. *Abortion*
       Turpentine Bush; Croton californica

IX. *Introduced illnesses*
Larrea mexicana, for consumption; Elderberry *(Sambucus pubens)*, for measles; White Sage, for measles; for Spanish Influenza and smallpox, a steambath. Herbs compounded for the steambath were *Artemisia tridentata, Larrea mexicana, Piperacea, Eriodictyon glutinosum californica,* and *Andiantum capillus-veneris.* An herb tea was made from *Ephedra* and *Sambucus pubens.*

Appendix 4.2. Edible Plants of the San Diego Region

Some portion of the following plants were consumed in the Indian diet

black oak, *Quercus kelloggii*
encina or live oak, *Quercus agrifolia*
white oak, *Quercus engelmanii*
scrub oak, *Quercus dumosa*
jack oak, *Quercus chrysoleois*
mesquite beans, *Prosopis juliflora*
yucca, *Yucca whipplei*
agave, *Agave deserti*
chia seeds, *Salvia columbariae*
prickly pear cactus fruit, *Opuntia*
thistle sage, *Salvia carduaceae*
white sage, *Salvia apiana*
wild oat, *Avena fatua*
wild peony, *Paenia californica*
filaree, *Erodium cicutorium*
pansy, *Viola pedunculata*
watercress, *Nasturtium officinale*
miner's lettuce, *Montia perfoliata*
lambs quarters, *Chenopodium album*
beavertail cactus fruit, *Opuntia basilaris*
fishhook cactus fruit, *Mammillari'a tetrancistra*
manzanita berries, *Arctostaphylos*
wild strawberry, *Fragaria californiaca*
wild blackberry, *Rubus ursinus*
wild cherry, *Prunus ilicifolia*
wild grape, *Vitis girdiana*
cattail, *Typha*
tule potato, *Scirpus*
mushrooms, tree fungus, clover, *Trifolium*
elderberries, *Sambucus*

Indian onion, *Allium*
pigweed, *Chenopodium*
screwbean, *Prosopis pubescens*
lemonade berry, *Rhus integrifolia*

References

Almstedt, Ruth. *Bibliography of the Diegueño Indians*. Ramona Ballena Press, 1974.

Barfield, Chet, "Casino Capital", *San Diego Union-Tribune,* June 24, 2002, pp. A1 and A8.

Barfield, Chet, "Indian Gaming Is About to Hit Growth Spurt", *San Diego Union-Tribune,* July 27, 2003, pp. A1 and A10.

Bean, Lowell and Lisa Bourgeault. *The Cahuilla.* New York: Chelsea House Publishers, 1989.

Carrico, Richard, *Strangers in a Stolen Land: American Indians in San Diego, 1850–1880*. Sacramento: Sierra Oaks Publishing Co., 1987.

County of San Diego. *Draft Update on the Impacts of Tribal Economic Development Projects in San Diego County*. San Diego, July 2002.

Hedges, Kenneth. *Santa Ysabel Ethnobotany*. Unpublished report, San Diego Museum of Man, 1968.

Heizer, R., ed. *Handbook of North American Indians, California.* Washington: Smithsonian, 1978.

Hyer, Joel. *"We Are Not Savages": Native Americans in Southern California and the Pala Reservation, 1880–1920*. East Lansing: Michigan State University Press, 2001.

Karr, Steven, "'Water We Believed Could Never Belong to Anyone': The San Luis Rey River and the Pala Indians of Southern California", *American Indian Quarterly*, 24, Summer 2000, pp. 381–399.

Keller, Jean. *Empty Beds: Indian Student Health at Sherman Institute, 1902–1922*. East Lansing. Michigan State University Press, 2002.

Loomis, Charles, "The Exiles of Cupa", *Out West,* Vol. 16, May 1902, pp. 465–479.

Loomis, Charles, "The Sequoya League: To Make Better Indians", *Out West,* Vol. 20, March 1904, pp. 281–284.

Pourade, Richard. *The History of San Diego: The Explorers*. San Diego: Union-Tribune Publishing Co., 1960.

Rawls, James. *Indians of California: Changing Images*. Norman: Univ. of Oklahoma Press, 1984.

Shipek, Florence. *Pushed into the Rocks*. Lincoln: University of Nebraska Press, 1988.

Shipek, Florence, ed. *The Autobiography of Delfina Cuero: A Diegueño Indian*. Morongo Indian Reservation: Malki Museum Press, 1970.

Sweeney, James, "No Sure Bets in Gambling Talks: Much at Stake for State, Tribes in Negotiations", *San Diego Union-Tribune,* March 16, 2003, pp. A1, A10, and A11.

Trafzer, Clifford, "Tuberculosis Deaths Among Southern California Indians, 1922–1944", *Canadian Bulletin of Medical History*, Vol. 18 (2001), pp. 85–107.

Trafzer, Clifford and Joel Hyer, eds. *Exterminate Them!: Written Accounts of Murder, Rape, and Enslavement of Native Americans during the California Gold Rush*. East Lansing: Michigan State University Press, 1999.

Valley, D. and D. Lindsay. *Jackpot Trail: Indian Gaming in Southern California*. El Cajon: Sunbelt Publications, 2003.

Internet Connections:
County of San Diego Tribal Inventory: *www.co.san-diego.ca.gov/cnty/cntydepts/landuse/tedp/tedp.doc*
Kumeyaay Nation: *www.kumeyaay.com/index.html*
Kumeyaay-Ipai Interpretive Center: *www.angelfire.com/falcon/kumeyaay*
San Diego Historical Society: *www.sandiegohistory.org/histsoc.html*
San Diego Museum of Man: *www.museumofman.org*

Chapter Five

Ernst C. Griffin and
John R. Weeks

Peopling the Region
San Diego's Population Patterns

For much of its history, San Diego was considered to be a sleepy "navy town" nestled around one of the world's most picturesque natural harbors. Over the past few decades, however, the area has come to be viewed as possessing one of the country's most attractive, desirable metropolitan environments, "America's Finest City" in the local promotional parlance. Even a cursory examination of Census statistics reveals that San Diego's population grew at an unusually

Ernest C. Griffin wrote the original text for this chapter while a professor in the Department of Geography at San Diego State University. John R. Weeks, a professor in the Department of Geography and Director of the International population Center at San Diego State University, prepared the present version for this edition.

rapid pace throughout the twentieth century. Since 1900 the county's population has climbed more than 8,000%, from slightly more than 35,000 to over 2.8 million (see Table 5.1), and the City of San Diego is now the seventh largest city in the nation. During this time span, the region has consistently exhibited growth rates significantly above those of California and dramatically above the mean for the United States. The state estimates that the county's population may reach 3,000,000 in 2005. This chapter will review San Diego County's population growth patterns since 1900, examine where people are coming from and why, outline changes in population distribution within the county, and summarize some of the major ethnic and racial components of our population.

TABLE 5.1. San Diego's Population Growth (thousands of inhabitants)

	1880	1890	1900	1910	1920	1930
County	8.6	34.9	35.1	61.7	112.2	209.7
City	2.6	16.2	17.7	39.6	74.4	148.0
City as a % of county	30.6%	46.4%	50.4%	64.2%	66.2%	70.6%

Source: United States Department of Commerce. Bureau of the Census. Censuses for 1880 through 1990.

TABLE 5.2. Percentage Population Growth by Decade

	1910–20	1920–30	1930–40	1940–50	1950–60	1960–70	1970–80	1980–90	1990–2000
United States	14.9	16.1	7.2	14.5	18.5	13.7	11.4	9.8	13.2
California	44.1	65.6	21.6	53.2	48.5	27.0	18.5	25.7	13.8
San Diego County	82.0	86.7	38.0	92.4	85.5	31.4	37.1	34.2	12.6
San Diego (city)	87.8	99.0	37.3	64.4	71.4	21.6	25.5	26.8	10.2

Source: United States Department of Commerce, Bureau of the Census. Censuses for 1900 through 2000.

An Overview

Most people are readily aware that California, generally, and Southern California, in particular, have long been among the fastest growing parts of the United States. From its entry into the Union, California possessed a mystique which lured people toward it. The Gold Rush, the aura of Hollywood, a sunny climate, unique economic opportunities, and a distinctive lifestyle among its inhabitants all have played a part in drawing people to the Golden State. During all but the last decade of the twentieth century the State of California has increased its population at least twice as rapidly as the national average. Until the 1990s, San Diego County's population growth rate was consistently greater than the state's average. But San Diego grew up in the shadow of the large, well-known urban blob to the north, Los Angeles. As a result, while the county's population growth has been consistently rapid, until recently this fact went largely unnoticed.

In the early decades of the 1900's, when the United States was experiencing population growth of about 1.5 percent annually and California about 5 percent, San Diego County grew at least 6 percent a year, or over four times the national average. These trends are summarized in Table 5.2. With the onset of the Great Depression in the 1930s, the U.S. annual population growth rate dropped to an all-time low of about .7 percent annually. However, San Diego's population expansion "fell" to a still healthy 3.25 percent a year, nearly five times greater than the country as a whole. During the "Baby Boom" years of the 1940s and 1950s, San Diego grew by almost 7 percent yearly, or about four times the national rate. In the era of declining growth rates which characterized the 1960s and 1970s, the county continued to grow two to three times more rapidly than the rest of the country. Not until the final decade of the twentieth century did San Diego's rate of growth drop below that of the state as a whole. This simply illustrates that the region's population growth was unusually rapid and sustained for a substantial period of time.

1940	1950	1960	1970	1980	1990	2000
289.3	556.8	1033.0	1357.9	1861.8	2498.1	2813.8
203.3	334.4	573.2	696.8	875.5	1110.5	1223.4
70.2%	60.1%	55.5%	51.3%	47.1%	44.5%	43.5%

Until recently, a very important component of San Diego's (and the State's) population increase had been internal migration. Population growth is measured by summing the rate of natural increase and net migration of a region. San Diego's population has fertility and mortality characteristics generally similar to the nation as a whole. Therefore, the rate of natural increase for our area is not significantly different than the national average. Yet our average annual growth rates had historically been significantly higher than for the United States. It is readily apparent, then, that migration to San Diego from other parts of the country, and recently from Mexico and the Pacific Rim, added enormously to growth.

Indeed, it is the latter migration that became predominant in the 1990s. Prior to that time, migration from elsewhere in the United States had been a major factor in San Diego's growth. However, in the 1990s and on into the twenty-first century, the number of migrants leaving San Diego for elsewhere in the U.S. has actually outnumbered migrants coming in from other parts of the country, whereas migration from abroad (especially from Mexico) has continued almost unabated. At the start of the twenty-first century almost all of the net increase in San Diego County's population is accounted for by immigrants and the children of those immigrants. In 2000, nearly every other birth in San Diego County was to a woman who had been born outside of the United States.

It is understandable that a "nation of immigrants" should be highly migratory. Perhaps our frontier heritage compels us to be a country of movers, seeking better opportunities in different places. California's population reflects this migratory character quite well. Many California residents consider themselves to be "almost natives" if they have lived in the state for over ten years. Native San Diegans are scarcer yet. In addition to out-of-staters, a very significant portion of the county's residents consists of transplanted Californians who now make their homes here.

When dealing with San Diego's population growth patterns, it is useful to keep two things in mind. First, when populations achieve a large size, the **percentage** growth rate often decreases while the **absolute** number of people represented increases. Second is the relative size of the City of San Diego to total population. From Table 5.1 it can be seen that the city had at least one-half of the county's total population until about 1975. The city's proportion of the total steadily increased from just over 50 percent in 1900 to 70 percent in the 1930s and 1940s. Since then, the growth of many satellite cities has outpaced that of San Diego. By 1990 the city of San Diego had less than 45% of the region's residents, but the county's eighteen incorporated cities together accounted for more than 80 percent of total county population in that same year. The relatively rapid growth of many of these suburban political entities has led to significant changes in population distributions and directions of growth in the county (see Chapter 14). They are presently the most demographically dynamic sections of the county.

Early Growth Periods

During the decades since the late 1800s a variety of factors influenced population growth at different times. Years of boom alternated with periods of stagnation or decline. It is helpful to remember that population change was not uniform within the periods selected for presentation here. These time blocks do represent eras of distinctive growth characteristics for the country which are definable in terms of the forces that attracted migrants to San Diego. This resulted in waves of people from various parts of the nation, and beyond, who had different needs to fulfill. Their impacts upon the landscape have varied and the demographic patterns of San Diego County reflected those differences.

1850–1920

San Diego became one of California's original counties in 1850 and its first census was taken in that year. just under 2300 people were counted and the manner in which the figures were reported gives us clues as to the social attitudes of the day (Table 5.3). At the time of its origin, San Diego County included all of southeastern California north to Death Valley, but it seems unlikely that the census included anything more than the area immediately around what is now the city of San Diego. For the next three decades the county's population increased sporadically and stood at 8,618 in 1880, although at the height of the county's gold rush a few years earlier, it was significantly higher than this.

San Diego county's first "population explosion" had its roots in the concerted efforts of land developers in the 1880s to entice people west-

TABLE 5.3. 1850 San Diego Census

Whites	248
"Tame Indians"	483
"Wild Indians"	1,550
Sandwich Islanders	3
Negroes	3
Total	2,287

Source: W. E. Smythe, *History of San Diego, 1542–1907,* San Diego: The History Company, 1907, p. 255. Quotation marks added.

ward. Men like Frank Kimball, Elisha Babcock, John Spreckels and others were convinced that San Diego would be *the* thriving metropolis of Southern California. Kimball, in particular, was certain that the western terminal for a southern rail route to California would end in San Diego and did everything within his power to bring about his dream, including the founding of National City. Land schemes were started and tracts of land were sold in San Diego's "New Town", in suburban subdivisions, and in newly founded satellite cities. Easterners anxious to escape the drudgeries of industrial cities and the miseries of winter were the primary targets of these developers.

The metropolitan area, centering on "New Town", the core of the current central business district of San Diego, grew rapidly during this period. The county's population expanded from 8,000 to 35,000 during the eighties. However, growth stagnated in the 1890s as Los Angeles was chosen as the West Coast terminus of the Santa Fe line and the economic opportunities available there overshadowed those in San Diego. Nevertheless, San Diego became a minor Mecca to many souls who had suffered through cold, raw eastern winters and wanted to escape to a haven of warm weather by the sea.

In addition to the growth of the metropolitan area, San Diego's backcountry received an influx of migrants as well. During the gold rush of the 1870s thousands of miners made the pilgrimage southward from the declining Mother Lode to the area around Julian to try their luck in the Cuyamacas and Lagunas. Short-lived though it was, many of these people stayed on after the mining boom and settled some of the more remote parts of the county. Other land schemes, tried in places like Escondido, met with little success.

By 1900, San Diego County's population had increased to over 35,000. Compared to San Francisco or even Los Angeles, this area was not much more than a dot on the southwest corner of the map. Mountains to the east had negated the county's one outstanding natural advantage, its harbor. San Diego was connected by rail to the East, but only via a spurline out of Los Angeles (see Chapter 11). Therefore, the region's hinterland was severely restricted as was its overland access.

During the first decade of the twentieth century, the city of San Diego accounted for nearly 80 percent of the total growth of the county, increasing its population from 17,700 in 1900 to over 39,500 in 1910. The increase was more than the entire county had held just ten years earlier. The great mass of population was concentrated in the New Town area, in Golden Hills, and around Old Town. Significant numbers of people were found in La Jolla, a somewhat separate enclave, Ocean Beach, Mission Beach, and Point Loma. Some of the smaller surrounding towns, like National City, Coronado, Chula Vista and La Mesa, also contributed to the growing "metropolitan" population (Figure 5.1).

The great Panama-California Exposition of 1915, dedicated to celebrate the opening of the Panama Canal and envisioned to compete with San Francisco's World Fair, attracted national attention to San Diego just prior to World War I. Centered in Balboa Park, which was developed expressly for the event, a tremendous amount of time, effort, and money was spent in staging the Exposition, which emphasized San Diego's Hispanic past and attractive climate. A visit by the Great White Fleet in 1908, while on its famous world voyage, heightened awareness of the strategic importance and potential of the San Diego Bay.

Rapid population growth continued during the First World War, particularly in the city of San Diego. The harbor's military potential began to be exploited as units of the Pacific Fleet were stationed in San Diego to protect growing American interests in the Philippines, Hawaii, Panama and Central America. By 1920 the county's population surpassed 100,000 with roughly 75,000 living in the core area of the city. Other areas of the county began to increase slowly but steadily. Farming and ranching activities, spurred by the introduction of citrus crops and the avocado, spread to interior valleys, especially El Cajon and Escondido.

Racially and ethnically San Diego was overwhelmingly white and European. The 1900 census indicated that only 406 blacks, slightly more than 1.15 percent of total population, lived in the county. By 1920 there were nearly 1200 blacks in the region, but this represented a drop to only slightly more than 1 percent of total population. Despite the area's strong Spanish-Mexican heritage, San Diego was home to fewer than 1,100 foreign-born Mexican citizens in 1900 and to some 2700 in 1920. It is impossible to determine how many Spanish-speaking residents lived in the county during this time period because such information was not considered important enough to ask about in the census.

Significantly, the county's Indian population fell from nearly 2,200 in 1900 to 1,350 in 1920 as a significant number of Indians left local reservations to seek urban employment opportunities.

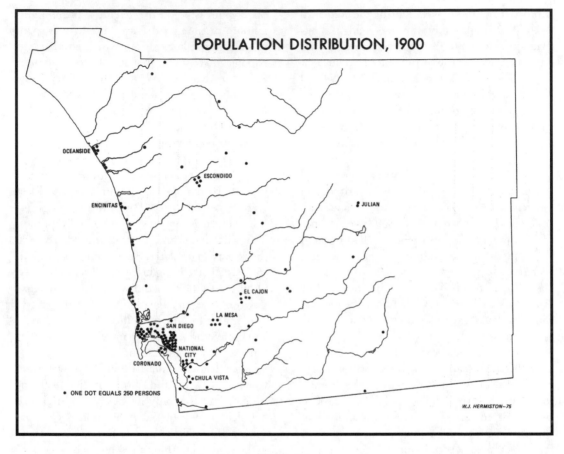

Figure 5.1.

The 1920s and 1930s

The 1920s represented a heady period as America emerged from the "Great War" as a legitimate world power which had achieved its goals of defending democratic ideals and prospering economically. Rich in physical resources, expanding commercially and experiencing a continuing technological revolution unlike anything known before, the nation roared into the twenties. The wanderlust inherent in the nation's people, stimulated by the war and easier modes of transportation, manifested itself as waves of migration from south to north and from east to west. As a result, Southern California and San Diego enjoyed unprecedented growth.

By the 1920s the United States had entered the auto age. Roads were built to link the East and West coasts as well as the major cities between them. It became 'easy' to cross the country. Individual mobility was increased tremendously as Easterners and Midwesterners began to drive to California to seek new opportunities. Certainly many migrants who wound up in San Diego got here via Los Angeles, but they could find jobs in a variety of new industries. Aircraft had proved their worthiness in the war and had taken a hold on the American imagination. An aircraft industry was developing in San Diego, in part because of the mild climate which permitted the assembly and storage of planes outdoors. By 1930 San Diego was home to a number of aircraft plants, the largest being Ryan Aviation and Consolidated Vultee, each of which employed hundreds of workers. Many smaller companies sprang up to service the aircraft industry, such as electronic and sheet metal working firms.

The military, which had made its initial appearance in the prewar years, expanded operations in San Diego during the 1920s and particularly in the 1930s. San Diego was unquestionably a "sailor's town," the best liberty port on the West Coast, particularly because of San Diego's proximity to Tijuana, where alcohol, gambling, and other pleasures were readily available. As the number of ships and shore installations increased, so did the economic opportunities in a variety of service industries. Additionally, the fishing industry expanded tremendously during this period, especially the tuna fleet which relied primarily on local marine resources (see Chapter 7).

As a result of these factors, San Diego's population grew substantially. During the 1920s the city of San Diego expanded from just under 75,000 to almost 150,000 residents while the county's total population reached nearly 210,000. The smaller incorporated towns surrounding the city continued to grow during the period as well. By contrast, rural areas increased relatively slowly as employment was limited in the ranching and orchard operations which dominated the back county.

During the 1930s economic conditions worsened throughout America and opportunities virtually everywhere were adversely affected. San Diego's growth rate fell sharply as compared to previous years, but the county's population still managed to increase by 40 percent during the decade. The major stimulant to new growth was the continued expansion of the Navy in San Diego. New bases and installations were built which increased the county's dependence upon military spending but provided many new jobs. Additionally, many so-called "Okies" and "Arkies", refugees from the Dust Bowl who fled to California to start life anew, found their way to San Diego. From the depressed urban centers of the East and Midwest came migrants who thought it better to be hungry in the warmth of San Diego and other California cities than to suffer in the cold of cities like Detroit, Chicago, and St. Louis.

By 1940 the county's population had reached 289,000. Nearly a quarter of a million people lived in the incorporated towns of the San Diego metropolitan region while the rural areas remained sparsely populated. The city had over 200,000 residents, more than 70 percent of the county's total. The black population grew roughly twenty times between 1920 and 1940, numbering 27,000 or about 9 percent of total population. Foreign-born Mexican-Americans also increased, numbering nearly 6,000, after declining greatly in the 1920's. The county's Indian population remained very small and essentially unchanged during this period, as the people who lived on the reservations were largely ignored by the urban dwellers to the west.

The Postwar Boom

With the economic stimulus provided by World War II and its aftermath, San Diego's population "exploded", large new suburbs appeared, and major shifts in the county's population distributions occurred. The period from 1940–1959 saw the greatest relative growth of the century, a trend that went uninterrupted until the early 1960s.

This era set the stage for San Diego's emergence as a nationally important growth center.

The 1940s and 1950s

San Diego experienced greater population growth during the 1940s and 1950s, in percentage terms, than at any comparable period in the county's history. San Diego became a major city and the metropolitan population nearly quadrupled in size, growing at an unprecedented average rate of 6.6 percent annually. Between 1940 and 1960, the county's total increased from under 300,000 to over 1 million people. New areas of the county experienced rapid growth and new patterns of settlement were formed. No longer was the city of San Diego the predominant area of growth, for this was the period when the satellite cities would begin to outstrip San Diego in terms of growth. The geographical distribution of the county's population began to change dramatically.

The onset of World War II had given San Diego a very strategic position. The Pacific Theater meant that training and supply bases would be needed and many existing facilities on the West Coast expanded greatly. Tens of thousands of military personnel came to the county during this period and their impact was twofold. First, their immediate presence increased the local population significantly. Second, many of the people who saw wartime service duty in San Diego were destined to return as permanent residents. Indeed, these returnees and their families formed the bulk of the county's growth during the late forties and throughout the 1950s. Moreover, large scale training facilities—"boot camps"—introduced a continuous flow of potential new residents to the county.

San Diego boomed economically as a result of the war. Thousands of new jobs were created in aircraft and related industries, shipbuilding, fishing and other pursuits. After the war a housing construction boom started almost immediately, which absorbed large quantities of labor and, along with aircraft and the military, provided economic prosperity which in turn attracted more people to San Diego.

Much of the county's growth was in the smaller cities. Oceanside nearly tripled in size between 1940 and 1950 as a result of the expansion of the U.S. Marine base at Camp Pendleton. La Mesa grew to over 10,000, Coronado doubled its population to 12,000, Chula Vista soared from 3,000 to 15,000, El Cajon began a fantastic growth spurt by tripling in population to 5,600, and National City doubled in size to over 20,000 during the decade. The city of San Diego grew substantially as well, increasing from 203,000 to 334,000. But its relative size decreased from 70 percent to 60 percent of total population, a trend which is still continuing. People were coming to San Diego from all over the nation, but the North Central and Southern states contributed most to the flow of in-migrants. Growth was further stimulated by the beginning of the "Baby Boom", one of the pleasantries of a country at peace after several years of war.

The tremendous increases of the 1940s accelerated in the first half of the 1950s. The Korean War was perhaps even more beneficial to the county's economy than World War 11, as military spending soared and the aircraft industry expanded to fulfill new contracts. The county's population grew by 120,000 people (over 20 percent) in 1950 alone, and by another 60,000 (nearly 10 percent) in 1951. After the Korean War wound down, San Diego continued to prosper. Advertisements were placed in newspapers around the nation imploring people to move to San Diego: "Let's all go to work at Convair, you'll earn more money there!" The advertising worked. By 1959 San Diego County had passed a million people. It was a major market in its own right, although still in the long shadow of

Los Angeles. A severe economic downturn gripped the region from the late 1950s through the early 1960s and this dramatically slowed, but certainly did not stop, the county's growth.

Burgeoning population growth was translated into the spread of settlement through much of the county. The city of San Diego had well over a half million residents in 1960 and expanded its political boundaries to accommodate future decades of urban sprawl. Major new tracts, such as Clairemont, Fletcher Hills and Serra Mesa were begun during this period, Cities like Chula Vista, El Cajon, La Mesa and Escondido all tripled in size during the 1950's (Table 5.4). Unincorporated areas grew as well, but generally at a much slower rate, partly because annexation by incorporated areas tended to bring newly populated areas into a municipality.

The vast majority of the population in the city remained white and largely blue collar. Blacks increased to 38,000 in 1960, an increase of about 40 percent over 1940, while total population leaped by over 300 percent. A largely black residential area developed in Logan Heights, the predecessor of Southeast San Diego, and most blacks were economically and culturally restricted to that neighborhood through racial covenants, racial steering, red-lining, and other practices used to reinforce racial isolation. Mexican-Americans and foreign-born Mexicans increased to over 70,000 in 1960, or roughly 6 percent of the county population, in part because of the "Bracero" program and the spurt in growth of Tijuana. Like blacks, Mexican-Americans were concentrated spatially in the southern part of the county but more particularly in the northern parts of National City and southeast San Diego.

TABLE 5.4. Growth of San Diego County Cities

	1940	1950	1960	1970	1980	1990	2000
Carlsbad	—	—	9,253	14,944	35,490	63,126	78,247
Chula Vista	5,138	15,927	42,034	67,901	83,927	135,163	173,556
Coronado	6,932	12,700	18,039	20,910	16,859	26,540	24,100
Del Mar	—	—	3,124	3,956	5,017	4,860	4,389
El Cajon	1,471	5,600	37,618	52,273	73,892	88,693	94,869
Encinitas	—	—	—	—	—	55,386	58,014
Escondido	4,560	6,544	16,377	36,792	62,480	108,635	133,559
Imperial Beach	—	—	17,773	20,244	22,689	26,512	26,992
La Mesa	3,925	10,946	30,441	39,178	50,342	52,931	54,749
Lemon Grove	—	—	—	19,935	20,780	23,984	24,918
National City	10,344	21,199	32,771	43,184	48,772	54,249	54,260
Oceanside	4,651	12,881	23,971	40,494	76,698	128,398	161,029
Poway	—	—	—	13,971	33,276	43,516	48,044
San Diego	203,341	334,387	573,224	696,769	875,538	1,110,549	1,223,400
San Marcos	—	—	—	3,896	17,479	38,974	54,977
Santee	—	—	—	20,902	40,039	52,902	52,975
Solana Beach	—	—	—	—	—	12,962	12,979
Vista	—	—	—	24,688	35,834	71,872	89,857

Source: United States and San Diego County census data.

The 1960s

In the 1960s San Diego County experienced a slowing of its percentage growth rate as total residents increased by about 325,000, or 31 percent, which represented the lowest percentage growth rate of any decade of the century to that time. However, much of this growth took place in the second half of the 1960s and presaged the period of massive absolute growth which occurred during the 1970s and 1980s. As odd as it may sound now, thousands of people "walked away" from the homes they had purchased in the late fifties and early sixties, losing their equity and leaving a stock of abandoned housing in the county. The sixties saw the spatial patterns of the county change radically as development sprawled into new areas. The patterns initiated during this decade accelerated as time went on.

The population boom of the 1940s and 1950s allowed the county to expand the scope of its economic diversification. As America made the transition into the "Post-Industrial" economy, San Diego was an early beneficiary. New industries, many producing high value items through the use of advanced technology, located in the region during the 1960s. Most of these companies were amenity oriented; they sought pleasant environments which would help them to retain their highly-educated, well-paid employees. San Diego County was seen as an ideal setting for such enterprises because of its desirable climate and attractive physical attributes. San Diego and many of its surrounding cities vigorously recruited such businesses and provided incentives, such as low cost land or tax credits, for locating here. Proportionately, the economic role of the military and the newly named aerospace industry declined.

In the latter half of the 1960s the county experienced a modest building boom. The construction of new housing tracts, to accommodate both newcomers and people moving from the older housing stock in the core of the city, brought about the development of new communities such as University City, Rancho Bernardo, and the initial planning for Mira Mesa and Rancho Penasquitos. This was accompanied by the rapid expansion of older communities including Santee, Poway, Vista, and Otay. Cities like Chula Vista, El Cajon, and Oceanside continued to grow rapidly. By contrast, the city of San Diego increased by just over 20 percent in the sixties and by 1970 had only slightly more than 50 percent of the county's total population.

During this time ethnic minorities expanded much more rapidly than other segments of the population. Blacks increased from 38,000 in 1960 to 62,000 in 1970. Although still highly concentrated in southeast San Diego, for the first time blacks were able to compete for more adequate housing in communities previously unavailable to them. Foreign-born Mexicans grew in numbers by roughly two-thirds and the Spanish surname population of the county increased to nearly 150,000, or about 10 percent of total inhabitants. The 1970 census identified 5,880 Indians in the county, though some local estimates were much higher.

San Diego as "Paradise Found"— 1970–1990

San Diego apparently entered the American psyche in a new form in the early 1970s and has become ingrained as an idyllic place to live, a "lotus-land by the sea" where the quality of life beckons like the proverbial siren's song. In a very real sense, San Diego came to be perceived as one of the nation's most desirable locations. This was reflected in the substantial growth rates and the very large increase in the county's absolute population during the 1970s and 1980s. During this period San Diego's population grew by 1.1 million people, an 84 percent increase. The region achieved "major-league" status and San Diego now aspires to be a "world class city".

In the seventies massive housing developments, such as Mira Mesa and Rancho Penasquitos, grew up in the northern quadrant of the city of San Diego while, simultaneously, large-scale housing and condominium projects blossomed in the county's northern communities. Numerous industrial parks and shopping malls, both large and small, were built in these areas and this further decentralized employment opportunities. Areas such as the Golden Triangle and Sorrento Valley were initiated and have since become primary development nodes (see Chapter 13). The population shift northward was in high gear.

The great increase in people moving into San Diego in the 1970s, numbering more than 500,000 for the decade, led to a rapid surge in property values throughout the county. In turn, this enhanced residential mobility within the region. Many homeowners saw equities appreciate at rates exceeding 10 percent a year. Many local residents bought bigger or "better" houses in more desirable locations and this, along with the demand generated by new arrivals, fueled the buying frenzy even further. In the early 1970s significant differentials were found for comparable housing units in various communities, but the general rise in home prices acted to lessen many of those variations.

By the end of the seventies, real concern was being expressed about "over-development" and the "Los Angelization" of San Diego. As a result, "slow growth" and "no growth" movements gained momentum in the county. Those groups garnered a good deal of political clout and by the early 1980s growth issues had become a central theme on political agendas throughout the region.

During the 1970s the number of minorities expanded greatly as well. Blacks exceeded 104,000 in 1980, just less than 6 percent of total population. The Hispanic population of 275,000 was up almost 86 percent during the decade and represented 15 percent of total residents. Likewise, the number of Indians enumerated in 1980 was just under 15,000, or nearly three times those reported in 1970. Asians and Pacific Islanders totaled just under 90,000, swelled especially by the first wave of Indochinese refugees. Those who identified themselves as "white" on the census forms, and this includes a percentage of the Spanish surname population, represented 1.5 million people, or 81 percent of the county's population. A rich variety of minorities comprised the remaining 19 percent.

A number of growth limitation measures were enacted by local governments in the late 1970s and the 1980s which placed some restrictions on development. The percentage growth rate in the eighties actually declined slightly from the seventies (from 37.1 percent to 34.2 percent). However, this still translated into a gain of more than 635,000 new residents for the region and a total population of just under 2.5 million by the 1990 census. The city of San Diego increased to over 1.1 million citizens in 1990, a little less than 45 percent of the region's total, making it the sixth largest city in America at that time. In the eighties growth continued to be centered in the north county, with the inland cities of San Marcos and Vista more than doubling their populations in ten years. While these cities led the growth parade, Escondido, Carlsbad, and Oceanside followed close behind. Oceanside, Chula Vista, and Escondido all exceeded the 100,000 mark during the 1980s.

As housing prices soared, the median price exceeded $200,000 in 1990, and affordable housing became a serious concern which has continued into the beginning of the twenty-first century. This led to large-scale building projects on land which was relatively easy to develop, much of it in previously undeveloped areas of south San Diego. Rapid expansion occurred in Chula Vista and the southern portions of the city of San Diego, where land values were significantly lower than in many parts of the region. In addition to price, proximity to the border may have been an attractive locational factor for the large Hispanic population which settled in these areas. Development continued in the northern part of the county as well, with the emergence of massive projects such as Carmel Valley, Carmel Mountain Estates, and Sabre Springs.

San Diego's Demographic Transition—1990 to the Present

San Diego's transition to a more ethnically diverse population began after the dramatic changes in U.S. immigration laws in the mid-1960s, which permitted a large increase in legal immigration from developing countries. This accelerated previous patterns of immigration into San Diego, especially from Mexico and Central America, and from the Philippines. By the 1980s this had become noticeable in San Diego, as it was throughout California, a state which was generally attractive to immigrants from Latin America and Asia. To the legal immigrants were added undocumented immigrants whose children, of course, were U.S. citizens if born in this country.

By the year 2000, Hispanics accounted for 26.7 percent of people of all ages, but in fact represented 38.1 percent of the population under age 18 (see Table 5.5). The non-Hispanic white population accounted for 59.8 percent of the population 18 and older, but only 41.3 percent of the under 18 population. Thus, the demographic transition taking place in San Diego is from a predominantly non-Hispanic white population to a population in which the older ages are largely non-Hispanic white while the younger ages are predominantly Hispanic, Asian, and African-American. The future will belong to those groups, but there will be considerable geographic variability within the county in the timing of the transition, with areas in the central and southern portions of the county becoming predominantly non-white

TABLE 5.5. Population of San Diego by Race/Ethnicity, 2000

	All Ages		18 and older		Under 18	
	Number	Percent	Number	Percent	Number	Percent
Total population	2,813,833	100.0	2,090,172	100.0	723,661	100.0
Hispanic or Latino (of any race)	750,965	26.7	475,519	22.8	275,446	38.1
Non-Hispanic						
White	1,548,833	55.0	1,249,632	59.8	299,201	41.3
Black or African American	154,487	5.5	107,228	5.1	47,259	6.5
American Indian and Alaska Native	15,253	0.5	11,300	0.5	3,953	5.5
Asian	245,297	8.7	188,799	9.0	56,498	7.8
Native Hawaiian and Other Pacific Islander	12,164	0.4	8,874	0.4	3,290	4.5
Some other race	5,822	0.2	3,715	0.2	2,107	2.9
Two or more races	81,012	2.9	45,105	2.2	35,907	5.0

Source: U.S. Census Bureau, Census 2000 Redistricting Data (Public Law 94–171) Summary File.

sooner than areas in the northern and eastern sections of the county.

Another interesting aspect of the 2000 census was the greatly differing growth rates of individual San Diego County cities. The common perception is that the county is "growing everywhere", but in terms of cities, this is not true. On the one hand, San Marcos grew by 41 percent and five other cities (all but one in North County) increased their population by 22 to 29 percent. Annexation of newly developing neighborhoods was often a major part of this.

On the other hand, ten cities (over half the total) had population changes of less than 8 percent, six cities grew by less than 2 percent, and two cities actually lost population (Table 5.6). This contrasts sharply with the 1980–1990 decade, in which every city but two gained in population by at least 10 percent (Table 5.4). This indicates that many cities in the county are nearing a "built out" condition, at least within their present city limits. These cities need to think about the long-term planning, fiscal, demographic, and infrastructure implications of their becoming built-out, "mature" cities.

Future Prospects

What does the future hold for San Diego in terms of population growth? That question is inevitably cloaked in uncertainties, since population forecasting is an imprecise activity at best. For example, estimates of the 2000 population for the county's incorporated cities, made in the early 1980s, underestimated the 2000 population of almost all of them (Table 5.7). For many cities (Chula Vista, for example), their 1990 population exceeded the year 2000 estimates (compare Tables 5.4 and 5.7).

Changes in birth rates and migration flows are difficult to forecast because they are influenced by such a myriad of factors. Indeed, SANDAG

TABLE 5.6. 1990–2000 Growth Rates of Cities

Growth rate:	Cities
>20%	Carlsbad, Chula Vista, Escondido, Oceanside, San Marcos, Vista
10% to 12%	Poway, San Diego
4% to 8%	El Cajon, Encinitas
0% to 2%	Imperial Beach, La Mesa, Lemon Grove, National City, Santee, Solana Beach
Loss	Coronado, Del Mar

Source: SANDAG.

deliberately increased its forecasts for the county in the 1990s, but a significant economic recession in the early 1990s, combined with greater than expected out-migration, led to an unanticipated slowdown in population growth in the 1990s (Table 5.2). Thus, SANDAG's forecasts for 2000 made in the 1990s tended to be higher than the actual 2000 census results. SANDAG has revised its forecasts in the light of the Census 2000 data and these figures for 2030 are shown in Table 5.7.

Another significant demographic change is San Diego's increasing senior citizen population. The 2003 population of about 345,000 residents 65 years of age or older is expected by SANDAG to increase to around 575,000 by the year 2020 (Figure 5.2). This will have important social, political, and fiscal implications.

While there is no unanimity of opinion as to what rate of population growth is best, a great many San Diegans favor efforts to limit population increases in some way. This attitude stems from perceived negative consequences of continued growth, including overcrowded beaches and parks, greater traffic congestion, greater noise and pollution, the loss of open space, and a general reduction in the perceived "quality of life". Additionally, periodic years of low precipitation (1987–1991 and 1999–2002) have created drought

TABLE 5.7. Urban Growth: Forecasts and Reality

City	1980 Population	1980 Estimate for the Year 2000	2000 Population	Estimated Year 2030 Population
Carlsbad	35,490	81,300	78,247	124,922
Chula Vista	83,927	106,300	173,556	282,664
Coronado	16,859	22,300	24,100	25,536
Del Mar	5,017	4,700	4,389	5,103
El Cajon	73,892	82,900	94,869	109,044
Encinitas	35,550	n.a.	58,014	78,762
Escondido	62,480	90,200	133,559	166,119
Imperial Beach	22,689	25,600	26,992	31,866
La Mesa	50,308	54,000	54,749	60,932
Lemon Grove	20,780	25,100	24,918	30,008
National City	48,772	52,100	54,260	67,430
Oceanside	76,698	133,700	161,029	214,696
Poway	33,439	n.a.	48,044	55,932
San Diego	875,538	1,136,200	1,223,400	1,613,355
San Marcos	17,479	37,300	54,977	106,772
Santee	40,298	59,000	52,975	69,221
Solana Beach	12,250	n.a.	12,979	14,411
Vista	35,834	47,000	89,857	113,969
Unincorporated Area	363,000	n.a.	442,919	718,862
County	1,861,800		2,813,833	3,889,604

Source: Columns 1 and 3, U.S. Census Bureau; Cols. 2 and 4, SANDAG.

conditions and heightened concerns over long-term water supplies.

For these reasons, many citizen groups support slow growth policies for the county. This is a difficult assignment, however. Could population growth be contained by limiting the production of new housing? This, unfortunately, might only exacerbate the already high cost of dwelling units, and increase the average number of persons residing in existing units. The conundrum is that we work hard to maintain high environmental quality in San Diego County, but the region's many attractive features will continue to draw in new residents.

On the other side of the debate are those who favor continued population growth. They assert that since in-migration probably can't be stopped, we must accommodate it. They view an increasing population as good for economic progress. They have faith in human ingenuity to resolve pollution and water supply problems.

The two sides in this debate find relatively little merit in their opponents' point of view. The one thing they would agree on is that in the short run the region's population is certain to continue to increase. Agencies involved with infrastructure adequacy struggle to keep pace. Their success is chronicled in subsequent chapters for such

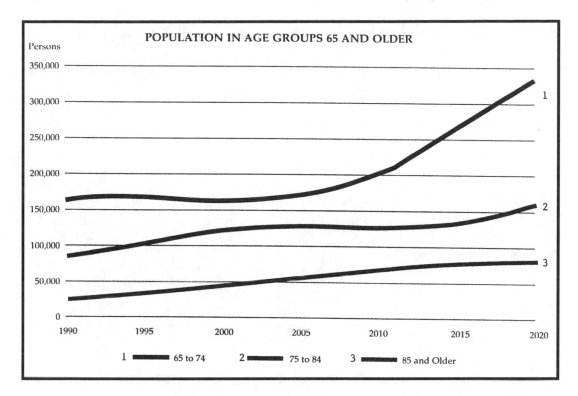

Figure 5.2.

topics as water (Chapter 8), pollution (Chapter 16), and open space and endangered species (Chapter 17).

There is no doubt that the twenty-first century promises to challenge the abilities of San Diego's planners and politicians to accommodate continuing growth while maintaining a high quality of life for the county's residents. San Diegans have created a unique set of lifestyles for themselves which center around outdoor activities and the use of public facilities and open spaces. Clean air, attractive beaches and bays, access to mountains and deserts, challenging golf courses, parks for picnicking, hiking, or jogging, bird sanctuaries and protected lagoons are just a few of the assets San Diegans take for granted. Population growth can present great economic opportunity but it also poses serious threats to the environmental attributes which have attracted so many to the county. Hopefully, we will have the wisdom to protect those things which have made San Diego a special place.

Appendix 5.1 California's Ten Largest Cities, 1880 and 2000

1880		2000	
1. San Francisco	233,959	Los Angeles	3,694,820
2. Oakland	34,555	San Diego	1,223,400
3. Sacramento	21,420	San Jose	894,943
4. San Jose	12,567	San Francisco	776,733
5. Los Angeles	11,183	Long Beach	461,522
6. Stockton	10,282	Fresno	427,652
7. Vallejo	5,987	Sacramento	407,018
8. Alameda	5,708	Oakland	399,484
9. Marysville	4,321	Santa Ana	337,977
10. Nevada (town)	4,022	Anaheim	328,014
20. (approximately) San Diego	2,637		

Source: U.S. Bureau of the Census.

References

County of San Diego. *San Diego County General Plan, Part II: Land Use Element* (Incorporates Regional Growth Management Plan). Latest revision.

Dumke, Glenn, "Bay 'n Climate, the Boom in the San Diego Area", in *The Boom of the Eighties in Southern California,* San Marino, CA: Huntington Press, 1944, pp. 132–152.

Ford, L. and Griffin, E. "The Ghettoization of Paradise", *The Geographical Review,* Vol. 69, no. 2 (April 1979), pp. 140–158.

Madyun, Gail and Larry Malone, *Black Pioneers in San Diego: 1880–1920.* San Diego: San Diego Historical Society, undated.

Pourade, R. F. *History of San Diego* (7 volumes). San Diego: Union-Tribune Publishing Co., 1960–1967.

San Diego Association of Governments, *INFO: Mapping the Census: Race and Ethnicity in the San Diego Region,* San Diego: SANDAG, April 2002.

San Diego Association of Governments, *Series IX Regional Growth Forecasts,* San Diego: SANDAG, 2001.

United States Census Bureau. *Censuses of California* (1880 through 2000). Washington DC: U. S. Census Bureau, various years.

Weisberg, L. and D. Washburn, "Comings and Goings", *San Diego Union-Tribune,* August 17, 2003, pp. A-1 and A-19.

Internet Connections:
United States Census Bureau: *www.census.gov*
San Diego Association of Governments: *www.sandag.org*
State of California demographic data: *www.dof.ca.gov/HTML/DEMOGRAP/Druhpar.htm*

Richard Phillips and
Lowell Lindsay

Chapter Six

Gifts from an Arid Land
Natural Resources of
San Diego County

Many parts of the world are richly endowed with natural resources. Too often, however, the resulting exploitation has led to environmental catastrophes, evidenced by denuded forest lands, unreclaimed heaps of mine waste, and residual pockets of human poverty. San Diego County, with its multiplicity of climates and diverse geology, is richly endowed with physical beauty and recreational resources. Natural resources, in the

This chapter was originally prepared by the late Richard P. Phillips, for many years a professor of geology and Coordinator of Environmental Studies at the University of San Diego. It was updated for this edition by Lowell Lindsay, past president of the San Diego Association of Geologists and CEO of Sunbelt Publications.

strict sense of those economic products of fields, mountains, and rocks, have generally been disappointing. Production of renewable natural resources, such as timber and range grass, has been strictly limited by the semiarid climate of much of the area. The nonrenewable resources such as gold, gems, and oil have produced flurries of interest, but no sustained industrial base. By far, the most valuable natural product of San Diego County has been the sand and gravel needed for its continuing development.

The USGS Minerals Yearbook for the year 2000 shows that California's non-fuel mineral production value was $3.3 billion. The state continued to lead the nation in the value of non-fuel mineral production, accounting for more than

8% of the total. It also continues to be the top construction sand and gravel producer, accounting for more than 13% of the U.S. mine production, and more than 17% of that commodity's total value. This same product was, by value, also the state's leading non-fuel mineral, accounting for nearly 29% of the value of the state's total non-fuel mineral production (Table 6.1).

The economic mineral wealth of San Diego County is almost exclusively construction sand and gravel, which accounts for 10.1 percent of California's total value of this product (Table 6.2). This category includes aggregate for manufacturing concrete, dimension stone for decorative applications, rip-rap for wave and flood control, and grus or decomposed granite ("DG"), as well as crushed/broken rock for the construction and road-building industries.

While there is an abundant supply of these materials in the county, the vast majority occurs in highly developed, developing, or environmentally sensitive river valleys. These latter land uses conflict with high-impact extractive industries such as sand and gravel mining. As a result, in the 1990s San Diego began importing sizable quantities of sand from northern Baja California. These and related issues are discussed in more detail later in this chapter, as well as in Chapter 16.

The term "natural resource" has been broadly defined to include all the resources available to meet human needs, including wildlife, plants, water, and soil, as well as the air we breathe and the quiet we enjoy. Many of these subjects are covered elsewhere in this book. This chapter will be primarily concerned with the nonmarine resources that can be, or have been, directly exploited locally for financial reward (marine resources are covered in Chapter 7).

Natural resources are traditionally divided into two classes: *renewable* and *nonrenewable*. The renewable resources are those (such as grasslands, forests, and wildlife) that can be

TABLE 6.1. Non-Fuel Mineral Production in California

	Quantity in 1,000 metric tons	Value in $1,000s
Asbestos	7,190	withheld
Boron minerals	1,070	557,000
Cement	11,384	864,100
Clay: bentonite and common	990	18,960
Gemstones	n.a.	1,500
Gold (kilograms)	17,200	155,000
Rare-earth metal concentrates	5	withheld
Sand and Gravel: construction	148,000	940,000
Sand and Gravel: industrial	1,810	45,200
Silver (metric tons)	9	1,390
Stone: crushed and dimension	59,733	378,790
Zeolites	n.a.	n.a.
Clays, other than above (a)	n.a.	308,000
Total		3,269,940

(a) including gypsum and feldspar in SD County.
Source: Adapted from Kohler, S., USGS Minerals Yearbook 2001, p. 71 ff.

TABLE 6.2. Construction Sand and Gravel, Year 2000

Description	California		San Diego County (District 12)		
	Quantity in 1,000 metric tons	Value in $1,000s	Quantity in 1,000 metric tons	Value in $1,000s	% of State in $1,000s
Concrete aggregate [a]	49,000	337,000	2,100	19,500	5.79%
Concrete products [b]	1,030	8,410	1,010	490	5.83%
Road base and coverings [c]	17,400	96,900	113	7,510	7.75%
Fill	6,870	36,200	857	3,200	8.84%
Other miscellaneous uses [d]	2,500	18,500	1,530	14,000	75.68%
Unspecified by end use	45,000	262,000	7,990	50,400	19.24%
Miscellaneous (not applicable in San Diego County)	26,200	180,990	0	0	0
Total	148,000	940,000	13,600	95,100	10.12%

[a] Including concrete sand.
[b] Blocks, bricks, pipe, decorative including plaster and gunite sands.
[c] Includes road base materials and other stabilization-cement and lime.
[d] Includes railroad ballast, and various other minor use categories.

exploited in such a way that their stocks do not diminish over time.

Mineral resources are, for the most part, non-renewable. Once mined, ores are gone forever, and only many millions of years of geologic time can create more. A very few minerals, such as salt extracted from the oceans, exist in such large amounts that in a single extractive operation we may think of the source as basically renewable. And of course, many fabricated mineral products, such as industrial metals, can and should be recycled.

Timber and Grass Resources

Trees are probably the first "renewable" natural resource that comes to mind. Unfortunately, in San Diego they are not very renewable. The trees that once covered Point Loma were quickly destroyed when every home was heated with wood, every meal was cooked with wood, and the demands of the hide-curing industry were

insatiable. Only the dedication and commitment of Ellen Browning Scripps and members of the San Diego Society of Natural History prevented the Torrey Pines from suffering the same fate.

From time to time the big trees of the mountains have attracted the interest of lumbermen. The mission records tell how the Padres visited Palomar Mountain in 1798 and carefully selected trees from which the great ridge timbers of the Mission San Luis Rey could be hewn. Those timbers have supported the roof now for over 200 years.

Commercial lumbering began around the Cuyamaca mountains in response to the building boom that came with the gold rush. Mills sold lumber at $30 a thousand board feet and helped change Julian from a tent city to a respectable town. In 1890 a sawmill was operating on Palomar Mountain, hauling timber down the wagon road that had been built by "Long Joe" Smith 25 years before. But San Diego lacked water to power its mills, and transportation from the mountains was so difficult that the local logs could not compete with timber that arrived by ship in great quantities, some of it from around the Horn.

In 1926 the area surrounding Laguna Mountain was essentially closed to any further lumbering when it was set aside as a recreational area by order of Agriculture Secretary W. M. Jardin. The order only made official what everyone already knew. Timber was not an economic resource in San Diego, but the mountain areas present an irreplaceable recreational resource that should be preserved. Even today, when it is necessary to remove large numbers of trees from the area either as a salvage operation after a fire or to remove diseased trees, it is difficult to find firms that will bid for the trees and log them off, and public opposition is apt to arise.

Protection is not enough, however, to insure the preservation of this valuable recreational resource. Scientists and foresters from the United States Forest Service must be vigilant and resourceful to prevent pests and disease from destroying the remaining pines. The infestation of bark beetles caused by the 1986–92 drought was one of the worst on record, killing many trees. The fungus which causes root rot has been identified, and the manner in which it spreads, inadvertently through human activity, has been recognized. A method of checking the spread of the dwarf mistletoe has been devised. Prescribed burning of the underbrush is now occasionally carried out. Careful management and adequate rainfall are required to maintain our local remnant forests.

If San Diego didn't have usable trees, the natural response would be to grow them, and what better tree than the wonderful import from Australia, the eucalyptus. From the 1875 plantings by Frank and Warren Kimball of National City to 1907 when the Santa Fe railroad planted 8,800 acres of their newly acquired Rancho Santa Fe with 3 million of them, San Diego was in a frenzy of eucalyptus plantings. The scientific and popular literature of the day praised the tree in every way possible. Not only was the wood "heavier than coal, and has an equal or higher thermal power, bulk for bulk, than coal . . ." (Scientific American, 1903), but from it could be built the best ships, indestructible piles for wharfs, and long lasting railroad ties. The oil from the leaves was reputed to be a wonder drug that could cure almost any human ailment. Just growing the trees drove away malaria which was a real threat in San Diego at the turn of the century.

But ships started to be made of steel, railroads were powered by oil, eucalyptus wood split when it dried, and food tasted funny if you used eucalyptus wood for baking. Thus, the tree became largely ornamental. Today we owe much of the charm (and shade) of San Diego to those trees brought over during the days of "bluegum mania." The various species of eucalyptus do grow well here, require little water, and have become almost a symbol of the metropolitan area.

Traveling south through California's coastal areas, an impressive amount of land is given over to cattle raising. However, the farther south one travels, the fewer head of cattle there are, since near San Diego the increase in aridity makes the land less suitable for range cattle. A study by the University of California indicated that it takes two acres of land to support a mature cow for one month in San Diego County, as compared to less than one acre in Santa Barbara County. As an economic resource, most of the natural range grass in San Diego County is fairly marginal, but it is still used. As Chapter 3 noted, introduced grasses have largely replaced native species in the county's grasslands.

Metals and Gemstones

Each of the episodes of San Diego's geological history has given rise to different mineral resources.

Some have been exploited, some are still being worked, and some may yet be waiting for future discovery and development. As an example, rocks formed from the sediments that were being deposited in the deep trench west of San Diego during the middle of the Mesozoic Era (see Table 2.1), sometimes called the Franciscan Assemblage, are hidden today beneath the Continental Borderland where they are under many feet of water and younger rocks. They are known only from bits and pieces dredged up by interested marine geologists. Yet, in northern California, where they are found on land, chromium, mercury, and asbestos have been mined from them. Present technology does not allow us to prospect these dark, submarine landscapes, but a wealth of these vital (albeit toxic) minerals may well be waiting to be used by future generations.

Industrial Metals

The discovery of copper- and iron-bearing veins in the Defiance District, about 12 miles northeast of San Clemente, led to the speculation that San Diego would become the Pittsburgh of the West. This was quickly followed by other copper discoveries: the Encinitas Mine four miles north of Rancho Santa Fe in 1887, and the Daley (Barona) Mine five miles south of Ramona in 1894 (Figure 6.1). These mines were small, producing less than 200,000 pounds of copper, most of it from the Daley Mine. This copper mineralization is associated with the metavolcanic rocks of the arc of oceanic islands that existed 150 million years ago where San Diego is now. It is not unusual to find copper in this environment. Some of the richest copper mines in the world are found in association with the volcanic rocks of Japan. In general, though, the grade of ore in the County is low, and traditional mining methods can only be used near the surface where weathering has concentrated the copper by "secondary enrichment." Eventually we might reinvestigate the volcanic beds

with an eye toward using modern mining methods that can profitably work large low- grade deposits.

Scheelite, a calcium tungstate, is the most abundant tungsten-bearing mineral in the County. It has been mined off and on, when the price is high, from several localities. The most productive, the Pawnee Mine about six miles northeast of Oak Grove along the boundary between San Diego and Riverside Counties, has produced about 3,000 units (a unit is 20 pounds) of tungsten trioxide. The scheelite is found in association with a rock called tactite, which is essentially a highly impure marble. The replacement and reaction of the calcium carbonate with the "juices" from the metamorphosing magma produces many interesting minerals, such as clinozoisite, garnet, and of course, scheelite. Locally these impure marbles have been a mineral seeker's dream, and such areas as the marble formations along Highway 8 east of Mountain Springs are a well-known "rockhound" hunting ground.

Gold

Fred (A. H.) Coleman had drifted down from the gold fields of the Mother Lode and was working as a cowboy in San Diego's back country. While watering his horse in a small creek on the flank of Volcan Mountain he noticed some yellow flakes, and so, early in February of 1870, San Diego's own gold rush started. The modern California State Highway 78 follows Coleman Creek from Wynola to Julian and passes close by the site of the original discovery.

Gold has been produced primarily from the metamorphic rocks. The schists around Julian and Banner contain goldbearing quartz that was mined early in the century. The mines of the Julian area were generally small and shallow. The Stonewall, which yielded about two million dollars worth of gold, was by far the largest, and it

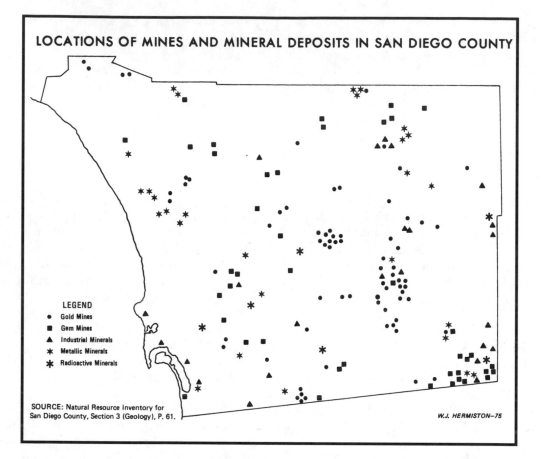

Figure 6.1. Mineral deposits in San Diego County.

went to a depth of only 600 feet. The miners in the Julian area were beset with problems. The ore was easy enough to treat. Most of the gold was obtained by "free milling," that is, by crushing the quartz fine enough so that the gold could be separated from it by simple methods. When ore was found it was quite rich, with values ranging from $75 to $520 in gold per ton being common (gold was then valued at $20 per ounce).

The problem was the "veins." They weren't like the veins that most of the miners were used to. Instead of cutting through the country rock

like a wall of quartz that could be worked in a systematic way, they pinched and rolled apparently at random. In addition, the veins were generally parallel to the layering in the country rock, and this made it hard to keep an opening from caving in.

Besides the troubles that nature had given the Julian miners, they had continuing financial problems. Outside capital could not be raised to finance the mines and allow their development in a businesslike way. The financiers from San Francisco recognized the highly localized nature of the deposits, and knew from bitter experience that once a pocket was mined out, the entire profit and more could quickly be expended looking for the next pocket. This not only made it impossible for the miners to raise needed capital, but indirectly forced them to develop their properties without the aid of expert engineering and geological advice. In San Diego, however, optimism ran high. Outside financing wasn't needed. In May of 1870 the San Diego Union crowed, "We have great faith in the ultimate value of these mines. They are no Humbug."

But gold is a nonrenewable resource. Once dug out of the ground there is no more to replace it. By 1876 most of the mines lay idle and inter-

est waned. New discoveries rejuvenated the Julian mining district in 1887 and Julian and Banner had a period of relative prosperity in the 1890s and early 1900s. By 1910 the district was inactive again and no major gold mining has taken place since. It is estimated that the total output of gold from San Diego County was less than $5,200,000. Only one mine, the Stonewall south of Julian, yielded over $1 million (Figure 6.2).

With the current high price of gold, people are beginning to take a renewed interest in the gold veins. In 1973 a small mine was reopened near Pine Valley and a new look is being taken at some of the properties in the Julian- Banner district. The fact that the veins don't look like the traditional quartz veins of other areas has

Figure 6.2. The old Stonewall Mine south of Julian, taken around the year 1900. Photograph courtesy of Historical Collection, San Diego Historical Society.

led some geologists to suspect that the "veins" aren't veins at all, but metamorphosed sand lenses from the original sediments, and that the gold was already there as placer deposits. Under the influences of heat and pressure, the quartz and gold migrated along the bedding to the crests of the folds, where the pressure was slightly less.

If this idea of the origin of the gold deposits has any validity, then a careful remapping of the Julian Schist may point to areas where new quartz rolls could be found, deposits not readily apparent from the surface, but present at depth, as indicated by geological clues.

Gold-bearing quartz is known in other areas of San Diego, but none but the Julian-Banner District has been very productive. The Beauty Peak District east of Palomar Mountain, the Deep Park and Laguna Mountain districts west of the crest of the Laguna Mountains, and the Metal Mountain District between Thing and McCain Valleys have all produced some gold from rocks similar to those found at Julian. In the Boulder Creek District, west of Cuyamaca Peak, the rocks are so highly metamorphosed that the original sedimentary character is hard to determine. Here both gold-bearing and barren quartz leads occur over a zone exposed for at least 1½ miles along the north side of Boulder Canyon.

Gems

Pegmatites are interesting rocks, and some of them are valuable. They are associated with the granitic rocks, and are often found cutting through them and the nearby metamorphic rocks as white bands called dikes. Pegmatite dikes are beautifully exposed on the side of Granite Mountain southwest of Earthquake Valley. You can drive right up to several large ones at Little Pass Camp Ground, about five miles southwest of Scissors Crossing on County Highway S-2. Pegmatites are characterized by crystals of large size. The minerals are similar to those found in the ordinary granitic rocks, but are often up to a foot in diameter. Occasionally pegmatites will contain ordinary minerals in sufficient concentration that they can be mined. The Pacific Feldspar Mine in Hauser Canyon north of Campo produced feldspar used in the manufacture of porcelain for bathroom fixtures. The mill where the feldspar was separated from the quartz still stands at Cameron Corners near Campo on State Highway 94.

The primary interest in the pegmatites, however, has been in the gems that they sometimes contain. Pala, Mesa Grande and Ramona are world famous for the tourmaline, morganite, garnet, kunzite, and other semiprecious gemstones that they have produced (Figure 6.3).

The pegmatites can be thought of as the last gasp of the solidifying plutonic magmas. As the magma cooled and congealed, the material richest in water and lowest in melting point would be concentrated into the final remaining liquid. This very fluid magma is thought to have worked its way into all the cracks and crevices that were available to it, and there cooled and hardened. This must have been a real alchemist's pot. In the hot magma, under great pressure, water rich, and rich in elements that are rare elsewhere, reactions could take place that formed not only large crystals, but the beautiful ones that are called gems.

One of the elements that is concentrated in pegmatites is lithium. It was lepidolite, the mineral source of lithium, that first brought mining to the Pala District. As early as 1892 this purplish, micaceous mineral was being mined from the Stewart deposit. The production of lepidolite continued intermittently to 1928, and over 23,480 tons, with a value of $432,800 was shipped. This production of a material that was used first as a medicine, later in metal casting, and most recently

Figure 6.3. Garnets recovered from surface deposits on Garnet Peak in the Laguna Mountains. Photo by P. R. Pryde.

in atomic energy, represents the most valuable product yet produced, in reported dollar value, from the "gem" pegmatites of Pala.

The presence of gem quality tourmaline had been reported from the pegmatites in 1870, when Henry Hamilton discovered some outstanding prismatic crystals of pink and green color on the southeast slope of Thomas Mountain in southern Riverside County. The Indians, too, had known of the tourmaline, and crystals have been found in many Indian graves. The first mining directed specifically at recovering the semiprecious gems of the pegmatites seems to have been in 1898 at the Himalaya Mine in the Mesa Grande District. In addition to tourmaline, fine transparent quartz crystals, beryl ranging from the blue aquamarine to peach colored morganite, spessartite garnet, spodumene represented by the pale rose kunzite and topaz have been recovered.

The gem market boomed through the early 1900s. By 1910 fifty deposits were being worked in the Pala District alone. From 1907 to 1909 the Pala District produced over 730 pounds of gem tourmaline with an estimated value of $61,500. But events far from San Diego were to pop the gem bubble. Lithia minerals were found in the Appalachians, much closer to the market and less expensive to mine. Then in 1912, and in the other direction, the Chinese dynasty headed by the dowager empress Tzu Hsi fell, and with it the market for tourmaline. The mines lay idle for many years, or were worked intermittently by "week-end" miners hopefully searching for new pockets of gems. Beginning about 1972, however, several of the mines were reopened and are being worked in a systematic way. The Pala District is again producing fine quality tourmaline and beryl specimens, as well as excellent gem-grade material. In 1974 it was reported that a considerable quantity of kunzite was found in the Tule Mountain area, the first gem material reported from there. Much of the recent output of the gem pegmatites is now sold to the growing army of mineral collectors and amateur gem cutters.

There are many other minerals of economic or recreational interest associated with the great batholith and its related metamorphic rocks. For instance, San Diego County is one of the few places in the world where native arsenic is found. Mica has been mined from pegmatites near Jacumba. The rare mineral dumortierite is found near Alpine just south of the Alpine-Dehesa Road. Nickel has been mined from a vein that cuts the gabbro just south of Inspiration Point on the Sunrise Highway. Molybdenite, found as bright, steel-gray flakes, has been mined from a fine-grained phase of the granitic rocks just north of Campo. Small amounts of lead, zinc, and even some uranium has been discovered in the county. Thus, the San Diego region has a rich variety of mineral wealth, but very little of it in commercial quantities.

Hydrothermal and geothermal resources are often associated with active fault and seismic zones, many of which are located in counties adjacent to San Diego. Major electricity producing geothermal plants are found in Imperial County (the second largest in California) and near Mexicali (second largest in the world). Riverside County hosts numerous commercially-operated recreational hot springs while San Diego has three: the Jacumba spa, Warner Springs, and Aqua Caliente County Park. All three are probably associated with the active Elsinore fault zone or its subparallel traces.

Rock, Sand, and Evaporites

During the Mesozoic Era, the west coast of North America was invaded by great masses of molten rock, rising from below the crust. In Southern California and Baja California these rocks, now cooled and crystallized, make up what is known as the *Peninsular Ranges Batholith*. Typically, these rocks have a "pepper and salt" appearance, consisting of closely interlocked grains of light (quartz and feldspar) and dark (hornblende and biotite mica) minerals. Although these rocks are often called "granite," very little is true granite. Granite is a very special type of rock, rich in potassium feldspar. The Peninsular Ranges Batholith is very poor in potassium feldspar, and the bulk of the rocks should be called *tonalite*. Since the composition of the various plutons ranges over a wide spectrum, and all of the resulting rocks look somewhat alike, the term often used to cover them all is "granitic," or granitelike.

The extraction of the granitic rock itself has been a leading part of the mineral industry of San Diego County since 1898. About thirty-seven quarries have been active in San Diego (Figure 6.4). Many of them were opened and mined for a single purpose, such as the Meadowlark Ranch quarry, about six miles north of Rancho Santa Fe, where stone for the Mission Bay Park project was obtained.

San Diego County has also been a source of decorative "granites" for monuments and building facing. Where the rock is dense enough, will take a nice polish, and is jointed in a way that allows quarrying into large angular blocks, quarries have been opened. The rock is mined, sawed with wire saws, and polished to later appear in graveyards or on bank fronts throughout the southwest. During the days of lower building cost and less expensive labor, two types, the "Silver-grey Granite" (technically a granodiorite) and the famous "San Diego Black Granite," were produced. In 1959, 34,700 cubic feet of finished granitic dimension stones were produced, with a value of more than $168,000, and San Diego

Figure 6.4. Rock quarry along Mission Gorge Road, San Diego. Photo courtesy of Sunbelt Publications.

County was the leading source in the State. The use of stone as a building material has declined in recent years and by 1975, the mining of the Silver-grey Granite had stopped.

The San Diego Black Granite, on the other hand, is still quarried and polished. This rock is technically a gabbro, that is, a granitic rock composed chiefly of plagioclase feldspar and hornblende with no quartz present. It takes a high polish, and has had a continuing popularity for monuments and building stone. Black Granite has been quarried from two areas, one west of Vista and the other southwest of Escondido.

An entirely new industry has developed around the gabbroic rocks. Precise industrial machining requires "surface plates" of extreme flatness and precise dimensional stability. Plates made from polished San Diego Black Granite have been found to be superior to almost any other material. In 1974 over 30,000 cubic feet of Black Granite was produced in San Diego County with a value of $330,000.[1] Most of this was used for surface plates.

Sand and Gravel

Far and away the most valuable mineral resource of San Diego County came here from Mexico. During the Eocene Epoch (40 to 60 million years ago) there was no Gulf of California, and no mountains where the Peninsular Ranges stand today. Rivers, rising in Sonora, Mexico flowed westward to the sea where they built extensive deltas of sand and gravel. Since the material had traveled a long way down the rivers, the soft, easily eroded rocks had been destroyed. What was left was hard, resistant material, perfect for use in construction. The conglomerate, a sedimentary rock made from the accumulation of sand and gravel sized pieces, that is exposed on the north side of Mission Valley is part of this delta.

Sand and gravel is essential to the continued growth and development of San Diego. Concrete is mostly sand and gravel; asphalt is sand and gravel held together by heavy oil and cement. The primary production area for many years was north of Friars Road in Mission Valley, but the end of the 1990s much of this area had been mined out and converted to commercial and residential uses (Figure 6.5). The material is mined, washed, crushed and screened before being stacked into miniature mountains awaiting selection and blending into the final products. While this operation may not have the romance of gold, or the allure of gems, in 1973 alone 9,892,000 cubic yards of material with a value of $15,919,000 was produced.[1] That is over seven cubic yards for every man, woman and child in San Diego County.

It would be misleading to give all the credit for our sand and gravel industry to the Eocene rivers. The present rivers have been very efficient in sorting, transporting and depositing sand of high quality and economic importance. The county's "River Sand Resource Study" projected a total volume of over 681 million cubic yards of construction quality sand in the major

coastal river basins of the county. Over half of this is in the north county market area (Table 6.3). Of the 488 million cubic yards located within the metropolitan San Diego market area, the Conservation Element of the San Diego County General Plan recognized only 110.8 million cubic yards as suitable for extraction.

The major problem facing the sand and gravel producers in San Diego is that they are being overrun by the urban growth that they help make possible. These low-cost, high-bulk products must be used near the source to be economically competitive. But pits and quarries tend to be dusty and noisy and generate heavy truck traffic.

In 1982, the California Division of Mines and Geology in its periodical *California Geology* concluded that "western San Diego County will face a shortage of approximately 330 million tons of construction-quality aggregate within the next 50 years," but "... plentiful aggregate resources do exist. Approximately 110 square miles were mapped as containing sand and gravel deposits. ... However, ... continuing urbanization and land-use decisions ... could result in these areas being closed or lost to mining."

TABLE 6.3. Sand Resources by Basin

River Basin	% of Total
San Luis Rey	31
San Dieguito	28
San Diego	19
Upper Basin	[15]
Lower Basin	[4]
Sweetwater	12
Tijuana (in USA)	1
Other	9

Note: The potential sand resource in the lower Santa Margarita river, while substantial, is not included as it is on Camp Pendleton and thus not available for commercial extraction.

Source: Dibble, 2003.

[1]In the 1980's, the county stopped gathering disaggregated data on local mineral production, hence more recent production figures are not available.

Figure 6.5. Homes constructed on former sand and gravel extraction area near Friars Road. Photo by P. R. Pryde.

The United States Geological Survey has suggested that there may be a potential source of sand and especially gravel located on the Continental Shelf approximately six miles off Imperial Beach. It estimated that the deposit could supply over one million tons of gravel per year for twenty years, and concluded that an operation of this type is technically and economically feasible.

Reflecting the decreasing production from Mission Valley, the importation of high quality sand and gravel from northern Baja California is a recent major development that started in the mid-1990s. This is an ironic parallel to the opening comment of this section which notes that almost all of this resource "came here from Mexico . . . during the Eocene Epoch." San Diego County produces or imports 3.5 million tons of construction sand per year. Of this, Baja California now contributes 530,000 tons, or fifteen percent, up from only a small amount in 1995. Of the total, another 670,000 tons is imported from elsewhere in southern California.

Baja California sand is preferred to other imported sand sources for its quality and transportation economics. Train transport from Tecate to Campo costs 3 to 4 cents per ton-mile and barge transport from Ensenada to San Diego costs 2 cents per ton-mile. This compares to 10 cents per ton-mile via truck from Los Angeles, Riverside, and Imperial counties. Primary source areas are the Guadalupe and Las Palmas valleys south of Tecate, Ojos Negros valley east of Ensenada, and the port area itself.

If current trends were to continue, the import from Baja California could double in the next couple of years. This "if" is very dependent on new environmental concerns south of the border. Just as San Diego has substantially restricted its own mining, so also are Mexican officials fearing negative impacts to valuable riverbeds and aquifers. By February of 2003, 46 out of 63 sand-mining operations in Baja California had recently been curtailed and shut down for violations of mining or environmental regulations. Scientific studies now in progress or proposed will influence policy decisions on the continued expansion or possible cessation of the importation of this valuable construction resource.

The sedimentary rocks of the Pacific Coastal region have supplied other mineral deposits besides sand and gravel for construction. Brickmaking was once an important industry in San Diego, with the quarries extracting clay from Rose Canyon and Sorrento Valley. Bentonite, a special clay used in oil well drilling and chemical filtration has been mined from the slopes of Otay Valley. It may well represent an unexploited resource within the county. Specialty sand (that is, sand not used for concrete or fill, but used in glassmaking, for sandblasting, for foundry sand, or in high grade plaster) has been mined from a quarry on Loma Alta Creek about 3½ miles east of Oceanside.

Salt and Other Evaporites

When seawater evaporates it leaves behind the load of minerals and salts that make it "salty." When the Gulf of California first formed, the sea extended northward through a series of basins to the head of the Salton Sea Depression, well into what is now central Riverside County. These basins formed natural evaporating pans, and today the minerals deposited in them form an economic resource that can be mined. The first mineral to deposit from seawater is gypsum.

Gypsum (calcium sulphate) is used to make plaster of paris and is a principal ingredient of wallboard used in construction. Today a large deposit is being mined by the United States Gypsum Company just across the county line in Imperial County near the mouth of Fish Creek Wash. The gypsum is moved by a narrow gage railroad to Plaster City, a mile north of Highway 8, where it is processed into wallboard (Figure 6.6). The extension of this deposit into San Diego County is primarily in Anza-Borrego Desert State Park, which lies immediately to the west. By traveling up Fish Creek and taking a short hike up the ridge to the south side of Split Mountain, caves and domes that have been eroded into the gypsum can be found.

Just east of the campground at Fish Creek Wash there is a hill standing out from the mountain front. The scars of roads and the ruins of buildings indicate that this hill was also the site of a mining venture in the past. This mine, the Roberts and Peeler strontium deposit, is a cap-like remnant of the gypsum beds, but here they contain celestite, a strontium sulfate. The source of the strontium in this particular area is not clear, but may have been associated with hot springs that flowed into the newly formed basins when the Salton Trough was forming.

What nature did in the desert, industry is doing in south San Diego Bay. Here, since 1869 salt has been produced by the evaporation of seawater. An area of about 1,200 acres is divided into 29 ponds separated by levees. Seawater contains about 3½ percent dissolved solids, most of it sodium chloride (common table salt). Water is admitted to the salt ponds during the high tide periods from mid-March to mid-December. The water passes through a series of concentrating ponds until evaporation has removed so much water that the remaining brine can no longer retain the total load of solids. The first mineral to crystallize is gypsum, followed by other sul-

Figure 6.6. View of the narrow gauge railroad that carries gypsum from the Fish Creek Mountains to the processing plant at Plaster City. Photo courtesy of Sunbelt Publications.

fides. This is allowed to deposit in the last of the concentrating ponds, and then, when the original volume of water is concentrated to about one-tenth of its original volume, it is pumped into the crystallizing ponds.

The next step is tricky. As the sun and wind continue to remove water, salt begins to crystallize out. If the concentration is allowed to go too high, though, magnesium sulphate will also deposit, and magnesium sulphate in common salt is highly undesirable. Periodically the magnesium rich "bittern" is withdrawn and new saturated brine is introduced. The bittern is processed in a neighboring plant to recover the magnesium chloride.

By the first part of June the layer of salt has built up thick enough to be harvested, and the pond is drained. The salt is collected, washed and stacked in the great white piles that can be seen near Highway 5 just past the South Bay Power Plant. Up to 100,000 tons of salt are produced annually by this method, to be used in water softening, food processing, soap making, chemical manufacturing, and a variety of other applications.

As noted earlier in the chapter, this industry is almost unique for it is a renewable mineral resource. In addition, the salt ponds form one of the most productive wildlife habitats in San Diego's coastal region. In 1999, these ponds became part of the new South San Diego Bay National Wildlife Refuge, but the salt operation will continue.

Fossil Fuels

Oil has never been produced in San Diego County, but that isn't because no one has looked. Since the Scott No. I well was drilled in 1916 to the drilling of the Robert Egger No. I in 1962, over fifty-five wells have been drilled in San Diego County looking for oil. Two of these are east of the mountains, just north of Highway 78 near Ocotillo Wells. A few others are scattered about the county in such unlikely areas for oil as Escondido and Lakeside. Most of them were drilled in the Pacific Coastal Plain from Oceanside south where the great thickness of sediments that had washed off the mountains in late Mesozoic time had been deposited. This thickness is indeed impressive. A well north of Oceanside was stopped at a depth of 3,300 feet and had not yet drilled into the basement rocks. East of Imperial Beach the San Diego Gas and Petroleum Company drilled 6,334 feet before they managed to get completely through the sedimentary rocks and encountered the volcanic rocks underneath. If all of these wells could be pulled out of the ground and hooked together, they would form a hole 22.7 miles long, and for all of this work, the investors found only three small "shows" of hydrocarbon. The continental shelf during the late Mesozoic Era just wasn't right for the formation of petroleum.

The recognition of the events of the Miocene Epoch, however, has reinterested the oil companies in exploring in Southern California. During the Miocene, the West Coast broke up into a series of basins, and in these basins were deposited marine sedimentary rocks that might just be what the geologists are looking for. These basins, now filled with sediment, lie on the Continental Borderland, that broken up region west of the shoreline, which extends the geologic San Diego region some 150 miles into the sea. Even though preliminary drilling tests in the Tanner-Cortez Banks area were disappointing, petroleum companies still believe there could be oil out there. The Department of Interior has in the past expressed its intent to grant federal leases for drilling in several of these offshore regions, but currently no areas off San Diego County being recommended for oil exploration.

As the railroads pushed westward across the continent, San Diego had a dream of being the western terminus. In an interesting way, the sedimentary rocks that had been deposited during the end of the Cretaceous Period played a part in keeping that hope alive. The one thing that railroads needed was fuel. West of Wyoming, the only fuel then available was wood. But in the sedimentary strata of Point Loma were strata of coal. This coal had first been prospected in 1856, when the Mormon colony in San Diego began sinking a prospect shaft on the west side of Point Loma about a mile and a half north of the present Coast Guard lighthouse. Before the present sewage treatment plant was built at about the same location this shaft could still be seen at the foot of the bluffs. It is reported that the shaft passed through five coal seams less than a foot thick and struck one four and a half feet thick at a depth of eighty-six feet. In spite of this promising show, the mine was abandoned because the porous sandstone let the seawater leak in and the mine had to be continuously pumped. A new try was made in the 1880s since coal was needed to smelt the newly discovered iron deposits, and again in the late 1890s to entice the railroad, the shipping, and the navy to San Diego. Some of the early mine workings were incorporated into the underground defenses that were installed as part of Fort Rosecrans. As late as 1965 it was possible to enter some of the old workings and sample the coal as part of a worldwide project to investigate the minor elements in coal.

Despite these periodic flurries of interest, San Diego has remained devoid of commercially exploitable fossil fuels. Time will tell if there are workable offshore oil deposits which could change all that.

References

Abbott, Patrick A. *Rise and Fall of San Diego: 150 Million Years of History Recorded in Sedimentary Rocks.* San Diego: Sunbelt Publications, 1999.

Bancroft, P., "Gem Mining in San Diego County", *Environment Southwest*, Summer 1989, pp. 14–20.

California Division of Oil, Gas, & Geothermal Resources. *Exploratory Wells Drilled Outside of Oil and Gas Fields in California.* Sacramento: California Department of Conservation, 1964.

California Geological Survey. *California Geology.* Sacramento: monthly from 1971 to 1991, bimonthly from 1992 to 2001.

Clifford, H., F. Bergen, and S. Spear. *Geology of San Diego County.* San Diego: Sunbelt Publ., 1997.

County of San Diego. *General Plan; Part X: Conservation Element.* Chapter 5 "Minerals" and Chapter 6 "Soils." Most recent revision.

Dibble, S., "Sand Exports from Mexico May Dry Up", *San Diego Union-Tribune*, Jan. 30, 2003.

Fetzer, Leland. *A Good Camp: Gold Mines of Julian and the Cuyamacas* San Diego: Sunbelt Publications, 2002.

Jahns, R. and L. Wright. *Gem and Lithium Bearing Pegmatites of the Pala District, San Diego County, California.* Sacramento: California Division of Mines, 1951.

Kennedy, M. and G. .Peterson. *Geology of the San Diego Metropolitan Area. Bulletin 200.* Sacramento: California Geological Survey, 1975.

Kohler, S., *USGS Minerals Yearbook,* 2001.

Lindsay, L. E., ed. *Geology and Geothermal Resources of the Imperial and Mexicali Valleys.* San Diego: San Diego Association of Geologists, 1998.

Murbach, M. and M. Hart, eds. *Geology of the Elsinore Fault Zone, San Diego Region.* San Diego: San Diego Association of Geologists, 2003.

San Diego Association of Geologists. *Annual Field Guides.* San Diego: annually since 1972.

Stanford, L. G., "San Diego's Eucalyptus Bubble", *The Journal of San Diego History,* Vol. XVI, no. 4 (1970), pp. 11–19.

Stroh, R. T., ed. *Coastal Processes and Engineering Geology of San Diego, California.* San Diego: San Diego Association of Geologists, 2001.

Walawender, Michael. *The Peninsular Ranges: A Geological Guide to San Diego's Back Country.* Dubuque, Iowa: Kendall/Hunt Publishing Company, 2000.

Weber, F. H. Jr. *Geology and Mineral Resources of San Diego County, California.* Sacramento: California Division of Mines and Geology, 1963.

Internet Connections:
California Geological Survey: *www.consrv.ca.gov/CGS/index.htm*
San Diego Association of Geologists: *www.sandiegogeologists.org/index.html*
San Diego Natural History Museum: *www.sdnhm.org*
Stewart Mine, Pala District: *www.mmmgems.com/stewart/index.htm*
Sunbelt Publications: *www.sunbeltbooks.com*

Chapter Seven

E. A. Keen

Beaches, Bays, and Boats
San Diego's Coastal and Marine Environment

Dove-sail regattas skim the shimmering bay,
Lacing the swift cross-currents of the day.
The copper sun of California burns
Misted Point Loma with its Navy bases,
Graveyard, and lighthouse where the wind
    erases
All Time and Memory in its circling turns.[1]

    The importance of the marine environment to San Diego is difficult to overstate, whether viewed from the standpoint of esthetics or economics. The inspirational views from Point

Elmer A. Keen is a professor emeritus of marine resources in the Department of Geography at San Diego State University.

[1]Harry Stiehl, "The Marine Graveyard on Point Loma," San Diego: Sea Vineyard Editions, 1971, p. 3.

Loma, the thrill of "hanging ten" on surfing waves, reeling in a sculpin from a fishing pier, watching the whales from a charter boat—all contribute greatly to satisfying the recreational needs of area residents. They also greatly contribute to tourism, one of the largest of local industries. Also, the many activities associated with commercial and naval vessels are central to the character of the region. Lastly, the moderating effect of ocean breezes on land temperatures and air pollution becomes clearly apparent to coastal residents when dissicating Santa Ana winds from the east replace these cooling breezes in late summer and early fall. Both San Diego's poets and its tycoons would agree that the regional quality of life and the structure of the economy is intimately intertwined with the ocean and its accompanying lagoons and bays. The following paragraphs will examine both the natural aspects of the marine environment, and the human uses of our marine resources.

The Marine Environment

Offshore Waters

The ocean is a vast reservoir of the nutrients essential to the growth of plants, which form the base of the food chain and thus support all animal life. However, most of these nutrients are at depths well below the upper layer of the ocean where sufficient sunlight penetrates to support plant life. Plants in the ocean, from microscopic phytoplankton to giant kelp, consume nutrients rapidly under the sunny skies of southern California. The productivity of the surface zone is directly proportional to the speed with which nutrients are replaced. Vertical mixing of the ocean water is by far the most important way nutrients are made available to plants, especially in the coastal waters off southern California where rivers bring limited nutrients from the land.

Currents, bottom topography, and winds act and interact to create vertical mixing of waters off San Diego well above that for the average of the world's oceans. In addition, steady winds blowing parallel to the shore or from land to sea cause nutrient-rich waters below to *upwell*. Ocean swimmers during a late summer Santa Ana wind are often painfully aware of this upwelling, as the easterly wind drives the warm surface water from the coast and causes colder, fertile water to upwell. However, the main season of upwelling is during the spring when strong, steady winds prevail from the north and northwest. Heavy plankton blooms can in turn result from this abundance of nutrients.

The biological productivity of the offshore area is enhanced somewhat by the areas of relatively shallow water found off the coast. In areas where the water is sufficiently shallow to have sunlight reach the bottom, nutrients can be utilized by plants on the bottom itself. Seaweeds of various kinds are able to attach directly to the bottom and provide food and cover for the animal life dependent upon them.

The San Diego region does not have much of a continental shelf; it varies from about two miles in width off Point Loma to no more than ten miles at its widest point off the Tijuana Estuary. However, seaward from the continental shelf extends a region of deep basins and intervening ridges. This wide, irregular region is termed the *Continental Borderland,* and is almost unique to the southern California-northern Baja California coast. Several of the ridges paralleling the coast out to a distance of about 200 miles come sufficiently close to the surface to be touched by sunlight. To the San Diegan, the most obvious evidence of these ridges is provided by the Channel Islands and Coronado Islands. Cortez Bank, Tanner Bank, Forty-mile Bank and other similar shallow parts of ridges are well-known in local fishing circles for the productivity of the waters over and around them.

If the volume of life in the open ocean is controlled by nutrient levels, the nature of the life is controlled more by temperature than any other single factor. As a consequence of the relatively cold California Current with its poleward origins, and the large amount of upwelled cooler water off the coast, waters off San Diego are well below the average temperature for the latitude. Two species of giant kelp, *Macrocystis pyrifera* and *Macrocystis augustifolia,* make up the expansive kelp beds in the near-shore area. They cannot survive prolonged periods of temperatures above 65° to 70°F, and would not be able to survive the warm waters found on the eastern side of our continent at the same latitude. Similarly, cool-water fish, such as the bluefin and albacore tunas found off San Diego in summer, would not normally be expected off the East Coast at the same season.

The overall productivity of the waters and the wide variety of habitats provided by the bottom topography means that a large number of species, as well as a large total *biomass* (the total volume or weight of living matter), are found off San Diego (Figure 7.1). The rocky bottom of the shallow coastal waters support a wide variety of sea plants. These in turn provide habitats for a wide variety of fish and crustaceans, such as the rock cod, giant seabass, and the spiny lobster, as well as the few remaining abalone. Among the fish species, the total biomass is dominated by *pelagic* (surface) species such as the anchovy, tuna, mackerel, and bonito. The pre-

dominance of pelagic fishes suggests the importance of plankton in the food chain in waters off San Diego, since these species depend primarily on plankton as the basis for their food supply.

Marine mammals are by no means lacking in the San Diego region. The best-known species is undoubtedly the California grey whale that passes San Diego in winter migrating to breeding grounds in Baja California and returns again in spring on the way north. The harbor seal, sea lion, and porpoise are also present in fair numbers. The sea otter was found until the turn of the twentieth century, but is now extirpated.

Finally, a surprising number and variety of pelagic species of oceanic birds (shearwaters, petrels, and even albatross and tropic-birds) may be found skimming the offshore waters.

Figure 7.1. Fish densities can be high in southern California's kelp beds; species include topsmelt, garibaldi, perch, and calico bass. Photo by P. R. Pryde.

The Littoral Zone

The area between the line where waves begin to drag the bottom, and the uppermost reach of waves on the beach or coastal cliffs, defines the *littoral zone*. Since waves usually begin to drag bottom at depths of about 30 feet, the seaward limit of this zone can be defined as the thirty-foot contour below the mean low tide line. This is the zone where wave energy is ultimately dissipated.

Possibly the most important aspect of the littoral zone is whether the bottom is rocky or sandy. Of the 76 miles of ocean shoreline in San Diego County (as opposed to the shoreline of coastal wetlands), 63.5 miles are classified as sandy beach and 10.7 miles as rocky beach. The small remainder is either permanent cobble or "protected by groins or breakwaters."

Rocky littoral zones are limited largely to two areas, La Jolla and Sunset Cliffs-Point Loma. The landward side is marked in both areas by sandstone cliffs ranging up to 200 feet in height. The intertidal zone is narrow for the most part with much of the wave energy dissipated directly against the cliffs. However, fairly extensive areas are exposed at very low tides in parts of La Jolla and Point Loma. The tidepools formed during these low tides are well known for the variety and abundance of plant and animal life exposed for easy viewing by visitors. The littoral zone beyond these rocky areas is even more productive biologically. A wide variety of seaweeds and grasses cling to the rocks in these turbulent waters and provide food and protection for numerous small fishes, crustaceans, and mollusks.

Erosion rates of the cliffs within the rocky beach area of the region vary from almost zero in parts of La Jolla to as much as an average of one foot a decade in portions of Sunset Cliffs. The presence of numerous joints and fractures in the sandstone of these areas has hastened erosion and led to creation of sea caves. Riprap or concrete seawalls have been placed along cliffs subject to severe erosion in the Ocean Beach-Sunset Cliffs area, along the Bird Rock area of La Jolla, and in Solana Beach. High waves associated with severe winter storms occasionally create bluff and beach erosion problems from Sunset Cliffs to Oceanside, and more detail on the causes of this erosion is given in Chapter 2.

The dominant feature of the sandy beach area is the constant migration of sand. This migration takes two forms: (1) an offshore-onshore migration dependent on the size of waves, and (2) along-shore (or "long-shore") migration created by littoral currents.

The offshore-onshore migration is a seasonal phenomenon. Winter waves remove sand from the beach proper and deposit it further offshore, but still within the littoral zone. Summer waves pick up the sand and gradually work it shoreward, with late summer the period of maximum buildup. This is illustrated in Figure 7.2, which shows seasonal beach profiles near the northern boundary of Torrey Pines State Preserve. Variations of six feet in sand depths in the upper part of the intertidal zone between winter and summer are not uncommon.

The longshore migration of sand depends on wave-induced currents created when waves strike the coast at less than a right angle. The angle of the waves is largely a function of wind direction. Both winds and waves may be either from the southeast, or from the northwest. Thus, the sand is transported back and forth along all beaches of the San Diego region depending on wind direction. However, the net movement north of Mission Bay is southward. Between the Mexican-American border and the entrance to San Diego Bay the net movement is northward, largely because of the protection provided in this area by Point Loma against wind generated waves from the northwest.

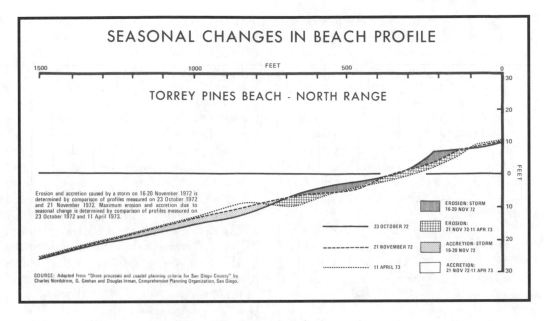

Figure 7.2. Seasonal sand movements.

The net volume of movement between on- and offshore sand migration appears to be essentially in balance for most beaches within the littoral zone. However, the long-shore migration is a different matter. Each of these separate areas, or sand cells as they have come to be called, has essentially its own sand budget. Movement between cells is prevented by topographic features in the littoral zone. Three major cells are recognized for the region, the Oceanside Cell, the Mission Beach Cell, and the Silver Strand Cell (see Figure 7.3).

The larger two of these, the Oceanside Cell and the Silver Strand Cell, constantly lose sand through transport by the longshore current. In the case of the Oceanside Cell, a net transport south of 200,000 to 300,000 cubic yards annually is estimated. Most of this is lost in Scripps Submarine Canyon. A small amount of sand bypasses this north arm of the La Jolla

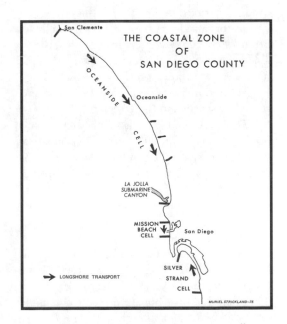

Figure 7.3. Longshore sand transport cells.

Submarine Canyon to feed Scripps Beach. Sand that enters the canyon sinks below the zone of wave action and ceases to be a factor in beach formation. The net northward transport along Silver Strand is considerably larger, being estimated at about 1.4 million cubic yards annually. Most of this sand is lost to further movement by wave action through transport to deeper water off the end of Zuniga Point Jetty, the jetty that forms the southern side of the entrance to San Diego Bay. However, a little passes through the jetty and is carried into the bay.

The smaller Mission Beach Cell (which covers portions of Pacific and Ocean Beaches as well) appears to have no major net loss of sand, primarily because of the holding action of the jetties protecting the entrance to the bay. As a result, sand is trapped by the jetties and a fair amount seeps through the riprap of the jetties into the entrance channel. This area must be dredged periodically because of this seepage.

Loss of sand from the Oceanside and Silver Strand Cells has become a matter of considerable concern within the region. The main external source of sand to replace that lost through longshore transport has been sediments transported by streams in those regions.

The Oceanside Cell was supplied by streams between Dana Point, at the northern boundary of the cell, and the La Jolla Submarine Canyon. As noted in Chapter 2, the damming of these streams, especially the San Luis Rey and San Dieguito rivers or their tributaries, has substantially lessened contributions from the land. Before the dams were built, the amount of sand added each year is believed to have been as large or larger than was lost into Scripps Canyon. At present, there is a net loss of approximately 60,000 cubic yards per year. The result is a slow but steady reduction in the total sand budget for this cell.

The Silver Strand Cell was supplied naturally by sediments transported by the Tijuana River. However, four dams upstream on this river have effectively blocked much of the sand transport. Constant large losses with almost no replacement had a predictable effect, and since the late 1960s, beach erosion has been a serious problem in this cell.

Sand dredged from San Diego Bay to deepen the ship channel was pumped to the Silver Strand Cell in the late 1970s. However, wave action speeded up by severe winter storms moved this sand rapidly northward and by the early 1980s, coastal properties remained under threat. Though expensive, return of these sands to the beaches by dredging may be the easiest way to protect the Silver Strand—and San Diego Bay.

Problems in the Oceanside Cell are likely to be even more expensive to correct. Winter storms have been especially destructive there and loss of the beach sands has exposed the relatively soft cliffs to erosion by waves. In 2001 the San Diego Association of Governments (SANDAG) supervised a major project to replenish two million cubic yards of dredged sand to 12 local beaches. This will not be a permanent solution, however, and similar efforts will probably need to be conducted in the future.

The Coastal Wetlands

All coastlines have indentations or irregularities that form quiet bodies of water that may or may not be fully tidal in nature. These irregularities are variously called bays, lagoons, sloughs, marshes, or estuaries, and collectively are referred to as *coastal wetlands*.

There are seventeen areas recognized as coastal wetlands in the San Diego region. They range in size from the 16.7 (formerly 21) square miles of San Diego Bay to the ten-acre Canyon de los Encinas Marsh located some four miles south of Carlsbad. Several of these possess wildlife habitats of critical importance. These include San Diego Bay, Tijuana Estuary, Mission Bay, Santa Margarita Estuary, San Elijo Lagoon, the San Diego River Estuary, Buena Vista Lagoon, and Los Peñasquitos Lagoon. In addition, San Dieguito Lagoon, once it is restored, will be an additional asset (Table 7.1).

Of these wetlands, only the Tijuana Estuary remains in relatively pristine condition, and in 1981 it was designated as a National Estuarine Sanctuary in recognition of its values as a natural ecosystem. The other wetlands have been substantially modified for one reason or another. Only five, San Diego Bay, Mission Bay and the San Diego River mouth, Sweetwater River and marsh, Tijuana Estuary, and Agua Hedionda Lagoon, are fully tidal at all times. Constantly connected to the ocean, these function as an integral part of the ocean ecosystem providing nursery areas for marine fish species such as the halibut and turbot, and supporting large waterfowl populations.

The *tidal prisms* (the amount of water that flows in and out with the tide) of the other coastal wetlands are not sufficiently large to keep sand from periodically blocking the entrances. As a result, they open to the ocean only when heavy rains build up sufficient fresh water within them to breach these sand berms, or when they are opened with earth moving equipment. Thus, they have a harsh environment caused by wide ranges in salinity and water quality. During winter rains, salinity levels may drop to near zero; in summer levels may reach sixty to seventy parts per thousand because of evaporation. Under these conditions only the most hardy forms of aquatic life can exist.

Many people advocate keeping the mouths of the most important lagoons open by periodic dredging. However, regardless of their salinity level, they are important resting and feeding stops for winter migrations of waterfowl and provide open space resources for the human inhabitants of the region.

Marine Resources

The abundant and varied nature of the marine resources of the San Diego region is implicit in the preceding discussion of the marine environment. The long expanses of sandy beaches with a variety of wave conditions are a joy to swimmers and surfers alike. Lengthy stretches of steep bluffs add to the scenic attraction of the coast and its beaches, but also cause coastal properties to be affordable only by those with well-above average incomes. In addition to scenic amenities, our coastal and offshore waters provide direct economic and employment benefits to the region as well. The purpose of this section is to bring out in clearer detail the importance of marine resources to the region.

Biotic Resources

Activities connected with extracting marine resource in the San Diego region fall into three categories: (1) commercial fishing, (2) sport fishing, and (3) kelp harvesting. Each of these makes a relatively minor contribution to the local economy, but their contribution to local color and to the particular life-style of the region is proportionately much larger.

Coastal waters, while relatively fertile, do not produce fishery resources adequate in numbers or variety to support a major commercial fishery. However, offshore albacore resources proved adequate to support the development of a pole and line tuna fishery. This in turn led to the development of a local tuna canning industry that has existed from the early 1900s. The more tropical yellowfin tuna range northward from their main habitat to the waters offshore from San Diego, and in the period between the

TABLE 7.1. San Diego County Coastal Wetlands

Name	Surface Area (acres)*	Salt	Type Fresh	Mixed	Tidal Status	Jurisdiction
San Mateo (marsh)	125 MA		X		Closed	Camp Pendleton
Las Flores (marsh)	60 MA	X	X	X	Generally closed	Camp Pendleton
Santa Margarita (estuary)	286 TLA	X	X	X	Generally closed	Camp Pendleton
San Luis Rey R. (marsh)	40 TLA		X	X	Generally closed	Oceanside
Loma Alta (marsh)	40 MA		X		Generally closed	Oceanside
Buena Vista (lagoon)	220 TLA		X	X	Generally closed	Oceanside; DFG; Carlsbad
Agua Hedionda (lagoon)	430 TWA	X	X	X	Open	Carlsbad; S.D.G,&E.
Batiquitos (lagoon)	600 TWA		X	X	Generally closed	Carlsbad; DFG; S.D. County
San Elijo (lagoon)	500 TWA	X	X	X	Generally closed	S.D. County; DFG; Encinitas
San Dieguito (lagoon)	300 TWA (W. of I-5)	X		X	Periodicaly closed	Del Mar; San Diego city; San Dieguito River Park
Los Peñasquitos (lagoon)	230 TWA	X	X	X	Periodically opened	San Diego city; State Parks
Mission Bay (bay; marsh)	2,228 MSL + 130 MA	X			Open	San Diego city
San Diego R. (marsh and estuary)	300 TWA	X	X	X	Open channel	San Diego city
San Diego Bay (bay, mudflats)	13,400 TWA	X			Open	Unified Port District; five cities around the Bay
Sweetwater R. (marsh)	150 MA (W. of I-5)	X		X	Open	National City; Chula Vista; USF&WS
Tijuana River (estuary)	1,100 MA	X		X	Open	USF&WS; Imperial Beach; State Park Dept.
Famosa Slough	31 TWA	X	X	X	Flushed at high tides	San Diego city

*MA = marsh area; TWA = total wetland area; TLA = total lagoon (or estuary) area; DFG = Calif. Dept. of Fish and Game; MSL = at mean sea level. USF&WS = U.S. Fish and Wildlife Service.

Source: Adapted primarily from California State Coastal Conservancy, *The Coastal Wetlands of San Diego County,* 1989.

two world wars their harvest increased the supply of tuna to the canneries. The tuna clippers expanded activities southward to take advantage of the large yellowfin stocks off Mexico and Central America. Yellowfin eventually replaced albacore as the main source of raw material for San Diego's tuna canneries.

The tuna clippers depended on a labor-intensive hook and line fishing method. After World War II, competition from foreign fishermen became increasingly difficult to meet. Development in the mid-1950s of the huge purse seines necessary to surround and hold a school of tuna reduced labor costs substantially, and by the early 1960s, the struggling clipper fleet had been replaced almost entirely by purse seiners (Figure 7.4).

The purse seiners proved competitive with foreign fishermen, and the California tuna fleet

began to recover. World demand for this increasingly popular fish grew steadily, and by the late 1960s tuna stocks of the eastern tropical Pacific, on which the fleet depended, approached full exploitation. Real prices received by fishermen began to spurt as the price of yellowfin tuna increased 425% between 1967 and 1981. The carrying capacity of the U.S. purse seiners operating in the eastern tropical Pacific Ocean, about 80% of which were based in San Diego, reached 121,000 tons in 1976. This was a fourfold increase over the entire U.S. distant seas tuna fleet in 1960.

Competition over the resource replaced the 1950s competition over the market as the main problem of the tuna fishermen. The San Diego fleet from its beginning depended almost entirely on resources off Mexico, Central America, and Ecuador. Latin American fishermen, attracted by

Figure 7.4. Boats of the San Diego based tuna fleet at the Embarcadero. Photo taken in the 1970s by P. R. Pryde.

the increasingly valuable tuna resources off their coasts, began to fish with greater diligence and efficiency from the late 1960s. Fear of overfishing resulted in annual quotas being imposed on yellowfin tuna in 1966, meaning that a fixed supply of yellowfin had to be divided between a growing number of vessels. Proximity to the fishing grounds and lower labor costs favored the Latin American fleet. But the real blow to the United States fleet dates from 1977.

In 1977, the United States extended its control over fishery resources *except* highly migratory species (primarily tunas) within 200 miles of its coastline. Mexico and other Latin American nations soon established their own 200 mile zones but included all fishery resources. A little over half of the tuna landed normally come from within 200 miles of the coast. Latin American nations imposed high fees and restrictions on foreign fishing vessels using their new exclusive economic zones. The California fleet's competitive position received a real blow. It landed two-thirds of the Eastern Tropical Pacific tuna in 1976, the year before the U.S. established a 200 mile zone. By the late 1980s, the United States and Mexican fleets each had about one-third each of the total landings. The carrying capacity of United States tuna seiners dropped to about one-third of the 1976 capacity.

The majority of owners of the San Diego based seiners transferred their vessels to Latin American registry during the 1980s or sold them to fishing enterprises there. Others moved to the new grounds opened up in the southwest Pacific where distance meant infrequent return to San Diego. In the early 1990's large tuna vessels still added interest to the San Diego Bay scene but were far less dominant than in the past. By 2000, the commercial tuna fishery was of little economic significance to San Diego.

With the loss of the tuna fleets, commercial fisheries in San Diego came to be truly local, and

of far less import to the economy. In terms of value of landings or numbers employed, the spiny lobster and the abalone fisheries used to be among the most important. Stocks of both of these luxury species are fully exploited, if not overexploited. The high value of both lobster and abalone and the difficulty of enforcing conservation measures allows considerable poaching of these resources. By 2003, almost all abalone take was prohibited, and white abalone was being considered for endangered status.

A wide variety of finfish other than tuna are taken commercially from local waters, but the aggregate volume or value is not high. Several species, including the yellowtail, barracuda, California halibut, giant seabass, white seabass, sardines, and Pacific mackerel, appear to be fully or over-exploited and restrictions have been or may soon be placed on their capture. A few such as the corvina, spotfin and yellowfin croaker, and grunion are reserved to sportfishing only.

If local fishery resources no longer contribute significantly to the local economy through commercial fishing, the same cannot be said of their contribution through sportfishing. The volume and value of the fish landed is small, but the total contribution of the sports fishery to the local economy is significant. Several large party boats and numerous small charter boats serve sport fishermen visiting or residing in the region. In addition, a good percentage of the pleasure craft berthed in local marinas, and of trailerable boats, are used for fishing. The economic impact of these boats, if not easily measured, is large. This does not include the expenditures for bait and equipment of surf and pier fishermen, or for the equipment and air of recreational divers. Not only the ocean, but San Diego Bay as well (which has greatly improved as a fishery in the past twenty years), attracts anglers.

But the significance of the local sportsfishery cannot be limited to economic aspects alone if one is to measure its total importance to the region. The local "way of life" is greatly enhanced for many residents by the availability of this recreational pastime. Is it any wonder that several species in local waters are reserved exclusively for the recreationist, and that additional ones have been considered for addition to the list?

The last category of marine resources to be discussed here is the giant kelp. Kelp have been harvested commercially in California since 1910. The state has defined individual beds, given each a number, and leases the right to harvest them to private companies. Of far greater importance to the region than this direct use, however, is the role played by the kelp forests in the local marine biotic community. Many species of fish and invertebrates depend on the kelp forests for food and habitat at some point in their life history to the benefit of recreational and commercial fisheries. Divers explore them for the sheer joy and wonder that kelp forests provide; university students and faculty use them as laboratories for training and research. Even surfers benefit as the giant kelp smooth out waves and improve their quality for surfing. These marine "forests" are indeed a natural resource deservedly cherished by residents of the region.

The beds vary widely in size over time and may at times disappear completely. Declines in size are associated primarily with El Niño events and with storms. Declines during the major El Niño events of 1957–58 and 1983–84 resulted in up to a 90% loss of kelp canopy in Southern California kelp forests. The main direct cause appears to be low nutrient levels associated with the El Niño, although wave action and higher water temperatures may be factors. Sea urchins also decimate kelp beds on occasion by eating through the stalk of the plant near the rock to which it is anchored. Controversy exists as to the degree that pollution from human sources affects the kelp beds, especially the one off Point Loma,

which is among the most studied in the world. While the studies are as yet inconclusive, pollution is believed to be a minor cause of variations in giant kelp abundance off San Diego County.

The company that harvests most of the San Diego kelp has, understandably, worked hard to maintain healthy beds and even to expand them. Kelp harvest consists of cutting the fronds to a depth of four feet, and processing the kelp for algin, a product with hundreds of uses. These are capital intensive operations. Years with 90% loss of canopy leaves equipment unused and markets unserved. Efforts to stabilize production range from restoration and expansion of beds to destruction of sea urchins with hammers. Problems with the urchins have been reduced in recent years with development of a local and export market for sea urchins for sushi fanciers. The larger problems associated with El Niño and storms are far less tractable. Widespread fluctuations in the size of San Diego kelp beds can be expected to continue because of these natural phenomena.

Uses in Place

Richard Henry Dana, writing in 1835, opens a window through which the reader may view a pristine coastal landscape in what would later be called southern California:

> The rocks were as large as those of Nahent on Newport, but, to my eye, more grand and broken. Besides, there was a grandeur in everything around, which gave almost a solemnity to the scene: a silence and a solitariness which affected everything! Not a human being but ourselves for miles; and no sound but the pulsations of the great Pacific! And the great steep hill rising like a wall, and cutting us off from all the world, but the

world of water. (From *Two Years Before the Mast*.)

"Today, the coastline below the headland that bears Dana's name has been drastically altered by the force of leisure time. Restaurants, marinas, and picnic areas, all perched atop fill dirt, now occupy areas of once-open sea. In its present configuration, Dana Point and vicinity reflect the status of outdoor recreation in general, as well as the priorities of coastal recreation in particular!"

The above quote from the recreation element of a planning study prepared by the San Diego Coast Regional Commission strongly portrays the impact of recreation, which is the most important "in place" use of the region's marine resources. Modification of the environment in order to intensify quiet-water recreational use has led to profound modification of Mission Bay and the north shore of San Diego Bay, and to construction of almost completely artificial harbors at Oceanside and Chula Vista.

The demand for this type of recreational resource and the popularity of the closely related residential marinas led to plans to develop almost all of the individual coastal wetlands of the county. Such plans once included a second entrance to San Diego Bay at its south end which would have facilitated development of marinas in that area by providing quicker access to the open ocean. Also proposed were a large marina in the Tijuana Estuary, and a residential marina

Figure 7.5. Competing industrial, recreational, and residential land uses of Agua Hedionda lagoon. Photo by P. R. Pryde.

for San Elijo Lagoon. None of these were built. Recreational uses currently share Agua Hedionda lagoon with SDG&E's Encina power plant (Figure 7.5).

Whether "undeveloped" coastal wetland resources are to be modified for more intensive recreational uses is among the most difficult resource use decisions before the region's governmental bodies. Intensive recreational uses of wetlands are usually not compatible with marine life and waterfowl habitat uses. Our undeveloped wetlands now serve an important function on the north-south flyway for migratory waterfowl. Those connected to the ocean have an important role in the marine ecosystem. Thus, supporters of more natural uses of these wetland resources have rallied to oppose those who would "develop" them for more intensive recreational and residential uses (see Chapter 17).

Of no less importance are the recreational resources of the open coastline. A survey of recreational activities of the region's inhabitants conducted by the county government revealed that "going to the beach" was the most popular recreational activity of all. This demand has led to increased conflict between swimming and surfing, the two most popular uses of the littoral zone. Regulations delineating the areas reserved for each have become necessary to separate these two activities.

Swimming, sunbathing, and surfing are the most intensive recreational uses of the open coastline, but surf fishing and tide pool study are quite popular as well. Excessive pressure by surf fishermen on the resource they exploit appears unlikely to ever become a serious problem. Not so with the tide pool "collectors." Local tide pools have been picked over and trampled by so many so-called nature lovers that many such pools now appear almost lifeless (at least when compared to their former biological abundance), despite the fact that such collection is strictly illegal under the California Fish and Game Code.

One should also consider the passive recreationist, the observer of nature, or simply the sightseer. Visitor and resident alike find themselves drawn time and again to the beautiful stretches of coastline such as the Sunset Cliffs-Point Loma area, the La Jolla-Torrey Pines area, and the Solana Beach-Encinitas area. Unfortunately, access to many of these cliff coastal viewpoints is impeded by private residential construction, although more beaches have been reserved to the public here than in most parts of southern California. San Diego Bay, with its many attractions, is also a major tourist magnet (Figure 7.6).

Some further comments about recreational boating in addition to those made earlier under sport fishing are appropriate in a discussion of recreational "in-place" resource use. Power boating, especially for towing water skiers, and sailboating have grown markedly in importance in recent years. The appeal of sailboat racing reached its peak in 1992 when the world championship America's Cup races were held in San Diego's offshore waters. Space requirements, both for mooring and operation of pleasure boats, are becoming difficult to meet. Participants can expect further regulations as to time and place of conflicting uses, such as water skiing, "jet-skiing", and small boat sailing, in the future.

Another in-place use is the development of San Diego Bay as a Naval port. As the largest naval base on the West Coast, the importance of the Navy's continued use of the area for national defense would be difficult to overstate. The Navy also contributes substantially to the local economy through generation of direct employment opportunities, and by its aggregate demand for local goods and services. Nor is the Navy fleet without recreational value. Certainly the large number of Naval vessels provide much

Figure 7.6. The Maritime Museum, featuring the Star of India (foreground) and the Berkeley (background) is a popular San Diego Bay attraction. Photo by P. R. Pryde.

color to San Diego Bay and can be counted among its tourist attractions.

Of less importance as a use in place are commercial shipping activities. This topic is covered in the chapter on transportation and will not be treated in detail here. Suffice it to say that San Diego's location relative to ocean transportation demand and competition from ports to the north simply has not favored large scale development, despite an excellent harbor.

The last in-place use to be discussed here is our use of the ocean to dispose of much of the region's wastes. Five major sewer lines discharge into the ocean in San Diego County, and the average discharge was about 280 million gallons per day in 2002 (see Chapter 16). What impact

this has on the marine environment is still the subject of much controversy. It appears likely that some damage is done by industrial wastes, especially chlorinated hydrocarbons and heavy metals. However, properly treated human wastes possibly are more beneficial than harmful to marine life as a whole. Human wastes contain a good balance of nutrients needed by marine plants and if properly distributed, probably increase the total biomass without seriously affecting variety.

Also controversial in its effects is the dumping of thermal wastes. Power plants along the coast have come under considerable fire from various environmental groups for possible adverse effects on the marine environment of their hot water discharges. Disposal of solid wastes is not permitted in the waters of this region; so garbage scows are not part of the maritime scene of southern California.

In summary, marine resources of the region are coming under pressures that, in some cases, have led to deterioration of the resource, and in others have created conflicts between different elements of society because the resource is no longer adequate to meet all needs. Pressures on the coastal zone itself have led to creation of governmental machinery, such as the California Coastal Zone Conservation Commission, to control and allocate uses in this important zone. The realization that better care must be paid to fishery resources if they are to continue to make a positive contribution is becoming more widespread.

Management of these common property resources to assure maximum benefits is extremely complex. Whether the realization of a need for better management can be channeled into development of techniques to maximize benefits remain to be seen. This problem strikes at the heart of a complex, dynamic, marine ecosystem that extends far beyond the boundaries of the region, and its resolution will require national and international efforts. Cooperation with Baja California for the joint management of the resources of the California Bight can pay off handsomely. Several jointly shared stocks of fish can only decline if this is not done.

The San Diego region contains some of the best human and laboratory resources for understanding the marine environment found anywhere in the world. The Scripps Institution of Oceanography is word renowned. These research resources, aided by a public educated to understand the problems involved, can help to assure the continued high quality contribution that the marine environment makes to the way of life of the region.

References

Browning, B., J. Speth, and W. Gayman. *The Natural Resources of San Diego Bay, Their Status and Future*. Sacramento: Department of Fish and Game, 1973.

California Department of Fish and Game (CDFG). *California's Living Marine Resources: A Status Report*. Sacramento, CDFG, 2002.

California State Coastal Conservancy. *The Coastal Wetlands of San Diego County*. Sacramento: State Coastal Conservancy, 1989.

City of San Diego, Department of Water Utilities. *Report of Ocean Studies off San Diego*. City of San Diego. December 1986.

Cunningham, Mark. *The San Diego Bay Marine Information System: The Application of a Real-Time Geographical Information System to Maritime Operational Decision Making*. (Master's thesis, Department of Geography). San Diego: San Diego State University, 2001.

Dana, R. H. *Two Years Before the Mast*. New York: P. F. Collier and Son, 1969.

Inter-American Tropical Tuna Commission (IATTC). *Annual Report of the IATTC, 1997*. La Jolla, CA: IATTC, 1999.

LaFee, Scott, "True Lagoon: Buena Vista's Vital Habitat Hangs in the Balance", *San Diego Union-Tribune*, May 2, 2001, p. F-1.

LaRue, Steve, "Death Beds: San Diego's Once-Rich Kelp Habitat Is in Serious Decline", *San Diego Union-Tribune*, April 23, 1997, p. E-1.

Lubrano, Gina, "Mood Is Grim as More of Tuna Fleet Heads into Sunset", *San Diego Union,* October 21, 1990, pp. B1 and B6.

Port of San Diego. *Annual Report 2001.* San Diego: Port of San Diego, 2002.

Southern California Coastal Water Research Project. *The Ecology of the Southern California Bight: Implications for Water Quality Management.* El Segundo, CA: 1973.

Warren, J. "The Lagoons", *Los Angeles Times* (San Diego County Edition), March 31, 1985, Part II, pp. 1, 4 and 6.

Weiss, K., "Industrial Fleets Have Caught 90% of All Big Fish, Study Says", *Los Angeles Times,* May 15, 2003, pp. A1 and A20.

Zedler, Joy. *The Ecology of Southern California Salt Marshes: A Community Profile.* Washington, DC. U.S. Fish and Wildlife Service, 1982.

Internet Connections:

California Coastal Commission: *www.coastal.ca.gov*

Inter-American Tropical Tuna Commission: *www.iattc.org*

Port of San Diego: *www.portofsandiego.org*

San Diego Regional Water Quality Control Board: *www.swrcb.ca.gov/rwqcb9/*

Chapter Eight

Philip R. Pryde

The Most Essential Resource
Water Supply for the County

San Diego County has been described as having every natural amenity necessary for "the good life" except one—drinkable water. The county does, of course, possess significant freshwater resources, but not in sufficient supply to meet the demands of the hundreds of thousands of new residents that have migrated into the region in the past few decades. Like all other areas of southern California, local ground water and surface water resources that were once quite adequate became insufficient to handle the needs of

Philip R. Pryde is a professor emeritus of geography specializing in environmental studies in the Department of Geography at San Diego State University.

a mushrooming population, and the county eventually had to look beyond its own borders for a source of imported water. In an average year, the county as a whole is about 90 percent dependent on imported supplies, depending on local stream run-off volumes.

Natural Water Supplies

San Diego County possesses greater water resources than the average resident probably realizes, and with proper management these resources could sustain a population of several hundred thousand without outside assistance. Due to the variability of local precipitation, however, substantial storage facilities and a certain amount of recycling capability would be necessary to achieve this. The current county population of about three million could in no way be accommodated without massive reliance on either outside water supplies, or expensive seawater desalting. We have chosen the former option.

Precipitation

In an average year, between three and four million acre-feet[1] of water fall on San Diego County. If all of this supply could be captured and stored, and if the amount received was reliable from one year to the next, this amount of precipitation would be sufficient to supply half of the urban needs of the entire state of California. Our precipitation is so variable, however, that the "average" will be exceeded or be deficient by as much as 30 percent or more in 45 years out of every 100. In the city of San Diego, which averages about ten inches of rainfall a year, the annual total has ranged from a high of 25.97 inches in 1883–84 to a low of 3.01 in 2001–02 (see Table 8.1).

In addition to annual fluctuations, our county's rainfall is highly seasonal as well, with over 85 percent usually falling in the six months from October to March and less than 15 percent falling between April and September. Summers can be even drier; for example, in 1973 only 2 percent of the year's precipitation (which was normal in amount for the year as a whole) fell between April and September. Thus, it has been deemed necessary to construct numerous reservoirs in the county to conserve the excess runoff of wet periods for use in drier ones.

[1]An acre-foot of water would cover a square parcel of land 209' on a side with one foot of water. An acre-foot equals 325,851 gallons, and is the standard unit of volume for fresh water supplies. It would supply two San Diego families with water for a year.

TABLE 8.1. Variability of Precipitation in San Diego (downtown)

Wettest years:	
Year (a)	Precipitation (inches)
1883–84	25.97
1940–41	24.74
1977–78	18.71
1921–22	18.65
1992–93	18.31
1982–83	18.26
1951–52	18.16
Average:	9.90
Driest years:	
1955–56	4.52
1933–34	4.26
1962–63	3.98
1862–63	3.87
1876–77	3.75
1960–61	3.46
2001–02	3.01

(a) A "rainfall year" in southern California extends from July 1 to June 30.

Runoff

Whether a year is relatively wet or relatively dry, the vast majority of the water that falls as precipitation will not be captured by the county's reservoirs for future use. Some will fall downstream from the dams and flow unimpeded to the ocean, but most will seep into the ground and be used for plant growth and to recharge our county's numerous underground aquifers.

Subsurface aquifer water, both from springs and from wells, was used as the first reliable supply for local residents, and if not overdrawn or polluted represents a high quality, renewable resource. Some of the county's many springs are mineralized, and some are popular hot mineral springs (Warner Hot Springs, Agua Caliente Springs, Jacumba Hot Springs, and just over the northern county line, Murrieta and San Juan

Hot Springs). Underground water reserves are difficult to measure, however, and an indication of their magnitude and maximum renewable rate of use can often be determined only indirectly by the average annual depth of water in the wells.

As was the case with precipitation, the runoff of San Diego County streams is extremely variable. For most American rivers an average runoff rate measured in cubic feet of water per second (c.f.s.) and an average annual volume of runoff can be calculated, but for San Diego County streams this is virtually impossible. If the type of average used to describe daily runoff is the mode (the value that occurs most frequently), then the average runoff for most county streams is zero, for most of the time they are dry.

Likewise, total annual discharge of county streams varies so much from one year to the next that to attempt to speak in terms of an "average" annual volume of runoff water is also rather meaningless. On the Tijuana and San Diego rivers, for example, the total runoff for particular years has varied from well in excess of a hundred thousand acre-feet to almost none.

Stream runoff contributes to usable local water supplies in two ways, by replenishing ground water and by filling reservoirs. Almost all of the major reservoirs in San Diego County were constructed with the primary purpose of capturing stream runoff and storing it for later use. But as noted above, in years of average or less than average precipitation, most of the runoff sinks into the ground and relatively little finds its way into storage reservoirs. For this reason, the majority of reservoirs in the county are less than 40 percent full most of the time. El Capitan Dam, the largest reservoir on the San Diego River system, did not overflow between 1941 and 1980, and in 1980 (after three consecutive wet winters) only a trickle flowed over it

for a few days. It has not overflown since. In 1978, 1980, and 1998, heavy runoff added well over a hundred thousand acre-feet of water to county reservoirs, but in many years the total inflow might be only a tenth that much. The estimated "safe yield" (the long-term average annual water yield) for the county has been calculated at around 134,000 acre-feet, about half of which would be from surface storage and about half from underground aquifers. Since the county uses over 600,000 acre-feet of water a year, it can be seen that except in extremely wet years local runoff would be greatly insufficient to meet the county's needs.

Early Water Supplies

The early history of San Diego County is virtually synonymous with the quest for water supplies. Most early settlers found springs and ground water to be adequate for their personal needs, but in order to expand irrigation the early Franciscan Fathers started building the first storage reservoir almost two centuries ago. By the end of the nineteenth century, San Diego County could accurately be described as one of the major focal points of dam construction in the world, and by 1923 every major drainage system in the county except the Santa Margarita included at least one reservoir.

The Nineteenth Century Dams

The San Diego River was the site of one of the first dam and water diversion projects undertaken by white settlers in what is now the United States. As early as 1792 a canal was constructed to bring water from upstream springs to the San Diego Mission de Alcala at the east end of Mission Valley. To provide still greater quantities of water, what we now know as Mission Dam at the eastern end of Mission Gorge was begun in 1807 (Figure 8.1). It required an aqueduct about six

Figure 8.1. Remains of old Mission Dam, shown during the flood runoff of 1941. It has undergone additional reconstruction since that time. Note sparcity of vegetation compared to present. Photo courtesy of Lauren Post.

miles long to bring the water to the fertile soils of Mission Valley, and was completed in 1816. It must be considered a major engineering accomplishment for its time and place, and today the remains of the dam are a registered National Historical Landmark. By the 1860s, however, the dam had fallen into disrepair and the local population was again entirely dependent on ground water until almost the turn of the century. The first piped water supply was put into service in the city of San Diego by the San Diego Water Company, formed in 1873.

In the ten years between 1887 and 1897 no less than six major dams were built on San Diego County streams, ushering in a half cen-

tury of reliance on local runoff to supply a fast growing county population. The first and smallest of the four was Cuyamaca Dam on Boulder Creek, completed in 1887. The dam may still be seen on the road from Julian to Cuyamaca State Park. It brought water to the lower San Diego River area through a remarkable wooden flume thirty-five miles long.

A reliable water supply was also needed in the National City-Chula Vista area, and to this end the San Diego Land and Town Co. began construction of a dam in the Sweetwater River Gorge in 1886. It was completed in April of 1888 and, at a height of 90 feet, was the highest dam in the United States at that time (Figure 8.2).

Despite the fact that the dam had been raised twenty more feet by 1911, the great flood of 1916 not only topped the spillway but eroded a portion of both abutments, causing great damage downstream and killing twenty-one persons (Figure 8.3).

Work on Lower Otay Dam was begun in 1887, but financial problems prevented its completion until about 1897. Operated by the Southern California Mountain Water Company, it supplied water to the South Bay area and to the new community of Coronado. Unfortunately, Lower Otay Dam was completely swept away by the great flood of 1916, also with loss of life. It was rebuilt in 1919 by the city of San Diego.

The fourth of the early dams impounds Morena Reservoir on Cottonwood Creek, a tributary of the Tijuana River. It was begun in 1895 but was not finished until 1912. Shortly after the dam was completed a flume was constructed to divert water from the reservoir into the Otay River and Lower Otay Reservoir. Both the Otay and Cottonwood systems were acquired by the city of San Diego just prior to the First World War.

The fifth project was a small dam on Escondido Creek, completed in 1895. Originally called Escondido Dam, it was completely rebuilt in 1924 and is now known as Wohlford Dam. Also completed in 1895 was La Mesa Dam, now lying beneath the water of Lake Murray formed by a new dam in 1918 (Figure 8.4).

The Twentieth Century Dams

Economic stagnation hit San Diego County in the 1890s, and not until after the turn of the century did it appear necessary to consider additional storage for local surface runoff. Including the reconstruction of Wohlford and Lower Otay, five dams were built in the six years between 1918 and 1924.

Figure 8.2. The original Sweetwater Dam under construction in 1886. Photograph courtesy of Historical Collection, San Diego Historical Society.

Figure 8.3. Break in Sweetwater Dam, January 30, 1916. Photograph courtesy of Historical Collection, San Diego Historical Society.

The first dam to be built in this period was on the San Dieguito River, and on its completion in 1918 formed Lake Hodges. Financed by the Santa Fe Railroad, it initially served Rancho Santa Fe and irrigated farming along the coast which included a newly imported tropical fruit, the avocado.

Three new reservoirs appeared between 1922 and 1924. The city of San Diego completed a second facility on Cottonwood Creek in 1922, Barrett Dam. It was also connected by flume (the Dulzura Conduit) to Lower Otay Reservoir. The largest reservoir in the county was formed the following year with the completion of Henshaw Dam on the upper San Luis Rey River. Wohlford Dam, as noted, was built on top of Escondido Dam in 1924. By 1925 the county

had a total of almost a dozen reservoirs of all sizes having a combined capacity of nearly half a million acre- feet (Table 8.2).

Yet this flurry of construction following World War I by no means solved the county's water problems. For one thing, the ambitious city of San Diego added more people between 1920 and 1930 than the entire county had held in 1910. For another, local runoff was still a fickle servant, and indeed three consecutive dry years occurred starting in 1922. San Diego had relied on groundwater until the 1890s when the first water was delivered through the flume from Cuyamaca Reservoir. In 1906 the city contracted for 7.8 million gallons of water a day from the Otay River system. In 1912 they purchased this system, and two years later also

Figure 8.4. The 1895 La Mesa Dam, here visible during a 1976 maintenance draw-down at Lake Murray. The Alvarado Filtration Plant is in right background. Photo by P. R. Pryde.

acquired Morena Reservoir. In the mid 1920s the San Dieguito system (Lake Hodges) was purchased. At the same time the city possessed a pumping capacity of 4 million gallons a day from underground aquifers in the San Diego River floodplain.

The city had a protracted fight with the Cuyamaca Water Company, however, over the right to build a large dam on the San Diego River at the El Capitan site east of Lakeside. It was not until the 1930s that the city won its case, and in frustration the city had sought approval in 1924 to build a large storage dam in Mission Gorge which the voters fortunately rejected. With its rights to the San Diego River secure,

the city quickly began constructing El Capitan Dam, the largest impoundment in its system, and finished it in 1935 just in time for a series of wet years that quickly filled it to overflowing.

The city also began Sutherland Dam on a tributary of the San Dieguito River in 1927, but foundation problems necessitated its relocation and it was not completed until 1954. Two other upstream dams were completed during the years of World War II, San Vicente north of Lakeside and Loveland on the Sweetwater River. These, together with the delayed completion of Sutherland Dam, ended the initial era of major reservoir construction in the county, although a few smaller ones exist near filtration plants or

TABLE 8.2. Major Reservoirs in San Diego County

Reservoir	Stream	Owner	Year Completed	Drainage Area (square miles)	Maximum Capacity (acre-feet)	Open to Use by Public?
Barrett	Cottonwood Creek	City of San Diego	1922	249	37,947	Yes
Cuyamaca	Boulder Creek	Helix Water District	1887	12	11,595	Yes
El Capitan	San Diego River	City of San Diego	1935	190	112,807	Yes
Henshaw	San Luis Rey River	Vista Irrigation District	1923	205	194,323	Yes
Hodges	San Dieguito River	City of San Diego	1918	303	33,550	Yes
Jennings	Quail Canyon	Helix Water District	1962	2	9,600	Yes
Loveland	Sweetwater River	California-American Water Company	1945	98	25,400	No
Lower Otay	Otay River	City of San Diego	1919*	99	52,345	Yes
Miramar	(unnamed)	City of San Diego	1960	2	7,184	Yes
Morena	Cottonwood Creek	City of San Diego	1912	114	50,206	Yes
Murray	Alvarado Creek	City of San Diego	1918*	4	5,742	Yes
Olivenhain	(unnamed)	Olivenhain M.W.D.	2003	1	24,000	yes
Ramona	(unnamed)	Ramona Municipal Water District	1988	2	12,000	No
San Vicente	San Vicente Creek	City of San Diego	1943 2008	75	90,230 142,330	Yes
Sutherland	Santa Ysabel Creek	City of San Diego	1954	53	29,684	Yes
Sweetwater	Sweetwater River	California-American Water Company	1888	182	27,700	No
Wohlford	Escondido Creek	Escondido Mutual Water Company	1924*	8	7,100	Yes

*Present dam, built over an earlier dam.

on minor streams (Figure 8.5). Although these many dams do provide additional water supplies to the county in wet years, it must be recalled that they may be contributing to problems on the beaches of San Diego County, as was pointed out in Chapters 2 and 7.

Towards the end of the twentieth century, some additional storage capacity was deemed necessary for assuring the adequacy of future local water supplies. To this end, a medium size dam was constructed in Ramona, and a larger one begun a few miles west of Lake Hodges by the Olivenhain MWD (see Table 8.2). Around the year 2010, it is planned to raise San Vicente Reservoir by an additional 54 feet, greatly increasing its storage capabilities. The latter two projects, plus some pipeline extensions, are part of the County Water Authority's Emergency

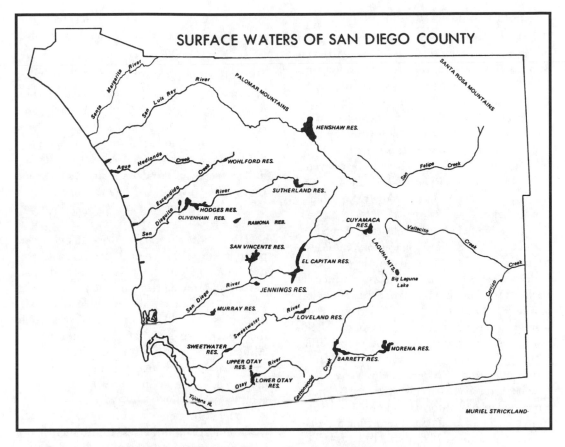

Figure 8.5. Major rivers and reservoirs of the county.

Water Storage Project (EWSP) to assure minimal water availability in the region in the event of major earthquakes elsewhere in southern California.

Other dams have been proposed for areas in north county, particularly two suggested for the Santa Margarita River north of Fallbrook, and the City of San Diego's proposed Pamo Dam on a tributary of Santa Ysabel Creek. These projects have all been rejected due to environmental constraints and other problems (see Chapter 17). The EWSP was the direct result of the abandonment of the Pamo Valley project.

Contemporary Water Supply

Although El Capitan was the capstone of the city's effort to conserve local runoff, it had not been completed for even a decade before the city realized it would have to look for much larger and more reliable sources of water. The "modern era" in the history of supplying water to San Diego County dates from the mid 1940s, with the formation of the San Diego County Water Authority and the first arrival of imported water from the Colorado River.

The Colorado River Aqueduct

All of southern California, with the exception of some high mountain areas, is a water-deficit region. The need to acquire outside water supplies for the region first became apparent in the Los Angeles area, and in 1928 the Metropolitan Water District of Southern California (MWD) was incorporated. Originally formed by thirteen cities in the Los Angeles basin, the primary function of the MWD has been to bring water from the Colorado River via an aqueduct and to distribute it among the cooperating member agencies.

The 242 mile-long Colorado River Aqueduct, one of the major engineering feats of its time, was begun in the early 1930s and completed in 1941. It draws water from Lake Havasu, formed by Parker Dam, and pumps it over the mountains to a series of distribution canals and a terminal storage reservoir in Riverside County, Lake Matthews. The aqueduct is capable of delivering 1,212,000 acre-feet of water a year to southern California, or over a billion gallons a day.

The water that we receive from the Colorado River is part of California's allotment of water from the Colorado, allocated according to agreements drawn up in 1922, 1929, and 1944. As a result of these agreements, the state of California is allowed to withdraw 4,400,000 acre-feet of water a year from the river. The MWD is only guaranteed 550,000 acre-feet a year from the Colorado, which means that the other 662,000 acre-feet which we transport via the aqueduct has consisted of water obtained from other states in the basin that are not using their full allotment (mainly Arizona). However, new regulations signed in 2001 require California to begin using only its basic 4.4 million acre-feet, and MWD only its base 550,000, starting in January 2003. The "lost" 662,000 acre-feet will have to be compensated for by other means. In 2003, an agreement was completed for San Diego to purchase 200,000 acre-feet of water from the Imperial Valley, including economic guarantees for Imperial County.

The San Diego County Water Authority

With the large increase in population that accompanied the outbreak of World War II, it became clear that local water supplies, previously quite adequate, would soon run out. Accordingly, the San Diego County Water Authority was formed in 1944 for the purpose of purchasing Colorado River water from the MWD and importing it into the county for local domestic and agricultural uses.

The County Water Authority is a public corporation, empowered to levy taxes, exercise eminent domain, and construct facilities for the purposes of transporting and delivering water, which it "wholesales" to its member agencies. It does not service all of San Diego County, only the western urbanized and agricultural areas. Although its twenty-three member agencies encompass only about a third of the county's land area, they take in over 95 percent of the county's population (Figure 8.6).

About 25 percent of the county's water is used in agriculture, and the rest for municipal and industrial purposes (Table 8.3). The Authority provides almost all the water used in the county today, as only a small percentage is still derived from local sources.

As soon as it was formed, the San Diego County Water Authority began the task of contracting for MWD water and constructing the facilities necessary to deliver it to the county. In late 1947 the first pipeline of the first aqueduct was completed. The timing was critical, for by February of 1948 the reservoirs storing locally collected water were almost dry. In 1954 a second pipeline, laid parallel to the first, was completed. Combined, they had a capacity of 196 cubic feet per second, or about 140,000 acre-feet a year. They

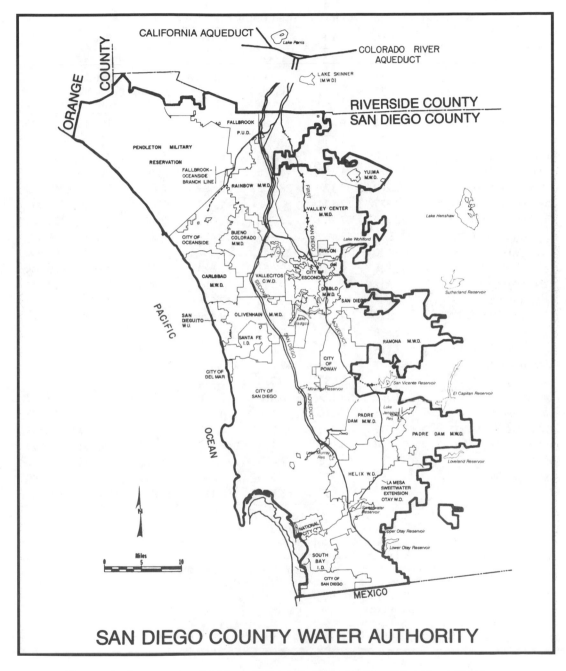

Figure 8.6. County water districts and aqueducts. Map courtesy of San Diego County Water Authority. The irregular dark lines is the eastern limit of the SDCWA service area.

TABLE 8.3. Water Use by Member Agency of the County Water Authority

	1997	1998	1999	2000	2001		
					Source of Water		
	Authority Supply Acre-Feet	Authority Supply Acre-Feet	Authority Supply Acre-Feet	Authority Supply Acre-Feet	Local Supply[1] Acre-Feet	Authority Supply[2] Acre-Feet	Total Acre-Feet
Carlsbad M.W.D.	16,011	15,449	17,286	19,952	1,414	19,016	20,430
City of Del Mar	1,518	1,440	1,465	1,566	17	1,416	1,433
City of Escondido	18,862	16,760	17,345	26,977	6,262	25,934	32,196
Fallbrook P.U.D.	14,021	11,582	14,176	16,824	764	15,066	15,830
Helix W.D.	36,202	29,172	28,485	38,483	2,661	37,419	40,080
City of National City	2,327	2,104	2	1,123	3,927	3,170	7,097
City of Oceanside	29,724	27,160	29,238	32,073	2,524	30,062	32,586
Olivenhain M.W.D.	15,234	13,680	16,165	19,433	250	18,586	18,836
Otay W.D.	24,560	22,874	25,442	29,901	850	30,002	30,852
Padre Dam M.W.D.	19,326	16,802	19,061	21,824	505	20,040	20,544
Camp Pendleton	112	88	119	105	13,505	68	13,573
City of Poway	12,659	11,223	13,270	15,625	73	13,604	13,677
Rainbow M.W.D.	24,134	19,051	25,403	29,929	0	27,427	27,427
Ramona M.W.D.	10,590	7,591	9,774	8,267	2,216	9,795	12,011
Rincon del Diablo M.W.D.	7,264	6,540	8,077	9,119	0	7,696	7,696
City of San Diego[5]	161,777	162,039	169,790	206,433	24,794	200,649	225,442
San Dieguito W.D.	4,509	4,080	3,875	5,112	3,663	4,690	8,353
Santa Fe I.D.	7,363	6,191	6,486	8,056	5,954	7,509	13,463
South Bay I.D.	8,715	7,376	6	4,392	6,447	11,177	17,623
Vallecitos W.D.	13,815	12,438	14,029	16,409	0	15,923	15,923
Valley Center M.W.D.[6]	38,744	29,301	39,195	48,550	0	44,598	44,598
Vista I.D.[7]	12,101	11,708	7,476	17,123	4,983	17,556	22,539
Yuma M.W.D.[8]	1,554	916	719	2,849	1,440	2,740	4,179
Total[9]	481,120	435,563	466,884	580,118	82,247	564,140	646,387

[1]Includes surface, recycled and groundwater supplies; does not reflect conserved water.
[2]Water use in a given year may differ from Authority water sales due to storage.
[3]Includes only amounts certified through the Interim Agricultural Water Program.
[4]Decrease in population attributed to revised census data.
[5]Excludes city of San Diego local surface water use outside of Authority service area.
[6]Excludes reclaimed groundwater replenishment extracted outside of Valley Center's service area.
[7]Excludes land outside of Authority service area.
[8]Excludes local supplies developed beyond Yuma's master meters.
[9]Numbers may not total due to rounding.

Source: SDCWA annual member agency data surveys.

delivered this water to San Vicente Reservoir, the major storage reservoir for imported water, which was completed in 1943.

The rapid growth in the county in the 1950s necessitated a second San Diego aqueduct, this one built along a different route that would take it somewhat closer to the coast. It has a capacity greater than the two pipelines of the first aqueduct combined, and a new reservoir, Miramar, was built to store and process the water it would provide. This third pipeline was completed in 1960, and in its final form includes an extension southward to Lower Otay Reservoir. Despite its large capacity, it proved adequate to handle the importation needs of the county for only a little more than a decade (Figure 8.7).

By the end of the 1960s, a fourth pipeline was under construction, this one again about as large as all previous ones combined. Eight feet in diameter, it was completed to its terminal point, Miramar Reservoir, in 1972. In 1980, a contract was awarded for the construction of a fifth pipeline, this one also eight feet in diameter, which was completed to its terminal point near San Marcos in late 1982. In the 1990's, as noted above, the system began to be enlarged, so as to handle a potential earthquake. The flow of water throughout the entire County Water Authority system is controlled from the Fred A. Heilbron Operations Center in Escondido.

At various terminal reservoirs throughout the county the water received from the Colorado River must undergo purification treatment before it is suitable for domestic use. The city of San Diego, for example, has three such treatment plants: a smaller one at Lower Otay Reservoir, and newer ones at Lake Murray and Miramar Reservoir. At these treatment plants, the water passes through sedimentation basins, where suspended materials settle out. The water is then filtered and chlorinated before being distributed for home use. These plants are unable, however, to remove the dissolved salts inherent in Colorado River water. These salts give our water a slightly mineralized flavor, but are not unhealthy. The situation improved slightly in the late 1970's when water from the California Water Plan began to arrive in the county.

The California Water Plan

Looking ahead to the future needs of California's rapidly increasing population, the state in the 1950s began planning a vast program for diverting water from northern California rivers and conveying it through hundreds of miles of canals and pipelines to areas of future need located mainly in the southern half of the state. It was approved by the legislature in 1959, and necessary funding for the California Water Plan was authorized by the state's voters in 1960.

The key element in the plan is Oroville Dam on the Feather River, a huge storage reservoir that can impound 3,500,000 acre-feet of water. From Oroville Reservoir, Feather River water flows via the Feather and Sacramento rivers to the San Francisco Bay delta area, and from there to a pumping plant near the town of Tracy which sends the water into the California Aqueduct and on its way to southern California.

That portion of the water destined for San Diego County leaves the main aqueduct in Antelope Valley north of Los Angeles and travels through San Bernardino to Lake Perris in southern Riverside County. From there a smaller canal takes the water to a junction point west of the town of Hemet, where blended water from both the Colorado Aqueduct and the Feather River are diverted into the various San Diego County Aqueduct pipelines.

An advantage of Feather River water for San Diego County users is that it has a much lower salt content than Colorado River water. The blended product water in 2000 averaged about 540 parts per million of dissolved solids.

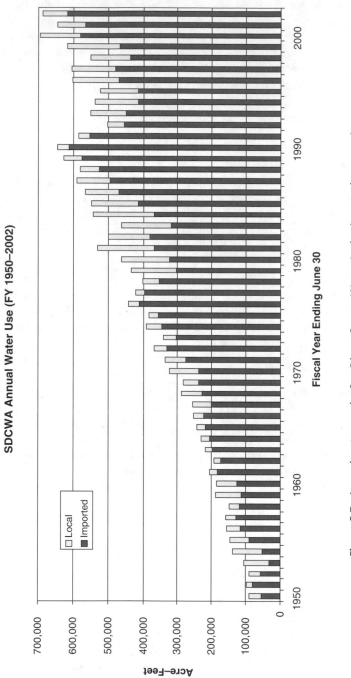

Figure 8.7. Annual water use by San Diego County Water Authority member agencies.

Water from the state project first arrived in San Diego County in May of 1978. However, in view of the major droughts of 1987–1990 and 1999–2002, it seems questionable whether present facilities will be sufficient to meet the county's water needs in the twenty-first century. This raises the question of providing for future water needs.

Water Conservation and Future Sources

The rapid increase in demand for fresh water in San Diego County that is illustrated by figure 8.7 results mainly from the country' rapid population growth. Major droughts stress the region's ability to meet water demands. The 1987–1990 drought forced the region to reduce its use of water. A call for a 10% decrease in water use during the summer of 1990 was followed by a 20% reduction requirement early in 1991. All 18 cities cooperated in efforts to decrease water use in homes, in landscaping and at work.

There are two techniques coming into increased use that greatly improve the efficiency of water used for irrigation. One is drip irrigation, now being used on many thousands of acres in the county (see Figure 9.5). In drip irrigation, the water seeps slowly out of a hose in the proximity of the plants' roots. In this way losses in the application of irrigation water are greatly reduced. The second approach is called *xeriscaping,* and consists of using drought tolerant *(xeritiphytic)* plans for landscaping, instead of plants (and lawns) that require a high volume of water. Many local nurseries now specialize in xeriphytic types of landscape plants.

Another very feasible way to reduce the need for new water supplies is to recycle (reuse) municipal waste water after it has been adequately treated. A well-known case where this has been done on a small scale for many years is at the Santee treatment plant, where water that has undergone secondary treatment is used

to maintain a series of recreational lakes. Elsewhere in the county, reclaimed water has also been used to water fields or landscaping in Escondido, Ramona, Fallbrook, the San Pasqual Valley, and at many other locations throughout the county. The potential for using reclaimed waste water for agricultural purposes is great, and the County Water Authority strongly supports a major effort to increase water reclamation capabilities in the region. However, the high salinity of our incoming water makes increased salt in the soil a potential problem wherever local waste water is reused.

Desalinization is the means of removing these salts. Desalinization is most often thought of in the context of removing salt from ocean water, and an experimental plant to accomplish this existed in Chula Vista from 1967 until 1973. Seawater desalinization, however, is extremely expensive. It is somewhat easier and cheaper to remove the smaller quantity of salts from reclaimed municipal or irrigation water. The latter usually only contain from 1,000 to 1,500 parts per million of dissolved salts, as compared to 35,000 for ocean water. The most commonly used system for desalinizing slightly salty water is a filter-like system called *reverse osmosis.* Small-scale reverse osmosis plants have existed for a number of years in many locations throughout the county.

Although reusing properly treated municipal waste waters for irrigation purposes is an option that can help decrease our future dependency on outside water supplies, it has been little used to date within the county due to the expense of the added treatment and distribution systems. However, the price of our imported water has gone up so much (Authority water rose in cost from $19 to $130 an acre-foot between 1961 and 1981, and rose to over $500 per acre-foot by 2002), that not only waste water reclamation but possibly even sea water desalting may become increasingly cost competitive during the 2000–2010 decade. In 2003, the SDCWA was considering building a seawater desalinization plant in Carlsbad.

After years of effort, a major agreement was signed in the fall of 2003 between the MWD, the San Diego County Water Authority, and the Imperial Irrigation District that would for the first time permit transfer (i.e., sale) of a portion of the IID's Colorado River water to the San Diego region. This was a very complex arrangement that could ultimately provide 200,000 acre-feet of river water to San Diego; a summary of its provisions is contained in the Gardner reference in the bibliography to this chapter.

One final word should be said about the need for water conservation. Many residents of San Diego County, some of whom may have recently moved here from more humid areas of the country, do not perceive of water as a scarce resource. They will use a garden hose, for example, to wash down their driveway when the same effect could be achieved just as efficiently and much more cheaply by means of a broom. A few people even bemoan our rainstorms, infrequent as they are, despite the many benefits that this scarce resource provides.[2] The reader can undoubtedly think of many examples of the imprudent or wasteful use of water by county residents and businesses. The severe drought conditions in the early 2000s should increase the perception of water as a scarce resource, and assist in the effort to reduce the local rate of per capita consumption and the need for future importations.

[2]The commercial value of the rain that falls on just the city of San Diego during the average winter is greater than all of the gold that was ever taken out of the hills of Julian!

Controlling Natural Runoff

The rivers of San Diego County, whose runoff is normally not large enough to be depended upon as a major source of municipal supplies, can on occasion be subjected to extremely heavy flooding. In the past, there have been very heavy flood flows on such rivers as the Sweetwater, San Diego, Tijuana, and San Luis Rey. The fact that the construction of upstream dams has helped to curtail the incidence of major flooding in recent decades does not mean that a storm of truly unusual proportions could not produce massive flooding again at some point in the future.

The Threat of Flooding

Floods are a natural part of any river system, and this is equally true for the rivers of San Diego County. Since accurate records began to be kept around the turn of the twentieth century, major floods have occurred in 1916 and 1927, and moderate sized floods in a number of other years, most recently 1998 (see Table 8.4). In dry years, however, the major streams of the county have on occasion had almost no runoff at all.

One unusual characteristic of the hydrology of San Diego County should be kept in mind concerning local flooding. The southern California-western Arizona area (with the exception of the highly controlled Colorado River) has the greatest variability of runoff of anywhere in the United States. Stated another way, the percentage differences in runoff magnitudes between the wettest years and the driest years are greater in this area than in any other part of the country. This reflects the fact that our rainfall is extremely variable, as noted above. The main implication of this is that even greater caution should be exercised in building in the floodplains of San Diego County than elsewhere in the country, since the size and frequency of

TABLE 8.4. Largest Floods of the 20th Century on the San Diego River [a]

Rank	Rain Year [b]	Month of Flood	Maximum cfs [c]	Rain Year Precipit'n	Rain Year Rank
1	1915–16	January	70,200	12.55	24
2	1926–27	February	45,400	14.74	15
3	1921–22	December	16,700	18.65	3
4	1936–37	February	14,200	15.93	9
5	1917–18	March	12,000	8.04	[d]
6	1982–83	March	9,590	18.26	5
7	1940–41	April	9,250	24.74	1
8	1931–32	February	7,400	13.18	20
9	1937–38	March	7,350	9.72	[d]
10	1994–95	March	6,010	17.12	8 [e]
11	1997–98	February	5,450	17.78	7
12	1925–26	April	4,540	15.66	11
13	1951–52	January	4,390	18.16	6
14	1914–15	February	3,960	14.41	17
15	1990–91	March	3,640	11.79	25
16	1992–93	January	3,460	18.31	4
17	1979–80	February	3,420 [f]	15.72	10
18	1966–67	December	3,400	10.63	ave.
19	1977–78	January	3,010 [f]	18.71	2
20	1981–82	March	2,900	11.50	27

[a] Actual years covered by available data are 1914 to 2001.
[b] In California annual rainfall is measured from July 1 to the following June 30.
[c] Cfs = cubic feet per second (at maximum flood flow).
[d] Annual precipitation for this year was below the mean.
[e] Note that 8 of the 10 largest floods occurred prior to 1942. This can be attributed mainly to the absence of dam storage capacity on the river at that time, or, in 1937 and 1941, to the fact that it was overflowing.
[f] The peak run-off data for Jan. 1978 and Feb. 1980 may be understated. It seems questionable that the peak flow of 1983 was three times that of 1978 or 1980. Water was so high in 1980 that Mission Valley was evacuated. No such emergency was declared in 1983. There was no recording gage in Mission Valley in 1978 and 1980.

Source: U.S. Geological Survey; U.S. Weather Bureau.

flooding on local streams is even more uncertain than elsewhere.

Nevertheless, today most of our major river valleys are either partially developed or are under continuing pressure for such development. This has caused floodplain landowners to demand some form of flood protection, as well as engendering a counterargument that they be left undeveloped as greenbelts. Either course of action is technically possible, depending on the desires of the local citizenry and their elected representatives.

Approaches to the Flood Problem

When a river valley is subject to occasional heavy flooding, as all are in San Diego County, there are several varieties of responses that can be made to the problem. If some development already exists, some sort of structural control is the most common option. In many parts of southern California, where dams have been constructed mainly for water conservation rather than for flood control, the primary type of response has been large downstream flood control channels. These are especially evident in the counties that make up the greater Los Angeles basin. If the flood threat is perceived as slight, and if cities are regulating floodplain uses, a nonstructural alternative is for property owners to invest in flood insurance, available through the federal government.

Increasingly, however, it is being recommended that floodplains not be developed. Despite billions of dollars in flood protection works built in the United States since the turn of the twentieth century, annual flood losses continue to rise. This is because once some form of structural protection is in place, landowners feel they are "safe" and much expensive development goes in. But there is no guarantee that the maximum runoff for which the dams, levees, or channels have been designed will not be exceeded, and when they are, massive losses will be incurred. This was exactly what happened, for example, in Harrisburg and Wilkes-Barre, Pennsylvania, during tropical storm Agnes in 1972, and on the Missouri River in 1993. Thus, the recommendations and policies that have been put forth in recent years by agencies and commissions of the federal government, the state of California, San Diego County, the San Diego Association of Governments, the city of San Diego, and the California Coastal Commission have all recommended against encouraging the development of flood-prone lands.

But if such lands are privately owned, how can landowners be prevented from developing them if they want to? One approach to this is to permit development, but only those kinds of development that are compatible with floodplains. By "compatible" is meant uses that will not be destroyed by a flood or that will not result in significant loss of property or lives should a flood come along. Such uses would include crop agriculture, golf courses, gravel pits, campgrounds, grazing lands, and a large number of other low-intensity activities. This is termed *floodplain zoning*, and it is being widely employed as a means of saving both property and taxpayers' money. Both the city and county of San Diego now have regulations in effect to implement such a policy.

Among the most critical floodplains in the county are those on the lower stretches of the San Diego, San Luis Rey, San Dieguito, and Tijuana rivers, and all have been the subject of recent controversies. The Tijuana River valley has been complex because of the concrete flood channel completed by the city of Tijuana in the mid-1970's, because a number of persons have built their homes in the floodplain, and because of the importance of the river's estuary. In 1993, a medium sized flood re-routed a portion of the river's main channel into an entirely new location. In 1978, a short "energy dissipator" facility was built on the U.S. side of the border, reflecting a decision to retain agriculture in the floodplain and to preserve the ecological values of the estuary. During the 1990s, the county acquired hundreds of acres in the flood plain for a new regional open space park.

Mission Valley, along the lower San Diego River, is likewise a complex case because of the extensive development that has already been permitted in the floodplain. Serious flooding occurred in the valley in 1978 and 1980, and the lower valley was evacuated in February, 1980 (Figures 8.8 and 8.9).

In 1976 the Corps of Engineers decided that federal funding for a channelization project in the Valley could not be economically justified, so the city and property owners between the 163 bridge and Qualcomm Way have cooperatively financed and built a natural-appearing ("soft-bottom") channel in this area. It would safely convey a flood the size of the 1980 one, but not the size of the 1916 flood. It is also worth remembering that the increasing urbanization taking place within the San Diego River watershed will tend to increase the size of the peak

Figures 8.8 and 8.9. The flood of January 1978 in Mission Valley. During high flows, property damage in recent years has amounted to several million dollars to businesses located in the floodplain. Photos by P. R. Pryde.

flood flows in Mission Valley, and that no extension of the mid-valley channel presently exists between I-5 and Route 163.

The response of a community to the question of floodplain management is significant anywhere, but particularly so in San Diego County. Recalling that floodplains serve as groundwater recharge areas, that our river valleys contain some of our best agricultural soils and wildlife habitats, that they represent natural greenbelts which are a desirable attribute for any metropolitan area, and that the uncertainty of flooding is greater here than in other parts of the country, it can be seen why professional planners and water use specialists have advocated that our floodplains not be developed. Implementing such recommendations, however, is not simple and represents a problem worth the attention of all citizens concerned with the future of the County.

References

City of San Diego. *The Urban Water Management Plan and Conservation Program for the City of San Diego*, City of San Diego , Water Utilities Department, 1990.

County of San Diego . *Water Supply Outlook for San Diego County, 1980–2000.* San Diego: County Department of Planning and Land Use., 1982.

Cranham, G. T. *Water for Southern California: Water Resources Development.* San Diego: Sunbelt Publications, 1999.

Gardner, M., "Accord Near on Landmark Water Deal", *San Diego Union-Tribune,* September 4, 2003, pp. A-1 and A-10.

Papageorge, N. T., "The Role of the San Diego River in the Development of Mission Valley", *The Journal of San Diego History*, vol. XVII, no. 2 (Spring 1971), pp. 14–27.

Pourade, R. F. *History of San Diego* (Vols. 4, 5, and 6). San Diego: Union-Tribune Publishing Co., 1964–1967.

Pryde, P. R., "A Coming Water Crisis in Southern California?", *The California Geographer* , Vol. 42, 2002, pp. 60–74.

San Diego County Water Authority. *2001 Annual Report*. San Diego: SDCWA, 2002.

San Diego County Water Authority. *San Diego Area Water Reuse Study.* SDCWA: September 1987.

San Diego County Water Authority. *Emergency Water Storage Project, Draft Environmental Impact Report.* San Diego: SDCWA, 1995.

San Diego County Water Authority. *To Quench a Thirst* (history of San Diego County water development), San Diego: SDCWA, 2003.

State of California, Department of Water Resources. *Ground Water Occurrence and Quality: San Diego Region.* (Bulletin no. 106-2), 2 vols. Sacramento: Department of Water Resources, 1967.

Walker, Dan. *Thirst for Independence: The San Diego Water Story.* San Diego: Sunbelt Publications, 2004.

Internet Connections:
City of San Diego Water Department: *www.sandiego.gov/water/*
Metropolitan Water District of Southern California: *www.mwd.dst.ca.us*
San Diego County Water Authority: *www.sdcwa.org*
San Diego Historical Society: *www.sandiegohistory.org*

Chapter Nine

Working the Land
Agriculture in San Diego County

Agriculture in San Diego County is a billion dollar business. In 2001, farmers, ranchers, stockmen, nurserymen, and beekeepers received about $1.29 billion for their products. Income from crop and livestock commodities ranks fourth in the county, after the military, manufacturing, and tourism. In addition to income derived directly from crops, an uncounted but large amount was received by truckers, packers, those who sell and service farm equipment and supplies, and others who serve the agricultural industry.

San Diego County agriculture exhibits great diversity. Around 60 separate crops and many

James D. Blick is an emeritus professor in the Department of Geography at San Diego State University, specializing in regional geography.

kinds of flowers and nursery products were harvested from 206,000 acres in 2001. About 28,000 head of beef cattle and calves ranged over more than 135,000 acres of rangeland, and millions of hens layed in excess of a billion eggs. Eighteen commodities had values in excess of ten million dollars each. In the last decade, agricultural income has risen by 25%.

A majority of the county's agricultural output is produced west of a line running northeasterly from Otay Mesa to Lake Henshaw. Most of the production occurs on land within twenty-five miles of the ocean. It is here that the various conditions of climate, land, soil, water, transportation, and other factors are most conducive to the high yields necessary to sustain the industry in an area of rising land values and costs of operation. Agriculture in the eastern two-thirds of the county, which consists mostly of mountains and deserts, is mainly on small irrigated parcels, but also includes extensive grazing of unirrigated pasture and rangeland.

Historical Development

The thousands of years of Indian occupancy saw no known agriculture. In early San Diego County the native inhabitants extracted their nourishment mainly from hunting and gathering. Many plants were used, but the oaks and mesquite were of greatest value (see Chapter 4). These foods were supplemented by dry seeds from grasses and annual forbs, wild fruits and nutlike seeds, leafy plants, and bulbs. Near the coast, fish and shellfish were taken from the coastal lagoons. Some game and birds were eaten to a small extent.

The last century and a half has seen profound changes in the agricultural make-up of the county. Initially, sparse settlement and long distances to markets were conducive to livestock, subsistence crops, and honey (at one time San Diego led the nation in honey production). Various citrus crops, especially oranges, appeared in the last quarter of the nineteenth century. In the twentieth century, other tree and vine crops, including avocados, grapes, tomatoes, and olives were the leading products. However, with increasing urbanization, desires for beautification, and higher costs of land and water, nursery and flower crops now lead in value. A portion comes from climatically controlled and carefully monitored greenhouse production.

The Mission Period

The Franciscan friars who arrived in 1769 were faced with the necessity of establishing selfsufficient missions in Alta California, and this required that they plant crops and graze cattle and sheep. Many of the Franciscans were from Spain where the Mediterranean climate is similar to that of California and where irrigation had of necessity been practiced for nearly two thousand years. Mission crops and agricultural practices resembled those of the homeland, with a few additions and some notable, but not very successful, experimentation.

Crops were planted in the nearby floodplain as soon as possible after the founding of Mission San Diego in 1769 and San Luis Rey in 1798. Corn was planted for tortillas and for atole (gruel) and pozole (thick soup with vegetables) to feed the Indians who did the work. Grapes for wine and brandy, wheat for bread, olives for oil, barley for general use, and various fruits such as pears, figs, pomegranates, and beans followed. Failures from flooding or drought occurred until an irrigation system could be built to bring a dependable supply of water. A dam was built on the San Diego River seven miles above the mission (Figure 8.1) and an aqueduct was delivering water by 1816. Mission orchards were often extensive. San Diego had three vineyards of 3,600, 5,000, and 8,000 vines and two olive groves of 167 and 300 trees. Both cotton and flax were attempted but were not successful.

Livestock was of major importance as a source of meat, tallow, soap, hides, and leather for mission use and for export. In 1822, the peak year, San Diego Mission owned 30,179 head of stock including 9,245 cattle and 19,000 sheep. At San Luis Rey, there were 57,330 animals including 27,500 head of cattle in 1832, its peak year. Mission lands were very extensive and sizeable quantities of stock and crops were to be found at places as far removed as Jamul, Santa Ysabel, and Pala where they were tended by Indians trained at the missions.

Mission agriultural practices were of necessity primitive. Plows were wooden, made of a suitable tree fork tipped with iron; grain was sown by hand, cut with a short sickle, and threshed with horses' hooves. Irrigation systems were gravity fed. That the Fathers could make both cement for construction and iron goods from a crude forge was to their credit.

The entire mission system collapsed between 1829 and 1835 when it was secularized under the Mexican governors. By the 1840s, only remnants were to be seen of either crops or herds. Mission gardens and orchards were abandoned. The Indians, who had been trained by the mission Fathers, did not long engage in agriculture except in a few isolated localities in the interior of the county. There are recorded small plots of corn, beans, wheat, and some fruit, but gradually the Indians became less dependent on planted crops and returned to the abundant supply of acorns, game, and other native products. Direct links between mission agriculture and that of the present are very slim; perhaps the best example is that of olives. Beginning in 1869, Frank Kimball purchased large quantities of olive cuttings from both Mission San Diego and San Luis Rey and, in all likelihood, a number of these still survive in the southwestern part of the county.

The Ranchos

Following the secularization of the missions, agriculture was characterized by cattle grazing on lands granted to certain individuals by the Mexican governors. Of the total of 553 grants made in California and subsequently approved by the Land Act of 1851, 32 were in San Diego County (Figure 9.1). Slightly over one-fifth of the total area of the county (560,530 acres) was awarded in grants. The ranchos ranged in size from little Cañada de los Coches with 28.29 acres to huge Santa Margarita y las Flores, the latter being the largest in the state with 133,441 acres. The average grant was 17,517 acres. Conditions on the ranchos were only a little different than during the Mission period. The great distances,

slow transportation to Mexican markets, and small local population precluded the sale of much meat. Rather, hides and tallow were sold, often illegally, to Yankee traders who arrived with increasing frequency in California waters. Planted crops usually included corn, wheat, barley, vegetables, grapes, and fruits and were mainly for use on the ranchos. The few hundred persons who then lived in the Pueblo of San Diego constituted a very small market for farm goods.

The ranchos and their cattle persisted after statehood in 1850, but most were soon to be either lost to their owners through legal actions, or sold. A few, however, still exist in some form, notably Santa Margarita y las Flores which is now Camp Pendleton, Cuyamaca Rancho, and Rancho Jamul which, until the turn of the twenty-first century, was operated as a ranch by the Daley family. This short period of only about two decades gave us not only traditions such as the barbecue and rodeo but set the stage for the early American occupancy of much of the county.

American Period—A New People on the Land

Agricultural settlement by the Americans began soon after the signing of the Treaty of Guadalupe Hidalgo in 1848. Except for a few isolated spots, farming was largely confined to more favorable sites in the valleys and low foothills. Most of the land was still under control of the ranchos or belonged to the Indians, and available farm land was limited. Even so, soon after 1850, there was a winery in San Pasqual Valley which utilized locally-grown grapes. Sheep were known in the foothills by the 1860s. It is safe to assume that the usual food crops such as corn, beans, wheat, vegetables, melons, and some fruit were grown for local consumption. Cattle were important at first but, following the drought of 1862–63, were of much reduced significance.

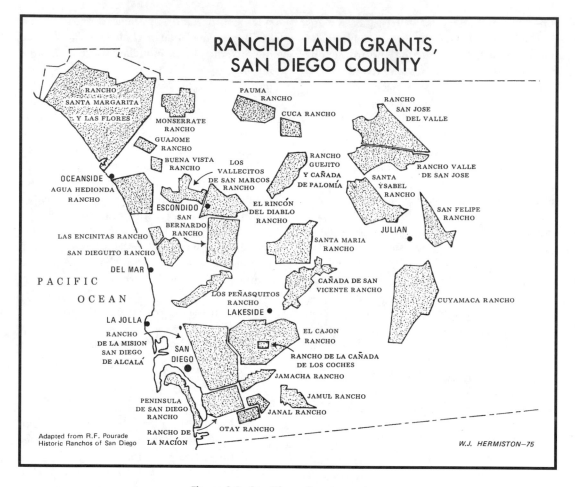

Figure 9.1. San Diego County ranchos.

A renewed interest in California occurred after the Civil War when footloose Southerners arrived to occupy many of the interior valleys. Longhorn cattle were introduced first, to be followed by black Angus, Durham, and other purebred stock. Napolean Bratton, after 1868, utilized the ample water from inland streams, and his cattle grazed freely in Lee, Lyons, Lawson, Bratton, Japatul, and various interior valleys. In 1865, Thomas Cameron established a sheep ranch in Cameron Valley and grazed his flocks on the open range in the summer and then drove them to the coastal terraces for winter feeding, lambing, and marketing. By 1871, sheep were grazed in El Cajon Valley. The early ranches were self-contained units with garden, orchard, pigs, and chickens for their own use.

The early settlers of the San Diego backcountry faced a number of formidable handicaps if they wished to farm. Arable land was limited to a few discontinuous valleys, sometimes already occupied by stockmen or Indians who also had claimed much of the available water. Most of the land is steep, rocky, and difficult to clear of its heavy chaparral. The weather was unpredictable. Droughts caused crop and native feed scarcities with consequent loss of stock. Floods, such as the "Great Flood" of 1862, washed out crops and irrigation works. Sometimes unusually cold or snowy winters killed new buds, nipped crops, and stranded stock. Predatory animals and discontented Indians caused problems from time to time. Lastly, roads were rudimentary until about 1900 and transportation of products to market was exceedingly difficult and slow. Self-sufficiency tended to be the rule with cash being obtained by marketing livestock in San Diego or providing food for travelers or the few small mountain communities such as Julian.

Bees were an important source of income for some of the early backcountry settlers. They provided a quick and high return and were easy to care for. Native chaparral species such as sage, California buckwheat, and others flower over a long growing season and enable bees to produce a high quality product. The honey could endure the rough travel to the coast and long overland or sea trips to market. The industry began in 1869 when John Harbison imported 110 colonies from Sacramento. By 1874 bees were kept at over 2,000 locations in the county and 200,000 pounds of honey were shipped.

Period of Expectation

The completion in 1869 of the transcontinental railroad, plus improved local sea and land transportation, attracted increasing numbers of people who settled on the former ranchos, on Indian lands (often as squatters), and in the embryonic towns. Agricultural possibilities attracted settlers to the arable lands, and new crops, some to be important later on, were introduced. Frank Kimball's acquisition and distribution of olives

from the missions beginning in 1869 has been noted. He also secured a few fig cuttings from the Mission and by 1872 harvested the first crop. Oranges were planted about the same time and lemons were introduced from Australia in 1875 to be planted in Paradise Valley. Limes from Hawaii were attempted but they were soon abandoned because of the lack of a market. Citrus experiments often were handicapped by low winter temperatures since orchard heating was not then practiced. In addition, water shortages and shipping difficulties plagued the growers.

Apples and pears were planted in the Julian area and near National City in 1876. In the drier interior valleys and on the terraces, grain replaced livestock and by 1876 there were 6,000 acres of wheat in El Cajon Valley alone. Unlisted amounts of milk, poultry, vegetables, grapes, and other crops were also raised by the remaining Indians and Californios and by the recent arrivals. By 1877, the majority of level, arable land had been planted to some crop. Cattle still grazed on Rancho Santa Margarita, and sheep and cattle were numerous in the remote interior of the county.

All the while, people anxiously awaited the coming of the railroad which had been talked about since 1850.

The Boom Years—Experimentation

The boom years of the 1880s saw the completion of the railroad to San Diego from the north in 1885 and the resulting influx of population, establishment of towns, and expansion of the market for agricultural products. Dams, reservoirs, and aqueducts from the mountains were built to bring water for irrigation and domestic use. Technological developments such as steam powered pumps (1872), cast iron irrigation pipe (1873), concrete pipe (1882), and electric powered pumps (1885) permitted the farmer to increase yields by better irrigation. Improvements in canning and packing helped place a higher quality product on the market. The so-called "no fence law," passed in 1872, forced the grazier to fence in his stock thus permitting farms to expand without danger from marauding livestock.

During the 1880s and 1890s some old crops were expanded and a number of new ones introduced, not always with success in spite of the often exorbitant claims made by proponents of the area's charms and advantages. Agriculture was often based on hearsay and trial and error. Probably no one did more to promote county agriculture than Frank Kimball whose horticultural activities included his great interest in olives, the introduction of many new fruit trees, founding of the San Diego County Fair in 1880, many lengthy trips around the country to promote local agriculture, and ten years (1888–1898) of service as the State Commissioner of Horticulture.

Grape acreage expanded greatly during the 1880s and large vineyards were to be found in interior locations such as San Pasqual, El Cajon, Cottonwood and Japatul Valleys, Alpine, Dehesa, and Jamul. Cuttings were imported from abroad, wineries (at least four) were in operation and thousands of young plants were set out. Raisins were produced as well as wine, but few grapes were grown for table use. Today, a few old gnarled vines and some abandoned terraces are all that remain of this venture.

Olives, which require about the same growing conditions as grapes, were also widely planted and were cured and sold locally or shipped out. For a while after 1886, an oil mill operated in National City. A number of deciduous fruits including pears, peaches, cherries, almonds, plums, and apricots were introduced at this time. Perhaps because of their need for winter chilling, all but apricots met with little or no success. Previously established crops such as wheat, barley, honey, and some others continued to be important.

The agricultural boom lasted into the 1890s, when a decline set in. Overexpansion in anticipation of a direct railroad to the East, the lack of tariff protection (especially for oranges from the Mediterranean), erratic rainfall, a loss of population following the real estate "boom of the eighties," and a nationwide financial crisis combined to seriously reduce crop yields and markets. Many farmers were broke and lands were abandoned.

An attempt was made in the late 1890s to grow mulberries and silkworms and to produce silk. The mild climate and long growing season were conducive to high yields of leaves. However, difficulties in providing sufficient leaves to feed enough worms to operate at the hoped-for scale, problems of markets, high labor costs relative to the Orient, and a general lack of interest soon ended the project in 1905. By early in the twentieth century, most of the crop types and cultivation patterns that can be observed today had been established. Recent innovations will be discussed later in the chapter.

San Diego's Agricultural Resources

Only a small fraction of the county (less than 3 percent) is planted to crops and another 15 percent is grazed. The remainder consists of desert, steep chaparral and forest-clad slopes, and expanding urban areas. A number of factors, both physical and cultural, influence where agriculture is practiced.

Several topographic zones occur, aligned in a northwest-southeast direction (see Chapter 2). The narrow coastal plain is largely composed of terraces, dissected by a large number of streams whose floodplains offer generally fertile but hazardous agricultural sites. The terraces themselves provide irrigable land for crops but are also being rapidly built upon. Inland, along the middle courses of the major rivers (Sweetwater, San Diego, San Dieguito, and San Luis Rey), are alluvial valleys which have natural conditions very favorable for agriculture.

The majority of the county is composed of the hills and mountains of the Peninsular Ranges and except for the few isolated valleys and gentler slopes, agriculture here is seriously handicapped by steep rocky terrain and inaccessibility. The eastern desert is characterized by steep rocky slopes and sandy lowlands which, when coupled with problems of water supply, present major hurdles to agricultural development.

The weather and climate of San Diego County has long been a major attraction to both farmers and nonfarm settlers. Precipitation is concentrated in the winter months, which results in major problems of water availability for the summer growing season. More of a problem than the amount of rainfall is its characteristic variability from year to year, and through more extended cycles of wet and dry years (see Chapters 3 and 8). The growing season is long and, inland beyond the immediate coastal zone, warm (Figure 9.2). The frostfree maritime belt near the coast is one of the county's main agricultural assets.

The mountain areas have cooler, wetter, and longer winters than the lowlands and it is only here that those deciduous fruits which require winter chilling grow well. Lack of suitable land restricts agriculture other than grazing to a very few small acreages. The desert area has a long growing season with a high percentage of available sunshine. Topography and water supply explain why it has not been more fully utilized for agriculture.

It is possible, from the standpoint of crop cultivation, to consider the climates of the county as consisting of five agricultural climatic regions (Figure 9.3).

I. Maritime. Occupies a narrow fringe along the coast and is dominated day and night by oceanic conditions—mild, without extremes, and subject to summer fog. Occasional hot dry Santa Anas upset the even maritime pattern. The area is ideal for vegetables and flowers.

II. Coastal. Adjacent to the maritime climate with greater range in temperatures and less fog—more sun; extends inland to the foothills.

III. Transitional. Includes coastal valleys (like El Cajon and San Pasqual), foothills, and mountains below about 2,000 feet. Occasional morning fog but mostly cooler in winter and warmer in summer than I and II; has occasional winter frosts and summer maxima over 100°.

IV. Interior. Wide daily and seasonal ranges of temperature; moist winters with occasional snow, summer hot and dry. Includes mountain areas from 2,000 feet to just east of the crest.

V. Desert. Lies in the rain shadow of the Peninsular Ranges; has greatest diurnal ranges, very hot dry summer with occasional thundershowers and mild winter with light, variable, cyclonic precipitation.

Specific considerations relating to agricultural needs explain the relatively minor differences that exist between these zones and the climatic regions discussed in Chapter 3.

Situation Factors Affecting Agriculture

A number of economic considerations are significant to agriculture in the county. Without large and accessible markets, crops and livestock would be produced here mainly to satisfy a smaller urban and subsistence need. The cut flower industry, for example, is almost wholly dependent upon being able to move its products by freeway and airplane. Four of the leading

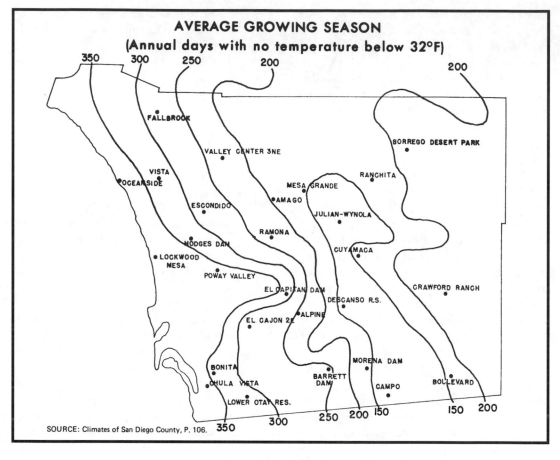

AVERAGE GROWING SEASON
(Annual days with no temperature below 32°F)

SOURCE: Climates of San Diego County, P. 106.

Figure 9.2.

products (tomatoes, eggs, avocados, and milk) are perishable and must be moved quickly to market. Agriculture has progressed from the complete self-sufficiency of the missions to the highly specialized nature it has today largely because of improvements in transportation. Once many goods (like hides) had to be dried to preserve them indefinitely, prior to their months-long trip to the East or Europe. Early steamers and sailing ships speeded things up a little. The opening of the railroad to the North

and East in 1885, trucks and concrete highways in the 1920s, fast trucks and freeways in the post World War II era, and now jet transport have all shortened delivery time and placed San Diego agriculture within reach of markets in all parts of the world.

The expanding population of the United States in general and California in particular has also helped agricultural sales. California in 1900 contained 1,485,053 people, about half of what San Diego County alone has today. Further-

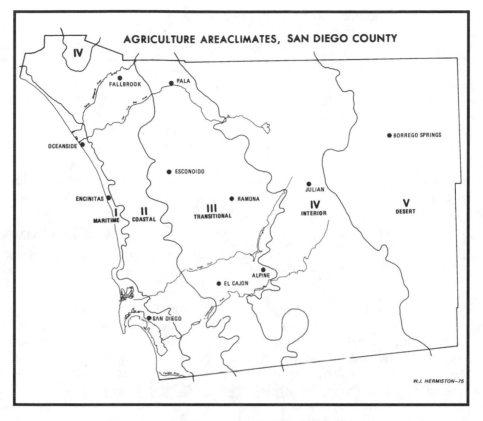

Figure 9.3. San Diego's Agricultural Climatic Regions.

more, at present, more than two million residents live in the northwest corner of Mexico and are part of the market for some San Diego County products.

Agriculture in the Present

In 2001 the income received by farmers and stockmen for their products was $1,289,000,000. The many commodities produced may be grouped into eight categories (Table 9.1). Agricultural income has almost tripled since 1982.

Major Commodities

As can be seen from Table 9.1, by far the largest "agricultural crop" in San Diego County is the category of nursery products and flower crops. In 2001, these types of crops accounted for just under two-thirds of all agricultural income. Commercial flower production is a part of this, but amounts to only ten percent of the total for the category. Almost eighty percent is accounted for by ornamental trees and shrubs, bedding plants, and indoor flower and foliage plants; in other words, servicing the local homeowner and the construction industry (Figure 9.4). The largest of

TABLE 9.1. Leading Agricultural Crops in San Diego County

Crop	2001 Acres	2001 $ Value	% of Total Value	1990 $ Value	1982 $ Value
Nursery Products and Flower Crops	8,829	855,138,931	66.3	491,353,000	92,544,000
Fruit and Nut Crops	44,363	230,001,032	17.8	267,583,000	128,125,000
Vegetable Crops	8,036	110,796,280	8.6	72,397,000	91,165,000
Livestock, Poultry Products		67,121,686	5.2	84,879,000	100,466,000
Livestock and Poultry		17,465,747	1.4	12,010,000	16,837,000
Field Crops (grain, etc.)	144,812	6,061,349	0.5	5,228,000	1,975,000
Apiary Products		1,888,129	0.1	1,259,000	1,987,000
Specialty Crops		442,658			
Total	164,357	1,288,915,812	100	934,709,000	433,099,000

Sources: For 2001: County of San Diego, "2001 Crop Statistics and Annual Report"; for 1990 and 1982, *San Diego: An Introduction to the Region,* 3rd ed., p. 147.

these sub-categories was indoor flowering plants, providing over $300 million income to San Diego's economy. Probably the best known industry in this category is the world-famous poinsettia business operated by the Paul Ecke family in Encinitas since 1924. The total value of local poinsettias sold in 2001 was over $42 million.

The majority of our flower crop is grown on the coastal terraces north of Solana Beach. From less than two million dollars in the early 1950s, the flower crop has expanded and amounted to $88 million in 2001. Carnations used to be one of the major crops, but between 1990 and 2001 the value of carnations produced dropped by over 80 percent. Today, no single type of flower dominates, as over forty varieties are grown. Roses are one of the most important, with over 4 million dollars in sales.

The favorable mild climate and available land attracted flower growers as far back as the early 1920s. Today, greenhouses are used to provide protection from heavy rain and provide precise control over growth and flowering. More rapid surface and air transportation allows truck delivery of flowers to the rest of the United States and next-day delivery to Europe.

Avocados are probably the "signature crop" of San Diego County. Fruit from the 25,922 acres harvested in 1990 yielded a gross return of $138,624,000 to the grove owners. For over a decade, avocados have been the top value food crop in the region. San Diego is the leading avocado producing county in the nation. Avocados were first planted commercially about 1915 in the northern part of the county and that area is still the center of cultivation.

Most of the production comes from groves near Fallbrook, Vista, Lilac, Pauma Valley, and Escondido, although scattered new acreage occurs on the hills around El Cajon and Crest. The avocado does best in the upper coastal and lower transitional area climates. Many groves are situated on hills which have the advantage of cold air drainage in winter, less susceptibility to root rot, and lower land cost. Some of them are on slopes as steep as 70 percent. Most trees are watered by a drip method to individual trees, which conserves moisture (Figure 9.5). San

Figure 9.4. High demand for nursery products and decorative flowers and plants has elevated them to the leading category of "crop" produced in San Diego county.

Diego avocados are marketed fresh in urban markets that extend into eastern U.S. Recent developments in freezing have served to expand the market and some of the crop is marketed as guacamole.

Eggs were at one time the leading commodity, but now account for less than four percent of agricultural income. In 2001, over 101 million dozen were sold for a total of $48,721,000. Egg ranches tend to be located on the periphery of the urban area where land is less expensive and often are in the foothills and lower mountain areas (Figure 9.6). Climate is not of great importance except that there are no egg ranches in the desert because hens lay poorly when it is very hot. The trend has been toward fewer but larger ranches. In 1957, 47.4 million dozen eggs were

produced on 750 egg ranches, but there were just 79 in 1982, and less than that in 2001. The ranches do not hatch their own chicks but buy hens nearly ready to lay. Seven pullet ranches specialize in raising chicks from the day-old to the laying stage. A large scale of operation is necessary, and the largest ranches have housed over a million laying hens.

Fresh market tomatoes have been of major importance for the last 40 years, formerly sharing the lead for value with eggs, though more recently both have been displaced by avocados. In 1990, tomatoes returned $40,062,000 to the farmers but by 2001 this had dropped by 25 percent to $30.6 million. The mild conditions prevailing in the maritime and coastal area climates are conductive to high yields. The bulk of the

Figure 9.5. Newly planted avocado trees in DeLuz. In the lower part of the photo may be seen drip irrigation lines and pumps that mix nutrients into the irrigation water. Photo by P.R. Pryde.

county, and in third place are cucumbers.

Dairy cattle have long been important in the county. The first settlers had their family cows and by the 1880s commercial creameries had made their appearance. Sales from milk amounted to $17,532,000 in 2001, a decline of almost 30 percent in eleven years. The dairies in the county have gradually been forced farther out by urban pressure and are mostly located along river valleys in the foothills. They are most numerous in the San Pasqual Valley and along the San Luis Rey River east of I-15, and a few still exist elsewhere (Figure 9.7). The county's dairies supply only a small fraction of the local demand for fresh milk, the rest must be brought in by truck from other areas of California.

No other crop so reflects the importance of the opening of the transcontinental railroads and more epitomizes Southern California agriculture than does citrus. It was the first crop of high value which was not only able to survive the long haul to the East Coast but also grew well in the region. Mild temperatures with freedom from severe frosts and ample water were and are the major physical attractions. Today, however, it is an industry in decline in the county.

Oranges and lemons were first planted commercially in the county in 1869. Expansion was rapid and reached a peak in 1939. A postwar decline because of urbanization caused acreage to fall to only 8,200 in 1960. It subsequently rose again to a peak of 16,821 acres, but fell again in recent years to just 8,245 acres in 2001, reflecting additional urban encroachment.

In 1990, income from citrus was $102,595,000 and accounted for 40 percent of all fruits and nuts, but by 2001 income had fallen to only $64,691,000. Summer ripening Valencia oranges are the major citrus fruit in value, accounting for $27,161,000 in 2001, but Table 9.2 shows their sharp decline. Lemons, once the leader, now account for $20 million.

producing acreage occurs on the marine terraces near urbanized areas, but this is precisely where development is rapidly replacing the tomato fields. Tomatoes in the county are started under cover to conserve heat and are grown on supports. Small field sizes, especially near urban areas, lend themselves to intensive farm practices and a good deal of hand labor is required for cultivating and harvesting. Nearly all of the crop is marketed fresh, mostly in the summer and fall. Surprisingly, mushrooms are the second most widely grown "vegetable" in the

Figure 9.6. Large "egg ranch" in Japatul Valley southeast of Alpine. Photo by J. D. Blick.

The majority of the citrus acreage is found in the northern part of the county, especially in the Rancho Santa Fe, Escondido, Vista, Bonsall, Fallbrook, San Pasqual, and Pauma Valley areas. Nearly all citrus in the county occurs below 2,300 feet on the coastal side of mountains and below 1,000 feet on the desert side. Valley bottoms are hazardous sites because of air drainage-induced frost, and are generally avoided. In addition, each citrus fruit also has certain limitations and does better in some areas than others. Oranges can withstand small amounts of frost and require sun for optimum development so they are found on hilly sites inland from the ocean, mostly in the coastal cli-

mate zone and in the desert. Lemons are a little more sensitive and are either found nearer the coast or in the desert. Limes are most sensitive and are found in warm sites near Vista and Fallbrook, as are tangerines and tangelos. Grapefruit require larger amounts of heat than oranges for highest quality and are best grown in the desert, below 1,000 feet.

Strawberries have been slowly increasing in importance. From 1963 to 1990 acreage increased from 109 to 834; their value in 1990 of $21,772,000 was over 60 times that of 1963. The strawberry income has stabilized since 1990, however, totalling $20,900,000 in 2001. The income per acre for strawberries is over $34,800,

Figure 9.7. San Pasqual Valley was acquired by the City of San Diego in the 1960s as a permanent agricultural preserve. It is the largest remaining agricultural district in the county. Photo by P. R. Pryde.

greater than any crop except nursery stock and cut flowers. Acreages are small and are scattered from the border to north of Vista. They require careful cultivation and handling and fast shipment to arrive at the markets in good condition.

The importance of beef cattle is declining in the county. Many beef cattle still graze on around 100,000 acres of unirrigated rangeland in the dry interior mountains and valleys, and on an additional 3,000 acres of irrigated pasture, for an annual return of around $15,000.000. The large ranches here continue a tradition begun by the first backcountry settlers over a century ago. Today, however, pasture use is regulated, cattle are purebred, supplemental feed and water are provided and they are trucked to feedlots for fat-

tening prior to sale. Chapter 17 will note a trend towards converting some large ranches to open space preserves.

Minor Crops

During the nineteenth century, grapes were a major crop and produced many tons of raisins and barrels of wine. Extensive acreage occurred in interior locations such as Alpine, El Cajon, Japatul, and San Pasqual. In the 1920s with Prohibition, production turned to table grapes. From the mid-1930s, acreage has generally declined.

In 2001, wine grapes were grown on 180 acres. Grapes are presently grown near Escondido and Julian, where local wineries use the full

TABLE 9.2. Trends in Leading Food Crops

Crop	2001 $Value	1990 $Value
Avocados	138,624,103	138,173,700
Eggs (a)	47,958,900	61,007,500
Tomatoes	30,578,337	40,061,500
Oranges, Valencia	27,161,019	46,028,400
Lemons	20,453,450	27,667,700
Strawberries	20,904,600	21,772,100
Mushrooms	16,926,000	10,064,300
Milk (a)	16,920,800	23,871,600
Cucumbers	9,009,170	10,968,300
Grapefruit	6,673,380	
Peppers (all kinds)	4,291,990	
Tangerine, Tangelo	5,003,010	
Oranges, Navel	3,799,026	

(a) 2000 data

Sources: County of San Diego, "Crop Statistics and Annual Report", for 1990, 2000 and 2001.

production. Other wineries in the county rely on grapes purchased elsewhere.

Apples for cider and fresh sale are produced in the Julian area, where most of the 450 acres are located. Despite their being an icon of the county mountains, income from apples is not large, less than a million dollars. Olives, which were once of major importance, are not now commercially grown in the county, but some herbs are produced.

Twelve vegetables returned income sufficient to be separately listed by the County Department of Agriculture. Another seventeen are included under two miscellaneous categories. Besides those already discussed, potatoes, beans, squash, corn, and peppers each return over $1 million. All vegetables are grown with irrigation in the maritime and coastal zones, in small plots of a few acres each. The county also produces the only macadamia nuts grown in the continental United States.

The amount of cropland in field crops was 144,800 acres in 2001. Hay and wheat are the leading field crops. Since yields are low, field crops returned only $6,061,000. Irrigated field crops include mainly pasture land. Usually, if land can be irrigated, other crops of higher value will be planted.

High cost of land, feed, and labor almost preclude fryer and broiler chickens being grown in the area. However, culling of the large layer population on egg ranches results in significant sales of meat chickens. In 2001 this was about six million pounds and returned about a million dollars. Some production in hogs and pigs occurs in a few places in the backcountry, and culled eggs are an important food for hogs. Buffalo are also commercially raised in the county, as are rabbits and ostriches. Bees and honey, of great importance a century ago, still are sold and brought in over a million dollars in 2001, double the 1990 value. The value of bees as pollinators should not be forgotten. Apiaries may be seen mainly in the chaparral-covered foothills, and in orchards.

Not included in the agricultural reports, but of some interest and importance, is the raising of thoroughbred horses.

The Future

Agriculture in San Diego County will continue to face a variety of interrelated problems. Unfortunately, many result in increasing costs for the farmer and rancher. Pressures of urbanization have been instrumental in the past in causing shifts in production: dairying is gone from Mission Valley; citrus and avocados are now of little importance around metropolitan San Diego; egg ranches have moved into the backcountry. Urbanization tends to push ever further outward, former orchards now sprout subdivisions, and it may be expected that in the future agricultural lands north of Escondido may become estates for the wealthy (Figure 9.8).

Farmland was once assessed and taxed as if it were urban land, because of its proximity to nearby developments or land in a higher zoning category. Costs of production then went up and the farmer was often forced to sell or move. In order to retain land in agricultural use by keeping taxes at a lower agricultural rate, the Land Conservation (or Williamson) Act of 1965 was passed by the state legislature. Under this act, a farmer or rancher agrees to maintain his land in agricultural use for ten years, and he is taxed accordingly. He then can continue his way of life, some open space is preserved, and valuable agricultural land is kept in production. At the same time, the taxes no longer paid by the

farmer would have to be added to the tax liability of the rest of the county.

From the first agricultural preserve established in 1967 in Encinitas, a total of several hundred thousand acres have been put into preserves. The great majority of the acreage is in grazing and occurs on rough land in the interior with little arable potential. Many farmers close-in have not applied for a preserve, perhaps because they fear it will prevent them from changing their land use and realizing a sizeable profit in so doing. Also, Proposition 13 in 1978 reduced some of the property tax strain. Another assist for local agriculture was the purchase of San Pasqual valley for a permanent agricultural preserve (Figure 9.7).

Figure 9.8. Conversion of an orange grove to a future commercial subdivision in the Bonsall area, a recurring theme in many parts of the county. Photo by P. R. Pryde

The spectre of ever-increasing direct costs of production faces the agriculturalist. Significant rises in the cost of fuels and water have been felt over the past few decades. The dairymen and livestock producers face higher feed costs. Labor costs are high, and mechanization is used where feasible. Costs for land, land preparation, pesticides, equipment, and all other inputs to production continue to rise.

The greatest economic threat of all may be the rapidly escalating cost of water. San Diego area growers pay more for water than farmers in any other region in the country, and how much longer they can afford to do so is a very serious question. Increasing costs are countered to some extent by an agricultural rebate for water used by farmers, but as water costs rise this may not be adequate. There is a limit to passing higher production costs along to consumers, as this will increase competition from other crops, other agricultural regions, or foreign imports. Much of the local flower industry, for example, has been lost to foreign competition.

An interesting trend in the county is an increasing number of organic farms in the region. Organic farms offer pesticide-free crops, and often sell their fruit and produce at local "farmers markets" and roadside stands (Figure 9.9). From almost none a few decades ago, their number had grown to 418 by the year 2000. San Diego County has one of the highest concentrations of organic farms of any county in California.

Agricultural land must be considered as a nonrenewable resource—once gone, it is gone forever. In the face of increasing population and decreasing available land, it is important that San Diego County's remaining agricultural land be preserved and the health of this key industry be maintained.

References

Close, D., D. Gilbert, and G. Peterson, eds. *Climates of San Diego County, Agricultural Relationships.* San Diego: University of California, Agricultural Extension Service, 1970.

Englehardt, Z. *San Diego Mission.* San Francisco: James H. Barry Co., 1920.

Fitzsimons, E., "County Crop Value Rises 1% in Tough Year", *San Diego Union-Tribune,* June 20, 2003, pp. B-1 and B-4.

Harlow, N. *Maps of the Pueblo Lands of San Diego, 1602–1874.* Los Angeles: Dawson, 1987.

McCain, Ella, *Memories of the Early Settlements: Dulzura., Potrero, and Campo.* National City: South Bay Press, 1955.

Pourade, R. F. *Historic Ranchos of San Diego.* San Diego: Union-Tribune Publishing Co., 1969.

Pryde, P. R., "Is There Any Hope for Agriculture in California's Rapid Growth Areas?", *GeoJournal,* Vol. 6, No. 6 (1982), pp. 533–8.

Snapp-Cook, Jonathon. *Sustainable Agriculture in San Diego County: An Exploration of Organic Farmers and Their Farms.* San Diego State University: Unpublished Master's thesis, Department of Geography, 2003.

San Diego County, Department of Agriculture. *1990 Crop Statistics and Annual Report.* 1991.

San Diego County, Department of Agriculture. *2001 Crop Statistics and Annual Report.* 2002.

San Diego County Farm Bureau. *San Diego County Agricultural Fact Sheet.* 1990.

Figure 9.9. Vegetables for sale at a roadside stand. Organic farming is a fast-growing component of San Diego's agricultural economy. Photo by J. D. Blick.

Internet Connections:

San Diego County Dept. of Agriculture: *www.sdcounty.ca.gov/cnty/cntydepts/landuse/agri/*

San Diego County Farm Bureau: *www.sdfarmbureau.org*

U.S. Department of Agriculture: *www.usda.gov*

Philip R. Pryde and
Frederick P. Stutz

Chapter Ten

Working the Cities
The Regional Economic Base

San Diego, long a "sleepy Navy town" in the Southwestern corner of the United States, has undergone a radical transformation of its economic base since the 1960s. The changes which occurred in the last few decades, both structurally and functionally, have ushered it into the competitive association of "new" Pacific Rim cities, which have forged strong interdependencies in response to an information and communication intensive era. San Diego's main economic advantages are its mild climate, its excellent deep-water harbor, its technological resources, its numerous

Frederick P. Stutz, a professor of urban and transportation studies in the Department of Geography at San Diego State University, prepared this chapter for the 3rd edition; Philip R. Pryde revised it for the 4th edition.

academic institutions, and its easy access to large regional (but not necessarily national) markets.

Early Economic History and Present Status

San Diego's early economic history was largely based on agriculture, and these efforts were described in the preceding chapter. Other important economic activities, such as mining and fishing, have been discussed in chapters six and seven. A faster pace of economic growth began in 1885 when the California Southern Railroad began service to the area, at last giving it rapid access to the rest of the country. Tourism, which today accounts for more than $5 billion in regional income a year, received its first major boost with the building of the Hotel del Coronado in 1888.

San Diego began its development as a defense industry center early in the 1900's, when two groups that would become natural allies in the field—the Navy and the aircraft industry—located here. The fledgling aircraft industry was lured by the climatic advantages that allowed open air storage, reduced heating costs, and almost year-round test flights. In 1920, the United States Navy, attracted by the excellent harbor and temperate climate, built a destroyer base on San Diego Bay. These two groups would soon dominate San Diego economically. Lindbergh's Spirit of St. Louis was one of the early aircraft built here by Ryan Aeronautical Company. Ryan continued to grow, later merged with the Teledyne Corporation, and the successor company is still an important part of San Diego's economy. Another early leader in the area's aircraft industry was Consolidated Aircraft (Convair). In 1953, Convair was merged with General Dynamics Electric Boat of Groton, Connecticut, to form a separate division of what is now one of the nation's largest defense contractors. The large General Dynamics plant on Kearny Mesa, however, was closed down in the 1990s.

World War II gave a significant boost to the military-based economy. Manufacturing employment nearly doubled during the war years, with most of the increase going to the aircraft industry. Many servicemen who passed through San Diego during World War II returned once the war was over, enhancing the city's skilled labor force. Because San Diego lacked the resource base for the development of "heavy" industry, post-World War II diversification within the economy has instead been oriented toward other major fields: light manufacturing, agriculture, tourism, research, and various high technology industries.

The San Diego economy at the start of the twenty-first century was characterized by diversity, ease of entry, and low unemployment. As was previously noted, it is a relative young economy, with most of the growth occurring after World War II. The San Diego Chamber of Commerce calculated the Gross Regional Product (the size of the county's total economy) in the year 2000 to be 113.7 billion dollars (Table 10.1), and it was expected to reach 126.7 billion by the end of 2002.

Ranked internationally, San Diego's Gross Regional Product would place the county thirty-fourth among the world's nations (the state of California would be seventh). The county has approximately the same Gross Regional Product as Finland; it's about one-third that of Russia's. Per capita income in San Diego County was $30,289 in 2000.

The former image of San Diego as largely a military town is today outdated; currently the services sector and the retail trade sector both employ more people than either the military or the government (non-military) sectors. The services sector is the largest, and in 2000 employed about 400,000 persons in the county. Over the past three decades there has been considerable diversification within the regional economy, with the industrial-research base now centered around biotechnology, scientific and medical research, communication technology, and higher education.

TABLE 10.1. San Diego County: Key Economic Indicators

Indicator	1977	1987	2000
Gross Regional Product (Billion $) [a]	25.6	41.5	113.7
Population (thousands)	1,711	2,288	2,814
Per Capita Income $ [a]	13,700	16,800	30,289
Employment (thousands)	602	1,011	[b] 1,097

[a] Not adjusted for inflation.
[b] 1997 data.

Sources: California Dept. of Finance; Union-Tribune Publishing Co.

San Diego isn't a major headquarters city for very large corporations, but a number of sizable companies have their head offices in the region. Sempra Energy (the parent company of SDG&E), Gateway, and Qualcomm are among the largest and best known (Table 10.2). These three, plus the consulting-services giant Science Applications International Corporation (SAIC) were the San Diego region's four entries on the Fortune 500 list of largest American corporations for 2002.

Population growth in recent decades has been rapid. As previous chapters have noted, San Diego is now the nation's seventh largest city, and San Diego County is nation's sixth largest county. The population in the county is slightly younger than the national average, although not significantly so (32.9 years compared to 35.3 years). Eleven percent of the county's population was over sixty-five, slightly less than the national average.

Regional employment has been strong during the 1990s and in 2003 San Diego was in better shape (in terms of low unemployment) than other California metropolitan regions. For example, in March of 2003, San Diego's unemployment rate was 4.3 percent, compared to 5.8 nationally and 6.6 for all of California. Indeed, between 2000 and 2001, San Diego recorded the fifth greatest increase in number of employees and regional payroll among all counties in the United States. Total employment in the county was about 1.1 million in 1997, and grew to around 1.2 million in 2000 plus another 100,000 military personnel.

Major Economic Sectors

The most important components of San Diego's civilian economy are services, government, and retail trade, which together make up 68 percent of the county's workforce. Other important sectors, in terms of employment, include manufacturing, finance and real estate, construction, and wholesale trade (Table 10.3).

Services

The Services sector is the largest source of employment in the San Diego region. It takes in a very wide variety of occupations, from medical personnel to hair stylists to garage mechanics to attorneys to gardeners. We all make frequent use of specialists in the services sector, quite likely several times a week. Money spent in the services sector typically re-circulates throughout the community fairly quickly.

This is an important sector not only for the number of jobs it provides, but also because it provides employment for thousands of new entrants into the work force annually. It is also one of the fastest growing sectors, with an estimated employment total in 2000 of 399,200.

Government and Defense

This sector includes government agencies at all levels—city, county, state, and federal—as well as military personnel. It also includes all of the public colleges and universities in the county. Table 10.4 indicates the importance of this sector in terms of major employment centers.

TABLE 10.2. Largest San Diego Region Companies (July 2000–June 2001 gross revenue)

Rank	Company	Revenue
1	Sempra Energy	9,425,000,000
2	Gateway	8,655,226,000
3	Qualcomm	2,672,748,000
4	Jack in the Box	1,785,062,000
5	Titan	1,096,430,000
6	Calloway Golf	853,799,000
7	Advanced Marketing Serv.	712,367,000
8	Peregrine Systems	642,403,000
9	Factory 2-U Stores	595,695,000
10	Invitrogen	511,241,000
11	Cubic	508,570,000
12	PriceSmart	448,432,000

Source: San Diego Union-Tribune, Oct. 30, 2001.

TABLE 10.3. Employment by Jurisdiction and Industry: 2000

	Agriculture and Mining	Construction	Manufacturing	Transportation Communication & Utilities	Wholesale Trade	Retail Trade	Finance, Insurance and Real Estate	Services	Government
Carlsbad	279	1669	9750	1483	3893	9253	2787	14990	3604
Chula Vista	165	1378	6051	1810	2069	11794	2290	11727	8814
Coronado		85		112	49	2005	370	3465	5299
Del Mar		253			40	1116	192	1709	
El Cajon		4380	6149		1673	9262	1341	8034	6943
Encinitas	1240	1253	349	180	416	6168	753	9008	2289
Escondido	552	6266	3578	1115	1664	12606	1726	13996	5508
Imperial Beach		112			28	686	172	712	1124
La Mesa		1740	201	344	202	7396	1531	9798	1493
Lemon Grove		639	317		97	2099	224	2585	
National City		1204	2318	509	1182	6559	718	4932	1175
Oceanside	1178	2004	4303	551	1247	8560	1635	11089	6674
Poway	73	2815	3017	485	899	3492	424	6376	2236
San Diego	1806	24730	74280	36404	28785	110411	48496	258268	129657
San Marcos		3231	6530	1409	2222	4378	719	6295	4227
Santee	75	3133	2121		1034	3208	400	2029	1504
Solana Beach		736	118	92	133	2187	866	2757	
Vista	130	2635	6895	381	2448	5284	1022	7904	4703
Unincorp	6275	11737	3095	4290	2919	10636	3834	23526	18558
Region Total	11800	70000	129200	50800	51000	217100	69500	399200	206600

Source: SANDAG.

Note: Some data may be suppressed for confidentiality reasons.

TABLE 10.4. Largest Employers in San Diego County in 2001

Rank	Employer	Workforce
1	US Navy—active duty	150,000
2	US Navy—civilian	52,000
3	County of San Diego	18,000
4	UCSD	17,800
5	City of San Diego	13,000
6	Qualcomm	10,000
7	Sharp Health Care	10,000
8	San Diego Unified School District	10,000
9	SDSU	8,056
10	Scripps Health	7,700
11	US Postal Service	7,000
12	Pacific Bell	6,000
13	Kaiser Permanente	5,800
14	Vons	5,200
15	Sea World	5,000
16	Sony	4,000
17	UCSD Health Care	3,700
18	Childrens Hospital	3,500
19	SAIC	3,300
20	Palomar-Pomerado Health	3,300
21	Sempra Energy (SDG&E)	3,200
22	Home Depot	3,100
23	USD	3,100
24	Target Corporation	3,000
25	Solar	2,900

Source: San Diego Regional Chamber of Commerce.

The defense industry has been a driving force behind the regional economy for decades. Total military spending in San Diego County totaled $13.6 billion in 2002, a 30 per cent increase in one year. San Diego County ranked third in the United States in terms of defense contracts received, at $4.6 billion. The local defense industry has been bolstered in recent years by the transfer of the U.S. Space and Naval Warfare Systems Command to San Diego.

San Diego weathered the 1990s without the base-closure upheavals experienced by other defense-oriented cities. Only one local base was closed (the Navy Recruit Depot near Lindbergh Field), and as of 2003 no other bases were targeted for closure. The largest military base in the county is Camp Pendleton, but far more visible are the naval ships at bases in National City and Coronado (Figure 10.1).

Non-military government employment in 2000 stood at 206,600. In addition, there were approximately 200,000 military personnel in the county, of which three-quarters were uniformed personnel and one-quarter civilians (Table 10.4).

Manufacturing

Manufacturing in the county is a larger employer than might be guessed, as many of the larger manufacturing enterprises are located in industrial parks that are not visible from the main freeways. The largest manufacturing companies in the region are Gateway, Qualcomm, Titan, and Calloway (Table 10.2). Total manufacturing employment in the county declined slightly between 1990 and 2000, from 134,000 to 129,000; part of the reason for this would be the closing of the large General Dynamics plant on Kearny Mesa.

In the important "high technology" sector of San Diego's economy (which includes both manufacturing and research and development activities), the fastest growing components during the 1990s were communications equipment, biotechnology, pharmaceuticals, and computer software. The only major decline occurred in defense manufacturing. The technology sector is assisted by research activities carried out at the region's major universities. In addition, the large military research and development effort should not be overlooked, as typified by the Naval Ocean Systems Center located on Point Loma.

Figure 10.1. Many Navy ships, such as these docked at the North Island Naval Air Station, are home-ported on San Diego Bay. Photo by P. R. Pryde.

Tourism

Tourism is not reported separately as an employment sector, but it is such a significant revenue generator for the San Diego region that it merits a separate discussion. This is an important "industry" because it brings in mainly outside money that greatly stimulates the economy. In 2002, an estimated 26.2 million visitors came to San Diego, of which 15 million stayed overnight. They spent an estimated $5.04 billion dollars in the county. It has been estimated that over 120,000 persons locally are employed in businesses that cater to tourists. Most of this employment would be included in the totals for the Services and Retail Trade sectors.

Tourism means any one who can be lured to San Diego, and includes two major components: regular tourists (families and others) who are here for sightseeing and pleasure, and convention and special event attendees.

The "regular" tourists are attracted by both natural assets such as the beaches, surf, climate, deserts, and mountains, as well as constructed attractions such as the Zoo and Wild Animal Park, Sea World, Legoland, golf courses, and more recently, casinos. With San Diego's climate,

tourism is a year-round business asset, and one that is remarkably little effected by business cycles. Another relatively new and rapidly expanding phenomenon are cruise ships, whose visits to the harbor increased from 16 in 1996 to 120 in 2002. In the latter year, the cruise ships brought in 307,000 visitors.

In terms of conventions, the enlargement of the Convention Center in the late 1990s has made a significant difference (Figure 10.2). San Diego now ranks first in California with 331 convention events in 2001; San Francisco (247), Anaheim (233), and Los Angeles (149) trailed behind. This provides a significant boost to the regional economy, with special benefits to hotels and restaurants; a study in 2002 concluded that conventioneers spent $184 million on lodging and $94 million on food and beverages in a single year. San Diego's hotel occupancy rate of around 68 percent was the third highest in the nation, behind only New York City and Oahu. The San Diego Convention and Visitors Bureau estimates that the downtown convention center alone hosted 332,000 visitors in 2002.

Special events include such periodic major activities as the Super Bowl, the America's Cup,

Figure 10.2. The new San Diego Convention Center on Harbor Drive. Photo by P. R. Pryde.

major golf and tennis matches, and the Del Mar race track and fairgrounds. Although most of these events occur at most once a year (and the first two less frequently), they provide a major economic stimulus while they are happening.

Retail and Wholesale Trade

Employment in these two sectors is reported separately, with 51,000 jobs in the wholesale component and 217,000 in retail trade in 2000 (Table 10.3). Together, they represent the second largest employment category. Although this sector is also an important one for providing entry-level employment, it is also one that is highly susceptible to adverse consequences from periodic downturns in the business cycle. Since a large segment of it caters to neighborhood customers (grocery stores, gas stations, etc.), it provides dispersed and localized employment and shopping opportunities that don't require lengthy commutes.

Construction

The Construction sector is one of the most visible, with new building seemingly going up everywhere. Employment in this sector was about 70,000 in 2000, or around six percent of the county total, but varies considerably from year to year depending on the state of the overall economy. This sector includes the major sub-contractors that are employed by the large building firms, and is a major supporter of the services and retail trade sectors.

New housing units continue to be completed in the thousands annually, mainly in North County, downtown San Diego, and East Chula Vista. However, in 2003 the most impressive focus of new construction was the East Village redevelopment district around the new baseball stadium (Figure 10.3). Chula Vista is also planning a major development of its Bayfront district (between E and F streets west of I-5).

Figure 10.3. Construction of the new San Diego Padres baseball stadium, and an adjacent new hotel, in the East Village redevelopment district. Photo by P. R. Pryde

Other Sectors

Grouped together into a single statistical category are the many financial, insurance, and real estate enterprises. These employ mainly professional people, and therefore do not provide many entry-level jobs. In 2000 these types of businesses collectively employed 69,500 persons.

Also grouped together statistically are the transportation, communication, and utility industries. These provide us with everything from water to electricity to trolley rides to long-distance telephone service. Lindbergh Field is one of the major employers in this sector, as is PacBell (SBC) and other communication companies. Collectively these businesses employed 50,800 persons.

The smallest statistical category is Agriculture and Mining, accounting for 11,800 jobs in 2000. Total employment in this sector varied only slightly during the 1990s, but has shown a long-term decline. With urbanization, agricultural output has shifted over the past two decades from an emphasis on field crops to being dominated by landscaping and ornamental plants. Agriculture in the county is described in Chapter 9, and mining in Chapter 6.

The International Component of San Diego's Economy

San Diego's international connections can be described under two main headings: exports to other countries, and daily cross-border economic interactions with Baja California.

The county's international trade is impressive, with over ten billion dollars in total exports going to foreign countries. Imports into the county are about 80 percent higher than exports, however. As would be expected, the largest single customer is Mexico, with about 43 percent of exports, followed at some distance by Canada, Japan, and the United Kingdom (Table 10.5). The largest customer in Europe, somewhat surprisingly, is the Netherlands, followed by France and Germany. In the Far East, South Korea ranks second behind Japan, followed by Singapore and Taiwan. The two main categories of exports are Electric and Electronic Equipment, and Industrial Machines and Computers; together they account for almost half of all exports.

The cross-border trade with Mexico is far greater than the average San Diegan probably realizes. Around the turn of the new century, up to 163,000 persons crossed the border daily at Tijuana and Otay Mesa (this figure declined somewhat after 2001). A survey in the 1980s showed that four-fifths of the border crossers lived in Tijuana and were commuting to jobs in the San Diego region. Most of these workers crossed daily, or at least more than once a week.

A fifth of those interviewed said they were crossing specifically to shop in the San Diego area. Sixty percent of these said they shopped in the U.S. at least once a week. Annually, they spend over a billion dollars in the county. The economic impact of this is huge, especially at retail stores near the border in San Ysidro and Chula Vista, many of whom employ bilingual salespersons. It has been suggested that the ratio of spending by Mexicans

TABLE 10.5. Leading Countries for San Diego Exports

Importing Country	Percent of County Exports
Mexico	43.0
Canada	10.2
Japan	5.7
United Kingdom	5.0
South Korea	3.7
Netherlands	3.5
France	2.9
Germany	2.4
Singapore	2.3
Australia	1.7
Taiwan	1.6
Others	17.9

Source: San Diego Chamber of Commerce.

in San Diego County, compared to spending by Americans in Mexico, is on the order of ten to one.

Energy for the Region

Energy is the lifeblood of industrialized societies. The San Diego region utilizes three main types of energy: electricity, and liquid and gaseous hydrocarbons. Most of our electricity is produced locally, but a great deal of what we use is also imported. All of the petroleum and natural gas products, including all the fuels used to run our electric power plants, must also be imported. Thus, it is important for San Diegans to be aware that almost all energy used in the region comes from outside; we are, literally, at the end of the pipeline.

Almost all the county's hydrocarbon energy supplies are imported into the region via pipelines in the form of either natural gas or refined petroleum products (mostly gasoline and fuel oil). The

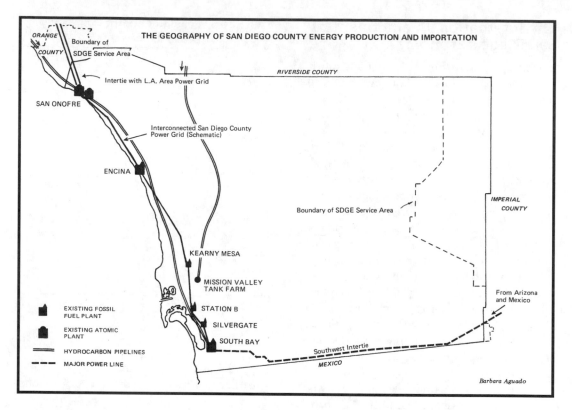

Figure 10.4. Energy sources and production sites in San Diego County. The Station B power plant no longer operates.

main exception is the uranium fuel that operates the reactors at the San Onofre Nuclear Generating Station. Coal is virtually unused in the county.

The liquid hydrocarbons arrive in a "products pipeline" from the Los Angeles area that terminates at the tank farm in Murphy Canyon just north of the stadium. The natural gas also arrives from the Los Angeles area in pipelines which parallel the I-5 and I-15 corridors (Figure 10.4). Most of the natural gas is used to heat our homes and businesses; a smaller amount is used in SDG&E's fossil fuel power plants. In 2003, Sempra Energy was negotiating with Mexico to build a large liquefied natural gas plant on the

coast south of Tijuana. The fuel oil is used both as a secondary fuel in the power plants, and as a source of on-site heat or electricity by private companies. We all know where the gasoline goes; the fact that it must be imported via pipelines accounts for some, but not all, of its high price here.

The electricity that we import comes from three sources: excess energy generated at the Palo Verde nuclear plant in Arizona, the same from the Cerro Prieto geothermal plant south of Mexicali, and power purchased on a variable basis from producers elsewhere in California and the Pacific Northwest. The first two are imported over the large high-voltage line that can be seen in places along I-8 in the desert. We will continue to import much of our electricity, as only limited new power plants are being proposed for construction within the county. One such plant was being proposed at the time of this writing for the Otay Mesa area. At the same time, the large South Bay plant in Chula Vista was being proposed for closure.

There is widespread agreement, at the philosophical level at least, that we should substitute renewable energy sources for fossil fuel ones wherever possible. We lack major rivers to produce hydroelectric power, and we don't have the high average wind speeds necessary for large scale wind generators (wind warms were built in the county in the 1980s, but weren't economically successful). However, we do have an abundance of sunshine. The San Diego region could be doing much more with solar energy than it is.

Solar energy can be used in three main ways. The most common is for solar hot water heating, and such systems are in use on thousands of homes in the county. It is likely that most every home in the county could save money from their use. The second way to use solar radiation is for space heating of homes and buildings. This is most feasibly done when a home is first being constructed (retrofitting is very expensive), and can provide 80 to 90 percent of home heating needs. When incorporated into new homes, it is very cost effective.

The third system involves the direct conversion of solar energy to electrical energy. This can be done in several ways, but the simplest is by use of what are called photovoltaic ("PV") cells. One individual cell does not produce very much current, but when hundreds of them are hooked together, the results are significant. If the south-facing roof of the average home were covered with PV cells, they could produce enough electricity to meet normal household needs (assuming, of course, that not everyone wanted to run a

hair drier and toaster oven at the same time). Pilot photovoltaic projects have been built in the county over the last three decades, the largest of which was constructed atop Mt. Laguna in the late 1970s (Figure 10.5). At the time, it was the largest PV installation in the world. By 2003, efforts were being made to expand the use of PV cells in the San Diego region, but overall their use is still very limited. This is a major San Diego industry waiting to be born.

In April of 2003, San Diego Gas and Electric issued a report warning of a possible energy shortfall by 2007. It said it would try to meet this challenge in four ways: reducing demand by conservation measures, increased use of renewable resources, new transmission lines to import more electricity into the county, and new electrical generating plants. San Diego will never be "energy independent", but we should strive to be more energy-efficient, and expand our use of renewable energy resources, as much as possible. In an uncertain world where we are at the end of the pipeline, it is very much in our best self-interest to do so.

In summary, the economy of the San Diego region at the turn of the twenty-first century is quite healthy, arguably the healthiest in California, and is favorably positioned for the future. This is because the economy is strongly oriented towards growth sectors such as information technology, computers, and biotechnology, augmented by a highly respected university research establishment. Also, the economy is developing stronger ties with the Pacific Rim countries, the tourism industry is strong and growing, and outside investor interest in the region remains high. San Diego will continue to benefit from the military presence, and the supply of workers is adequate to meet regional needs. The region's economy should be able to weather the occasional economic slowdown, and in good economic times realize a high level of prosperity.

Figure 10.5. A portion of the demonstration photovoltaic electricity facility on Mt. Laguna. Photo taken in 1979 by P. R. Pryde.

References

Bigelow, B. V. "Defense Spending Here Has Shifted", *San Diego Union-Tribune*, April 15, 2003, pp. C1 and C5.

Dickerson, M. "San Diego Is on the Rise with Help from Developers, Tech", *San Diego Union-Tribune*, January 2, 2003, pp. C1 and C2.

Kinsman, M., "San Diego Getaway Still a Popular Choice", *San Diego Union-Tribune*, February 27, 2003, pp. C1 and C4.

Millar, M., "The Whole World Has Interests in San Diego", *San Diego Union-Tribune,* May 19, 1991, pp. 1, 6 and 7.

Rose, C. D., "SDG&E Tells Its Strategy for Meeting Power Needs", *San Diego Union-Tribune,* April 17, 2003, pp. C1 and C8.

San Diego Association of Governments (SANDAG). *Creating Prosperity: San Diego Regional Economic Prosperity Strategy*. San Diego: SANDAG, undated (ca. 1998).

San Diego Association of Governments (SANDAG). *Demographic and Economic Forecast 1960–2010.* San Diego: SANDAG, Source Point, 1987.

San Diego Association of Governments (SANDAG). *Indicators of Sustainable Competitiveness: San Diego Region.* San Diego: SANDAG, June, 2002.

San Diego Regional Chamber of Commerce, Economic Research Bureau. *San Diego 2002 Regional Economic Overview.* San Diego: Greater San Diego Chamber of Commerce, 2002.

Union-Tribune Publishing Company. *Review of San Diego's Business Activity, 1990. San Diego: Union-Tribune* Publishing Co., 1990.

Washburn, D., "Defense Spending Soars in County", *San Diego Union-Tribune,* September 18, 2003, pp. C-1 and C-5.

Internet Connections:

San Diego Association of Governments (SANDAG): *www.sandag.org*

San Diego Regional Chamber of Commerce: *www.sdchamber.org*

San Diego Regional Economic Development Corporation: *www.sandiegobusiness.org*

Unified Port District: *www.portofsandiego.org*

Chapter Eleven

Imre E. Quastler and
Philip R. Pryde

San Diegans on the Move
Transportation in the County

Transportation has always been a matter of concern to San Diego County residents. To some local Indian groups, for example, access to fishing grounds via water transportation was important well before Columbus' first voyage. With the coming of European settlement in 1769, the area's relative inaccessibility, both from Mexico and later from the rest of the United States, was long a major factor in the development of what is now San Diego County. Certainly one of the main concerns of county residents in the second half of the

nineteenth century was how to improve access to the rest of California and the nation.

Beginning with the twentieth century, local human settlement patterns have been strongly influenced by transportation modes, first by the streetcar and later by the private automobile. Each change in dominant mode has been associated with new problems, as, for example, automotive exhaust emissions. Currently, there is much discussion about the possible future directions of public transportation investments in the county, including the expansion of a rail rapid transit system and the possible need for a new site for the county's major commercial airport. The abundance of these questions and the widespread interest they arouse assure that transportation will remain an important topic of local public debate.

Imre E. Quastler is a professor emeritus of transportation studies in the Department of Geography at San Diego State University. He authored the first four sections of this chapter; Philip R. Pryde prepared the last two sections for this edition.

Regional transportation planning involves some very complex issues, and we still do not have answers to many of even the most basic questions. To illustrate, what is meant by the often used statement that a particular transportation innovation has been *successful*? Should success be measured primarily in terms of air pollution, accessibility to jobs, or numbers of riders diverted from their cars? Perhaps a broader definition, such as a transportation change that leads to a measurable improvement in some indicators of the quality of life over the long run would be more acceptable. Rather than try to give definite answers to these larger questions, the main goal of this discussion is more modest. It will be simply to provide a chronological outline of local transportation developments since Indian times and to raise, in the process, some pertinent questions about the influence of transportation on people in San Diego County.

Period I, Before 1769

Before 1769, the sole residents of present-day San Diego County were various Indian tribes and bands. Perhaps the most sophisticated mode of transportation available to these Indians were "tule balsas" (rafts built of reeds), the standard water craft for Indians along much of California's Pacific coast. This mode was evidently used primarily in lagoons and bays, both for fishing and for personal transportation. Tule balsas may also have been used for short ocean trips, for some trade was carried on between local Indians and groups in the Channel Islands. It appears that most longer distance Indian trade was carried on in an east-west pattern, for there is evidence that contact was also maintained with Indians in the deserts to the east. Overland transportation was of the most basic type, including walking for personal transportation and carrying goods in nets. The horse was not available to local Indians until after 1769.

Although California was not settled by Europeans until late in the eighteenth century, the first explorers came to San Diego Bay only fifty years after Columbus' first voyage. In 1542 Juan Rodriguez Cabrillo sailed into the bay from the south, and sixty years later Sebastian Vizcaino explored California's coast. Other Spanish vessels, notably the yearly Manila Galleon, sailed the coast during these early years, but there is no convincing evidence that they landed in present-day San Diego County. Thus, the two earliest visits were probably not repeated for well over 150 years; in fact, until 1769, all of California remained a remote and poorly defined part of Spanish America.

California's isolation and lack of European settlement before 1769 can be ascribed, above all, to problems of transportation. It was extremely difficult and costly to reach this area from New Spain (Mexico), the base from which California was explored and later settled. Headwinds were encountered for a long distance along the coast, and much desolate countryside intervened between Upper California and settled portions of Mexico. Although the sea route was difficult, the land route was even more so. Particularly before the systematic settlement of Baja California, overland travel from Mexico involved a long and arduous journey through an area of few watering holes and many hostile Indians.

Period II, 1769–1847

Throughout California's Spanish and Mexican period, most contact with the outside world was maintained by sea. In spite of the difficulties of navigation, this was the easiest way to maintain ties with external areas. Sailing vessels from San Blas in Mexico came regularly from 1769 to 1810, bringing various supplies needed in San Diego. From the start, San Diego's port was one of the more important in the province; since San

Diego Bay is one of three excellent natural harbors in California (along with Humboldt and San Francisco Bays). Within the bay, ships would unload not at docks but, rather, vessels would lie at anchor off the shore and small boats would be used to load and unload commodities. An advantage of San Diego Bay was that ships could anchor in deep water close to shore. Such were the conditions when the *Betsey,* the first American ship to visit San Diego, stopped by for wood and water in 1800.

Early in the nineteenth century, ocean ties with Mexico began to be supplemented by regular visitors from other nations. Between 1800 and 1828, thirty-one merchant ships arrived at San Diego, of which sixteen were American. The Russian brig *Baikal* visited San Diego every year between 1825 and 1830. Most of the earlier arrivals were in the sea otter and whaling trades, but by the 1820s the hide and tallow trade with New England became California's chief contact with the outside world. This trade received widespread publicity in the United States with the publication of Richard Henry Dana's *Two Years Before the Mast.* The New England traders brought to California a wide variety of products, and their vessels have since been referred to as floating department stores. Dana's ship called at San Diego several times in 1835, and he made some interesting observations about the settlement. Of the bay he said the following:

> For landing and taking on board hides, San Diego is decidedly the best place in California. The harbour is small and landlocked; there is no surf; the vessels lie within a cable's length of the beach, and the beach itself is smooth, hard sand, without rocks or stones. For these reasons it is used by all the vessels in the trade as a depot; and indeed, it would be impos-

sible, when loading with the cured hides for the passage home, to take them on board at any of the open ports, without getting them wet in the surf, which would spoil them (Dana, p. 120).

He also described the hide-houses that had been constructed there by a number of Boston trading firms. In San Diego the crews could also relax, for the ships were relatively safe from damaging winds, in contrast to other ports such as San Pedro and Santa Barbara.

During this period, long distance overland transportation in California was relatively simple, as it had to be considering the condition of roads. Even the famous El Camino Real, which traversed the county along the coast, was undoubtedly little more than a cart trail. The main modes of overland transportation were the saddle horse, the oxdrawn carreta (wagon) and the mule train.

Several important overland explorations crossed what is now San Diego County during this period (Figure 11. 1). After helping to establish the San Diego Mission, Gaspar de Portola continued exploring north to the vicinity of San Francisco Bay. Pedro Fages of the San Diego Presidio explored the Borrego desert via Coyote Canyon in 1772. Two years later he was followed by Captain Juan Bautista de Anza. Satisfied with his initial exploration, de Anza crossed the Borrego desert and proceeded northward in 1775 with a large group of soldiers and settlers, some of whom later helped to found San Francisco.

As described by Dana, San Diego was certainly no more than a small village. As such, it can be assumed that almost all transportation within the village was on foot or by horse; the distances involved would hardly have warranted much else. Dana also noted that horses could be rented cheaply for trips in the immediate

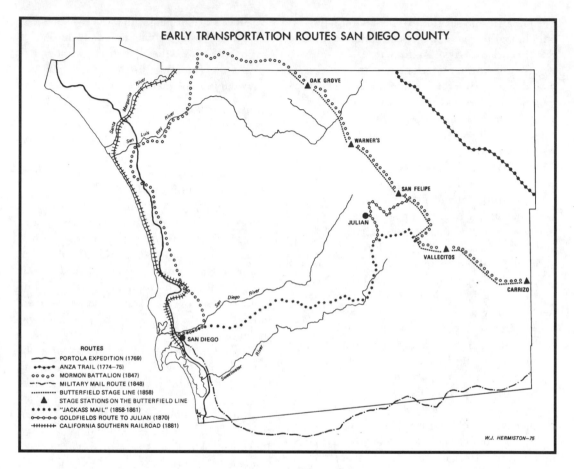

Figure 11.1.

vicinity. Evidently by the 1830s horses were so common that almost anyone could afford to keep one or more.

Period III, 1848–1880

The American takeover of California led to a number of important changes in transportation. For one, the whole orientation of the former province was altered from a view toward the south to eastward and northerly links with the rest of the United States. It is not surprising, therefore, that pressure for improved overland transportation connections soon increased. Both rail and road connections were sought, but the main effort was to attract a transcontinental railroad and thereby to make San Diego the metropolis and major port of southern California. As no railroad had actually been built by 1880, this can also be characterized as a time of paper railroads.

While community attention was focused particularly on railroads, in practice most important external ties remained via the sea.

Water links to California improved impressively with the American takeover and the Gold Rush. One of the most important innovations was the fast and reliable steamship, the first of which arrived in San Diego in 1849. The predominant destination for vessels coming to California was San Francisco, but by an act of Congress (1847), San Diego was made a point for mail pickup and delivery for the subsidized Pacific Mail Steamship Company. Of greater practical significance were the coastal sailing vessels and steamers out of San Francisco, which started service to San Diego in 1851. By 1854, the California Steam Navigation Company started to serve the bay, a service continued for decades by this company and succeeding firms. In 1880, the Pacific Coast Steamship Company was scheduling a steamer to San Diego every fifth day, handling both passengers and freight.

The first wharf in San Diego Bay was built in 1850, near what is today the intersection of Market Street and the Pacific Highway, and lasted until 1860. In the late 1860s two new wharves were built in San Diego, and National City also had one by 1871. The latter was used by the cargo/passenger vessels of the Pacific Mail Steamship Company until just after World War I. Lumber and coal were the leading commodities brought in by sea during this period. In addition, many hardware items and "notions" were sent here from San Francisco. As roads in the vicinity were poor, there was also a moderate amount of intracity water transportation in the 1860s and 1870s, primarily between San Diego and National City.

With the Gold Rush, Americans brought to California large Concord stages and freighting wagons that soon largely replaced the older Mexican equipment. As no gold was found in San Diego County prior to 1870, however, no important overland immigrant route came here. Intercity roads remained sparse; an 1869 map shows but two relatively important roads in present-day San Diego County. One extended along the coast from San Diego to Los Angeles via San Luis Rey, while the second came over the mountains from Yuma via the San Felipe Valley, Warner's Ranch, and the San Luis Rey River, and followed the route pioneered by the Mormon Battalion in 1847. In the 1870s, four privately owned toll roads were in operation in the eastern part of San Diego County.

The first overland connection to San Diego was a military mail run from Yuma, started in 1848 (Figure 11.1), which in part went through Mexico. The earliest scheduled overland service to San Diego was started in 1857 on a monthly basis as Birch's stage line from San Antonio, and constituted the first transcontinental stage service. In 1858, this service was taken over by John Butterfield's "Great Overland Mail," and it was changed to a Tipton (Mo.) to San Francisco route which bypassed San Diego. The fifty miles from the Vallecitos stage station into San Diego then had to be handled by mules; hence the famous name "jackass mail." Seeley and Wright also ran a stage line between San Diego and Los Angeles, taking two days, starting in 1867 and lasting until the coming of the railroad.

San Diego railroad efforts between 1848 and 1880 were largely centered around the proposed southern transcontinental, or 32nd parallel, route. Such a route had long been discussed at the national level, commonly with a terminus in San Diego. A far less attractive alternative was for a coastal railroad to San Francisco, connecting there with a transcontinental line. A basic problem was that only enough capital could be raised in a place like San Diego to secure a charter and to do some surveying. Thus, it was imperative for community leaders to solicit outside capital.

The first of the so-called railroad "booms" began in 1854, when the incredibly named San Diego & Gila Southern Pacific & Atlantic was organized to follow the 32nd parallel route east. A preliminary survey was carried out, but the lack of funds prevented further progress.

The second San Diego railroad boom extended from 1869 to 1873, when it began to look as if the county would finally get its transcontinental line. This boom started in 1869 when plans for the Memphis, El Paso and Pacific (MEP&P) line to San Diego were widely publicized, but the MEP&P went bankrupt in 1870. Hopes were revived in 1871 when a group of entrepreneurs obtained a charter for the Texas and Pacific (T&P) Railroad to build a line from Marshall, Texas, to San Diego. Before the project had made much headway, however, the Panic of 1873 intervened, making it impossible to market T&P bonds.

While these plans were being made the leaders of California's Southern Pacific (SP) were making competing plans to build eastward along the T&P's projected route. The interests that controlled the SP were closely identified with the cities along San Francisco Bay. The last thing this powerful group wanted was the development of a competing deepwater port in San Diego. In the ensuing struggle over the 32nd parallel route, the Southern Pacific was the winner, and the T&P was operated no farther west than El Paso. The SP route followed the relatively easy gradients via Beaumont and Indio to Yuma. This ensured that San Diego would not be the terminus of a transcontinental route and also contributed greatly to the growth of Los Angeles. By 1876, Los Angeles was connected by rail to San Francisco and the national railroad network, thus gaining an advantage in its urban rivalry with San Diego that it would never relinquish.

By the late seventies San Diego's leaders began to recognize that a direct connection eastward via the SP or T&P was unlikely. As a result, they began to pursue alternate railroad plans. In particular, hopes began to revive when it became clear that the Santa Fe (SF) Railroad would soon build a line to California. Community railroad strategy was therefore quickly revised to try to convince Santa Fe officials to locate their main terminus on San Diego Bay. These efforts were led by the Kimballs of National City, who envisioned their city as the actual terminus. In 1879 they persuaded the SF leadership to build from Yuma to San Diego Bay, but ultimately the Santa Fe decided on a more northerly route into the state via Needles and San Bernardino. Thus, a new agreement was worked out under which the SF was to support the construction of the California Southern (CS) Railroad between National City and San Bernardino. By the end of this period, however, no actual construction had taken place.

The largest community in the county in 1880 was San Diego, which had a population of only 2,637. As a result, major investments in urban transportation were unneeded, and most people moved around town on foot, supplemented by buggies. Essentially, however, by 1880 urban transportation was but little advanced beyond what it had been during the Spanish and Mexican periods.

Period IV, 1881–1929

This period can be described as a time of streetcar and railroad dominance in San Diego County. The completion of the first railroad link in 1881 contributed greatly to the real estate and population boom of the middle eighties. This population growth was so substantial by the late eighties that major private investments in public urban transportation systems also began to be feasible.

Initial railroad construction began in June, 1881, when work was started on the California Southern Railroad. Progress was rapid, and by the following year the first trains began to operate from Colton to National City. The route followed the coast northward to Oceanside, where it turned inland along the Santa Margarita River (up Temecula Canyon) and on through the Perris Valley to Colton (Figure 11.1). Fallbrook was one of the towns that developed rapidly with the coming of this railroad. In 1883 the CS was continued to San Bernardino, and by 1885 it had been extended to Barstow, where a connection was finally made with the Santa Fe. In November, 1885, the first transcontinental passenger train arrived in San Diego, and a dream of at least three decades was finally realized.

Unfortunately for local leaders, the completion of this link did not prove to be the great boon that was anticipated. In the first few years of its existence, the Southern Pacific refused to interchange traffic with the CS. By the time the line was finally completed, Los Angeles had such a head start in urban growth that it was the logical main terminus for the Santa Fe. Thus, Los Angeles and not San Diego was the prime "beneficiary" of the famous boon of the 1880s, when low railroad fares from eastern points contributed to an enormous influx of people.

In addition, the location of the line through Temecula Canyon proved to be a major mistake. Thirty miles of line were washed out for nine months in a winter storm in 1884. An alternate line along the coast to Los Angeles was finished in 1888 and when the rebuilt line through Temecula Canyon was again washed out in 1891, it was abandoned. The portion of it to Fallbrook was retained as a branch; another branch to Escondido was finished in 1887. The Santa Fe later moved its shops and offices, initially located in the San Diego area, to San Bernardino and Los Angeles. Thus, the CS line between Los Angeles and San Diego became little more than a branch.

This period also saw the construction of two other intercity railroads. In 1889 work began on the San Diego, Cuyamaca & Eastern (SDC&E); this was planned as the long sought direct line to the East. That year the line was opened to La Mesa, El Cajon and Lakeside (Figure 11.2). It was soon extended another three miles to Foster (near San Vicente Reservoir), but that is as far east as the SDC&E ever got.

In 1906, interests associated with the Southern Pacific began to take active steps to build the San Diego & Arizona Railroad. Because of some delays, the line was not completed to El Centro until 1919. This railroad followed a winding and difficult route via Tijuana, Tecate and the famous Carrizo Gorge. It is ironic that the formerly hostile Southern Pacific finally provided the county with its long-sought direct line to the East. By 1906 the SP had new management and was no longer interested in "protecting" the ports on San Francisco Bay.

Although this was a period of railroad dominance in San Diego County, water transportation continued to play an important role. In fact, most of the materials needed to build the California Southern Railroad were brought in by ocean vessels. It even appears possible that through the first half of this period, San Diego had the busiest port in southern California, as much traffic for Los Angeles was evidently transshipped here. In 1887, steamers brought 60,152 passengers to San Diego, which probably compared favorably with the numbers that came by rail. The port's importance declined dramatically, however, with the completion of the artificial harbor at Los Angeles in 1912.

Scheduled passenger service by water evidently started in 1885 with the first ferry operation to

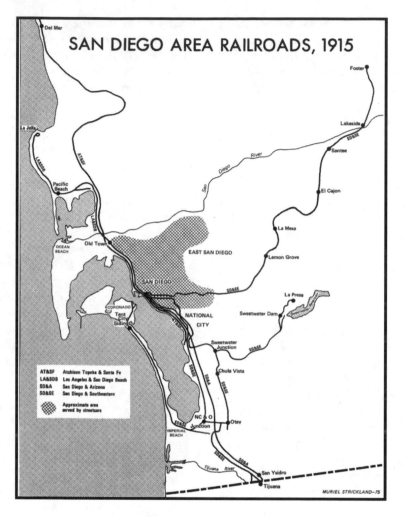

Figure 11.2.

Coronado. By 1888 a steamer provided regular services from downtown San Diego to Roseville, La Playa and Ballast Point. Runs to the Point Loma area lasted until 1919, when they were replaced by a trolley line. The ferry service to Coronado was the longest-lived, not to be replaced (by the Coronado Bridge) until 1969.

The years 1881–1929 also saw the construction of much intraurban rail mileage. With the rapid population growth of the 1880s, the outlines of the present city began to take shape, and average trip lengths increased. Construction of streetcar, cable car, and "steam interurban" lines proceeded rapidly in the late 1880s. By the early years of the next decade, the San Diego metropolitan area was interlaced with a considerable mileage of rail passenger lines (Figure 11.2).

The initial major investments were for horse-drawn streetcars. The first such line (1884) was the Coronado Beach Railroad, which ran between the ferry landing in Coronado and the Hotel Del Coronado, then under construction. Two years later horsecars were operating in San Diego, and by 1887 the first (albeit short-lived) electric streetcar line was in operation (Figure 11.3). In the late eighties and early nineties, many competing passenger lines were built, and in 1890 San Diego even constructed a cable car line from downtown to the bluffs on Adams Avenue overlooking Mission Valley. In 1891 the San Diego Electric Railway (SDER) was organized, and eventually most streetcar lines were brought under its control. Much of the streetcar mileage

was actually built in conjunction with real estate developments. An interesting example of real estate-transportation interaction was provided by a Coronado real estate company, which gave 120 single-trip tickets per month for a year on the Coronado Ferry, the Coronado Railroad, and the SDER to anyone who spent $1,000 on land bought from the company.

Perhaps as interesting as the streetcars were the steam-powered interurban lines that were built in and near the city of San Diego. These were primarily passenger lines, providing service over somewhat greater distances than was normal for streetcars. Two such lines were started during 1887 from downtown San Diego, one to Old Town (later extended to Pacific

Figure 11.3. Streetcar of the San Diego Electric Railway Company at 5th and Market, September 1892. Photograph courtesy of Historical Collection, San Diego Historical Society.

Beach and La Jolla), and one to National City and Sweetwater Dam. In 1888, the Coronado Railroad was extended around the bay via the Silver Strand to San Diego. Because of flood damage and competition from trolley lines, cars and buses, much of this mileage had been abandoned by 1920.

Early in the twentieth century, rail passenger systems began to be supplemented by highway transportation. This change reached important proportions in the decade 1910–20, but during the next decade it became more like a flood. Public transportation agencies were soon hard-pressed to retain their customers in the face of competition from the private automobile. By the early 1920s, mass production techniques made new cars available at remarkably low prices, and the shift from public to private transportation began to accelerate.

The rapidly increasing role of highway transportation necessitated a road paving program, and early in the century many streets within the city of San Diego were paved. Beyond the city limits, however, most were still dirt roads. The first major county road to be paved with concrete was the Coast Route (later U.S. 101) from San Diego north to the county line, completed about 1912. During the 1920s, a massive road improvement program was started that essentially has not yet stopped. A milestone occurred in 1928, when the paving of the Coast Highway was completed to Los Angeles. This development evidently did much to accelerate San Diego County's role as a regional recreation center.

During the last decade of this period, commercial air transportation also began to serve San Diego. On March 1, 1925, Ryan Airlines initiated a scheduled passenger service to Los Angeles. This operation has been called the first year-round air passenger service to be operated over the mainland United States. By the end of the 1920s, several other airlines had operated, or

were operating, into San Diego, both from Los Angeles and from the East via Yuma and El Centro.

Period V, 1930–Present

With little exaggeration, this may be labeled the "era of highway dominance" in San Diego County transportation, particularly since 1945. The private automobile accounts for over 80 percent of all passenger trips (if walking, bicycles and school buses are included) within the county, and for about 99 percent when only the car and public transit are considered. Even for long-distance trips outside the county, automobiles probably account for over 90 percent of travel. Similarly, for both long and short distance freight movements, the dominant mode in San Diego is the truck.

Automobiles dominate passenger travel because they offer unmatched speed for all except the shortest trips, and when two or more riders are involved, they are relatively cheap. The auto offers privacy, comfort, and psychic satisfaction, and is well suited to serving the dispersed trip patterns of low-density cities like San Diego.

The dominance of the car has several drawbacks, however. One is the immobility of those who cannot drive. Buses are available, but low demand makes it hard to maintain adequate routes and frequency of service. Other criticisms of the car include the high land needs of roads, freeways and parking lots, high accident rates, the need to import oil, and air, noise, and visual pollution. Additionally, in the 1990s, freeway congestion greatly decreased the convenience of automobiles, especially on I-5 and I-15.

These criticisms notwithstanding, there is no question that highways are the most important part of our transportation system today, and are likely to remain so for the foreseeable future. In 2000, there were about 7,600 miles of roads, streets, and highways in San Diego County, plus many miles of dirt roads. Virtually all residents rely on these roads and freeways for their regional mobility.

San Diego's first freeway, Cabrillo (officially, State Route 163) was opened from downtown San Diego to Mission Valley in 1948. Freeway construction began in earnest with the start of the Interstate system in 1956 (Figure 11.4). Today the numerous freeways are the most heavily used routes in the county. By 2002 there were over 300 miles of freeway, and this is expected to increase to 334 miles by 2010. Freeways account for over half of all vehicle-miles traveled.

Several freeway extensions are planned for the early 2000s, including State Route 52 east to connect to Route 67, the extension of 905 to the Otay Mesa border crossing, opening Route 125 between Routes 94 and 54, and the completion of Route 56 (Figure 11.5). The I-5–805 merge is to have additional lanes constructed. One controversial planned freeway extension is a privately financed continuation of Route 125 south to Tijuana. In addition, portions of other freeways will be upgraded by widening, interchange improvements, ramp metering, and the like. A few may have HOV (High Occupancy Vehicle) lanes installed; these are special lanes set aside exclusively for buses and other vehicles

Figure 11.4. Construction of Interstate 805 across Mission Valley in October, 1969. Photograph by P. R. Pryde.

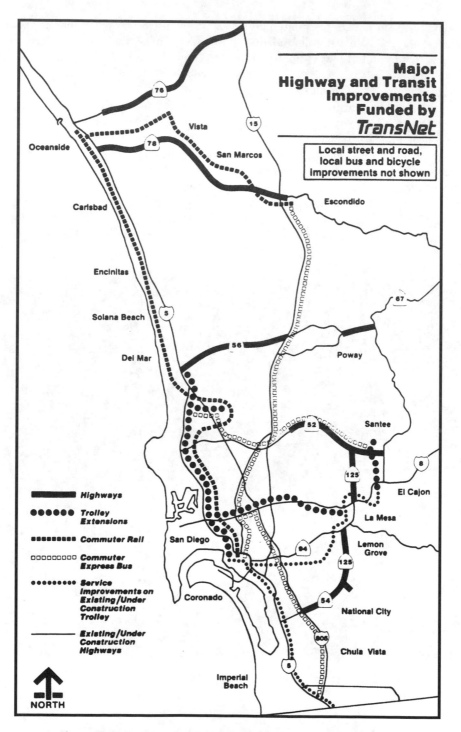

Figure 11.5. Transporatation improvements planned for 1990–2010.

carrying two or more passengers. At the start of 2004, however, many of these projects were threatened with delay by budget deficits and spending cuts.

Although new and expanded highways will be needed, efforts are also being made to improve the efficiency of the existing system. The two most successful efforts are freeway ramp metering, and the synchronization of traffic signals on city streets. Another option is to spread traffic out more evenly throughout the day by encouraging businesses to use more flexible work schedules for their employees.

Despite all the foregoing, it is likely that highway congestion will increase in the future. In 1988, there were 26 miles of heavily congested freeways in the county; this increased to 77 miles in 1998. It had increased still further by 2004.

Public Transportation

As noted above, public transportation in San Diego is limited. The last time it played a large role was during World War II, when restrictions on the use of cars contributed to a 600 percent increase in transit riders. With the coming of peace, ridership declined sharply and the company was sold in 1967 to the City of San Diego. In 1985 it was taken over by the Metropolitan Transit Development Board (MTDB), which also operates the San Diego Trolley.

In 1999, the county's 12 fixed-route transit systems (buses, trains, ferry, and trolley) carried over 90 million passengers, as compared to only 55 million ten years earlier. The largest bus operation is San Diego Transit, which serves the metropolitan area with 32 routes, and averages about 100,000 passengers daily. The second largest is the North County Transit District (NCTD), based in Oceanside. The County Transit System serves the suburban and rural eastern parts of the region. The weekday volume of fixed-route transit riders increased from 161,000 in 1989 to about 200,000 in 2000, with the hope that this might double to 400,000 by 2020.

The most publicized local transportation development in recent years is the ongoing construction of the San Diego Trolley. The first 16-mile segment from the downtown Santa Fe (Amtrak) railroad station to the Mexican border at San Ysidro, was opened on July 26,1981. It was built by the MTDB and is operated by San Diego Trolley Inc. Most of this first segment uses the right-of-way of the San Diego and Arizona Eastern (SD&AE) railroad, which the city purchased in 1979 for the bargain price of $18.8 million. The sale included 108 miles of track, consisting of the SD&AE line to El Centro (minus the Mexican portion), plus branches to El Cajon and Otay.

In the mid-1980s, the MTDB began extending the system. The "East Line" involved converting a freight line from downtown to Lemon Grove, La Mesa, and El Cajon. The route initially extended from the Santa Fe depot to the new El Cajon transit center; it was later (1994) extended to Santee. The extension was opened in 1989, and cost (including new cars) about $142 million.

In 1990 a third route was added with the completion of the 1.5 mile Bayside line. This segment starts at the Santa Fe depot and loops southward past Seaport Village and the Convention Center, and then rejoins the main line at 12th and C streets. In 1993, the first 3.8 miles of the North Line from the Santa Fe depot to Old Town was opened.

Mission Valley was added to the system with the 1998 opening of the line from Old Town to just east of the Stadium. By 2005 this line will be extended past San Diego State University (SDSU) to a connection with the East Line in La Mesa. This extension will be the most expensive transportation project in San Diego history. When completed, the San Diego Trolley system will have over 60 miles of track. A future extension is planned from Old Town to University City (Figure 11.6).

While the San Diego Trolley has been widely praised as a success, it is unlikely that the system will greatly lessen congestion on parallel freeways. Ironically, trolley ridership *depends* in part on congestion; the more clogged the highways, the more likely people are to seek public transportation. The trolley's main function will probably be to absorb some of the increase in regional traffic, especially for trips downtown, to SDSU, and the border.

In addition to these fixed-route transportation systems, there are also several demand-responsive networks in the county, some of which are specifically designed to service the elderly and disabled. Typical of such systems is dial-a-ride, where the customers call for service, are picked up at home, and taken to their destination. Such services are usually provided by private operators, and many are subsidized, but for the elderly and disabled, they provide welcome mobility. They served almost 700,000 passengers in 1999.

The county's main rail line is the 128 mile coastal route from Los Angeles, operated by the Burlington Northern Santa Fe Railroad (locally still referred to by its historical name, Santa Fe). In 2003, this line carried eleven passenger trains in each direction daily, operated by Amtrak (as compared to only three in the mid-1970s).

Figure 11.6. The San Diego Trolley at the Seaport Village stop on the Bayside Line. Photograph by P. R. Pryde.

Several of these runs connect to long-distance trains leaving from Los Angeles. In 2001 there were about 1.6 million riders. By 2010, it may be necessary to double-track much of the railroad within San Diego County.

In 1995, a new rail commuter service, called Coaster, began service. Operated by the NCTD, it utilizes the Santa Fe tracks between Oceanside and downtown San Diego (Figure 11.7). Its nine daily round trips are the first regular commuter trains within the county in many decades, and in 1999 Coaster carried 1.2 million passengers. Without this service, traffic congestion on parallel Interstate 5 would be even worse than it is at present.

Plans are being made to add a light rail (trolley) operation to the existing Oceanside to Escondido freight rail line. This trolley line would parallel State Route 78, and absorb some of the traffic that cannot easily be accommodated on that Route. At Oceanside the trolley would terminate at the transit center, where it would connect with buses, Coaster, and Amtrak trains. This is another project that could be delayed by budget deficits, however.

In 2003, the transit planning and development functions of the MTDB and NCTD were consolidated and transferred to the San Diego Association of Governments (SANDAG). The two existing transit organizations will continue to operate their respective systems, however.

Bicycles are a popular form of transportation around San Diego, both for recreation and commuting. In 2000 there were 73 miles of bike

Figure 11.7. The "Coaster" commuter train follows the I-5 corridor to its terminus at the Santa Fe depot in downtown San Diego. Photograph by P. R. Pryde.

paths, 665 miles of marked bike lanes, and 228 miles of designated bike routes in the county. This network is to be expanded to about 1,160 miles by the year 2004.

The County of San Diego has approved the creation of a multi-purpose trail network, which will serve bicyclists, hikers, and equestrians (Chapter 15). Additionally, a "walkable communities" program has been initiated in the urbanized area.

Air, Sea, and Freight

Since its start in 1930, air transportation has also grown substantially. The county has one major international airport (Lindbergh Field), four military air bases, and several of the nation's busiest general aviation fields (Montgomery, Gillespie, Brown, Palomar). Smaller landing strips exist in Oceanside, Ramona, Fallbrook, Borrego Springs, and elsewhere. Favorable aviation weather has made small aircraft attractive for both business and recreational use.

Almost all scheduled civilian passenger flights use Lindbergh Field. In 2001 Lindbergh handled about 15 million passengers, compared to 5 million in 1980. Most major airlines and several smaller companies utilize this central airport. In December of 2002, control over Lindbergh Field was transferred from the Port of San Diego to the newly created San Diego County Regional Airport Authority. The 9,400 foot main runway at Lindbergh can handle all sizes of aircraft, but is not long enough for take-off by the largest wide-body aircraft such as the 747 at maximum load. In practice, this has not proven to be much of a handicap.

In part because of Lindbergh's cramped location, because it has only one runway, and because ridership is expected to increase to 28 million by 2020, the relocation of San Diego's principal airport to a more spacious site has been advocated and studied for over 30 years. No agreement

exists, however, as to *where* a new airport should be sited. This topic will be discussed further in the next section.

Trucks and trains are the main means of moving freight within San Diego County. Trucks have long been the dominant mode since they provide the same mobility and convenience as do automobiles. The Burlington Northern Santa Fe Railroad (BNSF) provides freight service daily to and from the Los Angeles region, with additional trains as required. The BNSF also provides less frequent service over its branch to Escondido. The San Diego and Imperial Valley line provides freight service southward to Tijuana over the lines of the San Diego trolley, and thence eastward to Tecate. The former service to El Centro on the old SD&AE line, which was suspended years ago do to track deterioration, was in 2003 being repaired and was scheduled to re-open to the Imperial Valley in early 2004.

Air freight operations at Lindbergh Field exceeded 100,000 tons in 1996. The main air freight companies are UPS, Burlington Air Express, LEP, Ryan, Evergreen, Federal Express, Emery Worldwide, and Airborne Express.

For ocean-borne commerce, San Diego is very much in the shadow of the much larger port facilities at Los Angeles—Long Beach. In 2000, the Port of San Diego moved less than two million tons of goods, about one percent of that moved at Los Angeles—Long Beach. However, freight traffic through the Port is expected to double by 2010. The mainstay of San Diego's port is the bulk loading facility at the 10th Avenue Terminal, which is augmented by a smaller facility in National City.

Pipelines also deserve to be mentioned. The one handling the greatest tonnage is the Southern Pacific Company's products pipeline, which extends from Long Beach to San Diego. It has two terminals within the city, the most visible being the one along I-15 north of the stadium. The ten inch diameter pipeline carries gasoline, diesel oil, turbine fuel, and other petroleum products. Two major gas pipelines also enter the county, along the I-5 and I-15 corridors. Water pipelines are discussed in Chapter 8.

Period VI, The Future

One of the most difficult problems facing San Diego governmental agencies concerns the future role of automobile transportation. Since the county's low-density communities are most conveniently served by car, it would be difficult to reduce its role substantially in the short run.

Still, many feel that efforts should be made to reduce the dominance of the automobile, for the reasons outlined earlier. Past proposals for accomplishing this have ranged from expanded bus service, to building extensive rail systems and bikeways, to radical new concepts in urban transportation (people-movers, bullet trains, etc.). In each case it is hoped that people can be *enticed* out of their cars by better public transportation.

All the proposed substitutes for cars have major weaknesses, however. In most cases, either the system itself or the right-of-way it would require are simply too expensive. Thus the lowly bus, with its flexible route structure and relatively low costs, may offer the most feasible prospects for future regional public transportation. Increased use of express buses and HOV lanes on freeways has led to improved service in some communities. Current and planned future extensions of the San Diego Trolley were mentioned earlier, and are summarized in Table 11.1. Late in 2002 SANDAG began circulating a draft of a long-term regional transportation plan that would guide improvements in the county until the year 2030.

More "futuristic" modes of transportation are being considered. In 1966, the California High Speed Rail Authority was created. It is evaluating a statewide system, which would extend to San Diego. The type of system has not been selected yet, but one possibility is the use of tracked levitation vehicles (TLVs). TLVs are capable, in some versions, of 300 m.p.h. Both the Japanese and the Germans have carried out considerable work with TLVs. The cost of such a system would be the main hurdle.

In the final analysis, however, the automobile will continue to move most of us for the foreseeable future. Only a huge increase in gasoline prices is apt to alter this pattern significantly. Because of this, many manufacturers are seeking

TABLE 11.1. Recent and Future Transit Improvements

Project	Cost (million $)	Completion Date
Santee trolley extension	109.4	1995
Coaster service to San Diego	242.5	1995
Old Town trolley extension	112.1	1996
Mission Valley West trolley	223.6	1997
Stadium—SDSU trolley extension	461.0	2005
Oceanside—Escondido rail	351.5	2005
Mid-Coast trolley to Balboa Ave.	134.2	2008

Source: SANDAG, 2002. Note: Funding and completion dates could change depending on future budget allocations.

to develop more fuel efficient power plants for both the family car and delivery vehicles.

The last major question about regional transportation beyond the year 2020 involves the question of relocating Lindbergh Field. The current airport site involves a number of problems, including a steep glide slope, a single runway, the difficulty of lengthening this runway, occasional fog closures, access problems, and the high noise impact on nearby residents. Further, air traffic has been growing rapidly and will eventually exceed Lindbergh's capacity.

After a lengthy study of many potential sites, early in the 1990s it was determined that the best alternative locations would be Miramar (then Naval) Air Station and Brown Field near the Mexican border. Brown Field has several problems including nearby mountains and the proximity of the Tijuana airport.

Miramar is the logical choice, with long runways and easy access. However, the current tenant, the Marine Corps, is not presently in favor of joint military-civilian use, and there is also the problem of aircraft noise over La Jolla. Other suggested sites, such as Borrego Valley, are too far away to be practical. A new facility probably could not be completed prior to 2020 in any event, thus Lindbergh Field will likely have to be expanded enough to meet projected demand for at least another decade or two.

Transportation is something we often take for granted, in large part because we have made the family car such a convenient mode of personal and family movement. But the increasing congestion on our freeways and possible increases in fuel prices suggest that we may need to be willing to think more seriously about alternatives to our transportation status quo.

References

Brown, Alan. *A Description of Distant Roads: Original Journals of the First Expedition into California, 1769–1770 by Juan Crespi.* San Diego: San Diego State University Press, 2001.

Dana, R. H. *Two Years Before the Mast.* New York: P. F. Collier and Son, 1969.

MacAfee, Ward. *California's Railroad Era, 1850-1911.* San Marino, CA: Golden West Books, 1973.

McMullen, Jerry. *They Came by Sea: A Pictorial History of San Diego Bay.* Los Angeles: W. Ritchie Press, 1969.

Metropolitan Transit Development Board. *Metropolitan San Diego Short-Range Transit Plan FY 2003–2007.* Metropolitan Transit Development Board, January 2003.

Pourade, R.F. *History of San Diego.* (6 vols.) San Diego: Union-Tribune Publishing Co.,1960–7.

Ristine, J., "Transit Planning Being Shifted to a Single Agency", *San Diego Union-Tribune,* July 7, 2003, pp. B-1 and B-4.

San Diego Association of Governments. *2020 Regional Transportation Plan.* San Diego: SANDAG, August 2002.

San Diego Association of Governments. *Mobility 2030: The Transportation Plan for the San Diego Region* (preliminary draft). San Diego: SANDAG, August 2002.

Internet Connections:

North County Transit District: *www.gonctd.com*

Port of San Diego: *www.portofsandiego.org*

Regional transit information: *www.sdcommute.com*

San Diego Association of Governments (SANDAG): *www.sandag.org*

Chapter Twelve

Lawrence R. Ford

The Visions of the Builders
The Historical Evolution of the San Diego Cityscape

No true secrets are lurking in the landscape, but only undisclosed evidence, waiting for us. No true chaos is in the urban scene, but only patterns and clues waiting to be organized.

Grady Clay

The modern American city often appears to be a chaotic thing with little or no identifiable character or structure. The skyscrapers, freeways, and shopping centers dominate to the point of nearly obliterating the visible evidence of the evolution of the city. Only in cities that have been frozen in time by lack of growth and in neigh-

Larry R. Ford is a professor of urban studies in the Department of Geography at San Diego State University.

borhoods preserved as historically or architecturally meritorious is the past highly visible. Nevertheless, the evolution of a city can still be read from its cityscape and often the "stream of time" becomes evident from what at first glance appeared chaotic. We can learn to read the cityscape just as we would read geologic history and from it we can see where we have been, where we are going, and at what speed we are traveling.

The purpose of this chapter is to provide a few clues for reading the San Diego cityscape and thus, hopefully, for understanding the historical evolution of the city. Perhaps in no city are such clues needed more, for San Diego is a new large city which is growing and changing rapidly, a city where most of the residents are from someplace else. This chapter will attempt to relate existing landscapes to the evolution of the city so that the reader can better understand the images, dreams, and practical considerations that have shaped San Diego's cityscape.

The Spanish-Mexican Heritage: 1769–1850

Before the coming of the Spanish in the late 1700s, the landscape of what is now San Diego was little affected by human occupance. Diegueño Indians were hunters and gatherers and had no significant agriculture and relatively few permanent structures. There are few remnants of pre-Spanish Indian culture still remaining in the San Diego city area, but some artifacts, such as the Piedras Pintadas (painted rocks) are still visible (see Figure 4.2), as well as a few important archeological "digs."

When the Spanish explorers first visited San Diego, they were unimpressed. Compared to the Indian cities of Mexico, Central America, and South America, all of California seemed desolate, underpopulated, and inaccessible, especially barren Southern California. Even though San Diego was "discovered" by the Spanish in 1542, it was not until 1769 that a handful of priests and soldiers settled in San Diego and attempted to "civilize" the local Indians by teaching them agriculture and Christianity. Although San Diego theoretically dates from this period, almost nothing remains in its original form from the Spanish period (1769–1822). The pueblo in what is now Old Town State Historic Park was little more than a collection of crude thatched or mud huts, plus a church. Spanish colonial architecture did not exist in this poor makeshift environment except at the most rudimentary level. In fact, at the end of the Spanish period, there was not a single

two-story house in all of the San Diego and dirt provided the only floor in every building.

Spatially, the city was divided between the presidio at what is now Presidio Park and the mission further inland in Mission Valley where the soil was better and water more plentiful. The restored mission and Padre Dam are about the only notable landscape features from the Spanish era. The San Diego cityscape in 1820 was almost totally lacking in both the architecture and vegetation that people later came to associate with Southern California. Except for a few vineyards and adobe huts, San Diego was a barren place.

During the Mexican Period (1822–1848), Old Town began to grow a bit, and slightly more impressive structures such as Casa Estudillo and the Bandini House were built (Figure 12.1). These houses remain today although their reconstruction in the early twentieth century may have been somewhat romanticized. It is also likely that fancier trimmings such as glass windows and balconies occurred only after there was considerable Yankee influence, since California was quite isolated from Mexico but Boston traders were a common sight by the 1840s. In fact, the first major building in San Diego was an Army warehouse built in the summer of 1850 out of wood and bricks shipped around Cape Horn from Portland, Maine.

The Transitional Period: 1850–1880

It was during this period that Old Town blossomed and grew, only to be deserted for Alonzo Horton's New Town (now downtown San Diego). Remnants from this era can be found in both "cities" but Old Town is more densely packed with reminders of the early part of the period. Although Old Town was originally laid out and built as a Spanish-Mexican town, Yankee influence became strong, especially after

Figure 12.1. Casa Estudillo in Old Town State Park. Photo by Larry Ford.

1850 when California became a state. The Whaley House in Old Town, for example, appears to be an attempt to re-create New England in Southern California and was the first brick structure in the state (1856) (Figure 12.2). Most of these new structures were not as functional as the earlier adobes for dealing with the hot sun but they were likely seen as helping to "Americanize" the landscape. The Yankees also expressed more interest in planting trees (and less in planting vineyards), but San Diego was still more brown than green as most of the exotic vegetation common today had not yet been introduced.

By the 1870s, the fate of Old Town appeared to be sealed and even prominent residents of the older community began moving south to "Horton's Folly" or New Town. Some houses there also used materials from New England

that were shipped to San Diego, such as the Davis House (1857) which is now located at 4th and Island. Since American influence in San Diego was chiefly from the East by sea, the city had an unusual sort of nautical New England look during this period. Americans had largely rejected the Spanish-Mexican landscape as outmoded and inappropriate.

Although most of the relics from this period have been demolished, a few good examples remain, especially in Old Town. Since Old Town was bypassed by growth (until recent years when freeway construction destroyed much of it), it is still possible to experience the early San Diego architectural ideal. The Gatewood House, the Derby House, and several small, typical structures remain to complement the earlier Whaley House. Meanwhile, in downtown San Diego, Pantoja Park makes a continuing statement

Figure 12.2. The Whaley House in Old Town, the first brick building in California. Photo by P. R. Pryde.

about the proposed layout of the new city, for it was supposed to be the urban core. However, it quickly became peripheral as activity moved north and east to Horton Plaza (Figure 12.3).

Although people had high hopes for San Diego and its fantastic harbor, growth through the 1870s was extremely slow. The population was still less than 3,000 (compared to about 200,000 in San Francisco). Large scale urbanization did not begin until the boom of the 1880s.

The Victorian Period: 1880–1905

During the boom of the 1880s, San Diego began to look like a city. Much of the waterfront was filled in and piers and warehouses were constructed along with impressive business buildings and neo-Gothic residences. Public transportation

expanded the city's built-up area and distinct neighborhoods began to emerge as people flocked in from the East via the new railroad connections. By the 1890s, San Diego began to have the structure and organization of a typical American city complete with a downtown commercial section, swanky residential "hills," and a busy industrial waterfront. Much of this era is still visible in the landscape of Downtown, Uptown, and the Golden Hill area.

Downtown

The waterfront was originally at the foot of Fifth Avenue, and Fifth from the waterfront to Broadway was the main business street of the city. Although there are few remnants of the early port activities (most of the port facilities later moved to the foot of Broadway), there are

Figure 12.3.

GUIDE TO LANDMARK NUMBERS

1. Casa Estudillo and Bandini House
2. Davis House (original location)
3. Whaley House, Derby House, and Gatewood House
4. New Town (Pantoja) Park
5. Horton Plaza
6. "Foot of Fifth"
7. Gaslamp District
8. Stingaree District
9. Long-Waterman House
10. Britt-Scripps House
11. Torrance House
12. Temple Beth Israel (now moved to Heritage Park)
13. "Victorian Neighborhood"
14. Heritage Park
15. Villa Montezuma
16. Hotel Del Coronado
17. Mission Cliffs
18. Prado
19. Santa Fe Station
20. Irving Gill Houses
21. Site of former Klauber House (demolished in 1979)
22. "Assyrian Tower"
23. Spreckles Building
24. San Diego Trust and Savings
25. Balboa Theater
26. Ford Building
27. County Administration Building
28. "Art Deco" Store

several examples of early commercial buildings in the "Lower Fifth" area, many of which have been declared San Diego Historic Sites (Figure 12.4). Buildings such as the Backesto Block, Hubbell Bldg., Marston Bldg., Nesmith-Greeley Bldg., Yuma Bldg., Keating Bldg., Horton Hotel, and several other historic and interesting structures have been renovated as part of the "Gas Lamp Quarter," similar to the lively restored districts in Seattle and San Francisco. These delicate, small scale structures provide an interesting aesthetic contrast to the glass-walled skyscrapers north of Broadway and contribute an element of depth to the urban fabric.

Figure 12.4. Restored Victorian office building on lower Fifth Avenue (Gaslamp District). Photo by Larry Ford.

South of Market Street, near the old waterfront, a few old warehouses and Chinese buildings have been saved and renovated as the focus for a small Chinese cultural district on lower Third Avenue, located in a formerly wild section known as the "Stingaree". This area was once home to numerous solid brick buildings—the first to be built in San Diego in any number. Although a few of the buildings were architecturally unique and listed as historic sites, most have been destroyed and replaced with upscale housing as part of the Marina Redevelopment District (Figure 12.5). While some of the older industrial structures close to the Gaslamp Quarter, such as the Spaghetti Factory at Fifth and K, have been saved and renovated, many more have been cleared for the new Petco Park baseball stadium. Chinese laundries and storefront churches are now a thing of the past, as the area has become a major tourist and nightlife district.

Horton Plaza with its fountain is a monument to this early era. However, its northern location (on Broadway) signaled the end of Fifth and Market as a core, as the Plaza soon became the city's major focal point (by the 1880s). With the opening of the Horton Plaza shopping center a century later in 1985, it has once again become the downtown's major focal point.

Although several Victorian relics in downtown San Diego were replaced by the fifteen-block Horton Redevelopment Project during the 1980s, most of the buildings on Fourth and especially Fifth Avenue have been fully restored and serve as the heart of the booming Gaslamp Quarter. This "South of Broadway" district was considered to be San Diego's skid row until renovations began during the 1970s. By the late 1980s, the area had become a major tourist destination. With the completion of the Horton Plaza Shopping Center (and its huge parking garage) and the massive convention center and

Figure 12.5. View west from 3rd and Island, heart of the renewed Chinese cultural district, with new hotel and condominium towers beyond. Photo by P. R. Pryde.

associated hotels at the foot of Fifth, the Gaslamp Quarter formed one of the biggest and liveliest historic zones in the United States. Architectural history, it would seem, can be an important dimension of an attractive sense of place. Most of the skid row activities, such as homeless shelters, have moved several blocks eastward onto less valuable land.

Uptown

Downtown was not the only area that experienced a building boom in Victorian times. Residential districts to the north and east thrived. Uptown, the area north of downtown, roughly bounded by Ash to the south, Balboa Park to the east, Walnut to the north, and I-5 to the west is one. The greater portion of Uptown, called Horton's Addition, was legally recorded in 1867 and encompassed land that had previously been an Indian reservation. The actual urbanization of the area, however, did not commence until 1888, twenty-one years later. Prior to that time, the only structure standing was the Florence Hotel, located at the corner of Third and Fir. The hotel was built in 1883 and, although considered to be "in the sticks", was still the showplace of San Diego during the eighties.

Fifth Avenue was graded as far north as Ivy in 1885, thus "paving the way" for development in the area. Date, Cedar, Elm, Third, and Fourth were also graded that year. The San Diego Street Car Company, offering horse or mule drawn cars on tracks, opened a line in 1886 and the route through Uptown went up Fifth to Fir to accommodate the Florence Hotel. By 1887, a route was constructed all the way to University thus allowing low density, linear development to occur as far as two miles from downtown during the boom of the late 1880s. In 1888, over a hundred new homes were built with many more people living in hotels and boarding houses.

Land in Horton's Addition originally sold for $125 per 50′ × 100′ lot and Horton would give, in addition, a free lot to anyone who would build a substantial house on the lot. During the boom of the eighties, however, land appreciated by the hour and reached fantastic prices before the inevitable bust followed. The boom ended long before all of Uptown could be developed. Development was fairly dense south of Laurel, but there was none north of Walnut until 1894. By 1904, only 23 percent of Uptown was developed, mostly single family houses. Sixth Avenue was not graded until the 1890s, but it soon became a prestigious location because it fronted on the newly planned amenity of Balboa Park.

Uptown was an ideal suburban, parkside location during Victorian times and six San Diego mayors lived there between 1873 and 1915, along with a former governor of California. Many of the beautiful mansions of this period remain, although many (such as the Klauber House) have been torn down to make way for the new high-rise office and condominium structures now going up. Most of the fancier Victorian mansions in Uptown were built in a neo-Gothic style, complete with towers, ornate surface textures, stained glass windows, and a variety of delicate, lacy trim. Wood was by far the most common construction material and the style is often referred to as "Carpenter Gothic." Some of the houses were essentially townhouses since their owners also had ranches in the California tradition. Many historic sites are located in Uptown such as the Long-Waterman House, Britt Scripps House, and Torrance House. Most of the remaining significant houses are widely scattered, but several nice groupings still exist, especially between First, Fir, Front, and Grape where seven Victorian houses stand side-by-side. The pressure for higher intensity development, however, is great and so many of these old houses may have to be torn down or moved to the county's Heritage Park adjacent to Old Town. The Sherman-Gilbert House has been replaced by urbanization at Second and Fir but the house has been nicely restored as a theme building in Heritage Park near Old Town (Figure 12.6).

All in all, the landscape of Uptown makes for San Diego's best temporal collage as remnants and relics from all of San Diego's eras can be seen there from 1887 mansion, to 1920s bungalows, to 1970s condominiums (Figure 12.7).

Golden Hill

Golden Hill, the area just to the east of downtown bounded by Balboa Park on the north, I-5 on the west, Commercial Street on the south, and 30th Street on the east, is in many ways a better reminder of Victorian San Diego than Uptown. Even though it is smaller, it has a great variety of old buildings from the incomparable Villa Montezuma (the Jesse Shephard house) (Figure 12.8) to rows of Victorian cottages.

Villa Montezuma, perhaps San Diego's finest monument to Victorian residential architecture, is located in the southern section of Golden Hill at 20th and K. Built for Jesse Shephard, a world-famous musician, in order to induce him to reside permanently in San Diego (an idea that

Figure 12.6. The Sherman-Gilbert House in Old Town's Heritage Park. Photo by P. R. Pryde.

failed), the Villa had deteriorated badly by the late 1960s. Concerned citizens made known the plight of the mansion and in the early 1970s it was completely renovated with the aid of HUD funds (and again in the 1980s following a fire). It now operates as a museum-community center. Tours of the interior are available.

Golden Hill was a delightful place during the Victorian era as it had a sweeping view of the bay, easy access to downtown via the Broadway streetcar, and the rural air of an early suburbia. Even though a great many apartments have been constructed in the last decade, Golden Hill has not really experienced the intense pressure for redevelopment that has so greatly altered Uptown.

Important structures were built in other parts of San Diego during the Victorian Era and a few can still be seen in Pacific Beach, East San Diego, and elsewhere. About the only place where a turn-of-the-century ambiance can still be felt, however, is in La Jolla. The Green Dragon Colony, for example, was built in the 1890s as an artists' colony and was an important cultural focal point in La Jolla for years (today, its site is used for office, commercial, and residential space). The Red Rest and Red Roost, two "bungalow style" houses across from La Jolla Cove, epitomize the Victorian "beach community" ambiance of San Diego and are significant as part of the beginning of western outdoor lifestyles. Like many other San Diego landmarks, they are under intensive pressure for removal as coastal land in La Jolla is very valuable, and they have been allowed to deteriorate and will probably not be saved.

Figure 12.7. North of the Central Business District are numerous "temporal colleges" that show building styles from many eras. Photo by Larry Ford.

Figure 12.8. Villa Montezuma, at 20th and K Streets, in the Golden Hill area. Photo by P. R. Pryde.

It is impossible to leave the topic of Victorian architecture in San Diego without some mention of the Hotel del Coronado, perhaps the finest Victorian structure on the West Coast. San Diego once had several fine Victorian beach hotels (such as the Cliff House in Ocean Beach) all of which are gone. Fortunately, the best one remains (Figure 14.3).

Parks, Vegetation, and Services

It was during the Victorian Era that San Diegans began to pay some attention to their parks, especially Balboa Park, and to the general lack of aesthetic vegetation in the city. In 1889, the ladies' annex to the Chamber of Commerce raised $500 to plant trees along the western and southern sides of City (Balboa) Park. In 1893, the city distributed 300 trees throughout the city for planting and beautification. Balboa Park began to emerge from its "untouched" condition in 1892 when the city leased thirty acres in the northwest corner to Kate Sessions for a nursery. Ms. Sessions introduced a wide variety of exotic vegetation to the park and to San Diego generally, including cork oak from Spain, camphor from Asia, rubber trees from the tropics, and Eucalyptus from Australia. She planted 100 trees a year in the park until she left in 1903. She helped turn the park, and indeed San Diego, into a garden spot and helped to end its image as part of the Southern California Desert. San Diego instead became what was called at the time "Our Italy," a mediterranean lotus land of flowers, trees, and fruit as people discovered the wide variety of things that would grow here.

The San Diego cityscape was also experiencing changes of a different sort during this time. Streets were being graded and paved, transit systems were continuing to expand, streetlighting and sewers were being installed, and signs of all types became more noticeable (especially "For Sale" signs during the land boom). During the 1890s, twenty-nine miles of streetlighting were installed and houses were "electrified" within an eight-mile radius of downtown. San Diego was getting trees just in time to help to hide the maze of wires.

Not everything was looked upon as progress. When all of downtown (as far northeast as Date and 12th) had been paved and concrete sidewalks added, there were a large number of complaints about glare and so a darkening substance was introduced, proving perhaps that you can't please everyone.

In 1886, bonds were passed for sewers which put an end to widespread cesspool use in the city. By 1889, forty-seven miles of sewers had been laid as far east as 24th Street. By the early 1900s, mass transit lines were creeping out Adams Avenue and University Avenue, and "suburban" developments such as Mission Hills and Normal Heights were coming into existence. By this time, homes were a bit less ostentatious than typical "high Victorian" mansions;.

San Diego spread out very quickly. Unlike Boston, Philadelphia and other older Eastern cities, San Diego did not fill in all available central land before "sprawling" outward. In 1906 alone, forty buildings were constructed as far out as Normal Heights in spite of the fact that much of Golden Hill and Uptown remained vacant land and low density. Some of this was no doubt due to topography. The hilly, western portions of Uptown, for example, were not built upon until recent decades and even today many vacant lots remain. Topography was a difficult problem in the days of mass transit as it was difficult to catch a trolley only a block away if there was an intervening canyon. One solution was to build foot bridges over the canyons to connect neighborhoods to trolley stops. Some of these bridges can still be seen in the Uptown area, as for example at 4th and Quince.

The Exposition, Irving Gill, and Mission Revival: 1905–1930

It was during this period that San Diego (along with the rest of Southern California) was transformed from simply a western version of the East into an exotic re-creation of the Mediterranean—"Our Italy" incongruously dressed up in "Sevillian" clothes. The Panama-California Exposition had perhaps the greatest impact on this new Spanish Moroccan-Italian cityscape. The Exposition was held in Balboa Park (no longer simply City Park) and the park was transformed from largely barren land into a magnificent "Spanish" city as the Prado area buildings were constructed. The entire Prado is now an historic site and one of the most widely recognized symbols of San Diego (Figure 12.9). Park Boulevard was cut through the park at this time to permit better access to the attractions of the Prado.

It was also during this period that the Santa Fe station was rebuilt to handle the crowds expected at the Exposition. It too was built in the Mission Revival style, and helped not only to set the tone for "Spanish" Southern California, but to start a fad for Spanish train stations all around the West.

The "new" California landscape was not limited to Balboa Park and the train station. Every San Diego neighborhood gradually became a bit more "Mediterraneanized." The most important pioneer in the development of a unique Southern California architectural style was Irving Gill. After having moved here from Chicago, Gill developed a relatively simple (compared to Victorian) stucco style which incorporated some Mediterranean influences along with a great deal of functionalism so as to form an original California ambiance. Most of Gill's houses (built between 1905 and 1915) are in the Uptown area near the park or

Figure 12.9. The Museum of Man on El Prado in Balboa Park, the beginning of "Mediterranean" San Diego. Photo by Larry Ford.

canyons—areas which were filled in a bit later than the Victorian "streetcar" suburbs. By far the best street as far as the Gill Era is concerned is 7th Avenue north of Balboa Park. Here, several Gill masterpieces stand side-by-side to create an early twentieth century ambiance rare in other parks of the city. Gill also designed the La Jolla Women's Club and Recreation Center and they too reflect the early "Californization" of the cityscape.

It was during the 1920s that San Diego's residential cityscape was truly Hispanicized. The restraint shown by Gill was forgotten in an attempt to make Southern California exotic (a la Hollywood). As new "suburbs" such as Mission Hills and Kensington were developed, the romanticized Spanish Colonial house became extremely popular (Figure 12.10). Streets were embellished with rows of slender palm trees, and other exotic vegetation such as bougainvillea gained wide use as yard decoration. Unlike earlier residential areas which were usually laid out for trolley access, these new developments had streets which were circuitous, often winding along the rim of a canyon. In some cases, overhead wiring was placed in the alley or at the rear of the lot to increase the aesthetics of the street. Kensington pioneered the idea of underground wiring.

As trolley lines were extended as far east as University and Euclid, a great number of modest bungalows were built (often for retirees) in such areas as North Park and East San Diego.

Many of these, especially by the late 1920s were also in the red-tile, Spanish stucco style.

There are no designated historic sites in these newer developments, but there are, nevertheless, many interesting structures and neighborhoods. Talmadge, for example, was developed originally as an area for movie star homes—an idea that never really caught on except for the Talmadge sisters. Another house in the Kensington-Talmadge area is said to be the model for the original Jehovah Witness Watchtower.

In some areas, Spanish Colonial was not exotic enough and so Egyptian and Assyrian models were utilized. There are many Egyptian remnants in the Park Boulevard-University Avenue area. Even though the Egyptian Theater has been drastically remodeled several times and is now derelict, there are still many apartments and commercial structures around it that were

Figure 12.10. "Spanish" houses built in the 1920s and 1930s have had great staying power, in that they conform to the popular image of California. Photo by Larry Ford.

shaped by this fantasy. Perhaps the best example, however, is the old streetcar turn-around (now a bar) at the corner of University and Euclid. An exotic "Assyrian" tower once stood by the Egyptian-inspired temple garage that still dominates the corner and represents the "Hollywood" days of San Diego of the 1920s. The statues on the old "temple" have now been painted in a bright yellow and green.

It was also during the 1920s that the old modes of transportation such as streetcars and horsecars, gave way to automobiles. Consequently "auto architecture" began to appear—gas stations and parking lots at first, but soon a neon-lit galaxy of drive-in attractions (especially by the 1940s). Many new streets were paved and old ones widened during the 1920s, but the last of the old gas stations and garages, which could still be seen through the 1970s, are now gone (Figure 12.11).

It is perhaps especially interesting to compare University Avenue (a street that grew up as a streetcar commercial strip) and El Cajon Boulevard (a street that grew up with the automobile). The two streets have an entirely different ambiance, density, and architecture, especially west of Euclid.

San Diego's beach communities became well developed during the 1920s. Trolley lines extended as far as Mission and Pacific Beach but the auto no doubt made such casual attractions more popular. Belmont Park opened during the mid-twenties, and its 1925 roller coaster (one of the last such remaining on the West Coast) is now an historic site. Many "beach cottages" and other small structures date from this era as well. Perhaps life on the beach first became generally acceptable during the "Roaring Twenties."

Downtown San Diego was no less exotic. In the years just preceding World War I, the first tall (twelve stories) eastern-style office buildings were built—including some very impressive ones such as the Spreckles Building (only six stories) and the city's first highrise, the St. James Hotel. The Spreckles Building included one of

Figure 12.11. Early gas station south of Broadway, downtown. Photo taken in the 1970s by Larry Ford.

the city's finest theaters, and it was here that the opera *Aida* was performed—complete with chariots—during the 1920s. By the late 1920s, buildings going up in downtown San Diego were being modeled after Florentine Palaces and Spanish towers. The Bank of America Building and the San Diego Trust and Savings Building both appear to be out-of-scale refugees from "Romeo and Juliet." Both have balconies, decorative trim, and impressive arched entrances. The San Diego Trust and Savings Building (now a Courtyard by Marriott hotel) has a lovely muralled lobby and a "Spanish cupola" as well. For some reason, San Diego residential structures seemed to copy mainly from Spanish models, downtown buildings from Italian models, and many commercial buildings from Egyptian models. All in all, the San Diego of the 1920s was a very "Mediterranean" place.

Perhaps the most exotic downtown building resulting from this era is the Balboa Theater-a Spanish-Moroccan tower complete with indoor fountain and gold-tile roof. This structure will eventually be renovated and integrated into the Horton Plaza shopping complex.

The Art Deco Years: 1930–1950

Just as the 1915 Panama-California Exposition paved the way for Mission Revival enthusiasm in San Diego and helped to "Hispanicize" the cityscape, the second exposition in the 1930s helped to popularize "stream-lined moderne." The Ford Building (1935) is one of a few historic sites from this era but throughout the older sections of San Diego, rounded corners and modernistic "Batman" towers decorating such things as skating rinks and department stores have served as reminders of the time (Figure 12.12).

It was also during the 1930s and 1940s that auto architecture really began to come into its own with drive-in restaurants, drive-in theaters,

Figure 12.12. The Art-Deco Tower Bowl on El Cajon Boulevard. Photo by Larry Ford.

drive-in motels, as well as a proliferation of gas stations, garages, and other auto-serving structures. A number of interesting old motels still exist on El Cajon Boulevard between 54th and the I-8 entrance in La Mesa, many with a kind of "Old West" ambiance not at all typical of the surrounding newer structures. Although most of these early auto-oriented buildings are too young to be looked at with much interest by most (none are historic sites, for example) they are, nevertheless, a vanishing breed. During the 1950s, chain restaurants and gas stations began to homogenize the nation's highways and today these "standard" structures are completely dominant. "Mom and Dad's" drive-in restaurants had a brief reign indeed.

Meanwhile, in the residential neighborhoods (such as Talmadge), the Spanish house was being simplified and streamlined so as to still look Californian but yet contemporary—less red tile and exotic trim. During the 1940s, military housing went up in the Linda Vista and Rosecrans areas, as well as an increasing number of apartments in many neighborhoods.

Large factories and military buildings made a big impact on the cityscape during World War II with such large industrial buildings as the Convair plant, which was several times as large as the red brick warehouses of earlier eras. (The Convair plant was camouflaged to look like Mission Valley during World War II.) Very little of this era is reflected in the downtown cityscape as almost nothing of any importance was built there between 1930 and 1960 (as in most American downtowns). Reminders exist primarily in the form of trim on small buildings, a few gas stations, and perhaps in the County Administration Building which is sort of transitional between the exotic 1920s and the streamlined 1930s (see Figure 19.2). Actually, due to the depression and to the scarcity of the war years, relatively little was built anywhere during this era. The best place to get a glimpse of the time, however, is on old thoroughfares such as old Highway 101 (e.g., "Fat City") and El Cajon Boulevard fairly close to the center of the city.

Suburbia Explodes: 1950–2000

In the years since 1950, San Diego City has grown from 330,000 people to about 1,300,000 people while the population of San Diego County has tripled to surpass the 2.9 million mark. The areal expanse of the urbanized landscape has been even more spectacular. The cityscape, once confined to a rather compact area south of Mission Valley (with the exception of the beach communities) has oozed outward in every direction (Figure 12.13). Metropolitan San Diego is now almost solidly built up from the Mexican border to Camp Pendleton along the coast and to Escondido inland. To the east, El Cajon, Lakeside, and beyond are all highly urbanized. It is therefore not realistic to include this era in a tour through time the way one might include Downtown, Uptown, Hillcrest, and Kensington.

The last twenty-five years have been characterized by a number of discordant trends including mobile home parks in Alpine, lowrise condominiums everywhere, highrise condo-

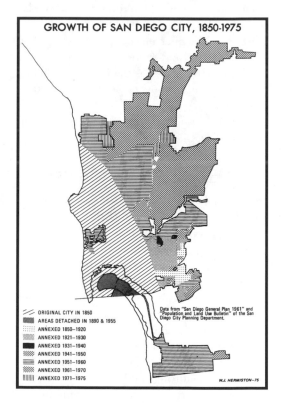

Figure 12.13.

miniums in the central city, a sea of tract homes in Mira Mesa, "new towns" such as Rancho Bernardo, and a tremendous increase in all types of apartment construction, shopping center construction, and office building construction. Home as well as commercial establishments are now designed around the automobile (Figure 12.14), a regrettably dehumanizing style of architecture. San Diego is no longer one city but rather a group of scattered subcenters, deliberately encouraged by the construction of new employment centers such as "the Golden Triangle" in University City. The land area of

Figure 12.14. The garage-dominant home: the typical housetype of post-1950 San Diego. The garage is moved forward so as to free the backyard for recreation, and perhaps to symbolize the dominance of the automobile. Photo by Larry Ford.

political San Diego (incorporated San Diego City) is over eight times larger than that of San Francisco and is within "catch-up" distance of Los Angeles. The sheer quantity of building of this period far outpaces all that went before it—where ever you go, there it is, new subdivisions, shopping centers, and "industrial parks," spreading outward at an impressive velocity.

Some efforts have been made to ameliorate the visual impact of exploding suburbia. Utility wires are being undergrounded, long range community plans are being drawn up, more walking and bike paths are being incorporated into the newer outlying subdivisions, and sign control ordinances of varying effectiveness have been enacted (Figure 13.9). The city of San Diego officially wishes to emphasize the central city, and the extent of urban renewal in the downtown area is truly impressive. Hopefully, measures such as these will help to mellow the more undesirable aspects of the existing urban sprawl. However, the nicer new accommodations in the more recent outlying subdivisions and downtown condominium towers come at a price well beyond the reach of the average citizen.

It must be left to the perspective of future urbanologists to determine what distinctive themes, if any, mark the exploding suburbia period, and what is of sufficient lasting value from this period to merit future historical preservation.

References

Brandes, Ray. *San Diego: An Illustrated History*. Los Angeles: Rosebud Books, 1981.

Carrico, S. and K. Ferguson, *San Diego's Historic Gaslamp Quarter: Then and Now*. San Diego: Goodway Printing, 1989.

Center City Development Corporation. *Urban Design Program: Center City, San Diego*. CCDC, 1983.

Johl, Karen. *Timeless Treasures: San Diego's Victorian Heritage*. San Diego: Rand Eds., 1982.

Kammerling. Bruce. *Irving J. Gill, Architect*. San Diego: San Diego Historical Soc., 1993.

Lynch, Kevin. *What Time Is This Place?* Cambridge: M.I.T. Press, 1972.

MacPhail, Elizabeth. *Kate Sessions: Pioneer Horticulturist*. San Diego: San Diego Historical Soc., 1976.

MacPhail, Elizabeth. *The Story of New Town San Diego and of Its Founder Alonzo E. Horton*. 2nd ed. San Diego: Pioneer Printers, 1979.

Morgan, N. and T. Blair. *Yesterday's San Diego*. Miami: E. A. Seemann Publ., 1976.

Pourade, R. F. *City of the Dream*. San Diego: Copley Press, 1977.

Pourade, R. F. *History of San Diego*. (6 vols.) San Diego: Union-Tribune Publishing Co., 1960–1967.

Sutro, Dirk. *San Diego Architecture*. San Diego: San Diego Architectural Foundation, 2002.

Internet Connections:

American Inst. of Architects, San Diego Chapter: *www.aiasandiego.com*

Center City Development Corp.: *www.ccdc.com*

San Diego Historical Society: *www.sandiegohistory.org*

Save Our Heritage Organization: *http://sohosandiego.org/*

Chapter Thirteen

Philip R. Pryde and
Frederick P. Stutz

"America's Finest City"
Communities of the City of San Diego

One of the things that contributes to San Diego's uniqueness is the variety of landforms on which its various communities have developed. The combination of beaches and mesas, canyons and valleys, peninsulas and hills have created numerous physical barriers which give geographic definition to the human communities. These barriers have allowed the communities to develop along individual lines, while retaining the characteristics that distinguish them from neighboring communities.

Historically, the city of San Diego developed by utilizing the closest and most easily developed land first. The terraces near the water and the gentler slopes adjacent to Old Town and Centre City were developed under a grid street pattern. As the population grew and more space was required it became necessary to link the mesa-tops and the outlying beach communities with improved roads and street-car systems (Chapter 11).

Suburbanization continued after the turn of the twentieth century, first with the annexation of Encanto and East San Diego (Figure 12.13). Along with Logan Heights, these were located on relatively flat upper-area land, and were laid out in grid patterns like the early communities. By the first third of the century the northern "suburb" of North Park and the mesa-top com-

Frederick P. Stutz, a professor of urban and transportation studies in the Department of Geography at San Diego State University, prepared the original version of this chapter; it was revised for the 4th edition by Philip R. Pryde.

213

munities of Hillcrest, Normal Heights and Kensington had developed along the south rim of Mission Valley, from Mission Hills eastward. First settled on streetcar lines, these areas are typified by Spanish style stucco and tile roof homes.

These areas of San Diego developed early and remain somewhat of a core for the city. They developed in a generalized ring fashion around the early commercial centers and differed from each other from the beginning. Although isolated, the first coastal towns were also developing at this time. Inland and to the south the independent towns of El Cajon, La Mesa, National City, and Chula Vista had appeared.

World War II brought a massive influx of new residents and new types of communities. The development of new highways and new earth moving techniques in the post-war era meant that housing construction was no longer at the mercy of the physical barriers which had kept outlying areas isolated. Slopes could be cut away, canyons filled, and natural runoff channels diverted to create a sprawling squared-off rolling hills form of suburbia. The previously isolated coastal communities found that with improved transportation they, too, would join the spreading suburbanization of the city of San Diego. More recently, outlying open space areas have been annexed by the city and have given way to another type of community, the "country estate" development with its internal golf course.

This chapter will depict in capsule form the various communities of the city of San Diego. We will look first at the downtown district of the city that likes to call itself "America's Finest".

The Center City Communities

These communities define San Diego's Central Business District (CBD). The CBD has the nat-ural boundary of San Diego Bay on the west, and the artificial boundary of Interstate 5 to the north and east. It enjoys the close proximity of such outstanding attractions as the Bay and Balboa Park. These, together with a moderate climate and thoughtful redevelopment, have enabled the CBD to become one of the most beautiful downtown areas in the world (Figure 13.1).

The Bay, of course, is the primary amenity of the CBD. Bay breezes create a natural air conditioning and also help minimize potential air quality problems. Bay frontage provides both recreational opportunities as well as dock access for commerce. The city needs to be careful, however, that increasing construction of high-rise buildings near the coast doesn't destroy views from other nearby neighborhoods. The CBD is most frequently accessed by the freeway network, but is also accessible by bus, train, and trolley, and enjoys perhaps the closest airport of any city center in the country.

Over the past thirty years, San Diego has done a commendable job of renewing and "reinventing" the CBD, which was in a state of lethargy and spreading decay in the 1960s. Before the initiation of redevelopment projects in 1975, the CBD was characterized by a low (and poor) resident population, vacant lots and old deteriorating buildings, relatively little office space for a city its size, and a less than vibrant venue for evening activities.

But by the turn of the twenty-first century, the CBD had been revitalized both socially and economically by creative redevelopment. The process was begun with the creation of the Horton Plaza Shopping Center, Seaport Village, and the Gaslamp District, and continues with the rebuilding of Little Italy (along India Street) and East Village near the Convention Center. As a result, the CBD pulses with the tens of thousands of people who work downtown, sev-

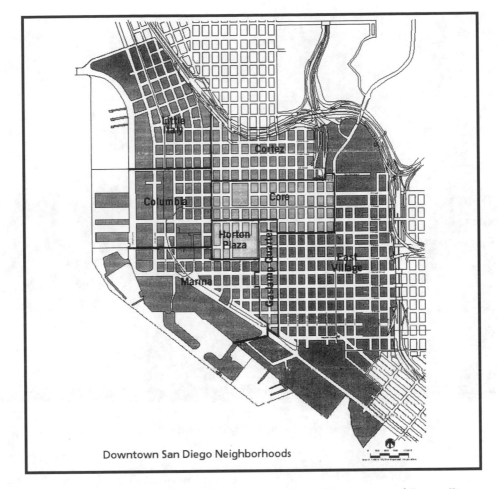

Figure 13.1. Communities of the Central Business District. Map courtesy of Centre City Development Corp.

eral thousand who live downtown, and thousands more who come to shop, sightsee, dine, or enjoy cultural amenities. Responsible for the CBD's revitalization is the Centre City Development Corporation (CCDC), which was created by the City of San Diego in 1975, and serves as the City's redevelopment agency.

The first, and in many ways the most important, downtown renewal effort was the fifteen-block Horton Plaza Redevelopment Project (Figure 13.2). Its focus is the Horton Plaza Shopping Center, completed in August 1985. But this is not just an attractive and innovative shopping center; its unique architecture and color scheme has inspired a complimentary architectural style throughout many parts of the CBD.

In the southwest portion of the CBD is the 125-acre Marina Redevelopment Project. This

Figure 13.2. Horton Plaza Shopping Center. Photo by P. R. Pryde.

is designed primarily to be an upscale residential district, but major hotels and commercial complexes lie on the periphery. Its attractions include Marina Park, the Convention Center, and Seaport Village, between which lie the Hyatt and Marriott hotel complexes.

The Columbia Redevelopment Project encompasses much of the original "downtown" area. Its goal is to connect the CBD in an attractive fashion to the waterfront, and it has become a prime location for high-rise office space. Its most eye-catching buildings are the hexagonal towers of the Emerald Shapery Center and the One America Plaza (Figure 13.3). The Santa Fe

Depot, Maritime Museum, and Cruise Ship Terminal also enhance this area.

The "Core" District extends eastward from the Columbia Project area to 12th Avenue. The western portion has been revitalized by high-rises, but the eastern half is still largely a zone of deterioration. The trolley line along C Street both provides access to, and divides, the Core. The Civic Center, which includes the City Administration building, Golden Hall, and the Civic Theater, forms the heart of this district.

North of the Columbia and Core districts are Little Italy and Cortez Hill. At the turn of the twenty-first century, both of these areas were rap-

Figure 13.3. The newly constructed skyline on the west side of San Diego's central business district. The Great American Plaza is on the left and the Emerald Shapery Center is to the right. Photo by P. R. Pryde.

idly undergoing a renewal process, with Little Italy especially taking on a distinct and lively identity as a unique commercial-residential district (Figure 13.4). The County Administration Center complex, dating from the 1930s, is also a familiar waterfront feature in this area.

The Gaslamp District Redevelopment Plan was approved in 1982. It emphasized the twin goals of preserving and restoring the many historic century-old buildings along 5th Avenue, while at the same time replacing undesirable commercial activities with attractive shops, restaurants, and offices. The effort has been hugely successful. The annual "Street Scene" music festival is one of San Diego's major "parties".

The East Village (formerly, "South College") District includes the area between the Gaslamp District and I-5, including the San Diego High School and City College campuses. Its southern sector was in 2002 a major redevelopment site, centered around the new Padres baseball park and related facilities. The area near 12th and Imperial is home to the San Diego Transit Corporation, and East Village also includes the waterfront industrial area south of the Convention Center.

Old Town

Old Town is the site of the original Spanish settlement in the state of California. It is not part of the CBD, but because of its historical ties to downtown San Diego it is convenient to mention it here. Old Town has a rich heritage that spans three culture periods—the Spanish,

Figure 13.4 The entrance to San Diego's "Little Italy" district on India Street. Photo by P. R. Pride.

Mexican, and Early American. Landmarks abound in Old Town, but the dominant one is the gleaming white Serra Museum atop the hill in Presidio Park. The Heritage Park victorian buildings in Old Town were discussed in Chapter 12.

Today, Old Town is a compact and distinct community that has undergone major changes. The 1960s and 1970s witnessed the transition of Old Town to a community focused heavily upon the historical buildings and recreational outlets that are found in Old Town State Park. The community Plan proposes that Old San Diego should be developed as a living, viable community rather than as a commercialized museum piece. In 1971, Old Town was designated as San Diego's first planned district. Today its streets are lined with small, artisan-type shops

and unique ethnic restaurants. The California Department of Transportation (Caltrans) District 11 headquarters remains the major incongruity in the community, and ironically, traffic congestion remains an unsolved problem.

These center city communities are a study in contrast. The western and southern portions have largely been transformed and revitalized since 1980, whereas the eastern portions are still in need of help. Overall, however, the improvement in the city's CBD over the past thirty years has been remarkable, and should be a point of civic pride. The renewal, efforts have greatly changed the city's skyline, which is now dominated by high-rises (Figures 13.5 through 13.7).

As the Center City redevelopment progresses, older hotels and apartment buildings which house many poorer San Diegans are

Figures 13.5, 13.6, and 13.7. Development of the San Diego city skyline from 1969 to 2003. In 1969 photo at top, the Union Bank Building is to the right of center and the Home Tower is at the right. In 1983 (center photo), the Columbia Centre building punctuates the skyline to the west (left), while the first tower of the Marriott Hotel rises in the center. In 2003, the Emerald Shapery Center peeks through the dominating towers of the Hyatt Hotel on the left, while the 41-story harbor view condominium towers extend skyward behind the Convention Center. Photos by P. R. Pryde.

removed or converted to new uses, and this forces the city to consider how to provide for the needs of these downtown residents. Also, as the CBD becomes more attractive for residents and tourists alike, problems of traffic and parking are apt to become more acute. The successful redesign of San Diego's central business district both cures old problems and produces new ones.

Central Residential Communities

North Park

North Park lies to the northeast of Balboa Park. The commercial activity of North Park is centered about 30th Street and University Avenue, a transfer point of the early trolley car lines. The shopping area remains much as it was when developed.

A grid pattern of streets divides the area into small blocks that contain a large number of new apartment buildings. The narrow, offset streets and the high population density combine to create traffic congestion of major proportions.

Nearly all the simple frame houses built in North Park during the 1920s had a horizontal-board exterior and two posts supporting the front porch roof. The ubiquity of this characteristic house style is the image of North Park that many people retain. The senior-citizen high-rises at Park Boulevard and University are another local landmark.

Immediately east of Balboa Park is an area with the older names of South Park, Burlingame, and Brooklyn Heights. The canyons and the resulting disconnected maze of streets work against the establishment of a viable "sense of community" over the larger area. Consequently, these communities tend to be rather small and somewhat isolated from one another. Most of the homes are single-family residences.

To the east of these communities is an area around I-805 and I-15 frequently referred as

City Heights or Mid City. In many ways it is a transitional zone between North park and East San Diego. Three canyons dissect the area, and the narrow ridges between the canyons contain complexes of single-family homes. Very little commercial activity occurs in City Heights and travel between residential areas is hindered by the canyons and freeways.

East San Diego

East San Diego had its beginnings during the 1880s land boom. It was incorporated in 1912 as the City of East San Diego and was called the Golden Rule City. At the time it was the second largest city in San Diego County. It lasted until 1923 when it was annexed to the city of San Diego. Although the boundaries are very ill-defined today, the center of the area is the intersection of Fairmont and University Avenue where the old East San Diego sign stood until 1968.

Although average incomes in the area are not high, East San Diego is still a viable community. Easy accessibility makes it attractive to persons looking for close-in housing. An influx of apartment building is replacing older singe-family homes, most of which were built in the 1920s. A new Vietnamese district has developed around 47th and El Cajon Boulevard. Property values are rising, population is increasing, and parking is becoming a major problem.

Southeast San Diego

Southeast San Diego is a large area with a variety of neighborhood, land use patterns, and socioeconomic characteristics. It is San Diego's largest community, with over 100,000 residents in 2000 (Table 13.1). Generally speaking, Southeast San Diego extends from Russ Boulevard and Highway 94 on the north to the National City boundary on the south, and from I-5 on the west to Lemon Grove on the east. Southeast San

TABLE 13.1. Largest Communities of the City of San Diego

Community	2000 Population
1. Southeast San Diego (includes Encanto)	105,319
2. Clairemont	83,117
3. Mira Mesa	77,277
4. Skyline-Paradise	72,396
5. City Heights (part of Mid-City Plan)	72,095
6. Otay-Nestor	64,673
7. Navajo	52,942
8. University	52,872
9. Penasquitos	51,245
10. North Park	48,690
11. Pacific Beach	42,159
12. Rancho Bernardo	41,886

Source: City of San Diego Planning Department, SANDAG, and City of San Diego Urban Analysis Section, 2000.

Diego is primarily a residential community with accompanying schools, parks, and shopping facilities, as well as many of the city's cemeteries. Its residents include a high percentage of minorities.

Throughout Southeast San Diego development occurred in a rather spontaneous manner which has resulted in portions of the community being isolated from surrounding areas. Some parks, schools, and shopping areas are separated by cemeteries, freeways, heavily traveled streets, drainage channels, canyons, undeveloped lands, or industrial uses from the area they were meant to serve. Housing varies from older, well maintained homes and newer multiple units to deteriorated structures.

Within the area described above are several identifiable subcommunities. Logan Heights, located between Imperial and National Avenues, is the community most commonly associated with San Diego's Black and Hispanic minorities. They are by no means confined to just this neighborhood, however. The murals in Chicano Park have become a focus of cultural identity for this area, and are well worth a visit (Figure 13.8).

Another identifiable community in this area is Golden Hill. This was San Diego's first suburban development—a very fashionable area containing mansions and Victorian homes. During the 1930s and 1940s housing values declined and changes occurred which has left Golden Hill an ethnically mixed area of rooming houses, apartments, and some smaller single-family homes. Golden Hill's outstanding landmark is Villa Montezuma, the restored Victorian mansion of Jesse Shepard (Figure 12.8). Residents of this community are more closely knit than in many other areas and have formed a homeowners association to preserve and improve the identity of their neighborhood.

Chollas Park is the name usually associated with the area between Wabash and 47th Street. Further to the east in Southeast San Diego is the community of Encanto. This is the least developed part of Southeast San Diego, despite being the first new area annexed to the city, and extends from 47th Street to Lemon Grove. It more nearly reflects the typical suburban pattern of single-family homes and extensive areas of undeveloped land.

To the south of Encanto are the communities of Paradise Hills and Skyline, separated from each other by Paradise Valley. They were developed prior to World War II with low densities and a semi-rural atmosphere. Although part of the city of San Diego, they also have considerable interaction with National City.

San Ysidro

Although physically separated from San Diego by National City and Chula Vista, San Ysidro is der station with over 20 million crossings annually. The San Diego trolley's southern terminus is located in San Ysidro, just yards from the border, and provides the easiest access for tourists to Tijuana.

The "greater San Ysidro area" extends west to the Tijuana River estuary (taking in the older community of Nestor), and east to Otay Mesa and Brown Field. The Otay Mesa area is slated for mixed residential, commercial, and industrial development, and will provide employment for thousands of workers in the south county, aided by increasing volumes of tourists and commerce at the Otay Mesa border crossing.

A large portion of the commercial activity of San Ysidro is located adjacent to the border and is particularly oriented towards Mexican shoppers. The latter spend hundreds of millions of dollars annually in San Diego County, ten times what Americans spend in Tijuana.

Mesa-top Streetcar Communities

These communities all lie south of I-8 and include Middletown, Mission Hills, Hillcrest, Normal Heights, Kensington, and the College area. All except the College area were once served by streetcar routes.

West of Balboa Park is the community of Uptown, also called Middletown. Freeways bound the area on three sides, providing excellent access and strong demarcation. Internal circulation is hindered by a series of canyons, but they create a feeling of openness. Middletown neighborhoods are characterized by a diversity of housing styles, although single-family homes predominate. Sprinkled throughout the community are older buildings with unique architecture and interesting pasts. The red brick Park Manor Hotel, as well as the William Clayton home at Sixth and Laurel, are among the buildings designated Historic Sites.

Figure 13.8. Some of the murals in Chicano Park (Logan Avenue at Crosby St.), depicting themes of importance to San Diego's Hispanic community. Photo by P. R. Pryde.

part of the city of San Diego.[1] It is adjacent to the United States-Mexico border, and has acquired an ethnic mix of people who live and work there. San Ysidro was originally a quiet border community in an agricultural setting, but today it is the location of the world's busiest bor-

[1] It is connected to the rest of San Diego by a narrow strip of "land" running southward through San Diego Bay.

Along 4th, 5th, and 6th Avenues is a medical-residential corridor sometimes referred to as "Pill Hill." The residences in the corridor vary from old single-family homes and older apartment to high-rise luxury condominiums such as those overlooking Balboa Park on 6th Street. Many well preserved Victorian and English-style homes are still occupied and maintained throughout Middletown, some as office or commercial ventures. West of First Avenue across Maple Canyon is Banker's Hill. This site was selected by the city's wealthy businessmen because of the physical amenities offered and its proximity to downtown.

Mission Hills

On the hills just above Old Town is one of San Diego's most prestigious communities. Mission Hill's first house was Villa Orizaba built in 1887. Few additional homes were built until 1908 when the San Diego electric Railway reached Mission Hills and a building boom began.

The convenient location, good views, and surrounding canyons give a "sense of place" to Mission Hills that is lacking in many other parts of the city. Stability is a key factor in maintaining the neighborhood, with many homes occupied by the second and third generations of the same family.

The curving streets, some lined with palms, the unique homes, and Presidio Park are all landmarks that distinguish Mission Hills. Mission Revival/Craftsman architecture is prevalent in the built landscape. In 1988 a 30-foot height limit was adopted for the "Western Slopes" of the Mission Hill Community.

Hillcrest

Hillcrest is "up the hill" from downtown San Diego. The heart of the community is located at 5th and University Avenues. Hillcrest's boundaries—Mission Valley, Mission Hills, and Park Boulevard—are fairly distinct.

A regular grid street pattern is broken up by numerous canyons. Traffic congestion and a lack of parking facilities are severe problems in Hillcrest, particularly during the peak hours. Many of the streets are narrow by today's standards and are a hindrance to movement by automobile.

The core area of Hillcrest is zoned for relatively high density; however, there are design guidelines in place to further promote and enhance the user-friendly pedestrian scale which is a key attribute of Hillcrest. The old commercial center is readily identified by the Hillcrest sign spanning the intersection at 5th and University. A newer shopping district now exists to the north in the vicinity of University and Richmond. Hillcrest is also a major medical center of San Diego, with two large hospitals and associated offices located north of Washington Street.

The area just east of Route 163 and south of I-8 is traditionally known as University Heights. Heavily dissected by canyons, it is often thought of as part of Hillcrest. In April of 1991 the old Trolley Barn Neighborhood Park at the north end of Park Boulevard was designated a historic site. Once slated for condominium development, this six acre park was once the "home base" for the electric trolley system.

Normal Heights and Kensington

Normal Heights is a very distinct community that is distinctively bounded by I-805, Mission valley, and I-15. Its commercial center is an almost continuous strip along Adams Avenue, which is also the antique store center of San Diego.

Immediately across I-15 is Kensington, which extends eastward to Fairmont Avenue. The southern boundary is not very distinct, but is generally considered to be either Monroe Avenue or El Cajon Boulevard.

Kensington has a very special character which deserves separate attention. In 1909, this area was selected by executives of the Santa Fe Railway Company for the building of a luxury subdivision. Far enough inland to escape the fog and dampness of the beaches, yet close enough to receive cool ocean breezes, Kensington was isolated on three sides by canyons. The man in charge, G. A. Davidson, was a Canadian with an affinity for English place names. This is reflected in current street names such as Marlborough, Middlesex, Edgeware, and others; even the name Kensington was taken from one of London's boroughs. Distinctive streetlights, a small park, and a ghost town for a motion picture set were part of the original development. In 1925, a "celebrity" subdivision was dedicated in the canyon-top area around Fairmount and Adams. The name Talmadge Park was lent to the community by the Talmadge sisters of silent movie fame.

Spanish-style homes with red tile roofs, palm lined streets, the park and library, and the Kensington sign are the easily remembered landmarks of Kensington. These familiar landmarks give a "sense of place" to Kensington, while the stability of residents, high degree of acquaintanceship, and pride in the community atmosphere give it a "sense of community." Normal Heights lacks the visual identity of Kensington as the houses are much more modest and lack the distinctiveness of the Spanish style.

The College Area

In 1931, State Teacher's College moved from a site on Normal Street, where the San Diego Unified School District's Education Center is now located, to a brush-covered mesa on the south rim of Alvarado Canyon. The original 125-acre campus and 1,500 students has grown to 275 acres and more than 33,000 students, making it the largest in the CSU system in enrollment, but unfortunately one of the smallest in land area. Despite San Diego State's present size and university status, the area is still known as the College Area Community. It is bounded by I-8 on the north, Montezuma and Collwood on the west, El Cajon Boulevard on the south, and 70th Street on the east.

The major problems of the community are those of campus enrollment growth, inadequate transportation facilities, almost no parks, and insufficient university-oriented housing. One result is a large number of students who live in rented single-family homes called "mini-dorms." Traffic and parking congestion can be severe. Some relief will arrive with the completion of the San Diego Trolley line through the campus in 2005.

The residential neighborhoods south of the College Area constitute the community of Rolando.

Coastal Communities of San Diego City

These communities include La Jolla, Pacific Beach, Mission Beach, Ocean Beach, and Point Loma.

La Jolla

La Jolla is often perceived as San Diego's most distinctive community (in fact, many think, erroneously, that it is a separate city). The ocean-oriented setting and the slopes of Mt. Soledad and the Muirlands combine to give a unique flavor to the community. The amenities and nationally renowned research facilities of UCSD and the Scripps Institute of Oceanography, as well as Torrey Pines State Park to the north, are other well-known attractions of La Jolla.

The physical barrier of Mt. Soledad kept La Jolla apart from San Diego until Ardath Road improved accessibility. The San Diego, Old Town, and Pacific Beach Railway served La Jolla from 1894 to 1919, and was the first major access to La Jolla. The loop of the rail line established the center of La Jolla as it exists today.

While La Jolla Cove and Park, UCSD, and Mt. Soledad are landmarks that distinguished La Jolla for many persons, the shopping area is equally important to others. The main commercial area above La Jolla Cove on Prospect and Girard Avenue contains many specialty shops, professional offices, import stores, and restaurants. It is a place for walking and browsing in the shop windows. The local sign control ordinance ads to the pleasantness of the surroundings (Figure 13.9). Although La Jolla is largely a pedestrian-oriented community, with a five-minute walk from the beach to downtown, the automobile presents a problem for pedestrians. Congestion and lack of parking facilities are ongoing problems in La Jolla. Nonetheless, La Jolla remains one of the true jewels of San Diego.

Pacific Beach and Mission Beach

The first major development to occur in Pacific Beach was a racetrack, in 1860, at the mouth of Rose Canyon. Following the 1889 recession, Pacific Beach was given over to lemon groves, and so it remained until the influx of defense workers in World War II created a large demand for housing. Traffic arterials that were built during the war gave form to the community and established the current pattern of commercial development. Today, Pacific Beach is an area of predominantly residential development enjoying water amenities on two sides. Bounded by Mission Bay to the South, and the Pacific Ocean to the west, the area is a draw for beach and water sports enthusiasts all year long. In the higher density areas, particularly the bay and ocean-oriented areas, parking and its attendant problems are serious.

Mission Beach had its beginnings in 1914 when it was subdivided into small lots for

Figure 13.9. Part of the main business district of La Jolla, illustrating the aesthetic benefits of that community's strict sign control ordinance. Photo by P. R. Pryde.

summer beach cottages. It was originally known as "New Tent City" since it served the same function as the Coronado "Tent City." During the years 1914–25, J. D. Spreckels built Belmont Park as an amusement center for San Diegans. This park, with its eye-catching roller coaster, divides the area into two distinct communities—North and South Mission Beach. Mission Beach is made up of very small lots that contains as many as thirty-five single-family residences per acre, and has population densities over 10,000 per square mile, the highest in the city. The population consists largely of young people, including many college students, who have a very strong "sense of community."

Future development of Mission Beach is a major concern to the residents, as well as to the city. Many people fear that the ocean front residential area will be turned into Miami Beach West. This led to the passage in 1972 of a height control initiative limiting structures to thirty feet. The high population density, a need for upgrading many of the houses, and the protective position taken by residents makes it difficult to reach agreement on the future of Mission Beach. The more than 6,000 residents combined with 10,000–20,000 weekend summer visitors create a traffic congestion and parking problem of major proportions.

The Point Loma Communities

Loma Portal was the first subdivision on or near the Point Loma peninsula, being founded in 1869. The western boundary is Nimitz Boulevard and the northern boundary is Midway Drive. Loma Portal contains a number of very stately Spanish colonial homes, and some streets are lined with turn-of-the-century gas lamp fixtures. A major new mixed-use development known as "Liberty Station" is being built on the former Navy Training Center property east of Rosecrans Street.

The Midway area stretches from Midway Drive to the intersection of I-5 and I-8. Dominating the entire area, from a visual perspective, is the Sports Arena. Unfortunately, traffic congestion and piecemeal development of incompatible land uses have created a chaotic environment. Most of the area is devoted to commercial and industrial uses, although a few apartment buildings and condominiums are interspersed throughout the area. Adding to the overall confusion is the frequent and deafening noise of aircraft departing from Lindbergh Field, also a serious problem in Loma Portal.

The historical promontory that separates the Pacific Ocean from San Diego Bay contains many expensive homes that have spectacular views, the campus of Point Loma Nazarene University and several military installations. The eastward view commands a stunning panorama of San Diego, the bay, and Coronado. The bayside of the Point Loma peninsula contains four significant features—historic Ballast Point (see Appendix 1.1), Cabrillo National Monument with its two lighthouses and tide pools, Shelter Island's boat facilities and restaurants, and Fort Rosecrans National Cemetery and adjacent naval installations.

Ocean Beach, on the west side of the peninsula, developed in the early 1900s as a summer cottage and resort community known as Mussel Beds. In 1910, the Wonderland Amusement Park drew San Diegans to the beach area via the Ocean Beach Motor Railway. During the 1920s and 1930s many of the cottages were converted to year-round residences, giving rise to the pattern of closely spaced, small homes. Today the population consists of two distinct groups—the older, established residents and the younger people that have moved to Ocean Beach and established a community within a community. The beach and pier, Sunset Cliffs, the sense of small community, and the youth culture are the most distinctive attributes of Ocean Beach.

All of Ocean Beach suffers from traffic congestion and parking problems which are especially intense during the summer beach season. Another vexing problem of Ocean Beach is the preservation of Sunset Cliffs. The cliffs are subject to extensive erosion by wave action, and various means of preserving the cliffs are being attempted.

Each of these coastal communities enjoys many water-related amenities and a high degree of community identity. They al seek to retain their desirable image, while coping with traffic and periodic water quality problems. Their location ensures that they will always be some of San Diego's most attractive real estate.

The Postwar Communities

These are the communities east of I-5 between Mission Valley and Miramar. Included are Clairemont, University City, Linda Vista, Serra Mesa, Navajo, and Tierrasanta. After World War II, the typical new tract community was laid out with curvilinear streets, giving a common appearance to these portions of the city.

Clairemont

Clairemont is San Diego's second largest residential community with over 80,000 residents in 2000. The northern and southern boundaries are San Clemente and Tecolote canyons, while the eastern and western boundaries are Interstates 805 and 5. Tract development began in 1950 in the subcommunity known as Morena, (or Bay Park), and continued on through the 1970s. The eastern Clairemont Boulevard-Convoy Street area (usually denoted as Kearny Mesa), has become the second most important industrial zone in the city. Also located in Clairemont are San Diego Mesa College, and Montgomery Field.

During the early 1970s the preservation of Tecolote and San Clemente canyons as open space and parklands was the lightning rod of community interest. As a result of these successful efforts, the community has over 1,300 acres of open space land.

University City

University City, to the north of Clairemont and San Clemente Canyon Park, dates from 1960. The impetus for University City was the decision of the Regents of the University of California to locate a campus on Torrey Pines Mesa. It wasn't until 1966–7 that direct access was made available when Genesee Avenue and San Clemente Canyon Road were opened. The area has achieved rather rapid growth in the past decade and is now considered San Diego's third "urban core." The area bounded by I-5, I-805, and Route 52 is commonly referred to as the "Golden Triangle" (Figure 13.10).

One feature which separates this community from others in San Diego is that the city and UCSD worked together to prepare a Community Plan before the community was built. The city and the university own sizeable portions of land, and the remainder was in large tracts held by a few owners. This restricted ownership has been a great aid in controlling the development patterns.

A major problem in University City is heard rather than seen. The Miramar Marine Corps Air Station lies to the east of University City, and the flight pattern brings military aircraft and their noise over portions of the community. Also problematic is the increased traffic associated with the rapid development.

Linda Vista

Linda Vista is located just above Mission Valley near the geographic center of San Diego. The focal point of the community is the Linda Vista Shopping Center, one of the first planned shopping centers in the United States.

Figure 13.10. View of a portion of the "Golden Triangle" district along La Jolla Village Drive west of I-805. This is the economic center of the northern portion of San Diego City. Photo by P. R. Pryde.

During World War II there was a need to increase housing to accommodate the influx of defense workers, and Linda Vista was created by the federal government as an "instant" community of 5,200 dwelling units in 1941. A year later, Eleanor Roosevelt turned the first spade of earth in groundbreaking ceremonies for the shopping center.

Today, Linda Vista is, in many respects, much like it was during World War II. One change is that a large Asian community has developed in the area. One of the dominant features of Linda Vista is the University of San Diego. USD is the city's largest private university, and contains one of the region's most distinctive architectural styles.

Across I-805, to the east, is the middle-income community of Serra Mesa. The eastern-most portion is sometimes referred to as Mission Village. Serra Mesa is a residential area of somewhat later vintage than Linda Vista. It has reached a high level of maturity and housing has stabilized at approximately 6,300 units, two-thirds of which are single-family residences. Since 1970 the population has remained stable at around 30,000, but a large contingent of Navy housing makes for a relatively high rate of housing turnover.

Navajo

Four subcommunities form the greater Navajo community—Grantville, Allied Gardens, Del Cerro, and San Carlos. Single-family homes are the major housing type throughout the Navajo area, which developed in the 1960s and early 1970s. The high topography and corresponding good views make this a desirable residential location. Grantville and Allied Gardens on the west side of the Navajo community comprise a commercial strip and a middle-class housing area respectively. On higher ground to the east is Del Cerro, an area of more housing on a hill overlooking the city, and further east San Carlos is situated around Lake Murray.

A variety of natural features adds to the uniqueness of this area. Elevations range from 100 feet above sea level in Grantville to 1,591 feet on Cowles Mountain, the highest point in the city. Grantville, at the mouth of Mission Gorge, was the first settlement in Mission Valley. This area was the hub of five early trails which have since grown to be the major arterials of Friars Road, I-15, I-8, and Mission Gorge Road. In the very early history of San Diego, the Mission San Diego de Alcala was moved to the strategic Grantville location and Mission Dam was erected upstream to supply irrigation waters. Allied Gardens, just above Grantville, was developed during the early 1950s. It has successfully fought to keep its major remaining open space, Navajo Canyon, from being developed.

With the 1974 acquisition by the city of Cowles Mountain, the Navajo community shares one of the nation's largest city parks with its neighbors. Mission Trails Park is 6000 acres of fishing, hiking, golfing, and exploring, and contains the deepest gorge found within any major city in America.

Tierrasanta

Tierrasanta was one of San Diego's main master plan developments of the 1970s and 1980s. Tierrasanta has planned for the preservation of the main canyons through the area, and with Mission Trails Regional Park immediately to the east, it should remain a very attractive community (despite the discovery in 1983 that live shells from World War II still exist there). Access has

been improved with the Santo Road connection to Route 52.

Mission Valley

This "Postwar" section cannot end without some mention of Mission Valley itself. Until the 1950s, Mission Valley was an agricultural floodplain, in which dairy cows probably outnumbered people (Figure 13.11). Large floods were not uncommon (see Chapter 8). In the 1950s, the first phase of the Mission Valley shopping center was begun, the road that is now I-8 was paved and widened, and the fate of the valley was sealed. Over the next 40 years, Friars Road was widened, sand and gravel operations were transformed into ever more shops and condominiums, the sports stadium was built and underwent several name changes, a trolley line was added, and the bucolic valley had become one of the prime mixed-use communities of the city. As a commercial venue Mission Valley is very convenient and lively, and all we need to do now is hope it doesn't rain in very large amounts.

The Northern Communities

The northern communities of the City of San Diego are those north of the Miramar air station, one group of which is located along I-15 (the "I-15 Corridor"), and the other just east of I-5. The first, and best known, of these is Rancho Bernardo.

Rancho Bernardo

Rancho Bernardo was the first of San Diego's outlying developments. It was heralded as a "new town" by its developer in 1966, and was pre-planned to include shops, open space, and industry in addition to housing. The community has promoted a recreation atmosphere, with the presence of golf courses, tennis courts, and

Figure 13.11. Mission Valley in 1954, when its major economic activity was still dairy farms. Note "rush hour traffic" on what is now I-8! View is to the east from Presidio Park. Photo by Lauren Post.

equestrian trails. These neighborhoods served originally as bedroom communities for San Diegans wanting to live "out in the countryside", but other subdivisions now envelop it.

The older portion of this community appears as a green oasis to the east of I-15 which bisects it; the newer portion is to the west. This western portion contains a large industrial park area, which provides employment for some residents, but also attracts thousands of commuters daily onto overcrowded I-15. Rancho Bernardo has one of the strongest community identities of any portion of San Diego.

Rancho Peñasquitos

The second new community in the "I-15 Corridor" was Rancho Peñasquitos, begun in the 1970s. It is located west of I-15, just north of the Los Peñasquitos Canyon Preserve. This canyon, and the conical peak of Black Mountain to the north (the second highest point in the City of San Diego), are the defining physical features of this spread-out residential neighborhood. The routing of Highway 56 through the community was very controversial, but its opening in about 2005 should help alleviate traffic flow through the area (until the drivers get to I-5 or I-15!).

Mira Mesa

Mira Mesa in the 1970s was one of San Diego's fastest growing communities. It is well defined by I-15 on the east, Miramar Naval Air Station on the south, I-5 on the west, and Los Peñasquitos Canyon on the north. Mira Mesa epitomized the overly hurried growth that occurred in San Diego during the '60s. Because of the resulting inadequate level of services Mira Mesa experienced, the city declared a moratorium on new housing until a growth plan could be developed.

Carmel Mountain and Sabre Springs

These two developments are on the east side of the freeway, opposite Rancho Peñasquitos, and complete the existing string of communities along the I-15 Corridor. Carmel Mountain was begun in the 1980s and Sabre Springs in the 1990s, on what was previously grazing land. Both abut directly on the city of Poway to the east, and are for the most part commuter communities, although Sabre Springs has a small light industry section.

The major problem of all these communities can be summed up very succinctly in one brief phrase: I-15. Well over 100,000 people live in these four I-15 Corridor communities, but expansions of I-15 did not keep pace. Today, the volume of cars trying to use I-15 (over 400,000 per day) greatly exceeds its capacity, especially at peak commuting hours, as anyone who has driven it in mid-morning or late afternoon is sadly aware. The small number of persons using bus service to these communities offers almost no relief, and there are no rapid transit options. Two HOV (high-occupancy vehicle) lanes for part of the route helps a bit, but only compounds the problem at the point where they end.

Improvements are being made to the freeway to help improve flow, but no rapid transit line is planned for the I-15 corridor. What is proposed is a "transitway", which may by 2020 exist as an exclusive bus-only route, but in 2004 it existed only in the conceptual stage. To make matters worse, another large-scale development, Black Mountain Ranch, may soon be built, which would also have to rely on I-15 for its commuting access.

The "North City West" Communities

In the 1970's, the development of a huge area of north San Diego was approved. This area, east of I-5 and north of Penasquitos Canyon, was originally referred to as North City West, but few people liked this name. As it began to be master-planned, the two main sub-areas took on the specific names of Sorrento Hills and Carmel Valley. Two existing neighborhoods west of I-5 are known as Sorrento Valley and Torrey Pines. The Carmel Valley neighborhoods will continue to be developed for many years yet.

Although these are mainly residential communities, a large new light-industry complex has been developed near the intersection of I-15 and Route 56. This employment center, combined with the existing one in Sorrento Valley, broke the back of I-5 in terms of capacity. The three-mile stretch between the merge of I-805 and Del Mar Heights Road is one of the worst traffic jams in the county, perhaps exceeding even I-15. The mystery here is, that unlike I-15, there is an excellent alternative: the commuter trains that run along the coast, paralleling I-5 (see Chapter 11). Although these trains are heavily used, and ridership is growing, it is mind-boggling why anyone would want to sit in traffic jams on I-5 when commuter trains are zipping past only a few feet away.

The San Dieguito River Valley

The northern boundary of the City of San Diego is, for a portion of its length, in or near the San Dieguito River Valley. A few exclusive neighborhoods exist here within the city limits, such as Fairbanks Country Club, but for the most part this valley remains rural, and there is a strong desire to keep it that way. Just east of Del Mar, the floodplain of the river is subject to periodic inundation, and plans are being made to keep it free of intensive development. Further east, the City of San Diego owns the land around Lake Hodges, which is managed by the City Water Department. Still further east, all of San Pasqual Valley is likewise owned by the City, and is leased to farmers for various agricultural pursuits. On the north slopes is the well known San Diego Wild Animal Park.

All of these areas (and more in other nearby cities and the county) are within the planning area for the San Dieguito River Park. This Park is an ambitious effort to create a linear open space park with a continuous trail system the entire length of the San Dieguito River corridor, from its source on Volcan Mountain to its estuary in Del Mar. By 2002, over 20 miles of trails had been opened.

This chapter has described a bit of the past and present of San Diego. Its future will largely reflect increasing density within the present city limits, as there is little unincorporated territory remaining nearby that could be annexed to the city. Thus, the current configuration of communities will most likely change very little in coming years. The challenge will be to maintain the attractiveness and livability of these communities as their demographic characteristics evolve over time.

References

Centre City Development Corporation. *Downtown Today* (Issue No. 40). San Diego: CCDC, Winter 2003.

City of San Diego. *Centre City Development Plan* (as updated). City of San Diego Planning Department. See also other community plans.

City of San Diego. *Progress Guide and General Plan for the City of San Diego.* San Diego City Planning Department, 1979, as updated (new edition expected in 2004).

Daly-Lipe, Patricia, and Barbara Dawson. *La Jolla: A Celebration of Its Past.* San Diego: Sunbelt Publications, 2002.

Higgins, S. J. *This Fantastic City San Diego.* City of San Diego, 1956.

Mendel, Carol. *San Diego on Foot.* San Diego: Arts and Crafts Press, 1990.

Peik, R. and L. Peik, *Discover San Diego.* San Diego: Peik's Enterprises, 1989.

Pourade, R. F. *History of San Diego.* (6 vols.), San Diego: Union-Tribune Publishing Company, 1960–67.

Randolph, H. S. F. *La Jolla Year by Year.* La Jolla: Library Association of La Jolla, 1955.

San Diego Association of Governments, *1990 Activity Centers,* San Diego: SANDAG, 1990.

Smythe, W. E. *History of San Diego, 1542–1907.* San Diego: The History Company, 1907.

Stutz, F. P. *San Diego Downtown Walking Guide.* El Cajon, R. V. Press, 1989.

Internet Connections:
Center City Development Corp.: *www.ccdc.com*
City of San Diego: *www.sandiego.gov*
San Diego General Plan: *www.sandiego.gov/general-plan/index.shtml*

Philip R. Pryde and
Frederick P. Stutz

Chapter Fourteen

Beyond the Central City
Other Communities and Towns of the County

Beyond the city limits of San Diego lie seventeen other incorporated cities and a larger number of unincorporated communities (see Figures 14.1 and 14.4). Incorporated cities (such as Oceanside and Chula Vista) are those that constitute separate legal entities that are self-governing within their specified city limits. Unincorporated communities (such as Lakeside or Julian) lack such self-governing rights and

Philip R. Pryde is professor emeritus of environmental studies in the Department of Geography at San Diego State University, and prepared the material in this chapter for the fourth edition. Frederick P. Stutz is a professor of urban studies in the Department of Geography, and wrote the original version of this chapter for the book's earlier editions.

are not separate legal entities; both their governance and their boundaries are determined by the County of San Diego through its Board of Supervisors. Due to the large number of both types of communities, only a brief sketch of each can be given here, with the hope of capturing a bit of the special ambiance of each. We will start with the cities and towns located south of the City of San Diego.

South County Communities

National City
National City is the second oldest city in San Diego County, having been incorporated in 1887

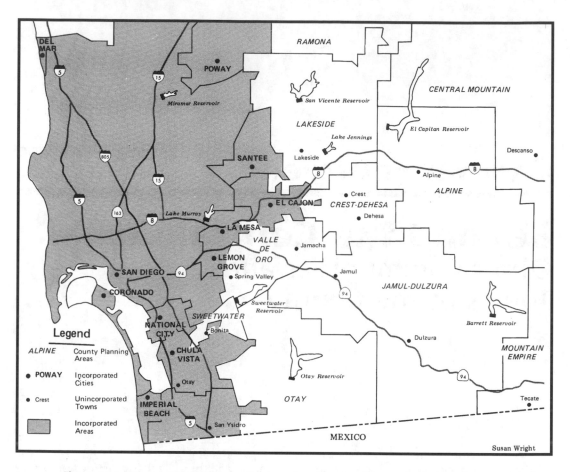

Figure 14.1. Communities of the southern and eastern San Diego suburban area, showing county planning areas and generalized boundaries of incorporated cities. Chula Vista has expanded east to Otay Reservoir since this map was compiled.

(Figure 14.2). National City is largely built-out, and its population increased only slightly between 1970 and 2000, to a total of 54,260. The city's economy is heavily dependent on Navy or civilian employees of the 32nd Street Naval Station. Other activities exist, however. The 24th Street Marine Terminal has attracted a number of related industrial firms, and a potential for further expansion exists. The southwesterly quarter of National City has been redeveloped

with new commercial and industrial uses. The area around 8th Avenue and National City Boulevard is being redeveloped with more intensive high rise commercial uses, and the Plaza Bonita shopping mall has helped the city's economic base.

The population is relatively young (25.8 years), and many are Spanish speaking. In many ways, National City resembles Southeast San Diego, which is the adjoining neighbor to the

Figure 14.2. The Frank Kimball house in National City, originally constructed in 1868, is one of that community's best preserved historic landmarks. Photo by P. R. Pryde.

north, and the two communities share many of the same problems.

Chula Vista

Chula Vista, which incorporated in 1911, has become the second largest city in San Diego County, with a 2000 population of 173,556. It continues to grow rapidly, and should reach 200,000 residents before 2010.

During World War II the Rohr Aircraft plant moved to Chula Vista from San Diego, and quickly became its largest industry. Chula Vista is the major urban center of the South Bay, and its economy benefits from its proximity to Tijuana and Baja California. Chula Vista's growing pains include traffic congestion and no identifiable downtown, but overall the city appears as a pleasant suburban residential community.

Currently Chula Vista is developing its waterfront, particularly around the J Street marina, and has plans for a large and somewhat controversial waterfront development on former agricultural lands between E and F streets which, if built as planned, would become Chula Vista's de facto city center. Chula Vistans hope that the fossil fuel power plant that dominates the waterfront near L Street can be retired and torn down in the near future.

Traveling east along E Street one drops down into the Sweetwater River Valley, and encounters the old rural residential community of Bonita. As the pressure for moderately expensive homes has increased, Bonita has grown to sizeable proportions, and portions of it have been annexed to Chula Vista. Bonita Road is now a major commercial strip. The proposed SR125 freeway is routed east of Bonita, and is intended to connect the east county with Otay Mesa. The highway will serve the rapidly developing eastern portions of the City of Chula Vista, such as Eastlake and Otay Ranch, which has encircled Southwestern Community College. Chula Vista also includes the blue-collar neighborhoods of Harborside, Castle Park, and Otay, which collectively are known as the Montgomery area.

Imperial Beach

Imperial Beach lies in the extreme southwest corner of both the county and the conterminous United States. It adjoins the Mexican border and fronts on the Pacific Ocean and San Diego Bay. The name was selected in the late nineteenth century to appeal to the residents of Imperial Valley; early subdividers envisioned Imperial Valley residents building a community of summer homes along the beaches. Imperial Beach remained a quiet seaside village until 1906, when ferry and railroad connections with San Diego were completed.

Incorporated in 1956, Imperial Beach is a residential and water-oriented community. Unfortunately, there is no identifiable city center, and an inadequate economic base is perhaps its major problem. Ream Field Naval Air Station is the major employer in Imperial Beach.

During the 1970s, the city had proposed that the Tijuana River could be changed into a recreational and residential marina; but many other people and organizations strongly opposed the idea (including the city of San Diego in which the estuary partly lies). It is now protected as a National Estuarine Sanctuary, and adjoins a still larger county maintained habitat preserve to the east that is within the city of San Diego.

Coronado

Coronado began in 1880s, as a popular venue for land speculators and rabbit hunters. It gained its lasting identity in 1888, with the completion of the famous Hotel Del Coronado (Figure 14.3). Three years later, Coronado incorporated as a city. In 1917, the federal government secured North Island for military purposes, and ever since the Navy has played a leading role in Coronado's history.

The prominent landmarks, most of which can be seen from locations all around the bay, are the Hotel, the Coronado Shores condominiums, and the Bay Bridge. On a smaller scale, one can notice the integration of architecture and vegetation, the curving boulevards, wide sidewalks, and distinctive business establishments. Throughout the residential area, especially along Ocean Boulevard and Alemeda, are many old and stately mansions. The natural amenities, wealth, and insular location of Coronado combine to make it one of San Diego's most pleasant and well-defined communities, with a very stable population of around 24,000.

With the opening of the Bay Bridge in 1969, Coronado's isolated situation was removed, to the displeasure of some local residents. Two major residential developments appeared during the 1970's, Coronado Cays and Coronado Shores (ten very noticeable 17 story buildings).

No freeways exist in Coronado, and the increased traffic generated by the Navy and tourism has created significant congestion of unprecedented proportions on the local streets. Walking is still a pleasure in the residential areas along the beaches. Despite its traffic problems, Coronado remains a delightful, albeit expensive, community.

Figure 14.3. The Hotel del Coronado, an outstanding Victorian landmark since 1887. It is on the National Register of Historic Sites. Photo by Philip R. Pryde.

East County Communities

El Cajon

The Spanish term "el cajon," meaning "the box," is a very fit description of the broad, level valley fifteen miles inland from the coast. El Cajon was the first incorporated city in the valley (1912), and is now the fifth largest in the county. The city limits encompass the greater portion of the valley floor, which historically used to serve as an agricultural and livestock grazing region. The community originated in the 1870s around the old Knox Hotel, which served as a stagecoach stop at the corner of Main and Magnolia. The Knox House and Museum, a few blocks to the north, date from 1876.

El Cajon is a classic example of an exploding suburb, as its population went from 5,600 in 1950 to almost 100,000 in 2003. However, its population has grown relatively little since 1990 as El Cajon (unlike other medium-sized cities in the county) has annexed very little surrounding land.

The rapid urbanization has depended almost entirely on the private automobile for mobility. Today the commercial center is the Parkway Plaza regional shopping center just north of the I-8 freeway. The old downtown is the location of the popular East county Performance Arts Center. El Cajon also has developed a growing industrial park of over 200 manufacturing firms, centered around Gillespie Field, which El Cajon annexed in the late 1970s.

Bostonia, one of San Diego County's oldest rural communities, lies on the edge of the city of El Cajon, but has not yet been incorporated into it.

La Mesa

La Mesa is a city whose topography has defied urban sprawl. It was founded in 1888, as one of Southern California's boom towns, and was advertised as the "Pasadena of San Diego." Originally known as Allison Springs, and later as La Mesa Springs, the area served as an operations base for the construction of a railroad. Incorporated as a general law city with a population of 700 in 1912, the city grew at a relatively slow rate until 1940. In the next forty years La Mesa grew from 4,000 to 50,000, and today is often referred to as one of San Diego's "bedroom communities."

A major landmark associated with La Mesa, but actually east of the city limits, is Mt. Helix. The small park on the summit affords (on clear days) an excellent view over much of the San Diego region. Easter sunrise services are held annually in the amphitheater just below the summit.

All of La Mesa is rather hilly and many homes have sweeping views in various directions, attracting a generally affluent population. The main commercial area is the Grossmont Shopping Center which, when it opened in the 1960s, threatened downtown La Mesa with becoming a near ghost town. However, La Mesa has revitalized its downtown district, and the city's annual Oktoberfest is held on the main street. It is one of the region's most stable cities.

Santee

North of El Cajon is the city of Santee. This former ranch was first subdivided during the 1880s, but in 1950, fewer than 2,000 people lived there. During the ensuing forty years the population has exploded to over 52,000. The city benefited in the 1990s by the extension of both the San Diego Trolley and state freeway 52 to Santee. A major commercial development has been built around the Santee trolley station.

A major attraction in Santee is the Santee Lakes Recreation Park, built around a water reclamation plant which received worldwide publicity in the late 1960s. Mast Park is another popular recreational facility along the San Diego River.

In the late 1990s, a spirited battle ensued over the proposed subdivision of Santee's last major open space area, Fanita Ranch. The outcome of this debate will have much to do with deciding the future urban character of Santee.

Lemon Grove

Lemon Grove is located eight miles east of San Diego and was one of earliest rapidly growing suburbs. The lemon groves for which it was named have been supplanted by thousands of housing units, and only a whimsical, huge yellow lemon mounted in the center of town gives a clue to how its name originated. The movement to incorporate Lemon Grove as a separate city was successfully concluded by a vote of the residents in 1977. As it is largely built up within its city limits, its 2000 population of about 25,000 will not increase rapidly. It is served by both the 94 and 125 freeways, and the San Diego trolley.

Spring Valley

East of Lemon Groove is the unincorporated residential community of Spring Valley. Located on generally hilly topography with attractive views, its 2000 population was 59,324, making it the second largest unincorporated community in San Diego county (Table 14.1). Like lemon Grove, it is accessible by state routes 94 and 125.

There are two subcommunities on the southern fringes of Spring Valley, the new Rancho San Diego and the much older La Presa. To its

TABLE 14.1. The Largest Unincorporated Communities in San Diego County

Community	Est'd 1990 Population	2000 Population[1]
Lakeside	49,800	72,370
Spring Valley	61,000	59,324
Valle de Oro	37,800	40,035
Fallbrook	38,000	39,585
North County Metro[2]	36,000	38,171
Pendleton/DeLuz	40,300	36,927
Ramona	27,700	33,407
Alpine	9,800	16,681
Valley Center	15,100	15,639
Sweetwater[3]	14,500	12,951
San Dieguito[4]	9,000	2,527
Crest/Dehesa	10,400	9,426
Jamul/Dulzura	9,600	9,208
Bonsall	n/a	8,864

[1]Changes in community populations between 1990 and 2000 may result from changes in the location of community boundaries and urban annexations, as well as demographic changes.
[2]North County Metro refers to the unincorporated enclaves and rural areas around the cities of Vista, Carlsbad, Oceanside, San Marcos and Escondido.
[3]Some of this area was annexed into the city of Chula Vista.
[4]The San Dieguito area includes Del Dios, Rancho Santa Fe, Fairbanks Ranch, and Harmony Grove.

Source: County of San Diego, Department of Planning and Land Use, 2002.

north is the Valle de Oro area. If Spring Valley continues to urbanize, its most logical future fate would be to incorporate.

Lakeside

Immediately north of El Cajon, and extending on both sides of state route 67, lies the unincorporated community of Lakeside. Lakeside is an older community that has a long-established core near Lindo Lake, which accounts for its

name. In the early part of the twentieth century, a railroad line reached Lakeside (see Figure 11.2). In addition to residential sub-divisions extending outwards from the old core, there is also a large rural area in the lightly-populated Lakeside backcountry. In this rural area is located the Barona Indian Reservation and the expansive Barona Casino, Lakeside's largest employer.

Several county parks and open space preserves, plus San Vicente, El Capitan, and Lake Jennings reservoirs, attract visitors from throughout the region. The San Diego River flows through the community, and an effort is underway to enhance it and create a river park along portions of it.

Lakeside was the largest unincorporated community in the county in 2000 with a planning area population of 72,370, and consequently growth management has become a major issue there. Like Spring Valley, all or part of Lakeside may eventually incorporate.

Alpine

Alpine is another old rural community that has grown tremendously in the last thirty years. The townsite dates from 1883, and still retains a few old buildings that remind the newcomers of its long history. On Alpine's eastern edge lies the Viejas Casino, campground, and factory outlet complex. Easy access via Interstate 8 encouraged rapid development in Alpine during the 1980s and 1990s, and its population has surged to over 15,000. Following the turn of the century, a spirited debate was underway concerning the extent, and pace, of Alpine's future growth, and the fate of the open space that surrounds it.

Ramona

Ramona is a rapidly growing unincorporated town in the foothills of central San Diego County, established in 1886. Its 1893 Town Hall still stands. This area was named for the heroine in Helen Hunt Jackson's classical novel of Indian oppression in California. It is now within the commuting sphere of San Diego, but is still connected to the metropolitan area by a single road that is still just two lanes in places. Despite this its population had exploded to 33,400 by 2000.

Like Lakeside and Alpine, Ramona covers a large rural area, and functions as a service center for a productive agricultural region in which eggs and horses are important specialty crops. Near Ramona is the extensive San Diego Country Estates development. Curbing the rapid growth of the Ramona region, improving access to and within the community, and deciding the future of the environmentally important Ramona grasslands are key issues for the initial years of the twenty-first century.

The North Coastal Cities

Prior to the 1970s the North Coastal region was predominantly a semirural residential area with large amounts of undeveloped land. As the area began to develop, several distinct communities became established over the years. These included Del Mar, Solana Beach, Leucadia, Cardiff, Encinitas, Carlsbad, Oceanside, Olivenhain, and Rancho Sante Fe (Figure 14.4). The lack of water held these communities to a rather modest rate of growth until the 1920s. The opening of Lake Hodges and later the availability of Colorado River water permitted growth to accelerate and the open spaces began to fill in.

Del Mar

Del Mar is a beautiful, small city with under 5,000 residents that embraces strict development policies. Because of its small size, Del Mar is close to being entirely developed within its city limits. It has many activities that add to its appeal, of which the best known are the Del Mar

Fairgrounds and the Del Mar Race Track. Not only do they bring Del Mar revenue, but they also provide much excitement (and congestion) in the summertime.

Starting in the 1990s, the restoration of the San Dieguito Lagoon has been one of Del Mar's highest priorities. The restoration of the natural functions of the lagoon is one of the key projects of the San Dieguito River Park.

Solana Beach

Solana Beach was incorporated in 1986, and mirrors Del Mar in being small in area and almost entirely built out. Although its 13,000 residents are highly urbanized, parts of the town retain a certain rural quality within an urban area. One noteworthy development in Solana Beach is the placement of a commuter rail station at Lomas Santa Fe and the Pacific Coast Highway (S21).

Encinitas

Encinitas, like Solana Beach, incorporated in 1986 and now has 58,000 inhabitants. It is comprised of five distinct communities; Leucadia, Old Encinitas, "New" Encinitas (east of I-5), Olivenhain, and Cardiff by the Sea. Olivenhain was one of the original agricultural settlements in the area, and although Olivenhain has been engulfed by subdivisions, the 100-year old Meeting Hall still stands. Encinitas enjoys the open space of San Elijo Lagoon, numerous beaches, and a small amount of residual agriculture, including the Paul Ecke poinsettia farms. Batiquitos Lagoon forms the northern boundary (Figures 14.5 and 14.6).

Carlsbad

Carlsbad is another old coastal community, dating from 1883. It originally was a mineral spa with a strong central European flavor. Although it didn't become a city until 1952, it has been very growth-oriented over the past decade, and now

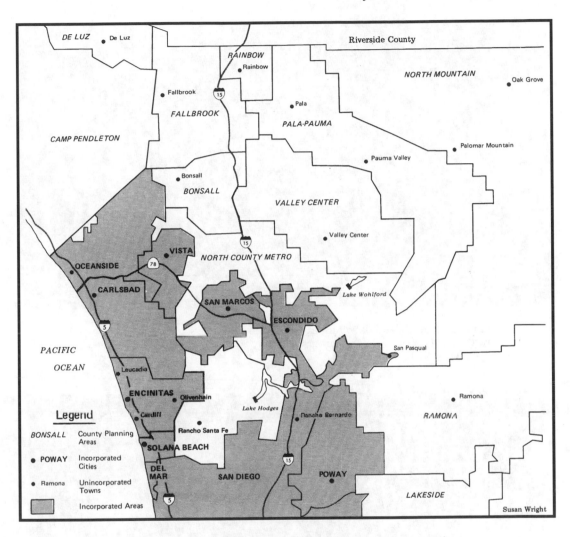

Figure 14.4 North county communities, showing county planning areas and generalized boundaries of incorporate cities.

contains over 80,000 residents. San Diego Gas and Electric's (Sempra Energy) Encina power plant used to be the only major industrial plant in the city, but today many new firms have located along the I-5 railroad corridor south of the power station, as well as near Palomar Airport. A major new tourist attraction built in the 1990s is the Legoland theme park. Nearby are the last remnants of the famous Carlsbad flower fields, still a major and highly colorful attraction each spring.

Figure 14.5. Leucadia and Batiquitos Lagoon in the early 1960s. I-5 is under construction in the upper left corner of the picture. Photo courtesy of the San Diego County Department of Agriculture.

Figure 14.6. Same area as above in 1980, showing intensive beach front development along the bluffs in Leucadia. Photo by Bob O'Brien.

The city of Carlsbad has expanded its borders greatly since the 1970s, annexing the exclusive La Costa development in the process, yet the city still lacks an identifiable downtown. To catch a flavor of the Old Carlsbad, visit the coastal area along Carlsbad Boulevard (Figure 14.7). The city's coastal strip also enjoys the open space of three lagoons—Bataquitos, Agua Hedionda, and Buena Vista, the later shared with Oceanside.

Oceanside

The most northern city in the county, Oceanside has been since the 1940s the major urban area serving the Marine Corps training facilities at Camp Pendleton. Settlement in the area dates from the founding of the historic Mission San Luis Rey in 1798 (Figure 14.8).

Oceanside was incorporated in 1888, and has lately annexed and expanded into former agricultural areas to the east. In 1970, the population of Oceanside was 40,494; by 1990 the population had tripled to over 128,000 and reached 161,000 in 2000. A portion of the new homes serve commuters who work in Orange or Riverside counties.

The principal economic activities of the community are retail trade, electronics, government services, tourist trade, and agriculture. More than a hundred light industrial companies are located here. Commercial developments along El Camino Real at Highways 76 and 78 have

Figure 14.7. The former Twin Inns, now a restaurant, in Carlsbad, another excellent example of nineteenth century Victorian architecture in north county. Photo by Philip R. Pryde.

Figure 14.8. The Mission San Luis Rey, in Oceanside. It is the second oldest in the county, dating from 1798. Photo by Philip R. Pryde.

boosted Oceanside's retail sales significantly. The city would like to expand and modernize its waterfront, harbor, and oceanfront facilities, but has a continuing problem with loss of beach sand. The influence of the military on Oceanside's economy will likely continue, as no reductions in Marine Corps operations at Camp Pendleton are likely in the foreseeable future.

Inland North County

Inland North County has been the fastest growing portion of San Diego County over the past twenty years. Orchards and farmland have given way to subdivisions and shopping centers, resulting in expansive urban growth and intolerable

traffic conditions on I-15. In 2004, an end to neither the growth boom nor the traffic problem was in sight.

Escondido

Escondido, an old incorporated city (1888) in north central San Diego County, has grown rapidly in the last thirty years. Escondido's population has increased from 36,800 in 1970 to 133,559 in 2000, mainly through the annexation of new residential developments on its periphery. It is now the county's fourth largest city, and the site of the California Center for the Arts.

The chief business activities are agriculture and retail trade, with the principal agricultural products being avocados, poultry, oranges and lemons. Escondido is a good example of a city serving a large outlying region, as its per capita retail sales are among the highest in the county.

The city enjoys the amenities of Lake Hodges, Kit Carson Park (with its spectacular Niki de Saint Phalle sculpture garden), and the San Dieguito River Park to the south, and Lakes Wohlford and Dixon to the north. It is also the entry way to the Wild Animal Park and new wineries in the San Pasqual Valley.

San Marcos

San Marcos has greatly expanded both its land area and population since its incorporation in 1963. The population exploded from 3000 in 1965, to almost 55,000 in 2000. The city has attracted much industry and has developed several new business centers. It could become an industrial center for North County. It is also the site of the new San Marcos State University.

Vista

Vista, like San Marcos, was incorporated in 1963, and is situated on the site of the old Buena Vista ranch. It is predominantly a residential community, essentially an eastward extension of Oceanside, and claims to have "America's best climate." Also like San Marcos, its population has grown rapidly from 24,700 in 1970 to over 90,000 in 2001. The growth of these cities has strained the capacity of Route 78 which connects them, and resulted in plans to add a commuter service on the rail line which runs from Oceanside to Escondido.

Vista's rapid growth has strained city services, which suffer from lack of an industrial tax base. Other planning challenges include a congested city center, and a lack of developed city parks. Nevertheless, the city continues to attract new residents, and its population is expected to exceed 100,000 within the decade.

Fallbrook

The history of Fallbrook goes back to 1869, when the Vital Reche family established a ranch just south of the present Live Oak Park. Over the years the community has developed into a picturesque, agriculturally-oriented town that combines both rural charm and a village atmosphere. The northern portion of the greater Fallbrook region is located among the rugged mountains which surround the Santa Margarita River. North of the river is the intentionally isolated community of DeLuz. Gently rolling hills covered with avocado and citrus crops predominate throughout the central part of Fallbrook. The southern portion is centered about the San Luis Rey River and is adjacent to the community of Bonsall, an area of rural homes surrounded by tree crops. In the 1990s, Bonsall became a focus of development activity, to the dismay of many older residents. Just east of I-15 is Rainbow, long the site of many nurseries and other specialized agriculture.

Fallbrook's population has increased twentyfold since 1940 when less than 2,000 people resided in the area. As of 2000, the population of the greater Fallbrook area stood at about 40,000, not including Camp Pendleton. Many of the residents are employed in the Fallbrook-Camp Pendleton area. Fallbrook turned down incorporation in 1981.

Pauma Valley

Stretching along the middle reaches of the San Luis Rey river and state highway 76 lies Pauma Valley. Although it contains only one village of the same name, it also is home to the densest concentration of Indian reservations in the county, which collectively have several thousand inhabitants. Although the valley remains largely agricultural, changes are clearly imminent, as no less than 5 casinos have been built

in this area. Of primary concern is the inade-
quacy of highways 76 and S-6 to handle greatly
increased volumes of traffic, as well as the
effects of potential private development on
nearby Palomar Mountain and its world-
famous 200-inch telescope. This valley requires
a great deal of thought as to the extent of its
future development.

Poway

Poway is a well-concealed pleasant suburb somewhat more isolated than Lakeside and Santee.
The community, which is a functional suburb
of San Diego, incorporated in 1980. Like
Lakeside, it was a prospering community well
before the turn of the century. Today, this history is largely confined to one small historical
museum which is well worth a visit.

Poway likes to call itself "The City in the
Country". It prides itself on good planning, and
has laid out an extensive open space and trail system. Although it grew rapidly between 1970 and
1990, its 2000 population of 48,044 is expected to
increase more slowly in the twenty-first century.
An industrial district has been created along
Scripps Poway Parkway.

Valley Center

To the Northeast of Escondido is the agricultural community of Valley Center. Although not
yet experiencing rapid growth, it could in the
near future. Valley Center embraces a large land
area mainly situated on a relatively flat plateau
which could be easily developed. For development to occur, a sewerage system would need to
be constructed, and road access to Escondido
and to I-15 would need to be improved. Valley
Center's 2000 population of 15,600 could double
by 2020, and many of its agricultural lands
urbanized, if the above infrastructure improvements are approved and built. The community
was hard hit by the 2003 Paradise fire.

The "Ranches"

Rancho Santa Fe was developed in 1922 as
exclusive country estates by the Santa Fe
Railroad. Originally, it was part of the San
Dieguito Ranch and was used by the railroad
to grow eucalyptus trees for crossties, but the
wood proved unsuitable for this purpose. Today
Rancho Santa Fe is a well planned, upper class
community with the highest average income levels in the county. Rancho Santa Fe has an active
and strong local homeowners association and
explicit covenants for the maintenance and protection of housing.

The above comments also apply to the nearby
Fairbanks Ranch, and the newer Crosby Estates.
Further south, the Fairbanks Country Club was
the site of the endurance trials for the 1984
Olympic Games equestrian event.

Rural Towns and Villages

The Highway 94 Communities

On, or near, state highway 94 lie a network of
small communities that collectively have a fascinating tale of county history to relate. Located
in some of the most scenic countryside in the
county, they stretch from Jamul to Jacumba.

Jamul and Vicinity

East of Spring Valley and Rancho San Diego is
the unincorporated community of Jamul. It is
characterized by low density, upper middle class
housing, a fiercely guarded rural lifestyle, and
an independent and engagingly non-conform-
ist citizenry. Like Alpine and Poway, it is close
enough to the metropolitan area to be a com-
mutable bedroom community, despite the hazards of the narrow and winding Highway 94.
Several large developments have been built in
Jamul in recent years, including the large Sycuan
Casino, but a strong desire exists to maintain the
rural character of the community. It remains to

be seen if the residents there can retain its present rural atmosphere in the face of strong development pressures.

A little further down Highway 94 is the village of Dulzura, which with Jamul forms the Jamul-Dulzura sub-regional planning area. The Jamul-Dulzura area had a 2000 population of 9,208. North of Jamul but still south of the freeway are the adjacent but split-level communities of Crest and Harbison Canyon. Crest is probably the best hidden of the nearby communities, where new avocado groves find their southernmost expression in the county. Harbison Canyon is an older community, and both it and Crest suffered huge losses of homes in the 2003 Cedar fire.

The Eastern Highway 94 Communities

Lying to the south of Highway 94, which runs close to the Mexican border, are the six small communities of Tecate, Potrero, Campo, Morena Village, Boulevard, and Jacumba. None have more than a few hundred residents, and none (with the possible exception of Tecate) want too many more. Campo and Jacumba are the two most historic of these communities; the Campo store historic site was built in 1886 (Campo was also the site of a World War II prisoner-of-war camp, and earlier housed troops of the famous "Buffalo Soldiers").

The Jacumba hot springs resort has been a landmark for decades. In the 1990s, a huge land development project was proposed for Jacumba; its fate was unknown as of 2002. Boulevard's proximity to I-8 may eventually encourage growth; a small Indian casino has been recently built at a nearby freeway exit. Tecate has controversial long-range growth plans based on its twin-city status with its nearby and much larger Mexican counterpart of the same name.

All county residents, on some of their eastward jaunts, should drive Highway 94 and enjoy the quiet beauty and rural charm of this often overlooked border route.

Pine Valley and Descanso

These communities both lie a short distance off Interstate 8. The freeway bypasses Descanso, but old U.S. 80 connects it to Pine Valley. Pine Valley and Descanso have thus far not suffered much from indiscriminate development. Descanso and Pine Valley (together with Julian) function as tourist service centers for the popular Cuyamaca and Laguna recreation areas. In addition to the threat of high-priced "estate" development, all lie in areas subject to periodic brushfires (see Chapter 3).

Julian and Other Mountain Towns

Julian is without question the most historic non-coastal community in San Diego County. Julian burst dramatically onto the county scene following the discovery of gold there in 1870, and soon was the second largest settlement in the county (see Chapter 6). It vied with San Diego to be the County seat. The gold boom lasted little more than a decade, however, and Julian once again became a quiet mountain village.

Today, this highest community in the county (4,100 feet above sea level) is a popular tourist stop and second home locale, with many gold rush buildings still standing (Figure 14.9). Thanks to a tremendous effort by firemen, these buildings and others in downtown Julian were spared in the great fire of October 2003. Of special interest is a delightfully disorganized country museum, and the old Witch Creek school, built in 1888, which is now a library. Julian is a must for anyone exploring the historic corners of the county. However, new tourist facilities and second home developments, are creating seasonal traffic problems. The population of the Julian planning area in 2000 was 3,100.

Figure 14.9. The Julian land office building, with the Julian Hotel visible at right. Both buildings date from the gold rush and are still commercially in operation. Photo by Philip R. Pryde.

A few miles west of Julian is the crossroads village of Santa Ysabel. Perhaps best known for an irresistible bakery located there, it was also the site of an early asistencia, or mission outpost, the original buildings of which no longer exist. Further north is the resort of Warner Springs, long a popular spot for those whose love of warm mineral baths is greater than their dislike of hydrogen sulfide vapors. In 1983 it was re-opened as a subscription-only private resort. A popular glider port is nearby as well as an early chapel from San Diego's Mexican period (see Figure 1.3). The villages of Mt. Laguna and Palomar Mountain handle tourist and local residents' needs on their respective mountains.

Borrego Springs

Basking in its scenic enclave within Anza-Borrego Desert State Park, Borrego Springs is the county's only town lying in the desert province. It has three functions, as a retirement community for sun lovers, as a center of services for vacationers and tourists, and as a specialized agricultural area (mainly citrus) (Figure 14.10). Both real estate promoters and agricultural interests have historically wanted to develop this valley along their respective lines of interest, and by the 1980s the developers had clearly won. Two large new developments, Rams Hill and Borrego Country Club, are slowly being built out. A major development factor could be the nature of the ground water resources of the valley; by 2002 it had become clear that water table levels were dropping in parts of the valley. In 2000 the Borrego valley had 2,582 resident, but enough individual land parcels already exist to raise that figure 4 to 5 times. Such an increase would put considerable pressure on the surrounding Anza-Borrego Desert State Park, which is in the process of developing its own master plan.

Almost all these rural communities have strong identities and strong feelings of community which should enable them to resist deterioration brought on by an influx of outsiders. Both Julian and Borrego Springs must also cope with the thousands of tourists that pass through them. Borrego Springs seems most susceptible to future growth. In the mountain communities particularly, most longtime residents consider any rapid change in community type a deterioration of life-style.

The county government has a strong obligation to see that these rural communities maintain their historic identities, and that they are not overrun by uncontrolled growth. Much of any region's charm lies in its older, smaller towns, and locally these represent assets which San Diego County should strive to preserve. The County's General Plan 2020 update, underway in 2003, will determine the fate of all these communities.

Figure 14.10. A new orange grove being planted in Borrego Springs in the 1980s. There is now concern about the adequacy of groundwater supplies in the Valley to sustain large-scale agriculture. Photo by Philip R. Pryde.

Appendix 14.1 Comparative Data for Cities in San Diego County

City	2000 Population	City Area (sq. miles)	Population Density (persons / sq. mile)	Median Age	Median Income $	Percent Ethnic Minority	Persons per Household
Carlsbad	78,247	39.1	2,001	38.1	52,297	21	2.60
Chula Vista	173,556	48.0	3,616	32.7	40,394	56	3.04
Coronado	24,100	8.3	2,904	27.8	57,758	21	2.43
Del Mar	4,389	1.8	2,438	41.9	68,231	7	2.35
El Cajon	94,869	14.4	6,588	31.9	32,414	24	2.84
Encinitas	58,014	19.4	2,990	36.5	53,966	22	2.72
Escondido	133,559	36.2	3,689	32.5	36,694	35	2.98
Imperial Beach	26,992	4.4	6,135	28.4	30,505	48	3.02
La Mesa	54,749	9.0	6,083	37.4	38,194	19	2.43
Lemon Grove	24,918	3.9	6,389	33.4	38,968	42	2.93
National City	54,260	7.6	7,139	25.8	27,464	78	3.41
Oceanside	161,029	42.2	3,816	32.2	39,492	43	2.97
Poway	48,044	39.1	1,229	34.9	63,234	17	3.23
San Diego	1,223,400	329.9	3,708	32.9	40,837	45	2.79
San Marcos	54,977	24.2	2,272	32.2	37,092	38	3.15
Santee	52,975	16.5	3,211	33.9	48,050	17	3.02
Solana Beach	12,979	3.4	3,817	40.0	58,969	22	2.54
Vista	89,857	18.6	4,831	31.9	37,854	38	3.07
Unincorporated Area	442,919	3,572.20	124	32.9	44,765	27	3.14
County	2,813,833	4,238.20	664	32.9	41,445	39	2.89

Sources: SANDAG, INFO: Profiling the Region's Jurisdictions, 1998; CA Dept. of Finance; population is 2000 U.S. census figures.

References

Adema, T. J. *Our Hills and Valleys: A History of the Helix-Spring Valley Region.* San Diego: San Diego Historical Society, 1993.

Ames, Meriam et al., eds. *Rancho Santa Fe: A California Village.* 4th ed. San Diego: RSF Historical Society, 2001.

Brigand, Phil. *Borrego Beginnings.* Borrego Springs: Anza-Borrego Desert Natural History Asso., 2001.

Dillane, Allan Perry. *A Historical Geography of the El Cajon Valley, San Diego County, California.* Unpublished master's thesis, San Diego State College, 1964.

Ewing, Nancy H. *Del Mar: Looking Back.* Del Mar: The Del Mar History Foundation, 1988.

Harmon, John B., Jr. *History of Carlsbad.* Carlsbad: Friends of the Library, 1961.

Julian Historical Society. *History of Julian.* Julian: Julian Historical Society, 1969.

LaForce, Beatrice. *Alpine, History of a Mountain Settlement.* El Cajon: Sunlight Press, 1974.

LeMenager, C. R. *Ramona and Roundabout.* Ramona: Eagle Peak Publishing Co., 1989.

McCain, Ella (Williams). *Memories of Early Settlements: Dulzura, Potrero and Campo.* National City: South Bay Press, 1955.

McHenry, Peter. *The History of Valley Center, California.* Escondido: GP Marketing, 1998.

Mendel, Carol. *San Diego . . . City and County.* San Diego: Arts and Crafts Press, 1990.

Peirce, Rollin. *History of Ramona, A San Diego County Village.* 1960.

Peterson, J. Harold. *The Coronado Story.* Coronado: Coronado Federal Savings and Loan Association, 1954.

Phillips, Irene. *The Chula Vista Story.* National City: South Bay Press, 1968.

_____ . *The Story of El Rancho de la Nacion.* National City: South Bay Press, 1959.

Ryan, Frances Beven and Ryan, Lewis C. *Yesterdays in Escondido.* Escondido: Frances and Lewis Ryan, 1973.

San Diego Association of Governments. INFO: Profiling the Region's Jurisdictions. San Diego: SANDAG, 1998.

Sherman, Lola. *A History of North San Diego County.* Carlsbad: Heritage Media Corp., 2001.

West, Norrie et al., eds. *La Mesa Through the Years.* La Mesa: La Mesa historical Society, 2002.

In addition, reference is made to the many community plans (San Dieguito, Julian, Fallbrook, etc.) which have been prepared by the San Diego County Planning Department; plus the city plans of the county's several incorporated cities.

Internet Connections:

SANDAG: "INFO" reference cited above: *www.sandag.org/uploads/publicationid/publicationid_649_834.pdf*

San Diego Historical Society: *www.sandiegohistory.org*

Also, all incorporated cities will have a web site; enter the city's name in the search box.

Chapter Fifteen

Fun in the Sun
Regional Recreation Facilities

The climate and varied terrain of San Diego County have given it outdoor recreational opportunities of a quality and variety rarely equaled in the United States. The climate over most of the county allows year-round recreation, and it would be possible on some winter days to bask on an ocean beach, ski in the mountains, and study desert wildflowers all in the same day.

The most accessible and popular of the county's varied landscapes is the coastline. Even within this narrow zone there is great variety, including flat sandy beaches, impressive bluffs and headlands, and rich estuaries and lagoons. From the Mexican border north to La Jolla, the

Bob R. O'Brien is a professor emeritus of geography specializing in recreational land use in the Department of Geography at San Diego State University.

beaches are predominantly flat and accessible, broken occasionally by river flood plains and estuaries. From La Jolla through most of North County, the beaches are often buttressed by bold cliffs, reaching a maximum of 300 feet in the Torrey Pines State Park area. Eighty percent of the county's coastline is publicly owned, but some of this lies within military reservations and is normally closed to the public (Table 15.1).

TABLE 15.1. Beach ownership, San Diego County

Private	15.00 miles	(19.8%)
Federal	24.50 miles	(32.2%)
State	20.25 miles	(26.6%)
City	15.00 miles	(19.8%)
County	1.25 miles	(1.6%)

Also within the urbanized western portion of the county are mesas, canyon valleys, and even some sizeable mountains. This rugged topography (together with civic foresight) has allowed for many types of scenic open space and recreational opportunities. In addition to the beaches, this coastal area also contains many important wetlands such as Mission Bay, San Diego Bay, the Tijuana River estuary (Border Field State Park), and the six north coastal lagoons. The recreational needs of tourists are accommodated both at the numerous city and state parks which dot the coastal zone, as well as at centers of commercial tourism such as San Diego Bay, Mission Bay, La Jolla, Del Mar, and Oceanside.

The coastal terraces and mesas are heavily dissected by canyons, which carry the county's intermittent stream runoff to the ocean. The river valleys and their floodplains, from the Santa Margarita in the north to the Tijuana River in the south, form some of the county's most attractive landscapes, and also contain some of its most important natural resources, both biotic and mineral.

There are a number of near-coastal peaks, detached from the main peninsular ranges in the county, which rise from 800 to 2,800 feet above the nearby suburban valleys. Like the canyons and the floodplains, they contribute valuable open space and scenic interest to the metropolitan landscape.

The primary mountainous areas of the county, the Palomar, Cuyamaca and Laguna ranges, offer a special bonus to the people of San Diego County. The mountains are high enough to contain a thick cover of mixed deciduous and coniferous trees, often of impressive size, plus seasonal snowfall. The landscape also contains enough level land to provide living space and recreational opportunities for camping, picnicking, sight-seeing, and hiking.

Desert-oriented recreation in San Diego County is of a quality equal to anywhere in the west. It is true desert, lying in stark contrast to the adjacent mountain area, rich in plant and wildlife, mostly undeveloped, with much of it preserved in the nation's largest state park—Anza-Borrego Desert State Park.

Metropolitan Area Parks

In order to describe recreational opportunities in San Diego County, it is necessary to recognize a large number of park categories and management goals, as well as differences between undeveloped, partially developed, developed, and potential parks. The recreation area classification that follows is a flexible one, and the most important point is to understand the reasons for the different management policies of our major recreation complexes.

San Diego City Parks

In 2002 the city of San Diego administered 215 park sites of 14,122 acres, and 61 open space areas of 21,560 acres. Most of the parks are less than ten acres in size but the five largest contain 70% of the acreage in the system. The larger parks are often classified as regional parks and thus are important to the recreational needs of the entire county, while the smaller ones are oriented to the immediate surrounding population. Regional parks are usually of large acreage and have special characteristics, whether they are highly developed city parks, natural landscapes, or reservoirs (Table 15.2). A few examples of such parks follow.

Balboa Park is nationally famous because of the San Diego Zoo, which contains one of the world's largest collection of animals (about 4,100 specimens of 858 species and subspecies). However, the zoo comprises only about 10 per-

TABLE 15.2. City of San Diego Parks and Open Space

Major Parks (over 40 acres)	Acreage	Major Open Space Areas (> 100 a.)	Acreage
Balboa Park	1,172	Black Mountain Park	1,076
Beyer	43	Carmel Valley	1,325
Canyonside Community Park	43	Crest Canyon	117
Chollas Lake Community Park	329	Fairbanks Ranch	573
Kate Sessions Memorial Park	79	Kensington	102
Kearny Mesa Community Park	71	Los Penasquitos Canyon Preserve	3,139
Lake Murray Community Park	52	Marion Bear Memorial Park	467
Mid-City Athletic Area	41	Mission Trails Regional Park	5,880
Mission Bay Park	4,236	Navajo Canyon Open Space Park	153
Mission Beach Park	80	Otay Mesa Community Park	434
Montgomery-Waller Community Park	59	Rancho Mission Canyon	237
Paradise Hills Community Park	40	Rose Canyon	279
Presidio Park	49	Sabre Springs	806
Sunset Cliffs Park	67	San Pasqual Open Space	2,350
Torrey Pines City Park	535	Scripps Miramar	509
		Soledad Natural Park	197
Underwater Park		Tecolote Canyon Natural Park	912
		Tierrasanta	794
La Jolla Underwater Park	5,977		

Source: City of San Diego, *Park and Recreation Inventory,* June 2002.

cent of the park area. County residents are also drawn in equal numbers to the Del Prado area with its various museums, the Palisades area with its indoor recreation opportunities, and the Morley Field area with its tennis courts, playing fields, and swimming pool. There are also good playgrounds, shuffleboard and roque courts, two golf courses, and facilities for youth group camping. Two hundred acres in Florida Canyon will be developed as a native plant preserve and the large adjacent former landfill is to be planted in grass and trees. Efforts are being made to reclaim some of the 400 acres that have been lost in the past to nonpark uses, such as the Naval Hospital and highways.

In Mission Bay, a large marsh was dredged and shaped to provide the country's largest aquatic city park (4,236 acres). Sandy beaches, boating, sailing, fishing, water skiing and biking, plus a number of tourist-oriented developments such as Sea World, with 4,000,000 visitors annually, and various hotel complexes are among the recreational activities there (Figure 15.1). Some of the bay is still to be developed and conflicts have risen between wildlife preservationists and private and public developmental interests, and between advocates of large-scale tourism versus locally oriented recreation.

On the ocean side of Mission Bay is one of the city's most popular beaches. Mission Beach provides excellent swimming, a broad clean beach, volleyball and basketball courts, green lawn areas, and a promenade for cycling and walking.

Other city property includes some of the most beautiful coastal areas in southern California—the bluffs and caves of Sunset Cliffs, the erosional

Figure 15.1. Mission Bay park during its early development. Fiesta Island is being created by fill; Mission Beach is in the background. Photo taken in 1969 by P. R. Pryde.

features of the La Jolla headland, and the vertical bluffs and roadless beaches between Scripps pier and Peñasquitos Lagoon.

The 5,880 acre Mission Trails Park, with additional land to be added by the county and state, represents a rugged island of open space in a sea of urbanization. The visual importance of the area might turn out to be its leading attribute, but the wooded slopes and bold rock formations, the still beautiful San Diego River, and the Mission Dam Historical Park in Mission Gorge all offer excellent potential for outdoor recreation. The hike to the top of Cowles Mountain, at 1,591 feet the highest prominence in the city, is one of the most popular activities in the new park. Lake Murray attracts joggers, walkers, fishermen, picnickers, and bicyclists, and the park's Visitor and Interpretive Center is one of the finest of its kind in the county.

Marian Bear Park, with 467 acres in San Clemente Canyon, offers a good example of streamside vegetation and opportunities for pic-

nicking and bicycling. A much larger park has been developed in Los Peñasquitos Canyon to the north, which contains one of the best assemblages of native wildlife of any coastal canyon in the county. It is an important area for archeology and history, as well as a popular area for bicycling and hiking. The city and county jointly administer it.

Population-based parks are meant to serve the surrounding neighborhood and consist of (1) neighborhood parks and playgrounds which contain play areas, multipurpose courts, and lawn areas, and serve a population of 3,500–5,000 people within a radius of one-half mile; and (2) community park and recreation centers serving 18,000 to 25,000 residents within a radius of one and one-half miles. For the larger community parks, thirteen to twenty acres is needed depending on the availability of an adjacent schoolground. Their facilities include tennis courts, a lighted sports field, parking, and a community center building for meetings. Forty-seven of the San Diego City parks are community parks, though without necessarily having all the facilities or acreage noted above.

The seventeen other incorporated cities of the county contain over fifty additional urban parks, with a combined area of almost 20,000 acres. Of these, Carlsbad and Poway have the most, with over 3,000 acres each Table 15.3).

County, State and National Recreation Areas

The county in 2002 operated fifteen regional parks, 23 community parks, 18 regional preserves and open space parks, and 6 historic sites (Table 15.4 and Figure 15.2). Not all of the county parks can be described here, but some of the more important or unusual should be noted.

Lake Morena Park, located in East County between Pine Valley and Campo, contains 3,250 acres and is available for camping, picnicking, boating and fishing. This is one of several recreation areas that have been or will be built around water conservation reservoirs. Others can be found at San Vicente, El Capitan, Lower Otay, Cuyamaca, Jennings, Murray, and Wohlford reservoirs. A large park is planned around and downstream from Sweetwater Reservoir, and similar possibilities exist at other large reservoirs throughout the county.

El Monte Regional Park is one of the most popular in the county. Its grassy lawns under

TABLE 15.3. Park Acreages of San Diego County Cities (1986)

City	Acres	Park Acres/1,000 Residents	% of city in Park/ Recreation Land
Carlsbad	3,097	39.6	12.4%
Chula Vista	2,846	16.4	9.3
Coronado	710[a]	29.5	13.4[a]
Del Mar	383[a]	87.2	33.2[a]
El Cajon	264	2.8	2.9
Encinitas	2,033	35.0	16.4
Escondido	1,263	9.5	10.2
Imperial Beach	918[a]	34.0	32.6[a]
La Mesa	202	3.7	3.5
Lemon Grove	36	1.4	1.4
National City	326	6.0	6.7
Oceanside	2,762	17.2	10.2
Poway	3,047	63.4	12.2
San Diego	40,561	33.2	19.2
San Marcos	616	11.2	4.0
Santee	591	11.1	5.6
Solana Beach	237	18.3	10.9
Vista	960	10.7	8.1

[a]For some cities, the park acreage figure includes both city owned parks and parks operated by other jurisdictions; in some cases (such as Del Mar and Imperial Beach) almost all the acreage is in non-city owned parks.

Source: San Diego Association of Governments, "INFO," July–August 1997, Table 4. (last two columns computed using Appendix 14.1)

TABLE 15.4. Major San Diego County
Regional Parks

Name	Acreage	Campsites
Aqua Caliente Springs	910	121
Dos Picos	78	60
El Capitan	2,839	
El Monte	90	
Goodan Ranch	324	
Guajome	569	34
Hellhole Canyon	1,712	50
Lake Jennings	45	90
Lake Morena	3,250	186
Louis A. Stelzer	315	25
Mount Gower	1,590	50
Oak Oasis	397	
Otay Valley	100	
Potrero	115	39
San Elijo Lagoon	830	
Santa Margarita River	173	
Simon	650	
South Bay Biological Study Area	27	
Sweetwater	570	54
Sycamore Canyon	1,819	
Tijuana River Valley	1,353	
Vallecito	71	44
Volcan Mountain	2,494	
William Heise	900	104

Sources: San Diego County Parks Department,
"The San Diego County Park System," 1990, and
undated pamphlets "Our Open Space Preserves"
and "Our Camping Parks".

huge live oak trees are especially favored by pic-nickers, while the precipitous slopes of El Cajon Mountain to the north add scenic interest and a challenge to qualified climbers. A number of smaller parks around the county such as Live Oak Park near Fallbrook and Felicita Park near Escondido serve similar functions.

An unusual county park near Encinitas is Quail Gardens. This is a beautifully landscaped botanical garden, having both native plants and a wide variety of exotic species.

A new regional park planning effort is the San Dieguito River Park, which will eventually provide a linear open space park and trail system from the San Dieguito estuary to Volcan Mountain. A similar effort is underway on the San Diego River (see Chapter 17).

The San Diego Zoological Society operates the Wild Animal Park near Escondido, in addition to the downtown San Diego Zoo. This 1,800 acre park enables the animals to be seen in a much more natural setting than in most zoos. There has been notable success in breeding endangered species in the park, including the California condor, and it has quickly become one of the county's most popular recreation facilities.

State Parks

A large amount of the California State Parks System is located in San Diego County (Table 15.5). Out of a total of about 850,000 acres in the system, 61 percent is in the county. This includes Anza-Borrego Desert State Park (about 472,000 acres within the county) and Cuyamaca Rancho State Park (24,677 acres).

State park use varies according to location and function—hiking and camping at the larger parks, for example, and beach use at the coastal parks. Generally, however, use of the state parks is more restricted than in the county or city parks. For example, portions of Torrey Pines are classified as a state preserve, thus limiting development and intensity of use. Two-thirds of Anza-Borrego Desert State Park and over half of Cuyamaca Rancho State Park are classified as state wilderness areas in order to protect their scenery and often rare flora and fauna.

There are eight state beaches in the county, most of which are small but receive large visitations because of their strategic access to the ocean. An exception to the small size is San

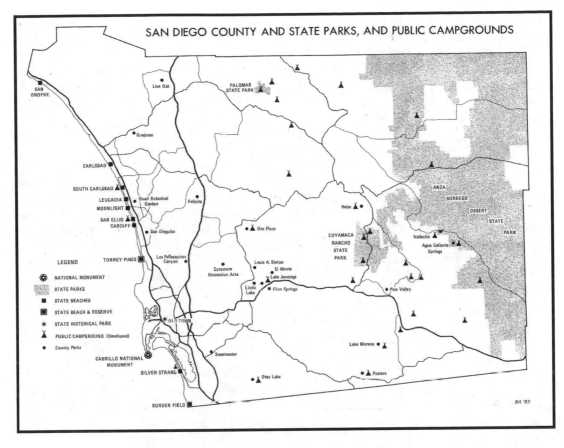

Figure 15.2. Some of the major county recreation areas.

Onofre, which at 3,036 acres is the largest California state beach. Camping near the ocean is a strong attraction here, as it is at San Elijo and South Carlsbad state beaches.

Inland from the beaches in several locations are environmentally critical fresh or salt water lagoons, some of which are protected by the state and other public agencies. Tijuana Slough, one of the finest salt water marshes in Southern California, is a good example. Slated for development in the 1960's it is now protected by Border Field State Park, by the Tijuana River

National Estuarine Reserve, and by a large new county regional park. Other cooperative agreements protect San Elijo Lagoon, San Dieguito Lagoon, and Buena Vista Lagoon in the North County. Recreation in these areas is confined to walking, bird watching and enjoying the tranquil natural scene.

Torrey Pines State Reserve protects large groves of one of the world's rarest trees, and also contains spectacular bluffs along the Pacific, fascinating narrow canyons cutting into those bluffs, and a wildlife-filled lagoon. Various measures

TABLE 15.5. Federal and State Recreation
             Areas

Area	Acreage	Campsites[a]
FEDERAL		
Cleveland National Forest[b]	288,060	463
Cabrillo National Monument	144	
McCain Valley (Bureau of Land Management)		46
STATE		
Anza-Borrego Desert State Park	600,000[c]	149
Cuyamaca Rancho State Park	24,677	166[e]
San Onofre State Beach	3,036	150
Palomar Mountain State Park	1,897	30
Torrey Pines State Reserve[d]	1,123	
Border Field State Park	680	
Silver Strand State Beach	428	133
South Carlsbad State Beach	135	222
San Elijo State Beach	39	171
Cardiff State Beach	25	
Moonlight State Beach	14	
Carlsbad State Beach	14	
Old Town State Historical Park	13	
Leucadia State Beach	11	

[a]Numbers understate capacity of sites; primitive areas are usually not included, and a group campground may accommodate up to 50 people, although it is counted as a single site.
[b]Portions of forest may be closed due to fire danger.
[c]Includes portions in Riverside and Imperial counties. About 472,000 acres are in San Diego County.
[d]Divided into Torrey Pines State Preserve, 1,082 acres and Torrey Pines State Beach 41 acres.
[e]These were damaged in the "Cedar" fire of October 2003.

have been adopted to limit the visitation to a number which can be supported without danger to the ecosystem.

Cuyamaca Rancho State Park offered a pleasant mountain environment containing a mixed conifer-deciduous forest with giant oaks, permanent streams, and space for camping, picnicking, climbing, hiking and horseback riding. The area is bisected by a highway, but there was room enough for a wilderness experience on the slopes of Cuyamaca Peak and East Mesa. Unfortunately, almost all of Cuyamaca State Park was consumed in the massive 2003 "Cedar" fire (see Chapter Three). Palomar Mountain State Park, though smaller, serves the northern section of the country in a similar way.

Anza-Borrego Desert State Park comes as close to being of national park stature as anything in the county. It is 25 percent larger than Sequoia National Park and is the last large Sonoran Desert area in California remaining essentially in its natural state (Figure 17.1). It contains a large and varied plant and animal population, including the endangered Desert Bighorn Sheep, the unique elephant tree, and spectacular desert scenery. The major uses of the area are for sight-seeing, off-road vehicles, hiking, winter and spring camping, and for a great variety of nature-oriented activities, especially in the Borrego Palm Canyon, Fish Creek, Font's Point, and Bow Willow areas (Figure 15.3). Box Canyon, a difficult passage along the Southern Emigrant Trail, is just one example of the fascinating history of the Park.

Old Town State Historical Park is of major interest to San Diegans, as it commemorates the first permanent settlement in San Diego. An interesting blend of reconstructed buildings and various thematic commercial activities, the park is in a continuing state of upgrading, a process which could continue for years as funds become available. San Pasqual Battlefield State Historical

Figure 15.3. Nature study, such as this miniature cactus garden, is one of the primary attractions of Anza-Borrego Desert State Park. Photo by P. R. Pryde.

Park near Escondido is another important historical site in the county, as are the various remnants of the Anza and Butterfield overland routes.

National Areas

Cleveland National Forest contains 288,000 acres within San Diego County, almost all of which (except during seasonal closures to prevent fires) is open for outdoor activities. Wildlife present include deer, coyote, bobcat, squirrel, racoon, mountain lion, and many varieties of birds and reptiles. Mount Laguna and Palomar Mountain are the two most popular recreation areas within the national forest.

The Laguna Mountain Recreation Area is located northeast of Pine Valley and consists of mixed conifers, oaks, and chaparral. In it one can find nature traits, campgrounds, spectacular views of the desert from the Sunrise Highway (County Route S-1), access to snow after winter storms, and a pleasant section of the Pacific Crest Trail. The Laguna Meadows., a beautiful grassy area with the mountain's only natural ponds, surrounded by forests, was purchased in the 1970s and added to the recreation area.

The Palomar Mountain area in North County affords long views into the surrounding countryside and access to the world famous 200-inch Palomar Mountain Observatory. One of the country's only natural trout population is found here, as is the 15,934 acre Agua Tibia Wilderness Area, the first federal wilderness area in the county. Three others were created by Congress in the 1980s (Chapter 17).

Cabrillo National Monument is the only unit of the National Park System found in San Diego County. It contains items of historical interest associated with both California's first European explorer and World War II, and has an unparalleled view of the city and bays of San Diego. Nature trails, wintertime views of seals and migrating gray whales, and access to tide pools are also popular attractions here (Figure 15.4).

Other Federal Lands Used for Outdoor Recreation

The Bureau of Land Management, the nation's largest administrator of federal real estate, is responsible for around 177,000 acres of county land (Table 1.1). Most forms of outdoor recreation are available on this land. A less utilized recreational resource in the county is Camp Pendleton, often mentioned as a model for military land management, with its miles of unspoiled beaches, stream courses, lagoons and mountains, some of which are open to public visitation, with prior approval for access.

Recreational Activities

The variety of outdoor recreational possibilities in the county is truly amazing. This is a result of the diversity of topographic forms, from coastal flatland to rugged mountains, of vegetation from desert to deep forest, of a settlement pattern from urban to wilderness, and a climate which allows year-around recreation.

Figure 15.4. San Diego Bay and the ocean areas near Cabrillo National Monument are popular sailing areas, and a good place to see migrating gray whales, sea lions, and tide pools. Photo by P. R. Pryde.

Recreational Travel and Camping

The variety of landscapes in the county inevitably make driving for pleasure an important recreational outlet in the county. Driving old Highway 101 through the coastal communities, the steep highway climbing to the summit of Palomar Mountain, heavily landscaped Cabrillo Parkway through Balboa Park and state Route S-2 traversing the spectacular scenery of Anza-Borrego Desert State Park are samples of what is available. The great number of people enjoying these vistas, however, might eventually pose a problem on some of these "backcountry" two-lane picturesque roads. Enhancement projects would include more roadside rests and scenic turnouts, and a prohibition on billboards.

The use of off-road vehicles, which includes motorcycles, trail bikes, dune buggies, 4-wheel drives, minibikes and others, has increased greatly in the county in recent years. Plans are underway to permit the use of these vehicles without damaging the landscape and without detracting from the quality of other recreational uses. There are hundreds of miles of unpaved backcountry roads in the county, and off-road vehicle parks are established in part with funds provided by ORV users. Ocotilla Wells State Motor Vehicular Recreation Area, east of Borrego Springs on the Imperial County line, presently contains 44,000 acres. Off-road vehicle parks, isolated from other users, offer the best future possibilities, and both private and governmental interests are planning for their development.

Bicycling has also exploded in popularity recently and better facilities are badly needed. Unlike off-road vehicles, there is little competition with other forms of outdoor recreation, and city streets can offer sufficient lower quality facilities until a network of separate bikeways can be made available. Provision for bikeways and bike paths is found in recreation and transportation plans at all levels of government, and these facilities are slowly being fitted into existing communities, as space and funds are available. Various guidebooks describe some of the best roads for cycling in the city and county, and several bike paths have been designated around the city, notably the routes from Mission Bay to La Jolla and from Presidio Park to Balboa Park. Two popular areas for mountain biking are Cuyamaca Rancho State Park and Los Penasquitos Regional Park.

Oddly enough, there are probably greater opportunities for recreational driving in the city than for walking. We seem to have considered walking obsolete in our transportation planning and wide, safe sidewalks are nonexistent in some communities. Still, the miles of sandy beaches and the dozens of pleasant communities and parks in the country make leisurely walking a pleasure in many areas.

Hiking is considered a little more serious pastime than simply walking, and major maintained trails in the county exist in the mountains or are in the planning stages. The public has access to the entire nonmilitary coastline below the highest tide line. The San Diego County segment of the Pacific Coast Trail, which stretches from Mexico to Canada, was completed by 1990. More impressive in concept is a proposed series of trails connecting the coast with the mountains through a number of river valleys such as the Pañasquitos, San Diego, San Dieguito, Otay, and others. One or more of these should be completed by 2010. The best existing system of trails is probably found within Cleveland National Forest, part of the old California riding and hiking trails system. Also, for the enthusiast, there are a number of dirt roads or unmaintained trails to the tops of some of the closer peaks in the area, such as Fortuna, Woodson, Cowles, Black and San Miguel mountains. Mountaineering on high peaks is limited, but rock climbing in Mission Gorge, on Mt. Woodson, near Jacumba, and in the Cuyamacas and elsewhere is of a high quality. More information on trails can be obtained by calling the San Diego Trails Council (619-563-5025).

Horses are a way of life in rural San Diego County, which has one of the highest per capita levels of equestrian use in the country. Despite occasional conflicts with hikers and bicyclists, horseback riders are credited with adding considerably to the county's network of trails.

Camping, both in recreational vehicles and in more simple styles, is greatly increasing in popularity. There are over 3,000 public campsites in the county, divided among county parks, state parks, and the national forest (Tables 15.4 and 15.5). There are also thousands of private facilities. This is far less than the demand for such areas on many days of the year, however, and further increases in demand can be expected in the future. The most heavily used sites are the coastal and mountain campgrounds in the summer and the desert in the winter.

Hunting is a limited activity in the county. Deer and game bird hunting is possible in the mountains, as well as duck hunting on some bodies of water and small game hunting elsewhere. Skeet practice and rifle ranges are also present in the county. Locally, habitat destruction far overshadows hunting as a cause of wildlife reduction.

Still, for an urbanizing county San Diego has an amazingly large amount of undeveloped land which serves as home to a wide range of wildlife. The grizzly bear is gone but the mountain lion is still here, and the Audubon Christmas bird count in the county is regularly one of the highest in the nation. Casual or organized wildlife and plant observation are popular recreation activities, and as noted in Chapter 3, San Diego County leads the nation in bird species, thereby attracting thousands of amateur ornithologists as tourists every year. Nature trails are becoming popular in areas like the Cleveland National Forest, and considerable wildlife habitat is also being preserved throughout the county (Chapter 17).

Although San Diego County might seem the last place to go for a wilderness experience, there are several sizable roadless areas present in the county, and four areas in the national Wilderness Preservation System. Anza-Borrego Desert State Park has a wilderness designation for Desert Bighorn Sheep habitat and other sensitive flora and fauna applied over much of the park. Wilderness areas existed as well in Cuyamaca Rancho State Park. Camping may be limited by the fire season and a wilderness permit issued by the Forest Service is required for all hikers in national forest wilderness areas.

Water-Based Recreation and Other Activities

"Going to the beaches" is the most popular activity in the county and in the state of California. The simple activities are the most popular and require the least expertise and equipment: swimming, wading, picnicking, photography, impromptu sports, reading, walking and "doing nothing." In the county there are many miles of easily accessible beaches with picnic tables, fire rings, outdoor play equipment, rest rooms and parking, and clean, moderately warm water with safe surf conditions. Opportunities for swimming are excellent, with the most popular beaches being at Ocean Beach, La Jolla Shores, Mission Beach and Pacific Beach.

San Diego has ample space for these activities for the next few years, but population increases, pollution, and reduced access by overcrowding and development pose a threat of a reduction in quality. The work of the California Coastal Commission is potentially the best hope of preventing future deterioration of the coastline.

According to a survey by the National Surf Life Saving Association of America there are thirty-eight "classic" surfing areas in San Diego County and thirty-seven "good" areas, making the county one of the country's most popular surfing areas. Surf enthusiasts have fought developments which would destroy prime surfing areas or close off access to beaches. Competition with swimming is a problem in some areas.

Snorkeling and scuba diving enjoyed an early start as a sport in San Diego and soared in popularity. The rocky sections of coast at La Jolla, Bird Rock and Sunset Cliffs offer beautiful off-shore diving possibilities and are the most heavily used in the county. Overfishing and overcollecting have reduced the marine life available in some areas, and preserving these resources, preventing pollution, and ensuring adequate access remain the main problems of the sport.

Boating is one of the most popular of all San Diego pastimes. Facilities for powerboats, sailboats, personal watercraft, canoes and rowboats have increased in recent decades with the cleaning up of San Diego Bay, the development of Harbor and Shelter Islands and Mission Bay, and the opening of water supply reservoirs to boating and fishing. Conflicts between powerboats and other crafts, overcrowding of certain areas, lack of access and launching facilities and lack of sheltered mooring spaces are some of the current problems. In the master plan for Mission Bay, an effort has been made to keep sail boats, water skiers, jet skis, and commercial marinas separated (Figure 15.5). There are few areas left for additional marinas, without conflicting with other shoreline uses.

Many kinds of track, court, and field sports benefit from investments made in city and county parks. Many city parks have a hard court for basketball, a softball or baseball diamond, a grassy area for soccer and football, and so on.

Jogging can take place almost anywhere but benefits from a pleasant environment and measured courses; Balboa Park, Mission Bay, Lake Murray and the beach areas give optimum conditions. Tennis has been one of the fastest rising sports in the country and the city of San Diego operates 112 courts. Golfers are well provided for, with a total of 88 public, private, and military courses in the county taking advantage of the year-round season. According to the San Diego Union-Tribune, the largest among them are the Navy's Admiral Baker Course, Torrey Pines (host to periodic PGA tournaments), Singing Hills, and La Costa. The total area of golf courses in the county is 11,768 acres.

Sight-seeing is a supplemental or secondary recreational activity with most of the forms of outdoor recreation mentioned above, and is one of the bases for the county's outstanding tourist trade. Spectator sports include professional football, baseball, hockey, and soccer teams, numerous university teams, high school sports and many special events. Qualcomm Stadium and the Sports Arena offer outstanding facilities for top sporting events, and a new downtown stadium has been built for the San Diego Padres. Winter sports are obviously reduced in number and quality, but one of the peak seasons in the mountains comes when thousands of people head into the hills for snow play, and there are ice skating rinks in the metropolitan area.

Tourism is a 5.1 billion dollar annual industry in San Diego, and tends to center on Balboa Park and the San Diego Zoo, Mission Bay and Sea World, the area's beaches, and our location on the route to Mexico. County residents sometimes complain about the 27 million annual tourists crowding recreational facilities, and the effects tourist promotion has on swelling the area's permanent population. However, the development of these local recreational facilities obviously owes much to the out-of-county

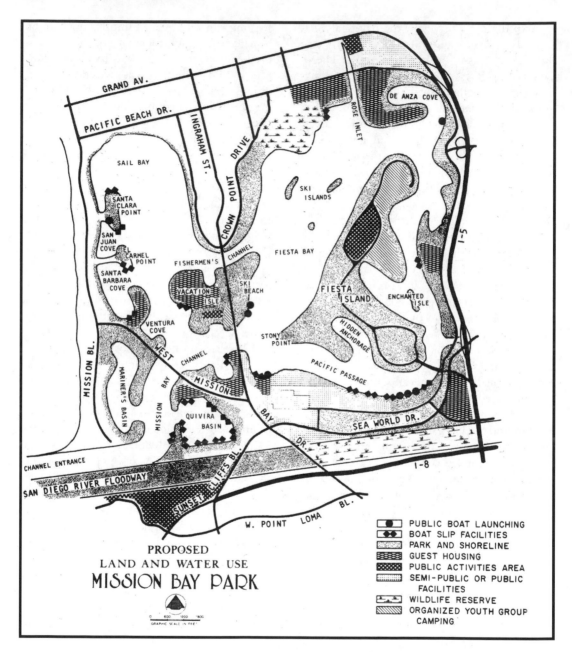

Figure 15.5.

demand for them, and taxes on tourist activities help pay for these facilities. The preservation of quality recreational areas benefits both resident and out-of-county recreationists.

As population rises in San Diego County, and there are few signs of its slowing down, efforts must be intensified at expanding recreational areas in the county, developing new facilities for population-based parks, and preserving the natural areas still present in the county. Preserving natural areas will be the most difficult, as pressures for increased commercial and residential developments are added to pressures for mass recreation (see Chapter 17). We owe it to ourselves and our heirs to make sure the work is done, and done with care.

References

California Department of Parks and Recreation (CDPR). *Anza-Borrego Desert State Park Preliminary General Plan*. Sacramento: CDPR, January 2003.

California Department of Parks and Recreation. *The California State Parks System*. Sacramento: CDPR (pamphlet periodic reissue).

Christman, F. *The Romance of Balboa Park* (4th ed.). San Diego: San Diego Historical Society, 1985.

Copp, N. and J. Schad. *Cycling San Diego* (3rd edition). El Cajon: Centra Publications, 2002.

Hill, C. *Fishing the Lakes of San Diego County*. Lakeside: Blueberry Hill Publ. Co., 1989.

Lindsay, L. and D. *The Anza-Borrego Desert Region* (4th ed.). Berkeley: Wilderness Press, 1998.

Mendel, C. *San Diego City and County*. San Diego: Arts and Crafts Press, 1990.

Hewitt, L. and B. Moore. *Walking San Diego* (2nd ed.). Seattle: The Mountaineers Books, 2000.

San Diego Association of Governments. *INFO*. San Diego: SANDAG, July-August 1977.

San Diego County Department of Parks and Recreation. *Destinations . . . San Diego County Parks*. San Diego: SDCDPR, Spring 2003.

Schad, J. *Afoot and Afield in San Diego County* (3rd ed.). Berkeley: Wilderness Press, 1998.

Schad, J. *Back Country Roads and Trails: San Diego County*. Beaverton, OR: Touchstone, 1985.

Showley, Roger. *Balboa Park: A Millennium History*. Carlsbad: Heritage Media Corp., 1999.

Internet Connections:

California state parks: *www.parks.ca.gov*
San Diego City parks: *www.sandiego.gov*
San Diego County Parks: *www.sdparks.org*

Chapter Sixteen

Philip R. Pryde

Keeping It Clean
Maintaining Environmental Quality

People have always been concerned about the quality of their immediate neighborhood and their local community. This concept is frequently termed the "quality of the environment". Deterioration of environmental quality often can be most pronounced in large metropolitan areas.

What are the elements of a quality environment? The term "environment" is very broad and encompasses, in addition to the physical environment, a variety of elements relating to the individual's social-economic environment. These elements include employment opportu-

Philip R. Pryde is professor emeritus of environmental studies in the Department of Geography at San Diego State University.

nities, crime rates, availability of housing and medical care, adequacy of schools, a stable home environment, occupational health and safety, and even the caliber and responsiveness of local government. Taken all together, the total concept is usually referred to as a "Quality of Life" index. Working with all of these factors for San Diego County would be a huge undertaking, and well beyond the scope of this chapter.

Since the central theme of this book has been human alteration to our natural environment, this chapter will look only at those factors that involve the county's physical surroundings. The other types of personal environments mentioned above are equally important, though, and shouldn't be overlooked.

It has been suggested that the level of pollution in any region is a function of three things:

the size (and density) of population, the level and nature of per capita consumption, and the types of technology employed in the society. San Diego County certainly represents a region in which both population and per capita consumption have increased sharply over the past few decades. This has posed the potential of significantly deteriorating the quality of our local environment.

How well have we in San Diego fended off these threats of environmental deterioration? To begin with, let's look at the quality of our air. This is one area where technology has come to our rescue.

Air Quality in San Diego County

Air quality represents a remarkable environmental victory in the San Diego region. In the 1950s, '60s, and '70s, air quality was so poor that driving from home to downtown or Mission Valley on a bad day would produce tears, red eyes, and shortness of breath. Los Angeles was even worse, not that that was much consolation. First stage health alerts were common (and second stage were common in the L.A. basin). Today, the air is reasonably clean, and health alerts are virtually unheard of. Why did the situation used to be so much worse in southern California than elsewhere, and how did we improve it?

The Potential for Air Pollution in San Diego County

The reasons that air quality in southern California was so bad 40 years ago was mainly due to two factors: cars were very dirty then, and southern California has the worst natural potential for air pollution in the entire United States. The latter problem is not well understood, so let's look at it first.

The reason that San Diego and Los Angeles have such high air pollution potential has more

to do with meteorology than with topography. The problem is that we have a great many atmospheric temperature inversions, and underneath these inversions the air is often relatively still. Meterologists would phrase it that our air basin has poor ventilation.

Why are inversions the most important factor? Normally, as you go higher into the atmosphere, the air becomes colder. A temperature inversion is the term applied to the situation where a layer of warmer air is encountered as one gains in elevation (Figure 16.1). The significance of this for air quality is that an atmospheric temperature inversion creates a "lid" under which the pollutants are trapped—they cannot rise above it (Figure 16.2). The more frequently an area has temperature inversions, the more frequently it is apt to have polluted air, and the lower the inversion, the more concentrated will be the pollutants. Unfortunately, San Diego has one of the greatest potentials for low-level atmospheric temperature inversions of anywhere in the United States (Figure 16.3).

Cool air off the ocean will frequently move inland through San Diego's many valleys, leaving warmer air up above the mesas. This creates a local temperature inversion, which can create strong temporary conditions for air pollution in the valleys. Unfortunately, freeways tend to be in these valleys, and morning rush hour traffic can concentrate emissions.

More stable inversions often occur around 2,000 feet, and the rising pollutants can become most concentrated just below the bottom of the inversion layer. Alpine is located at about 2,000 feet, and this explains the tendency to have high average pollution readings there. The problem is not limited to Alpine, of course, but could also be found at other locations at about the same elevation. Alpine just happens to be where the monitor is located.

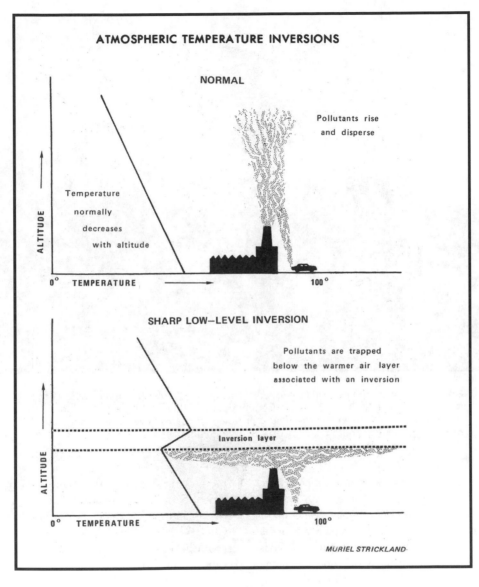

Figure 16.1.

Figure 16.2. A sharp inversion layer over El Cajon, with Cowles Mountain rising above it. In the 60s and 70s, such inversions frequently trapped unhealthy, eye-stinging pollutants beneath them. Improved auto emission standards have greatly improved regional air quality. Photo taken in 1971 by P. R. Pryde.

Damage to vegetation from air pollution, though of secondary importance to human health, is easier to identify. In past years, minor damage to Jeffery and Ponderosa pine trees in the Mt. Palomar, Cuyamaca, and Laguna areas has been observed, as well as occasional damage locally to crops such as tomatoes and lettuce. Fortunately, air pollution levels are no longer high enough to be doing significant damage to crops.

The geographic distribution of air pollution within San Diego County conforms in the main to population concentrations, but with some unexpected exceptions. In 2001 there were ten monitoring stations in the county—two in the city of San Diego (downtown and on Kearny Mesa), and in Oceanside, Escondido, El Cajon, Chula Vista, Del Mar and Alpine, plus two more recently installed stations on Otay Mesa and Camp Pendleton.

Downtown San Diego, where one might expect pollution to be highest, has relatively moderate average readings, because of the almost daily breeze off the ocean which tends to blow pollutants elsewhere. The same holds true for Chula Vista. North coastal communities (from Oceanside to Del Mar), however, can

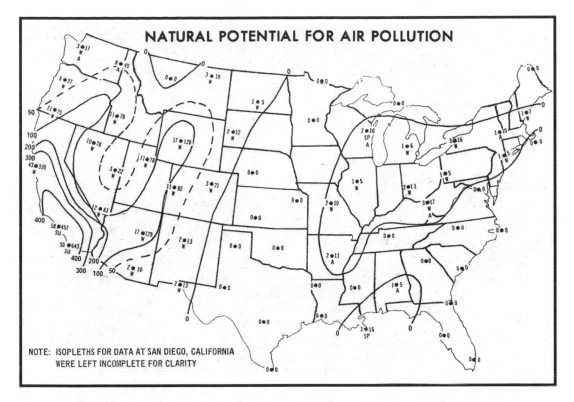

Figure 16.3. Isopleths of total number of episode days in 5 years with mixing heights ≤1000m, wind speeds ≤6.0m sec −1, and no significant precipitation—for episodes lasting at least 5 days. Numerals on left and right give total number of episodes and episode-days, respectively. Season with greatest number of episode-days indicated as W (winter), SP (spring), SU (summer), or A (autumn).

Adapted from: G. C. Holzworth, "Mixing Heights, Wind Speeds, and Potential for Urban Air Pollution Throughout the Contiguous United States" (EPA, 1972).

record very high one-day readings under Santa Ana conditions, when smog from Los Angeles is blown out over the ocean, later to drift back in towards northern San Diego County. In 1990, smog transported to San Diego County from Los Angeles and Orange counties was accounting for about half of all our region's high air pollution days (see Figure 16.4).

Types of Local Air Pollutants

There are a great many different types of air pollutants, and some are of more concern in the San Diego area than others. Most are produced by automobiles and other transportation sources, which account for over 75 percent of all air pollutants in the county. The main pollutants locally are carbon monoxide, hydrocarbons, oxides of nitrogen, and especially ozone.

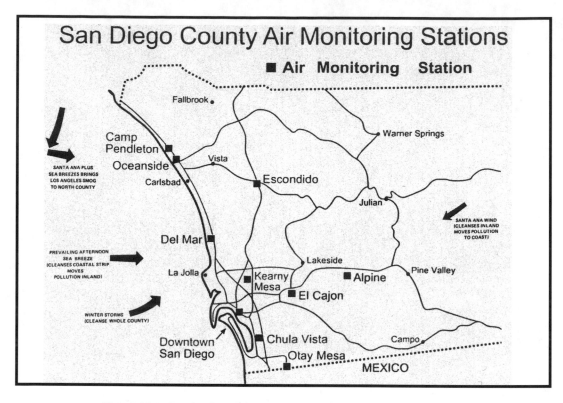

Figure 16.4. Monitoring stations and wind effects in San Diego County.

Most people know that carbon monoxide exhaust fumes from cars can be lethal if they become concentrated in an enclosed area, such as a garage. By tonnage, they are our largest single type of pollutant, and almost all come from motor vehicles. Despite this, they are not considered to be the worst problem locally. Except for persons in close contact with operating vehicles (policemen, garage mechanics, etc.), atmospheric concentrations of carbon monoxide rarely approach a potentially dangerous level.

Hydrocarbons, oxides of nitrogen, and ozone are more of a problem. When they are present on a sunny day (which means most of the time in San Diego), they go through a series of complex chemical changes in the atmosphere. The final effect of these changes is to produce an eye-stinging brownish haze which has been termed photochemical smog. Most smog-producing pollutants (55%) come from motor vehicle operations, but the largest single source of nitrogen oxides is direct fuel combustion, meaning mainly electrical power plants. Ozone is the most easily measured of these gases associated with photochemical smog, and the hardest to deal with.

Improvements to automobile engines and their associated pollution control technologies have produced a marked reduction in air pollutants in southern California since the 1970s.

As a result, San Diego was able to meet California standards (which are more strict than federal standards) for all pollutants except ozone. Further improvements during the 1990s, however, meant that in 2001, for the first time, San Diego attained the reduction in atmosphere ozone necessary to comply with state standards. The improvements in ozone levels over the past two decades is shown in Table 16.1. The table also illustrates the unique problem faced by Alpine, which was explained earlier.

Other types of common air pollutants are particulate matter, lead, and sulfur dioxide. Most particulate matter (solid and liquid aerosols) in the atmosphere, although acting to limit visibility, are not a health problem. Blowing dust and sand accounts for most of the larger particulates. Very small particulates, called PM_{10} and defined as those smaller than 10 microns in diameter, are a serious potential health problem, because they can lodge deep in human lungs. The federal standards have never been exceeded in San Diego County, but the stricter state standards are not being met in most areas of California.

One of the most serious particulates used to be atmospheric lead, produced by the burning of gasolines that contain tetraethyl lead. With the removal of lead from gasoline, it is no longer a problem. Sulfur dioxide is among the worst of pollutants, and is usually associated with concentrations of heavy industry. Fortunately, San Diego County has only small amounts of sulfur dioxide and lead; both are at much lower levels than either state or federal standards.

Improving the Quality of the Air Resource

Who is responsible for clean air in San Diego? The answer is that the federal government, the state of California, the county of San Diego, and, of course, the individual citizen all have important roles to play. For the San Diego County air basin, the Board of Supervisors itself also acts as our local Air Pollution Control Board (APCB).

In 1967, 1970, and 1988, the federal government and the state of California passed significant air pollution control legislation. Both established sets of air quality standards, and the county was required to devise a plan, called the

TABLE 16.1. Ozone Levels in San Diego County
(number of days with one-hour average levels exceeding the State standard)

Monitoring Station:	1980	1985	1990	1995	2001
Oceanside	54	36	14	5	1
Del Mar	65	48	25	12	0
Escondido	72	43	26	12	4
Downtown San Diego	25	23	26	3	1
Chula Vista	29	28	21	7	2
Kearny Mesa	42	48	30	8	9
El Cajon	45	48	46	17	3
Alpine	127	128	121	77	22
Otay Mesa				17	0
Camp Pendleton					2
Entire Air basin	167	148	139	96	29

Source: San Diego Air Pollution Control District, various annual reports.

Regional Air Quality Strategy (RAQS), to meet them. By 1991, as noted earlier, it was determined that within the county the standards for oxides of nitrogen, sulfur dioxide, carbon monoxide, and most particulates had been met, but not the standard for ozone. Improvements to all types of motor vehicles have now enabled us to meet ozone standards as well.

A little more should be said about hydrocarbons. In addition to motor vehicles, there are many other sources of hydrocarbons, such as paint application, restaurants, dry cleaning establishments, and even the family lawn mower, that must be taken into account. Cumulatively, their contribution is considerable, and regulation to control emissions from all these varied sources have been developed by the state APCB. Open burning used to be common in the more rural areas, but since 1973 open burning has been banned in the county.

The power plants at Carlsbad and Chula Vista produce almost no carbon monoxide or hydrocarbons, but they do produce most of our nitrogen oxides and sulfur oxides. They are generally required to burn low sulfur fuel oil (containing less than 0.5 percent sulfur) when natural gas isn't available. Since natural gas is currently plentiful, it is their primary fuel, and as a result their sulfur dioxide emissions are within recommended limits. Controlling oxides of nitrogen is not easy, for they are always produced when fuel is burned in air at high temperatures, and there is no inexpensive way to eliminate them. Fortunately, the county meets the standard for these emissions.

The individual has a major role to play in all of this. By use of the telephone, anyone may obtain air pollution information (858-650-4777, or look in the directory under San Diego County), or may report what they feel to be a violation. Each county resident has the responsibility to drive their car as efficiently as possible, to keep the engine in tune, to investigate joining a car pool, to check on the nearest bus route, to support better public transportation systems, and to let public officials know that they expect better air quality for themselves and their families. Since the family car is, collectively, the largest single source of air pollution in San Diego County, only with the cooperation of its driver will the quality of the air we breathe improve.

Maintaining Water Quality

In general, the quality of San Diego County's inland water bodies is reasonably good, particularly if compared to those of many other large metropolitan areas. However, problem areas do exist.

Our incoming drinking water, as Chapter 8 pointed out, is of high biological quality, but still has a relatively high dissolved salt content. Our treatment plants are first rate (although they can't remove salts), and if continued care is taken to avert any potential problems, San Diego's drinking water should be of good quality for years to come.

As in most metropolitan areas, the potential for pollution posed by waste waters from urban runoff and industrial sources is the primary area of concern. Much improvement in controlling water pollutants has been realized in recent decades (Figure 16.5). Nevertheless, it is in these areas that some problems still remain in the county.

Controlling Waste Effluents

Most waste effluents in the county are processed in one of several treatment plants located throughout the county, and then discharged into the ocean. By far the largest of these plants is the Metro sewage treatment plant on Point Loma. This regional facility handles the waste water from most of the San Diego metropolitan area,

Figure 16.5. Prior to the requirement for biodegradable detergents, the old non-biodegradable varieties produced huge accumulations of suds in local streams. This picture of the San Diego River at Mission Dam was taken in 1960 by Lauren Post.

and processes almost 200 million gallons of municipal wastes a day (Figure 16.6). Built in 1963, it replaced an inadequate, older plant which had discharged into San Diego Bay, greatly polluting it.

Other large treatment plants are in Carlsbad (the Encina plant), Oceanside, and Escondido (Table 16.2). Present policy is that all treated wastes from these large plants should be discharged into the ocean, rather than into internal bodies of waters such as streams or lagoons, as was formerly done. One major reason for this is that some lagoons (such as San Elijo and Bataquitos), tend to become stagnant during the summer months, with a corresponding loss of wildlife habitat, and nutrients from treated waste water would aggravate this problem.

A controversy that has surrounded the large Metro plant on Point Loma involves whether or not it should be expanded to include a higher degree of treatment (called *secondary treatment*). This would remove almost all the remaining biodegradable matter from the discharged effluent water, and most of the smaller treatment plants in the county now have this type of treatment. The argument for a secondary facility at the Point Loma plant is that it would enable fewer pollutants to be discharged into the ocean,

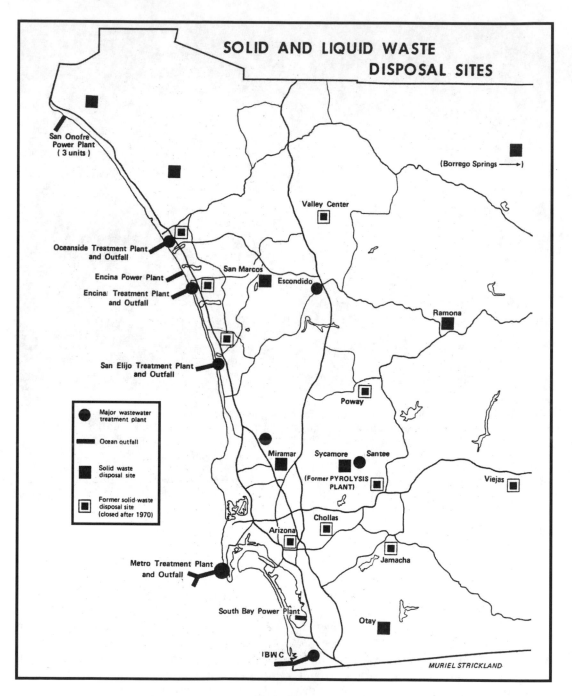

Figure 16.6.

TABLE 16.2. Major San Diego County Wastewater Treatment Plants

Agency Name	Facility Name	Highest Level of Treatment	Reclaimed Uses?	Discharge to:	Design Flowrate (MGD)	Current Flowrate MGD)(1)
Buena Sanitation District	Shadowridge WRP	Tertiary	Yes	Encina Ocean Outfall	1.16	0.82
Carlsbad MWD	Carlsbad WRF	Tertiary	Yes	Reclaimed water use	4.00	0.00
Encina Wastewater Auth.	Encina WPCF	Secondary	No	Encina Ocean Outfall	36.00	23.44
Escondido, City of	Hale Ave. WW Trtmt. Plant	Secondary	No	San Elijo Ocean Outfall	17.50	14.70
Fallbrook P.U.D.	Plant 1	Tertiary	Yes	Oceanside Ocean Outfall	2.70	1.24
IBWC (2)	South Bay IWTP	Advanced Primary	No	South Bay Ocean Outfall	25.00	23.90
Oceanside, City of	La Salina WWTP	Secondary	No	Oceanside Ocean Outfall	5.50	3.60
Oceanside, City of	San Luis Rey WWTP	Secondary	No	Oceanside Ocean Outfall	10.70	9.30
Otay MWD	Ralph W. Chapman WRF	Tertiary	Yes	Reclaimed water use	1.30	1.05
Padre Dam MWD	Padre Dam WRF	Tertiary	Yes	Excess to Sycamore Creek	2.00	1.87
San Diego, City of	North City WRP	Tertiary	Yes	Pt. Loma Ocean Outfall	30.00	25.00
San Diego, City of	Point Loma Plant	Advanced Primary	No	Pt. Loma Ocean Outfall	240.00	175.00
San Diego, City of	South Bay Water Recl. Plant	Tertiary	No	South Bay Ocean Outfall	15.00	5.00
San Elijo J.P.A.	San Elijo WPCF	Tertiary	Yes	San Elijo Ocean Outfall	5.25	2.91
USMC, Camp Pendleton	4 Separate Plants	Secondary	Yes	Santa Margarita River	6.31	2.92
Vallecitos WD	Meadowlark WRP	Tertiary	Yes	Encina Ocean Outfall	2.25	1.65
					404.67	292.40

(1) As of November 2002.
(2) International Boundary and Water Commission.

Source: San Diego Regional Water Quality Control Board, November 2002; personal communication.

and that secondary plants are the national standard. The city's counterargument is that the ocean can provide this form of biodegradable decay itself, and that no evidence of ocean water deterioration, or harm to marine life, has yet been demonstrated. The city has requested, and received, a waiver from the secondary treatment requirement. However, the Environmental Protection Agency still feels secondary treatment is necessary.

The San Diego ocean environment has one ongoing problem, which occurs all too frequently throughout southern California. That problem is periodic beach closures due to contamination of the near-coast waters. The main causes are broken or malfunctioning sewer lines or pumping plants, and contaminated surface run-off.

For example, in 1999, there were 720 beach closure days (from all pollution sources) in San Diego County. In 2000, the total number of times that county beaches were either closed or had warning signs posted was 1,349, although this number was reduced considerably in 2001 and 2002. In 2001, the San Diego Regional Water Quality Control Board recorded 602 problems with sewer lines, most quite minor, but a few involving major polluted discharges.

The result of all the above is that all too often many of our beaches are closed temporarily to recreational activities for public health reasons. Our sewerage infrastructure is old in many areas, and while the city has an ongoing improvement program, many years and much money will be needed to fully correct the problem. To encourage quicker corrective action, the city in 2001 was sued by two conservation groups, and the suit later joined by the federal Environmental Protection Agency, over the 1,500 spills that had occurred the previous five years.

San Diego is fortunate to have relatively little industrial pollution. This is in part because we have few industries whose processes involve large amounts of wastewater, and in part because many of those that we do have (such as food and kelp processing plants along San Diego Bay) have had their effluents hooked into the Metro treatment facilities. However, there is a problem of pollution of the bay from boats, both naval and private. Both are required to utilize holding tanks that discharge wastewaters to shore facilities (Metro). However, it will probably never be feasible to entirely eliminate oil leaks, floating debris, or peeling paint from boats. The sediments on the bottom of the Bay also remain polluted from a variety of contaminants that have been discharged into its waters over the years.

One potential problem area which San Diego has in common with almost all other metropolitan areas is that of waste heat, or thermal effluents. By far the main source of heated water discharges in the county are the power plants of San Diego Gas and Electric Company, particularly those at San Onofre, South Bay, and Encina. Each of these plants takes in and discharges more than one-half billion gallons of cooling water every day. The San Onofre nuclear plant and the Encina plant discharge into the Pacific Ocean; the South Bay plant into lower San Diego Bay. There have been no reports of major problems resulting from these thermal discharges, but concern has been expressed at fish kills occurring at the cooling water intakes at the San Onofre nuclear plant. At both South Bay and Encina experiments have been carried out in the use of the heated water for "aquaculture," which is the growing of shellfish at faster rates in the warmer waters. Consideration is being given to closing down the South Bay plant, which would eliminate this heat source.

An expanding county population needs new water supplies, and the metropolitan area must dispose of its wastewater. One way of resolving (at least in part) both problems simultaneously would be to expand the practice of water reclamation and reuse. This would be most feasible in terms of using treated wastewaters for landscaping and agricultural irrigation, and this has been done on a small scale in many places in the county already. Areas where reclaimed water is being used for irrigation can be identified by bright purple piping and values.

If salts in the water are not too high, or can be removed at a competitive price, reclamation could result in a significant reduction in the need to import more water into the county from external sources. A large plant has been built in the northern part of the city of San Diego along I-805 (Figure 16.7). A major problem in using the product water from plants such as this is that water demand is seasonal—high in summer but low in winter. This creates problems in terms of the economics of producing reclaimed water, if wintertime customers can't be found.

Reclaimed water from the North City wastewater treatment plant could be used as a permanent, guaranteed source of additional feed water into the aqueducts that provide water into our municipal water supply treatment plants. This has proven to be politically unpopular, as most people don't see this as a suitable source of raw water for our potable water treatment plants. This is both unfortunate and ironic, for the water leaving the North City plant may be cleaner than incoming water from the Colorado River, our present primary supply of feed water into these same plants.

Using reclaimed water as widely as possible makes great sense and should be encouraged by all jurisdictions in the county, but it is expen-

Figure 16.7. San Diego's North City Water Reclamation Plant treats municipal wastewaters and reclaims them to a quality suitable for irrigation and other non-potable uses. Photo by P. R. Pryde.

sive. To bring all wastewater in the county up to irrigation standards would be economically infeasible.

Problems of Land Disruption

Perhaps San Diego's most visible environmental problem is the widespread scarring of the landscape resulting from residential and commercial development. In part this is a legacy of what were the commonly accepted cut-and-fill construction practices of the past. Fortunately, there has been some improvement in the governing ordinances, and somewhat stricter grading and landscaping regulations are now in effect. However, the scars of the past will remain with us for years, if not decades, to come. In addition to construction, other landscape-transforming activities carried out in the county include solid waste disposal and mining.

Solid and Hazardous Waste Disposal

Most solid wastes in the county are disposed of at sanitary-landfill sites. In 2002 there were eight of these in the county, which handle over five million tons of trash per year (Figure 16.6). In a sanitary landfill operation, the trash is deposited in a cleared area, leveled, and then buried under a thin layer of dirt (providing a challenge for hundreds of scavenging seagulls). Subsequently, more layers of trash and cover will be added, until the disposal site is eventually filled up. Then the site must be used for non-structural purposes, as the land will slowly undergo an uneven settling process (termed *subsidence*) for years.

A more complex problem is presented by the 93,000 tons annually of county generated hazardous and toxic wastes which must be handled with great care (Table 16.3). In the past, the county merely transferred them to the West Covina toxic waste dump, but the West

TABLE 16.3. Hazardous Waste Generation in San Diego County

Jurisdiction	1986 tons	1986%
Carlsbad	1,683	1.8
Chula Vista	3,776	4.1
Coronado	57	0.1
Del Mar	67	0.1
El Cajon	2,008	2.2
Encinitas	221	0.2
Escondido	1,185	1.3
Imperial Beach	34	0.0
La Mesa	340	0.4
Lemon Grove	202	0.2
National City	17,897	19.2
Oceanside	1,072	1.2
Poway	179	0.2
San Diego	40,948	43.9
San Marcos	1,508	1.6
Santee	221	0.2
Solana Beach	4	0.0
Vista	184	0.2
U.S. Navy	21,034	22.6
Unincorporated	528	0.6
Total	93,100	100.0

Source: *County of San Diego Hazardous Waste Management Plan,* 1989.

Covina facility was closed in 1984. In 1989, nine industrial sites in the county were approved to process hazardous waste. A 1986 law requires every county to have a plan for minimizing and recycling hazardous and toxic wastes, and a local disposal site. The county has prepared such a plan, although so far no disposal site has been selected. The extent of the problem locally is illustrated by the fact that in 1990 twelve different sites in the county were federally listed as major toxic waste problem areas qualifying for 'superfund' clean-up monies.

Some substances classified as hazardous wastes, such as used motor oil can (and should) be recycled. For information on disposing of chemical wastes around your home, call the San Diego Household Hazardous Materials Hotline at 858-694-7000.

It is often pointed out that solid wastes, like municipal wastewater, can be viewed as a potential resource. These wastes contain significant amounts of glass, steel, aluminum, and other recyclable products. Aluminum is the most valuable, but in terms of bulk the most plentiful and useful "raw material" is paper and cardboard fibers (Table 16.4). Although recycling municipal wastes is expensive, many cities, including San Diego, have established "curbside recycling" programs, whereby solid wastes that can be transformed into new products are collected by the city. In addition, over 60 recycling centers are located around the county. A list of these centers can be obtained by calling 858-694-7000, or by contacting the "I Love a Clean San Diego" organization.

Mineral Extraction

Despite the fact that San Diego County has relatively few high-value mineral deposits, large areas within the county show the effects of surface mining. This is almost all the result of sand, gravel, and rock extraction, and the effect is heightened by the high degree of visibility of much of these operations (see Chapter 6).

Three main types of products are extracted: alluvial sand from river floodplains, sand and gravel from coastal formations such as conglomerate, and hard granitic or metavolcanic rock which when crushed can be used in construction or for decorative purposes. Over 5,000 acres of land are controlled by local extractive industries.

Making a sand-and-gravel operation aesthetically pleasing is a difficult task at best. In

TABLE 16.4. Waste Analysis for San Marcos Landfill

	Percent of San Marcos Waste Tonnage:
Cardboard	5.61%
Newspaper	2.63%
High grade paper	0.98%
Mixed waste paper	5.41%
Tin cans	0.90%
Glass	1.57%
Hard plastics	1.68%
Film plastics	1.57%
Aluminum cans	0.14%
Yard waste	15.12%
Wood waste	5.42%
Diapers	1.10%
Non KIMS/misc/etc	20.41%
Concrete	5.99%
Dirt/rock/sand	12.33%
Asphalt	1.89%
Mixed waste with demo/construction	17.28%
Total	100.01%

*Source: San Diego County's Waste Characterization and Market Study August, 1990.

some cases the remains of old sand-and-gravel operations are positive in appearance, such as the lakes that can be seen in the San Diego River channel in Mission Valley and Santee. More often, however, the pits, dust, noise, and truck traffic associated with these operations leave an unfavorable impression on the observer.

Both the city and the county use a discretionary permit system in licensing such operations, and have regulations governing noise, safety, aesthetic screening, and rehabilitation. Basically, however, mineral extraction necessarily involves some manner of "hole" in the landscape which in some form will have to remain for the life of the project (perhaps 30–50 years). It would be difficult to attempt to phase these operations out of the metropolitan region, because their products' low values requires them to be produced close to where they'll be used. Thus, screening and landscaping may be the best that can be done during the life of the project. Post-extraction reclamation plans for these sites are now mandatory, although many (especially in Mission Valley) have been transformed into commercial and office building complexes.

Construction Activities

As any San Diego resident is aware, the amount of earth moving that accompanies a major local building project is often monumental. The reason for so much reshaping of the landscape is understandable best in engineering and economic terms: The unconsolidated coastal terrace deposits are very easy to move around and, by so doing, more dwelling units can be built on a parcel of a given size.

Most canyon sides in the San Diego metropolitan area occur at a natural slope of between 1½ to 1 (about an angle of 34°) and 2 to 1 (27°). Such natural slopes will usually be sparsely vegetated if south-facing (into the sun), but may be heavily vegetated if north-facing (away from the sun). In the past, cuts made for the purpose of constructing subdivisions or highways were often of a 1 to 1 slope (45°). In San Diego's climate, such slopes will rarely revegetate themselves naturally (Figure 16.8). Even if irrigated, it may be difficult to establish an adequate ground cover on 1-to-1 slopes. Erosion problems are common, and if the cut has been made through a layer of conglomerate, rocks may tumble down onto the road or yard at the bottom, creating a significant hazard.

In recent years there has been a considerable effort to strengthen grading ordinances. New regulations typically require that cuts be con-

toured and revegetated at a slope no steeper than 1½ to 1. These regulations will prevent a recurrence of past abuses such as in Figure 16.8, but these older cuts will remain as a barren reminder of the limits of natural revegetation for many years to come.

Other Environmental Considerations

Several other common types of environmental problems are of importance in San Diego County, too. One would be the proper use of pesticides. The most widely used pesticides in the county are soil sterilants and fungicides, used in agriculture. Large amounts are also used by individual homeowners, generally for insect control. Pesticide use is controlled by both local and state agencies. Perhaps the most appropriate caution concerning pesticides is to be sure that their use is absolutely necessary, to seek out viable alternatives, and to follow the label directions governing any pesticide that is used at home or work.

Figure 16.8. Efforts to stabilize an eroding, excessively steep slope (1:1) slope on 54th street in San Diego. Photo by P. R. Pryde.

Occasionally a major program, such as the 1990 spraying for Mediterranean fruit flies in and around El Cajon, will engender considerable controversy. Both Mediterranean and Mexican fruit flies appear periodically in the county, and pose a major threat to the county's multi-million dollar fruit crop (see Chapter 9). A serious infestation of the Mexican fruit fly occurred in Valley Center in December of 2002. The standard treatment for both types of flies is aerial spraying of the short-life organic phosphate pesticide Malathion. For organic farmers who wish to avoid chemical pesticides such as Malathion, the organic (bacterium) based pesticide Spinosad has been approved.

Another environmental ailment of growing concern in urban areas is noise. Freeways, airports, motorcycles, construction activity and even dogs all contribute to increasing decibel levels in urban areas such as San Diego. In recent years, many homes have been built in high noise areas such as around Miramar Air Station. In some older parts of the city, noise levels rose as freeways were put in and jet aircraft replaced piston planes (as around Lindbergh Field). Both the city and county of San Diego have now passed noise control legislation, and each has a noise abatement office to respond to citizen complaints. Although these laws are a good start, some local noise sources (such as aircraft and motor vehicles) will be difficult to bring under full control because they are regulated mainly by state and federal agencies. An additional problem is that existing noise ordinances are not always enforced because of insufficient funds.

Efforts to eliminate "visual pollution" have not fared very well. Although both the city and the county have sign control ordinances, they have inadequate enforcement capabilities. Thus far the outdoor advertising industry has been successful in blocking efforts to remove billboards from city and county roadways, but there have been occasional local successes in controlling signs (see Figure 13.9). Efforts to eliminate litter have also had limited effect thus far.

Utility wires are required to be placed underground in new urban subdivisions, and SDG&E devotes a certain percentage of its earnings to undergrounding existing wires. As there are hundreds of miles of wires to be "buried," it will be many years before the utility wires will be removed from even the major thoroughfares in San Diego. Nevertheless, in those areas where this conversion has been completed, the improvement is striking.

Most of the above environmental problems are tightly interconnected with other quality-of-life considerations, and require a comprehensive approach in order to find a satisfactory solution. For example, air pollution is obviously tied in with transportation decisions, water pollution with industry and recreation, and noise with population density. To maximize the quality of life in the various communities of the San Diego metropolitan region, these many considerations require careful, integrated planning. This topic will be examined in Chapter 19.

References

Balint, Kathryn, "Crisis Looms at Dumps", *San Diego Union-Tribune*, Feb. 16, 2003, pp. B1, B4.

City of San Diego. *General Plan and Progress Guide*, Conservation Element. Most recent revision.

City of San Diego. *2002/2003 City of San Diego Recycling Guide*. San Diego: City of San Diego Environmental Services Department, 2002.

County of San Diego. *Hazardous Waste Management Plan, 1989–2000*. San Diego County, Department of Health Services, 1989.

County of San Diego. *Integrated Solid Waste Management Plan* (Final Draft). San Diego, 1995.

County of San Diego. *San Diego County General Plan,* Conservation Element. Most recent revision.

McDonald, J., "Water Quality Data Show Local Beaches Cleaning Up", *San Diego Union-Tribune,* August 14, 2003, pp. B-1 and B-6.

Pryde, Philip R. "San Diego Environmental Issues", *Environment Southwest*, No. 488 (Winter 1980), pp. 14–17.

Regional Air Quality Strategy (joint City-County-CPO report). San Diego, 1976, revised 1989.

Rodgers, Terry, "Polluted Waters Listed", *San Diego Union-Tribune*, Nov. 6, 2001, pp. B1 and B4.

Rodgers, Terry, "Growers Go into Action in Fruit Fly Infestation", *San Diego Union-Tribune*, December 12, 2002, pp. B1 and B3.

San Diego Association of Governments (SANDAG). *Measuring the San Diego Region's Livability*. San Diego: SANDAG, 2000.

San Diego County Air Pollution Control District. *2001 Annual Report: "Air Quality in San Diego"*. San Diego: San Diego County A.P.C.D., 2002.

Internet Connections:

Air Pollution Control District: *www.co.san-diego.ca.us/cnty/cntydepts/landuse/air/*

Environmental Health Coalition: *www.environmentalhealth.org*

San Diego City Environmental Services Dep't: *www.sandiego.gov/environmental-services*

San Diego Regional Water Quality Control Board: *www.swrcb.ca.gov/rwqcb9/*

Chapter Seventeen
Philip R. Pryde

Saving the Pieces
The Effort to Conserve San Diego's Biodiversity

Chapter Three emphasized the vast biological diversity of San Diego County, a diversity that results from the abundance of natural zones found in our region. It also noted that we have lost most of a number of different habitat types in the county (Table 17.1).

Why is conserving biological diversity so important? This wealth of biological diversity (often shortened to simply "biodiversity"), is not just something to enjoy as we drive along our highways and byways, it is of immense practical importance to us as well, providing us with

Philip R. Pryde is professor emeritus of environmental studies in the Department of Geography at San Diego State University.

an abundance of services at no cost. As previous chapters have noted, rivers provide our reservoirs

TABLE 17.1. Loss of Key San Diego County Habitats

Habitat Type	Percent Remaining	Percent Lost
Vernal pools	2	98
Native perennial grassland	5	95
Freshwater marsh	9	91
Maritime succulent scrub	10	90
Coastal salt marsh	12	88
Southern maritime chaparral	18	82
Coastal sage scrub	28	72
Riparian woodland	39	61

Sources: U.S. Fish and Wildlife Service; Table 3.4.

with drinking water, floodplains collect our well water, plants stabilize our soils, birds consume harmful insects, soils purify biological pollutants, and forests ameliorate our climate.

But at the invisible level, the genetic information contained in plants and animals may be the most important of all. To give just one telling example, the anti-cancer chemical taxol is derived from Pacific Northwest yew trees; until recently yew trees were routinely destroyed in the effort to log larger and more economically remunerative fir and cedar trees. Then, the great hidden benefit to people they contained was discovered. We don't know what other plants might have similar secrets, but it only makes sense not to carelessly eliminate any elements of the natural environment, since they all may harbor benefits not yet discovered. Biotic preservation is based on a combination of aesthetic, moral, and practical considerations.

This chapter will outline San Diego's efforts to conserve its considerable natural wealth.

The Earliest Efforts (pre-World War II)

The earliest efforts to preserve pieces of San Diego were based on aesthetic and recreational considerations. The San Diego region was big, the population was small, and there was not yet any sense of an impending loss of resources of value.

The first significant open space preservation action came in 1868 when Ephraim Morse and Alonzo Horton selected a large parcel of land for the young town of San Diego to use for a city park. It is now known as Balboa Park. At that time it was scrub land on the outskirts of the city; today it is an emerald gem in the heart of a city of a size that even the promotional Mr. Horton could not have dreamed. Originally a mile and a half on a side (1,440 acres), the portion north-

east of 6th and Ash was subsequently split off for development, so that today the park encompasses 1,172 acres.

Any discussion of the early park history of San Diego must include the contributions of Kate Sessions. Starting in 1892, this energetic volunteer operated a nursery in Balboa Park for many years, and much of the landscaping of this and other early parks was carried out under her direction (see Chapter 12). She is honored by a park in her name in La Jolla.

One major event occurred prior to the end of the nineteenth century in San Diego's backcountry, and that was the creation of what is now Cleveland National Forest. In its early form, it was known as the Trabuco Reserve, an area that was set aside in 1893. This area was brought under the management of the new Forestry Service in 1907, and it was enlarged and renamed Cleveland National Forest in 1908 by President Theodore Roosevelt. It is today both an important biological area and a four-season playground for thousands of urban San Diegans. It contains our most extensive conifer and oak forests and the highest natural lakes (which fluctuate greatly in size in dry years).

In the early twentieth century, the initial thrust was on "beautification", an effort led by Kate Sessions, George Marston, and others. The "greening" of San Diego was also spurred on by the two international expositions in Balboa Park—the Panama-California in 1915 and the California–Pacific in 1935. This was a period of widespread planting of trees and flowers, which involved the introduction of hundreds of non-native species into the region, a process that is now causing considerable concern (Chapter 3).

Perhaps the most important year in the first half of the century was 1933, in which both Cuyamaca and Anza-Borrego Desert State Parks were created. Cuyamaca Rancho State Park was created out of part of the old Cuyamaca Rancho land grant dating from the Mexican era in the county. It contains some of the best forests in the county, as well as its second highest peak (Table 2.2), which is easily seen from the urban area on clear days.

Anza-Borrego Desert State Park is among the largest state parks in the country. It began with the donation of a few thousand privately owned acres in 1932. It became much larger the following year as the result of congressional legislation that transferred 185,000 acres from the federal Bureau of Land Management. It was further expanded to 448,840 acres in 1936. Initially called the Borego (sic) Palms Desert State Park, it has grown steadily to its present size of approximately 624,000 acres. Small portions of it extend into both Riverside and Imperial counties (Figure 17.1). Best known for its spectacular displays of wildflowers (in wet years, at least), it is also a wonderland of biological, geological, archeological, and historical treasures waiting to be discovered.

A New Look at Our Public Lands and Rivers

The creation of Anza-Borrego Desert State Park was important in one other respect: it opened the way to viewing our public lands as resources that were important for protection as both recreation areas and protected natural areas. In the 1970s, the focus was on wilderness.

In 1970, there were no statutory wilderness areas anywhere in San Diego County. The federal Wilderness Act of 1964, however, mandated that the Forest Service review suitable areas for such a designation. Thus, Cleveland National Forest began taking a look at the existing Agua Tibia Primitive Area, which was established in 1931 and straddles the San Diego–Riverside county line north of Pauma Valley, for possible wilderness status.

It was quickly determined that the area was suitable, and that it contained no conflicting mining, logging, or grazing leases. However, the Forest Service wanted a limited wilderness area established (11,920 acres), arguing that such an area could not include any existing roads, even if the roads would subsequently be closed to the public and used only for emergency purposes. The fight for a larger wilderness area was led by the Sierra Club, which argued that the dirt road in question, if closed to the public and used only by fire and rescue vehicles, was really only a wide path, and that therefore a much larger area of 16,400 acres was justified. With the assistance of then Senator Alan Cranston and Congressman Clair Burgener, the citizens prevailed, and the larger area was enacted into law in 1975. San Diego County had its first official wilderness area.

Since then, three other Forest Service wilderness areas have been created within the county: Pine Valley, Hauser, and San Mateo. Two are located south of I-8, in the roadless area between the freeway and Barrett Reservoir. The third (San Mateo) is in the far northwestern portion of the county between the community of DeLuz and the southwest corner of Riverside County (in which it partly lies).

However, the largest wilderness in the county by far is that which has been delineated in Anza-Borrego Desert State Park. Twelve separate state wilderness areas exist in the Park, separated by paved highways and major dirt roads. They protect numerous important wildlife habitats, archeological sites, geological formations, and areas of outstanding natural beauty. At present they total 405,100 acres; this may be expanded under the 2003 proposed General Plan for the Park to 463,000 acres.

A very large *de facto* (but not statutory) wilderness area has been created along the border in the Otay Mountain—Tecate Peak region.

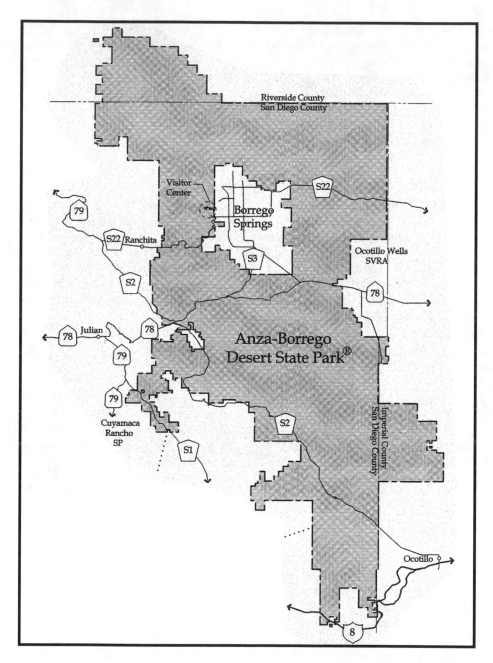

Figure 17.1. Outline map of Anza-Borrego Desert State Park, showing the location of the visitor's center and the off-road vehicle area (SVRA). The town of Borrego Springs is located in the "donut hole" in the center.

Termed the Otay Mountain-Kuchaama Cooperative Management Area, it takes in over 40 thousand acres of mountainous terrain that is mostly publicly owned by a number of federal and local agencies. The area is rugged, relatively pristine, and an important habitat for such rare species as the Tecate Cypress (Figure 17.2). On the other hand, it has very little access, is fire prone (much of it burned in 2003), and is heavily used by border patrol personnel. Still, it constitutes one of the largest blocks of undeveloped terrain within the county, and will be perpetuated as a highly diverse habitat preserve.

Another interesting development, which began in the 1980s, was the large-scale transference of federal lands to local jurisdictions and,

in at least one case, to a private conservation group. Such transfers had been possible for some time under existing federal legislation, but had been little used in San Diego County. The act provides that federal lands officially declared "surplus" (that is, having no identified use by the federal agency owning them) could be offered to, in order of preference, other federal agencies, state agencies, local government, and lastly for sale to private organizations, in all cases for public recreational purposes.

The initial gambit was by a private conservation group, San Diego Audubon Society, which worked for seven years to effect a transfer of 101 acres from the Bureau of Land Management (BLM) for addition to its Silverwood Wildlife

Figure 17.2. Tecate Cypress growing amid spring wildflowers in the Otay Mountains Cooperative Management Area. Photograph by P. R. Pryde.

Sanctuary in Lakeside. This sale was finally completed in 1984. Once the potential of the federal act became known, many other BLM parcels were transferred, mainly to local governments for park purposes. These transfers included several open space preserves for the county, similar preserves for the city of Poway, Spanish Landing Park in the city of San Diego, and numerous others. This act has proven very beneficial for the cause of open space and habitat protection within the county.

Saving the Rivers

Another emphasis of the 1970s and 1980s was on keeping San Diego County's rivers free flowing. In the 1970s the focus was on the San Diego and Tijuana rivers; in the 1980s it centered on the Santa Margarita River and Pamo Valley.

The first effort was to preserve the San Diego River. In the 1960s, the Army Corps of Engineers, which is in charge of structural flood control projects, proposed a large concrete flood channel for Mission Valley. It would have been almost identical to the large concrete channel on the Los Angeles River in the center of that city. By the early 1970s, however, environmental concerns had risen much higher on the public agenda, and it was soon clear that most San Diegans, including most landowners in the Valley, didn't want a local re-creation of the Los Angeles channel.

The new National Environmental Policy Act forced the Corps to do a review of their proposal, and the author of this chapter prepared a technical study showing that the Corps' run-off methodology was flawed. By the mid-1970s, the new studies, based on local precipitation data, concluded that no variant of a channel in the valley, or a new dam in the mountains, would be cost effective. This essentially ended Congress' interest in funding such a project. Subsequently,

a smaller, "natural" channel was developed between Route 163 and Qualcomm Way. The larger channel west of I-5 had been completed in 1953.

The remaining bits and pieces of riparian forests in Mission Valley (just east of I-5, the "natural" channel east of Route 163, and near the stadium) continue to provide habitat for a surprisingly large assortment of birds and animals. However, the stretch of the river's floodplain in Fashion Valley lacks any significant channel and remains a flood hazard zone.

A similar battle on the Tijuana River began in the mid-1970s. The issue was more complicated here, because the river enters San Diego from Tijuana, and the latter city was intent on building a very large concrete channel through the center of the city to provide flood protection. The question was, should San Diego do the same? After a heated debate and the completion of studies similar to those done for the San Diego River, it was decided that the floodwaters could be conveyed to the Pacific by building what was termed a "dissipater system" near the border to spread out and slow down the floodwaters, and then convey them to the ocean via the natural floodplain. There was some risk in this, as there are numerous houses and horse operations in the valley, and indeed they received considerable damage in the medium-sized flood of 1993 (and both access bridges were knocked out). Following this flood, improvements were made to the river's floodway, some of the most endangered houses were purchased, and new and higher bridges were built.

Currently, the Tijuana River valley in the U.S. is a significant habitat area for birds, and a key breeding area for the migratory and endangered least Bell's vireo. More recently, the county has been in the forefront of efforts to create a large open space preserve in the Valley, which will connect to Border Field State Park.

The major battle of the 1980s was to keep the Santa Margarita River natural. Although the most spectacular part of the Santa Margarita gorge lies just over the Riverside County line, the better wildlife habitat lies in our county, north of Fallbrook and on Camp Pendleton. A small reservoir (Vail Lake) exists on an upstream tributary, but the main part of the river through the Gorge and across Camp Pendleton is still free flowing (Figure 17.3).

For many decades there had been a proposal by the Bureau of Reclamation to build a two dam project in the middle course of the river—

Figure 17.3. View of the Santa Margarita River as it emerges from the gorge west of I-15, showing the extensive riparian forest along it. Photograph by P. R. Pryde.

a Fallbrook Dam on the stretch north of that city, and a De Luz Dam on Camp Pendleton. The stated purposes would be flood control and water for irrigation, but the amount of available water would be small, and flood control on the military base could be provided much more cheaply by alternative means. An examination of the Bureau's cost-benefit analysis showed that the purported monetary benefits were considerably overstated, and that if calculated more accurately, the project would not generate enough income to cover its costs. As a result, Congress rejected the authorizing legislation in 1985. Although a few proponents of a dam still exist, a large San Diego State University research reserve has been created in the gorge area, and the likelihood of a dam being built there is small.

The last major battle to preserve a natural stream course was the fight over Pamo Valley. This little known valley is located a few miles due north of Ramona. It is drained mostly by Temescal Creek, which in the southern portion of the valley flows into Santa Ysabel Creek (which further downstream becomes the San Dieguito River). Because of its relative isolation, Pamo Valley is one of the most natural of all remaining coastal-slope valleys in the County. Ironically, the reason for this is that the City of San Diego had reserved this valley many decades ago for the eventual construction of a major water storage reservoir, and thus the only permitted use of the valley was for a small amount of cattle grazing.

In the early 1980s the City and the San Diego County Water Authority decided that the time was right to build the dam. The public notice of this engendered a huge outcry to not flood the last unspoiled major foothills valley. As a result, the Water Authority initiated a search for a suitable alternative to the proposed dam, a process they called the Emergency Water Storage Project (see Chapter 8). This process worked very well, and after almost two years of study, an alternate project was approved that included the smaller, already approved, and non-objectionable Olivenhain Dam, plus eventually raising the existing San Vicente Dam. This is an excellent case study in cooperative "win-win" planning, in which both sets of objectives were met: the needed water storage was provided for, and Pamo Valley could remain natural. Pamo Valley is today a part of the San Dieguito River Park planning process.

Along with our coastal rivers, mention should also be of their terminal water bodies, the county's coastal lagoons and estuaries. All are significant refuges for wintering ducks and shorebirds. In 1970, only one or two of the region's estuary's had even partial protection; a small section of Buena Vista lagoon was in conservation ownership, but there was little else. At the time, there were plans to turn the Tijuana River estuary into a marina, and SDG&E wanted to build a nuclear power plant in Penasquitos Lagoon! Today, due to the efforts of citizens, environmental groups, and far-sighted elected officials, every coastal wetland is under some form of protected status, and most have their own citizen "watchdog" group. There are still problems – sedimentation and pollution head the list—but a remarkable turnaround in perception and management goals has largely kept our remaining coastal wetlands natural.

The New "Big Park" and "Big Open Space" Era

After the setting aside of Balboa Park in 1868, over a century went by before other big parcels of land were to be preserved in the urban area. The development of Mission Bay (1953) was noted in Chapter 15, but this was primarily a commercial recreation development, one that resulted in the loss of most of the natural marsh habitat that existed in the former False Bay (Figure 17.4). Only a small wetland on the north shore (the Kendall-Frost marsh) was retained as wading bird habitat. Unintentionally, however, the much larger San Diego River flood channel wetland on the south side of the park has evolved into one of the very best intertidal wetland and wintering bird area in all of California.

Another battle worth mentioning was the fight in the 1960s to prevent the widening of State Route 163 through Balboa Park. This was San Diego's first freeway, built in 1948 with only two lanes in each direction. By the 1960s, the freeway planners were assuring us that unless more lanes were added immediately, gridlock would be imminent, getting downtown would be a nightmare, and adverse economic consequences would ensue. The public, however, did not want the attractive landscaping around this scenic highway destroyed in order to widen 163, and after a spirited battle led by the new conservation group Citizens Coordinate for Century 3 (C-3), a decision was made to preserve the scenic route. History has shown that, except for minor delays in the afternoon where northbound 5 merges into 163, the predicted traffic jams have not occurred. Still, about once a decade, someone again sounds new Cassandra warnings about gridlock and advocates widening the road. Thus far, common sense has carried the day, and 163 remains a beautiful parkway (Figure 17.5).

The first new "big park" to be created in the metropolitan area was Mission Trails Regional Park. It contains the highest point in the city (Cowles Mountain at 1,591 feet), its deepest gorge, and one of its oldest historical monuments (Mission Dam). This scenic mountain range, being planned for estate development in the manner of Mt. Helix, was saved by a joint city-county acquisition effort that succeeded in acquiring the entire mountain range in the mid-

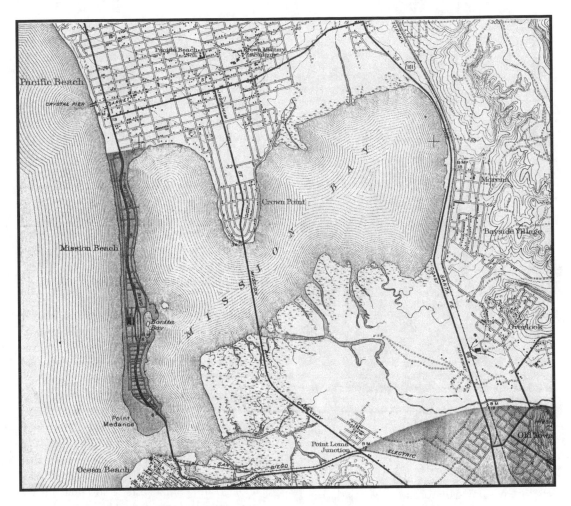

Figure 17.4. Mission Bay in 1943, prior to its transformation into Mission Bay Park. The former extensive marsh areas on the south shore can be seen. From 1943 USGS topographic map, La Jolla quadrangle.

1970s (Figure 17.6). Today, Mission Trails Regional Park, at 5,880 acres, is one of the largest city parks in the United States, and the riparian woodland through the gorge is one of the most important wildlife corridors and habitat preserves in any urban area. The city has built

a first-class visitor's center there with a spectacular view into the gorge.

Following the efforts, described above, to save local rivers from dams or channelization, people began to think bigger. Why not acknowledge the importance of our rivers as natural amenities,

Figure 17.5. State Route 163 as it winds through Balboa Park. Efforts to widen it have so far been defeated. Photograph by P. R. Pryde.

floodplains, wildlife areas, and recreational outlets, by envisioning one or more river parks running along major watercourses from the coast all the way to their headwaters? Why not protect the entire river valley, rather than just disconnected pieces? The idea took hold fairly quickly.

Before the end of the 1980s, the first major river park effort was under way, along the San Dieguito River. This is a joint planning effort (officially, a Joint Powers Authority—see Chapter 19) among the cities of San Diego, Poway, Escondido, Solana Beach and Del Mar, plus the County of San Diego. The San Dieguito River Park will eventually provide both recre-

ational trails and a wildlife corridor all the way from the river's estuary in Del Mar to its source 55 miles inland on Volcan Mountain. Several historic sites and archeological resources will be preserved along the route as well, and numerous interpretive facilities installed. A major restoration of the San Dieguito Lagoon and surrounding intertidal and upland habitats is planned. A Citizen Advisory Committee exists to extend advice on the park's development.

By 2003, about 18,000 acres had been acquired or otherwise preserved for the River Park, in addition to public lands that were already owned by the City of San Diego and various federal agencies. Key acquisitions have included most of the privately owned portions of Volcan Mountain, Bernardo Mountain near Escondido, Boden Canyon, and Edwards Ranch in Santa Ysabel (Figure 17.7). Eventually, the park's trail system will continue down the east side of Volcan Mountain to connect with the Pacific Crest Trail and the Anza-Borrego Desert State Park trail system.

Efforts were soon underway in South County to preserve valuable habitat on two shorter waterways, the Otay River and the U.S. portion of the Tijuana River. On the Otay River, an effort similar to San Dieguito's but on a smaller scale was entered into by the adjacent cities of San Diego and Chula Vista. The Tijuana River is only five miles long on the U.S. side, but it has very high wildlife value. A number of endangered species call the valley home. Following the decision not to build a concrete flood channel, the County and San Diego City have jointly worked to create a regional open space park and habitat preserve in the valley. It will be aided by other open lands owned by California (Border Field State Park) and the federal Fish and Wildlife Service.

In the 1990s, a long overdue campaign began to create a river park along the San Diego River.

Figure 17.6. View to the Cowles Mountain Range from the San Carlos area of San Diego. These mountains today form the core of the Mission Trails Regional Park. Photograph (taken in the 1970s) by P. R. Pryde.

In its initial stages, this proposed parkway would extend from the ocean inland as far as El Capitan Dam. However, a study regarding the integrated management of the resources of the entire watershed is also under way, and ultimately the open space park is envisioned to extend to the river's headwaters near Julian.

The San Diego River effort does not involve a formal Joint Powers Authority as does the San Dieguito River Park, but rather is a coalition of several separate organizations active in efforts to protect and restore the river. These include the San Diego River Park Foundation, San Diego River Park Coalition, San Diego River Park Alliance, San Diego River Park Lakeside Conservancy, Mission Trails Regional Park, San Diego River Watershed Workgroup, and the newly created (2003) San Diego River Park Conservancy. In addition, a large number of other supporting groups are involved, including (in part) the Friends of the Mission Valley Preserve, Friends of Famosa Slough, San Diego County Trails Council, Audubon Society, Friends of Adobe Falls, Friends of Dog Beach, and the various cities, parks, planning groups, and other interested organizations located along the river. These, collectively, constitute the Coalition. State monies are available for land acquisition by the two Conservancies, and efforts are underway to acquire suitable parcels in San Diego City, Lakeside, and elsewhere. In 2003, the creation of a state-chartered San Diego River

Figure 17.7. View to Bernardo Mountain across a portion of Lake Hodges. Most of the mountain was acquired in 2002 as an addition to the San Dieguito River Park. Photograph by P. R. Pryde.

Conservancy provided the river park with additional recognition and funding opportunities.

A Still Broader Picture: Saving Sustainable Habitats

With an increased recognition of the importance of conserving biodiversity and genetic information came an increased emphasis on preserving larger habitat areas. Specifically, what was desired was a means of saving large portions of key biomes, sufficient in size to house a sustainable population of rare or threatened species, and indeed of all species utilizing the area. The biomes of primary concern were coastal sage scrub and coastal wetlands, since the oak and conifer forests were under Forest Service supervision, the desert was under State Park protection, and most of the main river corridors and estuaries were being conserved by the river park efforts described above.

The Multiple Species Conservation Plan (MSCP)

Towards the end of the 1980s, an effort began in the City of San Diego to identify and preserve a large area of contiguous coastal sage scrub habitat that would suffice to protect certain threatened species, such as the California gnatcatcher, that depend on this type of vegetation. This effort was advanced by a state law—the "Natural Communities Conservation Program" (NCCP) —passed in 1991, that mandated this type of process. This effort was strongly supported by the building industry, who disliked having to deal with endangered species on a project-by-project basis; their goal was a program that would set aside adequate habitat for these species, so that the protection issue wouldn't have to come up with each project they wanted to build. In the San Diego metropolitan area, this effort is known as the "Multiple Species Conservation Plan", or MSCP.

By raising habitat planning to a regional level, the MSCP program has become a very large and complex planning effort. Years of work eventually resulted in the adoption of the Final MSCP Plan in 1998. It covers the area south of the San Dieguito River (but takes in all of San Pasqual Valley), and eastward to the outer edges of suburbanization. Similar programs covering the rest of the county are described below.

The idea was to map, using a Geographic Information System (GIS) program, the areas of highest habitat value in the MSCP's Multiple-Habitat Planning Area. A total of 93 species of plants and animals were selected for study, and used to determine core areas where the highest habitat value areas were located (Figure 17.8). A line was then drawn around the most important portions of this area, to take in as much of the prime habitat as possible; this became the MSCP preserve area. It was determined that 85 of the 93 studied species could probably be adequately protected ("covered") by a preserve of this size; the others would require additional help. The total area within the preserve when created in 1995 was 171,917 acres; this could change slightly in either direction with time.

Some of this preserve area was in public ownership, some in private. The agencies owning the public lands were expected to cooperate in the program; the privately owned lands were more complex. In some cases, willing sellers of the some of the private land could be found, and state bond issues, or other funds, could be used to acquire it. Where the private owner was intent on developing the parcel, a formula was devised to indicate how much of the privately owned portion within a given jurisdiction could be developed, and how much placed into the preserve.

Both the development community and the environmental community have concerns about the implementation of the plan, and how effective it will be many years down the road. Some of these questions are: what happens if a new species of plant or animal is added to the endangered list in the future, do we assume the preserve takes care of it? What if it is found mostly outside the preserve area, but a portion is inside it? How confident are we that the preserve will really protect a sustainable population of all 85 of the "covered" species? What about the eight species that were not adequately "covered"? How will priorities be determined for granting

permits for the limited development allowed within the preserve? The program is very complex in its implementation, and these are not the only difficult questions that are being asked. Nonetheless, there is a general consensus (though far from unanimous) that the MSCP program is the best "deal" that could be devised, and that we should work diligently towards its implementation. It seems likely, at least, that it ought to prove preferable to having no plan at all.

To complete habitat projection coverage for the county, two other large programs also exist. In the north coastal portion of the county, there is the Multiple Habitat Conservation Program, which is very similar to the MSCP program to the south. The County has its own Multiple Habitat Conservation and Open Space Program, which will take in the unincorporated portion of the county east of the main urbanized area. Between the three programs, all of the county will have been studied and will have multiple-habitat preserve areas in place.

These habitat preservation efforts involve a new strategy termed "mitigation banks". Large new developments that will destroy habitat are legally required to "mitigate" this habitat loss by restoring or acquiring other areas of similar habitat. One way of accomplishing this is to identify a large area worthy of preservation, and allowing new developments to satisfy their mitigation requirements by buying portions of it for a habitat preserve. Such an area is termed a "mitigation bank". Sometimes a public agency (or a land trust) will acquire the land to be "banked" in advance, and subsequently "sell" portions of it for mitigation credit. About a dozen such mitigation banks existed in the county in 2002.

Another widely used technique is the purchase of conservation easements. With this technique, landowners can retain title to their properties and continue to live on it, while earning income (and tax relief) by selling the right

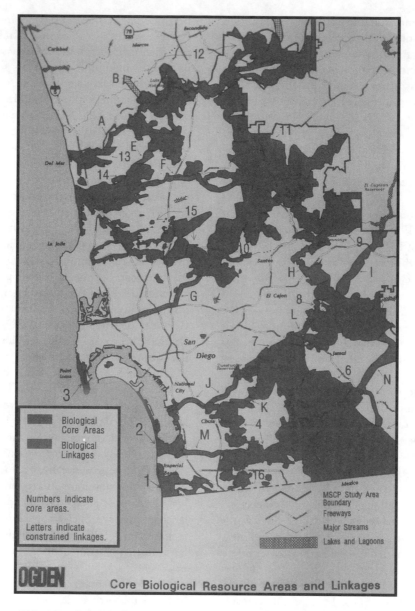

Figure 17.8. Map showing the core biological areas of the MSCP planning region. Photograph of MSCP map by P. R. Pryde.

to subdivide the parcel. The sale of these rights produces a conservation easement on the parcel, the title to which is usually held either by a governmental agency or a private land trust organization. The conservation easement is permanent, thus guaranteeing that the parcel will never contain more than one dwelling unit, and that most of it will remain in natural vegetation.

San Diego National Wildlife Refuge

A little known but highly significant large-scale habitat preservation project has been taking place in South County since the early 1990s. This is the creation of the San Diego National Wildlife Refuge, under the supervision of the U.S. Fish and Wildlife Service (F&WS). The purpose of the Refuge is to provide quality wildlife habitat for coastal wetlands, vernal pools, and coastal sage scrub biomes, and the many species, including endangered ones, that inhabit them. It was officially established in 1996.

It exists in three sections. The largest is termed the Otay-Sweetwater Planning Unit, and will take in coastal sage, grassland, chaparral, and riparian habitats in an irregularly shaped area south of I-8, east of Sweetwater Reservoir, and extending south past Lower Otay Reservoir to the Otay Mountain Preserve. It will be an important component of the MSCP, described above. This unit will include the Jamul, McGinty, and San Miguel Mountains, and the recently acquired Rancho San Diego. This planning unit takes in approximately 44,000 acres. The diversity of wildlife it will protect includes the California gnatcatcher, mountain lion, red-legged frog, San Diego horned lizard, and Quino checkerspot butterfly.

Smaller, but equally important, is the South San Diego Bay Planning Unit, approved in 1999. As noted previously, much of the original, extensive intratidal wetlands in San Diego Bay have been dredged or filled for economic purposes (Figure 17.9). Located in the southernmost portion of the Bay, the South San Diego Bay unit extends southward from the existing Sweetwater Marsh National Wildlife Refuge. Control over this portion of the bay was turned over to the Fish and Wildlife Service by the Port Authority. It includes the evaporation ponds of Western Salt Company, which have become a major wintering, feeding, and summer nesting area for a wide array of endangered and unusual bird species, such as least tern, Belding's savannah sparrow, gull-billed tern, peregrine falcon, snowy plover, black skimmer and many others. Even sea turtles make use of this area. It will take in around 4,000 acres.

The third planning unit is the Vernal Pools Stewardship Project. This is a bit more complicated, as it includes many remaining vernal pools located on the Marine Corp's Miramar Air Station, as well as on both public and private land in scattered locations from Del Mar to Otay Mesa. About 8,000 acres are involved, but many of these would be managed by the existing landowners, such as the Marine Corps.

The new Refuge is being administered out of the headquarters complex of the existing Tijuana Slough National Wildlife Refuge. A management plan for each unit was being developed at the turn of the new century, and land acquisition occurs on a regular basis as opportunities present themselves. By the start of 2001, over 7,000 acres of the Otay-Sweetwater unit had been purchased from willing sellers, and about 60 percent of the planned area was in some form of preserved status.

The three units of the new San Diego National Wildlife Refuge, together with the older Sweetwater Marsh and Tijuana Slough NWRs, collectively provide a large and hopefully effective preserve system for many of the

Figure 17.9. This was the north end of San Diego Bay in 1937. The County Administration Building can be seen under construction at lower right. At upper center is Loma Portal. The new fill to the right of center is the Coast Guard Station. Beyond (west of) the Coast Guard Station, the flat area to the right of the straight (dredged) water passage is what is now Lindbergh Field; immediately to the left of the channel is what is today Harbor Island. The remainder of the tidal flats in the upper center were dredged to make Harbor and Shelter Islands. Photograph courtesy of the Unified Port District.

coastal components of San Diego County's rich array of flora and fauna.

A New Mission for the Ranchlands

Chapters One and Nine noted that almost two centuries ago, the Mexican governors of what is now San Diego County divided up much of the region into large land grants, or ranchos (see Figure 9.1). With time, some of these went into other uses (Camp Pendleton, Cuyamaca State Park), but many retained something of their original boundaries and purpose, and passed through various ownerships while still remaining as large ranches. For a while they were reasonably profitable, but today, for various reasons, that is not always the case. Many are up for sale.

Although some have been split up or even sub-divided into "ranchettes," many of the ranching families do not want to see the open spaces that they have worked, sometimes for generations, being turned into more rural subdivisions. Even if they can't afford to operate them any longer, they would still like to see them remain reasonably natural. This means that various environmental organizations and governmental entities have had the opportunity to acquire large parcels, or in some cases entire ranches, for use as permanent open space. They have seized upon this opportunity to a remarkable degree.

Since about 1990, dozens of parcels greater than 100 acres in size, many of them exceeding 1,000 acres, have been acquired for addition to the county's open space network. The creation of the San Diego National Wildlife Refuge, the San Dieguito River Park, and the MSCP, all discussed above, have helped spur this effort along, but the county and other agencies have also been instrumental in acquiring available land. Where have the funds come from to acquire this land? The largest single source has been monies made available from State open space bond issues, but

some federal funds have been used as well.

In many cases, the initial purchasers are land trusts, such as the large national organizations The Nature Conservancy (TNC) and the Trust for Public Lands (TPL). In addition, there are several local land trusts active in the county, typically identifiable by the words "Land Trust", "Foundation", or "Conservancy" in their title. The advantage of land trusts is that they can act quickly when land goes on the market, acquire it, and then sell it later to a public agency that would have been much slower to gather together the needed acquisition funds or to work its way through the approval process. An excellent example was the purchase of Bernardo Mountain on the north shore of Lake Hodges in 2002, which had a very short deadline for the completion of its sale; its purchase was expedited by the efforts of the San Dieguito River Valley Conservancy (Figure 17.7).

In all, tens of thousands of acres have been acquired since 1990 by such purchases of large parcels; some of the largest are summarized in Table 17.2. More ranchlands remain available for purchase from willing sellers, to be added to our endowment of protected habitats and open space.

Are We Winning?

We may conclude this chapter with two questions for the future: what still needs to be done, and will our visions be fulfilled?

With regard to what yet needs to be done, the short answer is "much". Although we have preserved a great deal of what needs to be protected in our region, there is still more to do. Many parks, for example, have private inholdings that are subject to development. There is still a lot of land to be acquired for the MSCP and similar habitat plans. The various river parks need to connect the protected areas that

TABLE 17.2. Some Recent Large Open Space Acquisitions in San Diego County

Name of Parcel:	Acreage:	Year Acquired:	Agency Buying/Managing:	Location and/or Significance
Cowles Mountain	1,369	1974	City/County of San Diego	Highest point with the City of San Diego
Elfin Forest	750	1985	Olivenhain MWD	Watershed protection and visitor recreation
Mount Gower Preserve	1,590	1980s	County of San Diego	Predominantly chaparral; transferred from BLM
Hellhole Canyon Preserve	1,712	1980s	County of San Diego	Predominantly chaparral; transferred from BLM
El Capitan Preserve	2,839	1980s	County of San Diego	Predominantly chaparral; transferred from BLM
Tijuana River Valley	1,355	1990–1999	County of San Diego	Wetland habitat for rare and endangered species
Blue Sky Ranch	2,773	1990s	City of Poway	City of Poway open space and Ecological Reserve
Rancho San Diego (part)	1,900	1995	US Fish & Wildlife Service	Riparian and wetland habitat along Sweetwater R.
Daley Ranch (Rancho Jamul)	4,800	1997	Trust for Public Land	Is part of the Multiple Species Conservation Plan
Daley Ranch (Escondido)	3,058	1996	City of Escondido	Multi-species habitat preserve and open space park
Sentenac Canyon	1,421	May, 1998	Anza-Borrego Desert S.P.	Important wetland habitat along Rte. 78 east of S-2
Boden Canyon	1,358	1998–1999	San Diego City & Cal. DF&G	Oak woodland and riparian habitat north of Ramona
Rutherford Ranch, county	2,650	1990–1998	County of San Diego	Connects Volcan Mtn with San Felipe Valley
Rutherford Ranch, DF&G	6,888	1995–2001	Calif. Dept. of Fish & Game	Volcan Mtn pine forests; western San Felipe Valley
Crestridge	2,650	1999	Calif. Dept. of Fish & Game	Flora and fauna habitat preserve in Crest foothills
Eichenlaub Ranch	1,340	1999	City of San Diego	Protects watershed near city's Barrett Reservoir
Las Montanas	954	2000	Trust for Public Land, F&WS	Coastal sage scrub (gnatcatcher) habitat
Edwards (Santa Ysabel)	5,406	1999–2000	San Diego County	Includes southwestern slopes of Volcan Mountain
Lucky 5 Ranch	2,675	April, 2001	Anza-Borrego Desert S.P.	Connects Cuyamaca and Anza-Borrego state parks
Daley Ranch—Jamul (part)	3,700	June, 2001	Calif. Dept. of Fish & Game	Is part of the Multiple Species Conservation Plan
Cuyamaca (Tulloch) Ranch	2,117	Jan. 2002	The Nature Conservancy	Protects shore and watershed of Lake Cuyamaca
Mason Valley Ranch	842	2002	Anza-Borrego Foundation	Good ranchlands; key buffer area for State Park
Proctor Valley parcels	1,446	Jan. 2003	Calif. Dept. of Fish & Game	Coastal sage scrub habitat to be added to the MSCP
Sloane Canyon Sand Co.	876	July, 2003	US Fish & Wildlife Service	Three miles of riparian habitat along Sweetwater R.
Honey Springs Ranch	1,978	Oct. 2003	Calif. Dept. of Fish & Game	Oak parkland habitat to be added to the MSCP
Vallecito Ranch	3,339	2003	Anza-Borrego Foundation	Pristine desert scrub, riparian woods, desert marsh
Total of above acreages:	61,786			

Source: Compiled by author from various sources.

have been acquired to date. More ranches may yet come on the market. New protected habitats for future endangered species, not yet identified, may need to be preserved. The job will never be entirely done, but we can be proud of what has been accomplished to date. Certainly the San Diego region has done more than most metropolitan areas, and this in the face of (or perhaps because of) one of fastest urban growth rates in the country.

In the long run our visions for biological and genetic preservation will be fulfilled on the basis of not just the quantity of our protected areas, but also the quality of them. That is, we must not only set the land aside, we must take care of it in perpetuity. It does no good to acquire "protected" land, and then through inattention allow it to be overrun by vehicles, non-native species, recreationists, or other forms of potential deterioration. This is sometimes referred to as ensuring the "integrity" of the parcel, making sure it will always be as functional as it was when acquired or restored. For large parcels, some from of maintenance endowment may be essential to guarantee their long-term integrity.

It can be argued that we are winning, but also that we are advancing down a never-ending pathway. Each succeeding generation will need to continue the conservation work, and we must instruct our children that this effort will be theirs to carry out, as well. It is appropriate to end this chapter with the oft quoted statement that:

"We will preserve only what we love; we will love only what we understand; we will understand only what we are taught".

References

California Department of Parks and Recreation (CDPR). *Anza-Borrego Desert State Park Preliminary General Plan*. Sacramento: CDPR, January 2003.

City of San Diego. *Final MSCP Plan*. San Diego: City Community and Economic Development Department. August 1998.

County of San Diego. *Management Framework Plan for Tijauna River Valley Regional Park*. San Diego: County Parks and Recreation Department, May 2002.

LaRue, Steve, "Fast-Growing Wildlife Refuge Continues to Acquire Acreage", *San Diego Union-Tribune*, October 13, 2000, pp. B1 and B8.

Lindsay, Diana. *Anza-Borrego A to Z*. San Diego: Sunbelt Publications, 2001.

Pourade, R. F. *The History of San Diego: The Glory Years,* San Diego: Union-Tribune Publ. Co., 1964.

Pryde, Philip, "Agua Tibia - San Diego's Wilderness," *Environment Southwest,* No. 464 (May 1974), pp. 3–5.

Pryde, Philip, "What Does the Future Hold for Mission Valley?", *Environment Southwest,* No. 452 (March 1973), pp. 6–9.

Pryde, Philip, "An Inventory and Evaluation of Natural Areas in San Diego County," *Yearbook of the Association of Pacific Coast Geographers* , Vol. 50 (1988), pp. 87-103.

San Dieguito River Park (SDRP). *San Dieguito River Park Concept Plan*. San Diego: SDRP, 1993.

Showley, R. M. *San Diego : Perfecting Paradise*. Carlsbad, CA: Heritage Media Corp., 1999.

Sunila, Joyce, "The Corps (Marine) and the Only Natural River", *Audubon,* Sept. 1987, pp. 115–123.

Internet Connections:

Anza-Borrego Foundation: *www.theabf.org*

City of San Diego's MSCP program: *www.sandiego.gov/mscp/index.shtml*

Conservation banks: *www.dfg.ca.gov/hcpb/conplan/mitbank/mitbank/html*

San Diego National Wildlife Refuge(s): *http://sandiegorefuges.fws.gov/*

San Diego River Park: *www.sandiegoriver.org*

San Dieguito River Park: *www.sdrp.org*

Chapter Eighteen

Barbara E. Fredrich and
Alan Rice Osborn

Tijuana:
Transformation on the Border

South of the Tijuana River National Estuarine Reserve, past parcels of agricultural land, horse farms, a binational wastewater treatment plant, and the U.S.-Mexico International Border, is one of the fastest growing cities in North America. In 1889, it was a frontier town, mostly a scattering of houses twenty miles south of San Diego. Today, high-rise office buildings, hotels, condominiums, and shopping malls dominate the skyline. A large variety of immigrants and their descendants have made Tijuana their home. Its residents include, in addition to people from all parts of Mexico, Chinese (early nine-

Barbara Fredrich is a professor of cultural geography in the Department of Geography at San Diego State University; Alan Rice Osborn is a lecturer in the same department.

teenth century), Spanish (1930s), European Jews (1940s), and more recently, immigrants from elsewhere in Latin America, North America, and Asia. Tijuana is a highly cosmopolitan city, with a population estimated at 1.2 million, and is linked physically, economically, and socially to the San Diego metropolitan area and the rest of Southern California.

Tijuana is situated within one of the largest international border metropolitan regions in the world. Every day there is a massive international journey to work in which tens of thousands of both legal and undocumented workers pass through the gates at San Ysidro (the busiest port of entry in the U.S.), or at Otay Mesa, to enter the United States. According to the Immigration and Naturalization Service (INS), in 2002 an average of about 150,000 people crossed the

Tijuana-San Diego border each day; about one fifth are pedestrians. A destination somewhere in the San Diego region is the goal for about 65 percent of those heading north.

Tijuana is a place that continues to attract and captivate visitors and residents. It is the point of contact where two very different cultures meet, and an inseparable and vital part of San Diego's social and economic landscape. This chapter will briefly examine the nature and complexity of this exciting city, and how it is changing in the present era. It will look specifically at the development and modernization of Tijuana, and the influences (from both sides of the border) that are working to define the character of twenty-first century Tijuana and link it to the San Diego region.

Tijuana Prior to World War II

One of the intriguing aspects of Tijuana is the uncertainty of the origin of its name. Some suggest it is a corruption of a Kumeyaay Indian tribal word, "Tijuan," which means "by the sea." The name "Llantijuan," "Lla Tijuana," or "Tijuana" appears in some mission records. Some Americans think the town was named for a popular Sonoran cook, "Aunt Jane", but this is unlikely. The spelling "TiaJuana", sometimes seen on American maps, is incorrect. In 1925, following the Mexican revolution, the city was formally named Ciudad Zaragoza, after the Mexican Independence leader Ignacio Zaragoza. Local residents, however, persisted in calling it Tijuana, and eventually the Mexican Congress acquiesced. Whatever its origin, in 1929 "Tijuana" became the city's official name.

Permanent settlement in the area dates to the 1820s. At first it was just a scattering of adobe huts along the Tijuana River, a part of the Rancho de Tijuana, which was the largest of six cattle ranches administered from San Diego.

The boundary between Mexico and the United States was fixed following the Mexican-American War in 1848, and since that time the social and economic history of Tijuana has been linked to the history of San Diego.

Unlike other Mexican border cities (Tecate and Mexicali, for example), Tijuana was always much smaller than its cross-border counterpart, so that economic and political events in San Diego had a very great effect on Tijuana. In the nineteenth century these included the railroad-related building booms in the early 1880s (the decade in which a twenty kilometer free trade zone, or *zona libre* was initiated) and the stagnation and decline of the 1890s. During that period, Tijuana probably had more *cantinas* than any other type of establishment.

The first gambling license for a Tijuana establishment was issued in 1915. In addition to casino operations, other gambling activities such as bullfighting, cock fighting, boxing matches and horse racing became extremely popular, especially with visitors from the United States. These business and entertainment activities subsided during World War I, but during the U.S. crackdown on vice during the Prohibition era (1920–1933), Tijuana's reputation as a "wild west" town flourished. Although it is largely undeserved today, in some peoples' minds that frontier-town reputation persists.

By 1930 the population of Tijuana was only about 11,000—embryonic compared to San Diego's nearly 150,000. However, significant numbers of Mexican citizens were repatriated from the U.S. to Tijuana during the Great Depression. The city began to diversify economically, and during the decade of the 1930s it grew at approximately 5 percent annually, about twice the Mexican national average.

In 1942, the *Bracero* program ("bracero" is Spanish for "arms") was initiated to allow a Mexican agricultural labor force to substitute for

Americans drafted into service during World War II. A pattern emerged: Tijuana was both an interim destination for migrant workers en route north, and a place to which they were deported whenever there were fluctuations in U.S. economic or political policy. The effects on Tijuana's population were dramatic; Tijuana's population grew from just 22,000 in 1940, to over 65,000 in 1950 (Table 18.1).

Post-War Population and Economic Patterns

By 1950 Tijuana ranked fifth among the Mexican border cities in size. Since then the city has grown at an astronomical rate, from about 65,000 (1950) to nearly one and a quarter million. This has partly been due to a high rate of natural increase, but mostly it has been caused by a massive rural to urban migration process. This migration continues; Tijuana's population is increasing by an estimated 78,000 residents per year.

The original urban nucleus underwent a process of expansion in a pattern typical of Latin American cities. It developed neighborhoods extending outward from the Central Business District (CBD) that followed major transportation corridors and which today reflect decreasing socioeconomic levels. Thus, a westward coastal extension occurs along the road to Ensenada and a southeastern extension toward Tecate. Further complicating the development pattern is the rugged and deeply dissected topography of the area (Figure 18.1). The rapid urban expansion has resulted in an eclectic development pattern with low income settlements and businesses often located within or near elite neighborhoods.

Tijuana's incorporated boundaries, like those of San Diego, have changed over time. The city's municipal area was first designated in 1921 and encompassed both Tecate and Ensenada. Tecate had become a separate city by 1950; the most recent change was the creation of Playas de Rosarita (Rosarita Beach) in 1995. The city's municipal (developed) area was 12,650 hectares (ha.) (about 49 square miles) in 1984. The city had a density of 119 persons per ha. (or 30,800 persons per sq. mile) in 1960, which increased to 134 by 1987.

Currently the total built area is estimated at over 20,200 ha. (78 sq. miles), with over 10,880 ha. (42 sq. miles) classified as "urbanized". Over 7,720 ha. (30 sq. miles) was calculated to be residential (comprising over 340 residential districts) in function. The latter figure was used to calculate the current average population density of 166 per hectare (or over 40,000 persons per sq. mile). Within this high overall density there exists much variation, as can be seen in Figure 18.2. Perhaps not surprisingly, the areas of lowest income show a remarkably uniform pattern, with the highest density areas corresponding to the lowest income neighborhoods. In contrast, the areas of highest income occur near the Agua Caliente racetrack (near the CBD) and the beach community of Playas de Tijuana (light areas in Figure 18.3).

TABLE 18.1. Growth of Tijuana

Year	Population
1930	11,271
1940	21,977
1950	65,364
1960	165,690
1970	340,583
1980	461,257
1990	742,686
1995	991,592
2000	1,212,232

Source: Griffin and Ford, 1976; Herzog, 1990; Instituto Nacional de Estadistica, Geografia e Informatica (INEGI) 1980, 1990, 2000.

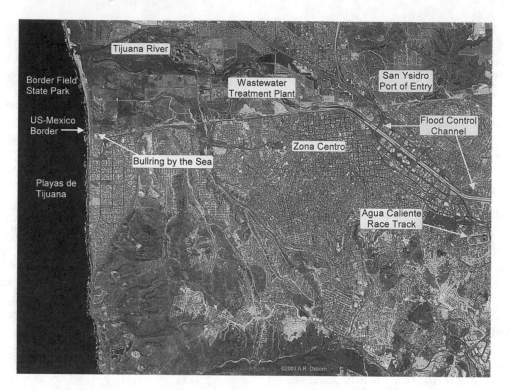

Figure 18.1. Aerial mosaic of central and western Tijuana (After *San Diego-Tijuana International Border Area Planning Atlas/ Atlas de Planeación del Área Fronteriza Internacional Tijuana-San Diego*, Figure 7-8).

Revenues from Mexican oil development in the 1970s funded an infrastructure building boom. For example, the Rio Tijuana was channelized to control flooding, and the zones of both its banks were cleared for the construction of government buildings, multi-story public housing, monumental statues (including the last Aztec ruler of Mexico, Cuauhtemoc), and a cultural center, which was completed in 1982.

The rapid growth of Tijuana over the last half-century can be attributed to several factors. First, the residents and recent migrants have taken advantage of a variety of employment opportunities ranging from high-tech professions to manual labor, in a region that has rela-

tively high employment and high federally established minimum wage rates. This acts as a significant stimulus for migration into Tijuana. In fact, Baja California is the second highest receiver of immigrants in Mexico, a rate of 8.5 percent in 2000. Not surprisingly, the mean age is twenty-three.

Second, the free trade zone (first established in the 1880s) allowed residents to purchase consumer and luxury goods, such as television sets, automobiles, cosmetics, and gasoline in the city at a cost lower than elsewhere in Mexico. Consequently, personal ownership of automobiles, television sets, and radios is higher than in the rest of the nation.

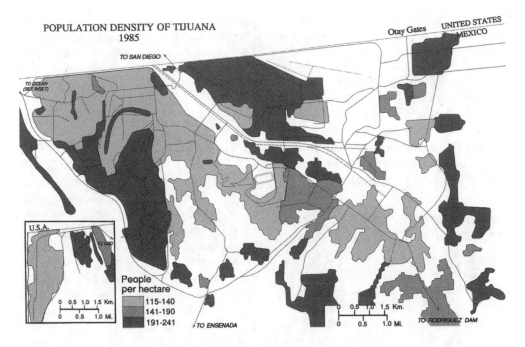

Figure 18.2. Population density of Tijuana. Map by Barbara Fredrich.

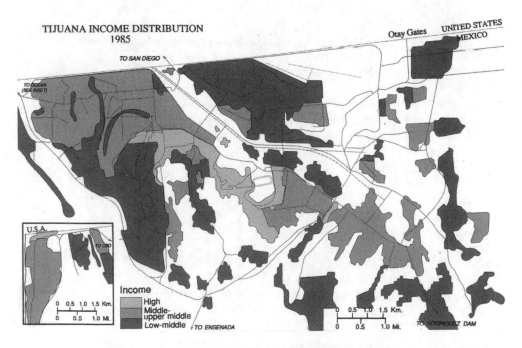

Figure 18.3. Tijuana income distribution. Map by Barbara Fredrich.

Third, the *Programa Nacional Fronteriza* (National Border Program) was initiated by the Mexican government in 1961, and was fully implemented by 1971. The goals of this program were to enhance economic diversification and development in Mexican border cities, increase investment, and reduce the outflow of capital to the United States. *Maquiladoras,* or tax-exempt enterprises that use inexpensive local labor to assemble finished products for export, became the foundation for the manufacturing sector.

The *Maquiladora* Landscape, and Other Economic Considerations

To understand the Tijuana economy at present, it is necessary to be familiar with the concept of *maquiladoras*. The Spanish word *maquilar* once referred to the portion of flour a miller kept in payment for grinding wheat. Today the term has evolved to mean a program in which foreign-owned goods are assembled at low-wage Mexican manufacturing plants, and are then shipped across the border into the US, paying only a nominal tariff. Under this economic structure foreign-owned companies in Mexico are allowed to import component parts, materials, machines and equipment without paying the heavy duties which would normally be assessed on such goods entering or leaving the country. *Maquiladora* companies produce finished goods such as electronic components, fabrics, medical goods, furniture parts or toys, for about one-tenth of the cost of those assembled in the United States.

This process, which initially included Asian nations such as Taiwan, Singapore, South Korea and Malaysia, has now gone global, and the term *maquiladora* is used in Latin America and elsewhere. Other terms, such as "twin-plants assembly" and "offshore production", are less used today. Both large and small companies have ben-

efited due to reduced labor costs, and Mexico benefited economically due to the huge increase in manufacturing employment and related jobs. In the mid-1990s, *maquiladoras* rivaled the oil industry as the Mexico's largest exporter. In Tijuana, *maquiladoras* grew from less than 100 assembly plants in the early 1970s with about 10,000 workers, to 772 plants in 2000 with 179,064 workers (Table 18.2).

The *maquiladoras* are dominated by electronics firms, including such familiar names as Sanyo, Sony, Matsushita, Samsung, Pioneer, Honeywell, and Hitachi (Figure 18.4). However, they include a wide variety of apparel and small manufacturing concerns as well. In the industrial district of La Mesa, scrap iron is melted to make manhole covers for U.S. streets. In other areas, products are made for such U.S. manufacturers of medical equipment and supplies as KenMex, Kelsar, Baxter International, Johnson and Johnson, and Colgate-Palmolive. In addition to the Hyundai plant near Rodriguez Dam, Toyota Motor Corporation is building a $140 million plant to manufacture truck beds for Tacoma pickup trucks.

However, critics charge that the system is exploitative and does not translate into real prosperity. They accuse manufacturers of taking advantage of very young workers to increase company profits in a weakly unionized setting, without lowering the product price for the ultimate consumer. There are accusations that young women, especially those from the inte-

TABLE 18.2. Growth of *Maquiladoras* in Tijuana

Year	Plants	Workers
Early 1970s	< 100	ca. 10,000
1985	> 200	> 25,000
1990	> 600	> 67,000
2000	772	179,064

Figure 18.4. The Sanyo plant in Tijuana, a typical maquiladora enterprise. Photo by Barbara Fredrich.

rior, are lured with offers of stable jobs and a better life. Too often they learn the hard way how costly it is to live in a border city such as Tijuana, perhaps the most expensive region of Mexico. New arrivals may have to work multiple jobs or seven-day weeks to meet basic needs. Homes for many workers may be small, crowded, and lacking in basic amenities. Additionally, the process may act to de-stabilize family relationships, since children and young women became less subject to family control when they leave school to work in Tijuana.

Some critics also charge that the unequal economic process continues Mexico's dependence on the United States, and contributes to the economic disparity within the binational region. Recently, concern has been expressed that American companies may be using the *maquiladora* plants to improperly dispose of hazardous waste in Mexico, as a way of evading stricter U.S. laws.

Such criticisms are usually countered with accounts of how *maquiladoras* have provided decent and stable jobs in an otherwise economically marginal area, and how they have aided economic development throughout Mexico. The signing of a free-trade agreement with the U.S. and Canada (NAFTA) in 1994 further stimulated capital inflow to Mexico. That agreement provides for the exchange of goods and services without the imposition of duties or quotas through the three nations. One particularly noteworthy result has been in the auto industry in Mexico, where some 3 million jobs from U.S. carmakers have been added as a result of NAFTA. But NAFTA has also been subject to many of the same criticisms as noted above.

However, the rapid growth of *maquiladoras* shown in Table 18.2 has abated in recent years. In Baja California these plants have had to cope with declining U.S. sales and delayed shipments because of heightened border security. Even before September, 2001, the economic growth rate of *maquiladora* exports had been sinking, necessitating closures and layoffs. Since 2000, manufacturing employment in Baja California has been lowered by twelve percent or about 35,000 workers, from a maximum of 291,000 workers in October 2000. In 2001 Tijuana lost nearly 12,000 jobs prior to September 11th. The number of *maquiladoras* has been reduced as well, with one estimate suggesting that there are now just 700 left employing 120,000 workers. As one example Hasbro, maker of Pokemon toys, has moved to China.

Other Aspects of Tijuana's Economy

The economy of Tijuana is very similar to the economy of the rest of the state of Baja California del Norte. Over two-thirds of the Baja California work force is employed in business, services, or government work. Less than five percent work in agriculture, fishing or livestock activities. About twenty percent were employed in manufacturing industries. Unemployment rates are estimated to be high, perhaps over 25 percent in Tijuana, and over 40 percent in the interior. However, to place this in context, the federal government's National Statistics Institute estimates that about 28 percent of working Mexicans are considered to be part of the "informal economy", that is, engaged in economic activities which are not registered for tax or social security purposes. This category includes street vendors, those who produce goods and services from home, and people hired occasionally to do work. If these figures are accurate, it is possible that about a third of Tijuana families pay no taxes. While this may mean a bit more income in the short term, it has important consequences, since those who pay no taxes have little access to health-care coverage.

The presence of light industries, luxury motels, lively discos, good restaurants, universities, a cultural center, and the famous Agua Caliente racetrack underscores the growing importance of retail and wholesale trade, services, banking, construction, and tourism to the economy of Tijuana. New stores display merchandise of highly varied quality that includes trinkets, quality crafts, clothes, leather goods, wrought iron, pottery, carved onyx and even blankets with U.S. logos. Tijuana residents tend to avoid shopping along Revolucion Avenue,

the favorite commercial venue for tourists. Instead locals shop at Blanco, Calimax, or Mesa de Otay's Commercial Mexicana, or at the new shopping centers such as the Plaza Rio Tijuana and Plaza Fiesta, and Pueblo Amigo in the Rio Tijuana zone. Residents may shop in a chic boutique at the Twin Towers (the two mirrored skyscrapers which dominate Tijuana's skyline) or they may prefer to take advantage of neighborhood swap meets (Figure 18.5).

However, recent financial crises and peso devaluations have greatly decreased the purchasing power of Mexicans. Until 1976 the exchange rate was quite stable, at 12.5 pesos to the dollar. But the peso was devalued in 1982, 1986, and 1992, and in the latter year the rate of exchange was 2,700 pesos to the dollar. A 1000:1 mid-1993 currency reissue made the exchange about three (new pesos) to one dollar. In early 2003 the rate of exchange was over ten pesos to the dollar, the lowest point since January 1999.

Notwithstanding longer border waits for security reasons, or the decreased value of the peso, Tijuana residents continue to shop in the San Diego area, especially at stores in San Ysidro and Chula Vista. A few are fortunate enough to have a Sentri lane permit (costing $129 for background checks) that allows a fairly quick entry—perhaps fifteen to twenty minutes or less. As might be expected, the number of people crossing the border declined precipitously after September 11, 2001. The average per day went from over 130,000 to about 80,000, while the number of pedestrians shrank to just 27,000. Despite this, because of heightened security most Mexican motorists wait over an hour or more to pass through the gates. For destinations close to the Border, many make use of the San Diego-Tijuana trolley. Recently a border mall within walking distance, La Puerta Las Americas, has opened.

Figure 18.5. Tijuana's "Twin Towers" overlook the Rio Tijuana commercial district and the residential neighborhoods on the hillsides to the north. Photo by Barbara Fredrich.

Socioeconomic Profiles

As in most Mexican cities, planning inadequacies are readily visible in the built environment—the juxtaposition of homes (rich and poor), businesses, and industry of all types reflects the paradox of prosperity alongside poverty. High-rise office buildings, hotels, condominiums and office malls have been built in the Zona Rio Tijuana, an area once known as "Cartolandia" because of the presence of numerous cardboard shacks. The great wealth visible in the mansions of Chapultepec hills contrasts with new squatter settlements that seem to spring up over night. The latter are found on less desirable or undeveloped margins of the urbanized area, and on the steep and sometimes unstable canyon slopes. In those places delivery persons, visitors, and postal carriers are challenged by the dearth of street signs and the absence (or sometimes multiplicity) of street numbers on homes (Figure 18.6).

Problems arising from Tijuana's urban growth are worsened by Mexico's centralized governmental structure, which tends to place local jurisdictions at the bottom of financial priorities. This factor, along with minimal resources, inadequate management, and insufficient personnel, creates an overwhelming burden for local government. The provision of basic urban amenities such as potable water and electricity (much less niceties such as clean streets) has been a challenge for decades. Management by crisis tends to be the *modus operandi*. Hence, urban planning, initially non-existent, is now challenged to keep pace with urban growth. Both state and federal agencies are financially constrained in providing basic services for permanent residents, transient workers, and visiting tourists alike.

A review of national, state, and Tijuana census data suggests the extent of the socio-environmental problems. Many homes in Tijuana are owner-built. The phenomenal rate of urban

Figure 18.6. A mix of mostly lower income housing on a Tijuana hillside. Typically, these homes will be renovated and improved over time. Photo by Barbara Fredrich.

growth over the past few decades makes renovations of these homes more difficult, as they must cope with inadequate building codes and zoning ordinances. Nevertheless, residents continue to be innovative in their house construction efforts, making use of whatever they can scavenge. By the mid-1980s three-fifths of the homes were constructed from used lumber, and another fifth was fashioned with drywall (both items largely obtained in the United States). The do-it-yourself home improvements, which permit a pay-as-you-go process, are a necessity for people whose economic means are marginal.

With time and economic stability, a more solidly constructed (brick or cinder block) home appears. The government eventually installs

water, sewage, and electrical service. Much of the family salary goes for rent and basic food items. Faced with daunting economic problems, the courage, spirit, and energy of many economically marginalized individuals and families carries them through.

Forty years ago the basic government standards for Tijuana's residential environments were described as "unmet" for four-fifths of the homes: about 37 percent of the homes lacked potable water and two-thirds were without a sewer line. A decade later about one-half of the homes had a water hook-up and fourth-fifths had electrical service. Currently over 97 percent have access to electricity, about 85 percent have a sewer line, and about 91 percent receive potable water, a higher rate than the national average of 89 percent. It is commendable that the rate of provision of basic amenities has increased, despite incredible urban growth.

Nevertheless an estimated 100,000 of the area's 1.2 million residents are dependent on 560 registered *piperos* (the traditional water-suppliers) to meet their needs, especially in eastern Tijuana. Their routes fluctuate in response to the degree of maturity of a community. As new residential neighborhoods spring up, delivery of water is generally first met by *piperos*; however, as the community becomes more developed and the city's pipelines are extended, the *piperos* shift their services to a more peripheral unplanned community. Not surprisingly under the circumstances, some of the poorest residents pay some of the highest prices for their water, in some cases as much as seven times more than a typical residential customer.

Meeting housing needs continues to be a major challenge for politicians and urban planners. In the early 1990s then-Governor Ernesto Ruffo Apel initiated a plan to offer lots, over a period of six years, to some 18,000 families. Recently Baja California was the recipient of a $110 million loan from Japan, matched by an equal amount from the Mexican government; to be used to catch up on laying water lines and storm drains. Even so, given Tijuana's growth rates, it will be difficult to have 100 percent coverage with water lines.

Limited water supplies have been an ongoing problem. Tijuana's water sources are wells near La Mision (limited supply), Rodriguez Dam (of little use in a drought), and imported water that arrives via a relatively small pipeline from the Colorado River (Figure 18.7). A former desalinization plant at Rosarita Beach has long since been shut down. In an emergency, a small pipeline from San Diego's Lower Otay Reservoir provides help. But even under the best of circumstances, Tijuana's water supply remains inadequate to meet the needs of its rapid population growth and commercial-industrial infrastructure.

Binational Cooperation

While the political systems of San Diego and Tijuana differ, the physical realities are similar, and many problems are shared. Current binational cooperation takes that fact into account when considering, among other things, the Tijuana River drainage basin, three-fourths of which lies in Mexico and one-fourth in the United States (Figure 18.8). This intermittent river passes through Tijuana, crosses the international border some six kilometers (four miles) from the ocean, enters an open floodplain, and terminates in the Tijuana River estuary in Imperial Beach, California. The river is partially regulated by the Rodriguez dam in Mexico and two others on the U.S. side, and by a large flood control channel built in the late 1970s through downtown Tijuana (Figure 18.9). Agreements crafted by the binational International Boundary and Water Commission regulate both countries' flood control measures, and a binational flood warning system was put in place throughout the basin in 2003. However, problems with uncontrolled sewage spills persist on both sides of the border.

Cross-border regional planning was virtually non-existent at a formal level until 1966 when the Comprehensive Planning Organization (later renamed SANDAG), was created (see Chapter 19). One contemporary example of cross-border planning is the Otay Mesa (San Diego)-Mesa de Otay (Tijuana) cooperative development. In addition to the flood control agreement mentioned above, the Border Environmental Cooperation Agreement (1983) addressed the problem of pollution in the border region. The United States-Mexico Border

Figure 18.7. Aerial view of Rodriguez Dam, east of Tijuana. The arid regional climate causes it to rarely be full. Photo by Larry Ford.

Public Health Association has increased public awareness of water quality problems, including regional flood and wastewater control.

The focus on wastewater led to the construction of an international sewage treatment facility in the Tijuana River Valley just north of the border. In addition, a privately financed sewage treatment plant, called the Bajagua project, has been proposed whose treated water would be sold for industrial uses to local *maquiladoras*. The importance of binational monitoring of water pollution at its source points, including that coming from the *maquiladoras*, is increasingly valued by all government agencies. In April of 2003, the United States and Mexico signed a ten-year environ-

mental agreement in Tijuana, called "Border 2012". It will seek to lower levels of air, water, and soil pollution, and reduce usage of pesticides and hazardous chemicals.

A major economic concern in the border region is the supply of energy for Tijuana and the rest of Baja California, especially in light of California's own recent energy crisis. Not surprisingly, there is a considerable bureaucracy for companies to deal with before they can build new power plants or other facilities. Mexico's Energy Regulatory Commission (CRE) is currently reviewing applications for the construction of liquefied natural gas (LNG) onshore receiving terminals. Marathon Oil, for example, wishes to construct a regional energy center,

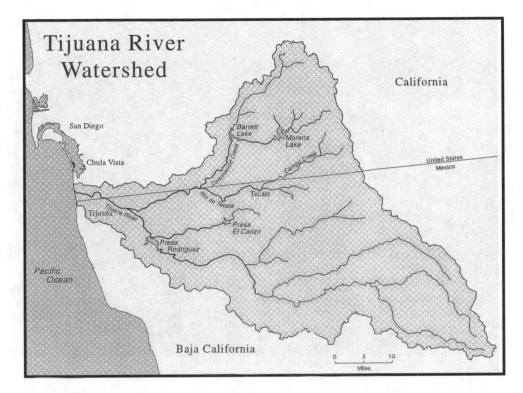

Figure 18.8.

including electrical power, LNG regasification, wastewater treatment, and desalination facilities, on a site south of Tijuana. An El Paso Corp.-Phillips/Conoco partnership has proposed the construction of an LNG terminal in Rosarito Beach, and both Sempra Energy and Shell Oil have plans to construct an onshore site at Costa Azul north of Ensenada.

The CRE's permits will only cover the development and operation of these facilities. Separate environmental permits must be issued by Mexico's federal environmental agency, which will be concerned with land alteration, unique species loss, and effects on the local fishing industry. The land use permits also require local government approval, an essential step for

approval of these projects. Also, the CRE is considering formulating rules for building and operating offshore terminals, partly in response to communities opposed to onshore facilities. All of this will take time; the manner in which these new rules and facilities may impact Tijuana's (or San Diego's) economic future remains to be seen.

Trucking Along the Border

An ongoing border issue is whether Mexican trucks have adequate safety and anti-pollution equipment to be permitted to operate in the U.S. In late November 2002, an Executive Order was signed that removed the much-disputed five-year NAFTA safety-regulation restrictions that

Figure 18.9. The Mexican flood channel along the Rio Tijuana through the center of the city. Photo by P. R. Pryde.

had prohibited Mexican trucks from hauling cargo on U.S. highways beyond the border zones. But in mid-January 2003 the 9th U.S. Circuit Court of Appeals ruled that the U.S. government must complete an environmental impact review before Mexican trucks are allowed beyond an existing 20-mile commercial border zone.

This topic continues to be politically controversial. The basic question is whether Mexican trucks pose a special danger on American roads. Studies by the Department of Transportation have indicated that nearly two in five Mexican Trucks failed basic safety inspections, compared with one in four in the U.S. and one in seven Canadian trucks.

Originally, NAFTA permitted U.S. and Mexican long-haul truckers access to the border states in December 1995, and to highways across the entire North American continent in 2000. Then the U.S., in response to concerns that Mexican trucks might compromise highway safety, imposed a moratorium that restricted carriers to the border zone. Thus, in California, some 4000 short-haul trucks (drayage carriers, sometimes called "mules") continue to convey products for the *maquiladoras* in the 20-mile commercial border zone.

Is safety a significant issue? Currently, failure rates (at California Highway Patrol inspection stations) are about the same for U.S. trucks and Mexican short-haul trucks (about twenty-six percent). The air quality standards for diesel trucks are the same in both nations; however, US regulations are scheduled to become more stringent in 2004 and 2007, while Mexico's standards are not scheduled to change.

The Department of Transportation (DOT) oversees trucking safety regulations, inspection sites, and personnel. In California, safety inspectors, auditors, and investigators are stationed at the Otay and Calexico commercial crossings. In the processing of applications, agents can permit provisional operation, depending on appropriate safety and financial records. At present Mexico does not want U.S. truckers to enter Mexico until there is equal adherence to the trucking agreement. As of mid-January 2003, some 170 trucking firms in Mexico (90 percent from Baja California) had filed applications with the DOT for permits to haul cargo on U.S. highways beyond the commercial border zones. These permits have not been issued. The entry of Mexican carriers on Anglo-American highways is likely to begin slowly and carefully for political, safety, and environmental reasons.

Immigration, Fences, and the Future

While the 1986 Immigration Reform and Control Act (IRCA) granted legal residence to about 2.8 million immigrants, many did not choose to take advantage of the program. Some researchers suggest that the 1986 law was not effective in stopping illegal immigration, due to a lack of enforcement of sanctions against companies that employed undocumented workers.

In August 2001 Vicente Fox, the newly-elected President of Mexico, went to Washington to discuss ways of using NAFTA to increase prosperity on both sides of the border, and increased safety for migrant workers. A proposal resulted that would provide for a guest worker program and a method to give legal resident status to some of the estimated three to five million undocumented Mexicans in the U.S. Many Mexican officials supported that goal. It was hoped that this process could reduce immigrant deaths in border areas and curtail immigrant-smuggling gangs. Mexico wants the U.S. to alter the existing immigration formula for Mexicans because it restricts permanent employment and family-based visas to about 25,000 per year. Agricultural interests suggest that guest worker status for Mexican laborers would benefit farms, workers, and the U.S. economy in general. They would move onto a "legal path," thereby improving relations with Mexico. But due to post-September 2001 security considerations, the U.S. placed the guest worker program on hold.

A partial alternative to the guest worker program is the *matricula consular*, which is a type of identification card issued by 47 Mexican consulates in the U.S. in an attempt to create a valid form of identification for Mexicans working in the States. However, there is considerable controversy as to its efficacy and underlying purpose. Currently, seven local cities, including Oceanside, Del Mar, Escondido, La Mesa, Santee, National City and Poway, recognize the card, but the city of San Diego and San Diego County do not.

Other issues relating to the border and immigration procedures are also controversial. For example, along San Diego's southern border is a seven mile fence, laced with holes through which *pollos* (undocumented immigrants), conducted by *polleros* or "coyotes" (people-smugglers who may charge hundreds of dollars per person) illegally cross into the U.S. In January, 2003, Ann Jarmusch, architecture critic for the San Diego *Union-Tribune,* voted the border fence as among the top 10 "intrusive and bombastic" structures in San Diego. It may get worse; in a controversial plan by the Homeland Security Agency, the present double-fence is proposed to be enlarged to a triple-fence, in an effort to make it impenetrable (Figure 18.10).

It is estimated that the Border Patrol intercepts about a third of the undocumented border crossings. "Operation Gatekeeper" was launched in 1994 to improve this ratio. Illegal migrants apprehended in Imperial Beach (historically the most heavily used entry), declined from over 185,000 in 1994 to about 75,000 in 1996, owing to the increased number of better equipped agents deployed. As a result, the most popular crossing point shifted from the flood-control area and sites near Border Field State Park (adjacent to the ocean), to the rugged terrain and mountains east of Tijuana, and to the deserts in Imperial County and Arizona. In the summer, this shift results in considerable peril, and a number of deaths every year, to migrants unfamiliar with the unforgiving nature of the Colorado Desert. The U.S. Border Patrol has worked to rescue several thousand migrants, and the agency continues to work with Mexico to advise potential immigrants of the dangers associated with illegal entry.

Nevertheless the migration continues. Operation Gatekeeper and other current border–tightening efforts have made it more difficult for the undocumented person to cross, but it has not stopped the flow of workers. Many immigrants take a chance on the services of the smugglers to help them cross the border (often with forged papers), and, if they're lucky, get to their final destination in the U.S.

In 2002 President Fox created an "Institute of Mexicans Abroad," which included a 120 member U.S.-based advisory council made up of 72 Mexicans immigrants plus 28 U.S.-born citizens of Mexican descent residing in 26 different U.S. states. The council also includes representatives from ten U.S.-based Latino organizations, and ten Mexican state governments. Three members are San Diego County residents. The council's purpose is to advise Mexican communities in the U.S. on immigration issues. Mexico is the source of 40 percent (eight out of twenty million) of all immigrants

Figure 18.10. The existing double fence along the Tijuana–San Diego border. It has been proposed to add a third layer of fence. Photo by Barbara Fredrich.

residing in the United States plus, as noted earlier, an estimated three to five million undocumented migrants. Many Mexican families living in the U.S. contribute financially to relatives and friends in Mexico; the current estimate is about $9 billion dollars. The politicians do not overlook that economic reality.

One by-product of heightened vigilance on the borders is an increase in drug arrests. U.S. Border Patrol agents stated that they seized illegal drugs worth $1.3 billion between September 2001 and September 2002. President Fox has vowed to crack down on the drug trade and its powerful leaders, and several significant arrests have been made in the border cities, and underground tunnels discovered. It is hoped on both sides of the border that the current effort to reduce the drug trade and related illegal activities will be successful.

Tijuana is a fascinating city in part because it is so complex. Seemingly a "poor" city, its wealth makes it a magnet for migrants from interior Mexico. It will also remain a magnet for American (and other) tourists, drawn to its shops, restaurants, race track, jai alai palace, cultural center, and other attractions. Commerce and trade, in both directions, will continue in huge proportions. Although the two cities appear quite different at first glance, each looks to the other to fulfill important social and economic needs (Figure 18.11).

Tijuana's social, environmental and economic history has long been closely aligned to that of

Figure 18.11. The different land use patterns on the two sides of the San Diego–Tijuana border are unmistakable. Photo by P. R. Pryde.

Southern California and the U.S. in general. Their histories have witnessed a series of boom and bust periods, through which both nations, and their various states and cities, have survived and expanded. We can expect a similar pattern for the twenty-first century, since the vast majority of Mexico's export income is linked to that of the U.S. Those linkages were well established prior to NAFTA, and as tariffs and restrictions disappear there will have to be what economists call "structural adjustments." Although many of these will be beneficial in the long run, others are likely to be painful, involving economic dislocations and job losses.

Many examples of binational cooperation exist, ranging from official and semi-official programs, to personal contacts. For example, San Diego State University's Institute for Regional Studies of the Californias promotes academic exchange and joint education programs. Faculty from other colleges and schools collaborate with numerous Mexican professionals on research and other projects. Increasing interaction and cooperation between Mexican and U.S. health care authorities is exemplified by the University of California at San Diego's International Surgical Program, which conducts, in conjunction with Mexicans doctor, free plastic surgery clinics. There is increasing collaboration, too, among citizen organizations, such as the binational groups Pro Peninsula and the Environmental Health Coalition.

Within this chaotic urban landscape, a renaissance of artistic expression is occurring, perhaps inspired by the city itself. Local artists, as well as those from Mexico City and elsewhere, are attracted by the unstructured nature of Tijuana and its environment. In addition, they can easily interact and communicate with artists and institutions in southern California. The city-managed arts center, the Casa de Cultura, is dominated by the giant, sandy-colored ball, and is a major focal point for expositions and communication. The roster of Tijuana artists includes poets, playwrights, actors, choreographers, dancers, tenors, painters, designers, photographers, architects, filmmakers and musicians— in short, an enormous number of people trained in a wide array of classical and modern traditions.

The Casa de Cultura contains a 1,100 seat theater, an IMAX movie screen, and the Museo de las Californias. In addition, it is home to a federally funded acting school, the Baja California Orchestra, and the Hispanic American Guitar Center. Internationally renowned artists perform there, and events are advertised in the San Diego *Union-Tribune* and the Los Angeles *Times*. There are also independently organized projects such as inSITE, which features art on both sides of the border and underscores cross-border ties, weekly published cultural reviews, and cultural cafes. Recently, a cadre of artists have catapulted Tijuana's name to Europe and an international sphere. The youthful Nortec Movement is a synthesis of *norteño banda* and contemporary Latin music, inspired by the urban sounds of Tijuana itself.

Like all major cities, Tijuana has a variety of urban problems, but these can be distorted in cross-cultural settings. There are obvious difficulties resulting from having to plan through two city, state, and federal governments, and two different economic systems. City officials on both sides have surmounted institutional barriers to achieve cooperation; for example, direct telephone lines exist between the two mayors' offices. It is acknowledged that mutual dependency necessitates more than ad hoc solutions to specific problems, since a fragmented approach will not resolve difficult cross-boundary challenges. The optimistic spirit and vitality of the people who work and reside in Tijuana, and who are creating a trend of growth, progress, and economic vitality, is an incalculable asset for Tijuana's future.

History and geography have made Tijuana and San Diego inseparable. Despite the artificial barrier of an international border and seven miles of metal and concrete fencing, the two cities are fundamentally connected. Although the two urban regions have enormous social, political and economic differences, they have at least as many characteristics that bind them together. It seems certain that Tijuana and San Diego will continue to grow, change and develop in concert, and that together they will continue to constitute one of the world's most fascinating and dynamic border regions.

References

Arreola, D. D. and J. R. Curtis. *The Mexican Border Cities: Landscape Anatomy and Place Personality,* Tucson: The University of Arizona Press, 1993.

Branscomb, L. W., "Binational Flood Warning System Is Set to Go", *San Diego Union-Tribune,* August 30, 2003, pp. B-1 and B-4.

Brown, C. and S. Mumme. "Applied and Theoretical Aspects of Binational Watershed Councils (*Consejos de Cuencas*) in the U.S.-Mexico Borderlands," *Natural Resources Journal*, Vol. 40 (Fall 2000), pp. 895–929.

Fredrich, B. E. "Tijuana: Modernization of an International Boundary Area," chapter 18 in P. Pryde (ed.), *San D iego: An Introduction to the Region* (3rd ed.). Dubuque: Kendall/Hunt Publishing Company, 1992.

Ganster, Paul. *Tijuana 1964: A Photographic and Historical View*. San Diego: San Diego State University Press, 2000.

Griffin, E. and L. Ford, "Tijuana: Landscape of a Cultural Hybrid," *The Geographical Review*, Vol. 66, No. 4 (1976), pp. 435–447.

Hanson, G. H. "U.S.-Mexico Integration and Regional Economies: Evidence from Border-City Pairs," *Journal of Urban Economics,* Vol. 50 (2001), pp. 259-287.

Herzog, L. *Where North Meets South: Cities, Space, and Politics on the U.S. – Mexico Border.* Austin: Center for Mexican American Studies, University of Texas, 1990.

Iglesias Prieto, N. *Beautiful Flowers of the Maquiladora: Life Histories of Women Workers in Tijuana*. Austin: University of Texas Press, 1997.

Instituto Nacional de Estadistica, Geografia e Informatica (INEGI). *X Censo nacional del poblacion y vivienda, 1990.* Aguascalientes: INEGI, 1991.

Jerrett, M. et al. "Environmental Accounting along the U.S.-Mexican Border," in P. Ganster (ed.), *The U.S.-México Border Environment. Economy and Environment for a Sustainable Border Region: Now and in 2020.* San Diego: San Diego State University Press, 2002.

Michel. S. M. and C. Graizbord. *Urban Rivers in Tecate and Tijuana: Strategies for Sustainable Cities [Los Rios Urbanas de Tecate y Tijuana: Estrategias para ciudades sustentables].* San Diego: Institute for Regional Studies of the Californias, 2002.

Pinera-Ramirez, D., ed. *Historia de Tijuana: Semblanza Central.* Tijuana: Centro de Investigaciones Historicas UNAM-UABC, 1985.

Pryde, P. R., "A Geography of Water Supply and Management in the San Diego-Tijuana Border Zone," in L. Herzog (ed.), *Planning the International Border Metropolis* (Center for U.S.-Mexican Studies Monograph # 19). San Diego: UCSD, 1986, pp. 45–54.

San Diego Association of Governments. *At the Crossroads: California-Baja California.* San Diego: SANDAG, 2002.

Smith, G. "The Decline of the Maquiladora," *Business Week*, April 20, 2002.

Sweedler, A. and O. de Buen. "Overview of the Energy Sector in the Border Region," in *Energy and Environment in the California-Baja California Border Region,* A. Sweedler et al. (eds.). San Diego: Institute for Regional Studies of the Californias, 1995, pp. 13–52.

Internet Connections:

Signature Group Internet Marketing. *Directory of San Diego Businesses* (1994–2003): *http://www.directoryof-sandiegobusinesses.com/directory_of_san_diego_businesses_largest-maquiladoras-in-tijuana.htm*

Gerber, J. and J. Carrillo. "Are Baja California's *Maquiladora* Plants Competitive?" Paper presented for San Diego Dialogue Forum Fronterizo, July 18, 2002: *http://www.cows.org/supplychain/pdf/gerber-carrillo.pdf*

LatinFocus Consensus Forecast, online at: *http://www.latin-focus.com/countries/mexico/mexmaquila.htm*

Lindquist, D. "U.S. Downturn, Strong Peso Bring Worst Year to Baja Plants," *The San Diego Union-Tribune*, March 27, 2002: *http://advancement.sdsu.edu/marcomm/news/clips/Archive/Mar2002/032702/032702baja.html*

The San Diego-Tijuana Interactive Atlas. 2000, online at: *http://cart.sandag.cog.ca.us/sdtij/intro.html*

San Diego-Tijuana International Border Area Planning Atlas/ Atlas de Planeación del Área Fronteriza Internacional Tijuana-San Diego, online at: *http://www-rohan.sdsu.edu/~irsc/atlas/atlashom.html*

Chapter Nineteen

Philip R. Pryde

Accommodating the Twenty-First Century
Planning San Diego's Future

In several of the preceding chapters, a review was presented of some of the main environmental challenges currently facing the county. All of these problems, as well as those of the socioeconomic environment, are the concern of one or more of the various administrative and planning bodies within San Diego county. It is to them that we look for an improved quality of life in the future. Who are these agencies, and how do they function?

Philip R. Pryde is professor emeritus of environmental studies in the Department of Geography at San Diego State University.

Basic Planning Units in the County

Most county residents live within the eighteen incorporated cities (see Chapter 14), but the County of San Diego has the widest jurisdiction of any governmental entity in the region (refer to Table 1.1). Although the county's Board of Supervisors has land use jurisdiction just within the unincorporated area, it is responsible for the entire county (and all its residents) in many areas of operation. These include, to name just a few, the registering of voters, air pollution control, the assessor and coroner's offices, agriculture, public health, and many others (however, the County Board of Education is independent of county government).

The county government is administratively under the guidance of the Board of Supervisors and the Chief Administrative Officer (CAO). The CAO is analogous to the City Manager of the city of San Diego; both are responsible for the day-to-day operations of all the agencies and departments under their jurisdiction. Most of the other cities in the county have a similar type of management structure. The CAO and the various city managers are appointed by the elected legislative body of the jurisdiction involved, that is, the Board of Supervisors in the case of the county and the city councils of the various cities.

The County of San Diego, as noted above, has legislative jurisdiction over the unincorporated portions of the county. Its administrative structure consists of a large number of operational departments, all under the supervision of the CAO (Figure 19.1). Some of the most important of these departments are those supervising public works, health services, planning and land use, agriculture, social services, and housing and community development. In addition, several other important county offices are headed by elected officials, such as the Sheriff, Treasurer, District Attorney, and various judges. Also elected, of course, are the five members of the Board of Supervisors themselves, each of whom is elected from within their own specific district. Districts 1, 3, and 4 represent primarily the urbanized western part of the county, whereas most of the rural and outlying suburban areas are included in districts 2 (east county) and 5 (north county).

All land use planning and environmental analysis for the county is carried out by the Department of Planning and Land Use. It has two main divisions, one dealing with the granting of permits and the regulation of development, and one dealing with long range planning, environmental analysis, and growth management. Other departments of the county, such as Public Works, Parks and Recreation, Agriculture, and Air Pollution, also have important roles to play in environmental planning. Review of environmental impacts associated with development projects is carried out by the Department of Planning and Land Use, frequently based on environmental impact reports prepared by outside consultants.

The Planning Department has a very wide geographic area of responsibility. It is concerned with both the generalized planning of the total unincorporated area of the county, as well as for drawing up specific plans for individual unincorporated communities, such as Ramona, Julian, or Fallbrook. However, it is an advisory body only, and has no power to implement its own plans. It presents its ideas, and those proposed by developers, to the county planning commission, which reviews the plans and gives either a favorable or unfavorable recommendation to the county Board of Supervisors. It is with the Board of Supervisors that legislative authority lies, and the ability to implement these plans. Public hearings before the Board take place in the County Administration Center, an architectural landmark on Pacific Highway (Figure 19.2).

Within the city of San Diego, the procedure is somewhat similar. For long-range planning, there is a city planning department, and additionally an environmental quality division responsible for preparing environmental impact reports. Like the county, the city also has a planning commission which makes recommendations on proposed projects. In the case of the city, the legislative body is the City Council, rather than a Board of Supervisors. Some of the other cities in the county are structured similar to the city of San Diego, but others have slightly different procedures for reviewing and implementing plans.

County of San Diego Organizational Structure

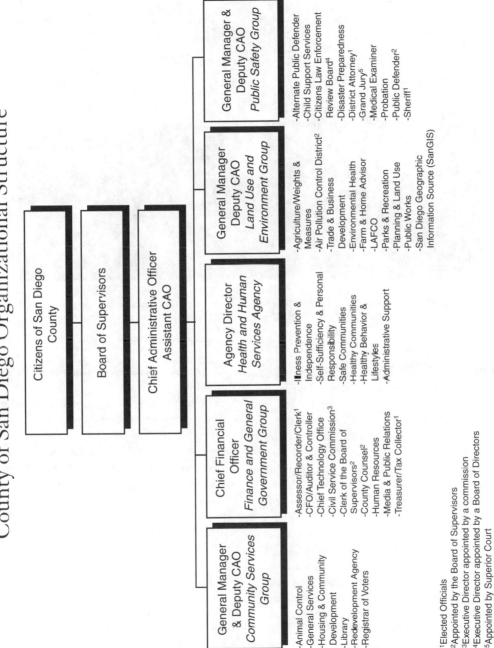

Citizens of San Diego County

Board of Supervisors

Chief Administrative Officer Assistant CAO

General Manager & Deputy CAO
Community Services Group
- Animal Control
- General Services
- Housing & Community Development
- Library
- Redevelopment Agency
- Registrar of Voters

Chief Financial Officer
Finance and General Government Group
- Assessor/Recorder/Clerk[1]
- CFO/Auditor & Controller
- Chief Technology Office
- Civil Service Commission[3]
- Clerk of the Board of Supervisors[2]
- County Counsel[2]
- Human Resources
- Media & Public Relations
- Treasurer/Tax Collector[1]

Agency Director
Health and Human Services Agency
- Illness Prevention & Independence
- Self-Sufficiency & Personal Responsibility
- Safe Communities
- Healthy Communities
- Healthy Behavior & Lifestyles
- Administrative Support

General Manager Deputy CAO
Land Use and Environment Group
- Agriculture/Weights & Measures
- Air Pollution Control District[2]
- Trade & Business Development
- Environmental Health
- Farm & Home Advisor
- LAFCO
- Parks & Recreation
- Planning & Land Use
- Public Works
- San Diego Geographic Information Source (SanGIS)

General Manager & Deputy CAO
Public Safety Group
- Alternate Public Defender
- Child Support Services
- Citizens Law Enforcement Review Board[4]
- Disaster Preparedness
- District Attorney[1]
- Grand Jury[5]
- Medical Examiner
- Probation
- Public Defender[2]
- Sheriff[1]

[1] Elected Officials
[2] Appointed by the Board of Supervisors
[3] Executive Director appointed by a commission
[4] Executive Director appointed by a Board of Directors
[5] Appointed by Superior Court
[6] Appointed by Juvenile Court
[7] Appointed by Five Court Districts

Current as of April 12, 2002

Figure 19.2. The County Administration Center on Pacific Highway has been an attractive architectural feature of San Diego's waterfront since the 1930s. Photo by P. R. Pryde.

State and Federal Planning Agencies

As noted in Chapter 1, the county Board of Supervisors and the various incorporated cities are far from the only agencies whose daily decisions affect the future form of the county. There is also the federal Department of Defense (Navy and Marines), the Department of Interior (Bureau of Land Management, Fish and Wildlife Service, National Park Service), Department of Agriculture (Cleveland National Forest), numerous Indian reservations, the State Park and Recreation Commission (Anza-Borrego, Cuyamaca, Palomar, and other state parks and beaches), the San Diego Unified Port District, the State Department of Transportation, various special districts (such as water districts), the California Coastal Commission, and a variety of other smaller agencies. The various agencies

listed above enjoy differing amounts of planning autonomy.

The agencies with the greatest amount of planning autonomy (other than the Indian reservations) are probably military commands such as the U.S. Navy and Marine Corps. The county has virtually no ability to tell the Navy or Marines what they can or cannot do within their various local installations. The county does not even have air pollution control authority over sources originating on military bases. However, the Navy and Marines have always endeavored to cooperate and coordinate to the maximum extent possible with local planning bodies. In fact, Camp Pendleton has won awards for its conservation activities such as protecting wildlife in the Santa Margarita River estuary, and it has been a leader in recycling water for use on the base. It also represents a permanent open space buffer between San Diego and the sprawling millions to the north in Orange and Los Angeles counties.

A somewhat lesser degree of planning autonomy would be generally the case for other federal agencies such as Cleveland National Forest (under the Department of Agriculture), and the Bureau of Land Management (under the Department of the Interior). Although their plans are drafted locally, they must be approved in Washington DC, and also undergo local public review. The lands in the mountains administered by the Forest Service are very popular recreation areas and are heavily used by local residents, and pressures for different types of recreational and economic uses for these lands make proper planning and land management a difficult task. Cleveland National Forest has its headquarters in Rancho Bernardo in San Diego, and includes three local ranger districts, of which two (Descanso and Palomar) are in San Diego County.

Similarly, state agencies have general planning control over their own land areas. By far the largest state landholder in the county is the Department of Parks and Recreation, which administers one-sixth of the county's land area in Anza-Borrego Desert State Park (the unincorporated community of Borrego Springs is not within the Park, and is serviced by the county government). In neither state-owned areas, such as Anza-Borrego, nor in the federally controlled areas, does the county have any type of veto power over projects that may be planned, but in all cases these agencies coordinate with the county (in some cases they are required to by provisions in such laws as the National Environmental Policy Act) before undertaking any major projects. Similarly, the county would coordinate with them before doing anything that might adversely affect their lands or activities. Such coordination is obviously important because, as illustrated in Table 1.1, over half of the total county land area consists of public lands.

Another state agency to be mentioned here is the California Coastal Commission, discussed in Chapter 7. Although having title to no land, the state commission has strong control over all development within about a half mile of the coast, and a planning responsibility within five miles of it. Local coastal plans are in place for the entire length of the San Diego County coastline.

The Unified Port District also has wide planning and development authority within the San Diego Bay portions of San Diego and the four other South County coastal cities. Until 2003, it operated Lindbergh Field, and has legal title to the tidelands of San Diego Bay. To further confuse the picture along the coast, the Army Corps of Engineers must issue permits for any filling that is proposed in wetlands (called "Section 404 permits"), and state and federal water quality control agencies keep close watch over any effluents that are discharged (Chapter 16). Obviously, close coordination is essential between all these agencies and the local community in which a proposed coastal development is to occur.

Another planning device that is used in the county is called a *joint powers authority* (JPA). This is a type of legally created body that unites two or more local governmental jurisdictions in a common ("joint") planning or administrative effort, such as a regional park or transportation system. One example would be the San Dieguito River Park JPA, which brings together the cities of San Diego, Escondido, Poway, Solana Beach and Del Mar, and the county of San Diego, in a joint effort to plan and manage a new 55-mile linear open space park along the entire length of the San Dieguito River (Chapter 17). The San Diego Association of Governments (discussed below) would be another example, and is the most important JPA in the region.

Special Districts

Most of those who live in the eighteen incorporated cities of the county have little familiarity with, or need for, special districts. The types of services that the special districts perform in the rural areas are usually provided by the urban dwellers' city governments. For those who live in the countryside, however, many of their basic needs are provided by these special districts. The districts provide such functions as fire protection, water supply, waste disposal, street maintenances, and even cemeteries. In all there are over a dozen different types of districts, and a total of 112 such special districts within the county (Table 19.1).

Who decides whether special districts should be formed? The body responsible for this is the Local Agency Formation Commission, or LAFCO for short. The seven member Commission holds hearings on all proposals for incorporating new districts, and has a staff which makes independent recommendations on such proposals. Without the approval of LAFCO, new districts (or annexations to existing ones) cannot be brought into existence, nor can existing districts be terminated.

Perhaps the most important function of LAFCO is to decide on the incorporation of new cities. At present San Diego County has only eighteen incorporated cities, as compared to about eighty in Los Angeles County. Many studies have cautioned about the problems that can result from having too many units of local government, too many potentially self-centered suburbs crowded around a central city, too much fragmentation in planning and decision making. Before a new city is approved, it should be able to be self-supporting in terms of its revenue base and physical size, and it should have logical geographic boundaries. It is LAFCO's responsibility to be certain these conditions are met. Since 1986, no new cities have been created,

TABLE 19.1. Special Districts in San Diego County

Type of District*	Number of Districts*
Cemetary	4
Community College/Education*	6
Fire	23
Flood Control	2
Hospital/Paramedic	6
Landscaping	2
Harbor maintenance	1
Park and Recreation	6
Road Maintenance	4
San Diego County Water Authority	1
Sewer	17
Sewer and Water	12
Soil Conservation	3
Unified Port District	1
Water	22
Other	2
Total	112

*Certain types of districts were not enumerated by the cited source, such as school districts and Joint Powers Authorities.

Source: Adapted from San Diego Local Agency Formation Commission, 2000.

and there have been only ten new ones established since 1912. Many observers believe that this "go slow" approach to suburb proliferation has been a healthy attribute of San Diego County, and represents a tendency that should be followed in the future.

San Diego Association of Governments (SANDAG)

Over the past three decades, local planning efforts have undergone two significant trends. The first is that a larger role is being played by the federal and state governments. The second is a realization that planning, in order to be effective, must often be done on a broader geographical scale than has usually occurred in the past.

The federal government feels it should have some say in how local planning is conducted because it disburses such large amounts of funds to local agencies. The same is true at the state level. In California, the state now supports regional coastal commissions, plans power plant siting, provides much of our water, operates state parks, requires environmental impact statements on all significant projects, and oversees local air and water quality, to name just a few of its activities in the sphere of local planning and administration. Both the state and the federal governments have encouraged the trend towards regional planning, as it has become clearer that many pressing problems (such as transportation, housing, air pollution, and numerous others) can only be adequately handled on a regional basis.

Regional planning in San Diego County (for the county as a whole) used to be difficult, for the several incorporated cities had most of the population of the county, but the unincorporated "backcountry" took most of the land area. The county government had little planning jurisdiction inside the incorporated cities, and the cities had essentially none in the unincorporated areas.

To resolve this problem, in 1966 a "council of governments" called the Comprehensive Planning Organization (CPO) was formed. In 1980, its name was changed to the San Diego Association of Governments, or SANDAG. It is made up of representatives of each of the incorporated cities in the county (usually their mayor or a city council member), and the county of San Diego is also a member. These representatives make up SANDAG's Board of Directors, the organization's decision-making body. The California Department of Trans-

portation (CALTRANS), the County Water Authority, the Metropolitan and North County Transit Development Boards, the Port District, and Representative from Baja California serve as advisory members. In addition, SANDAG has a professional planning staff which prepares regional plans and information reports, and makes recommendations to the Board (Figure 19.3).

SANDAG's main areas of concern are problems that are intrinsically regional in nature. These include transportation, open space, energy, housing, regional growth forecasts, and water, sewage and flood control facilities. SANDAG, working closely with the eighteen cities in the county, has prepared regional plans concerning each of the problem areas listed above, and updates them periodically. These reports are available to the public.

In an effort to coordinate the planning efforts of its member jurisdictions, SANDAG is preparing a "Regional Comprehensive Plan." A preliminary draft is scheduled to appear late in 2003.

In addition to drawing up plans, SANDAG has one other important function. The federal government requires that a regional council-of-governments or planning body, such as SANDAG, review and comment on all local applications for federal funds, to be sure that such proposed projects are consistent with regional goals and plans. This type of project review is another important function of SANDAG, one that is mandatory for all large metropolitan areas in the United States.

SANDAG also operates a separate non-profit corporation called "SourcePoint," which for a fee provides a wide range of statistical and informational services to both public and private customers. SourcePoint has its own board of directors.

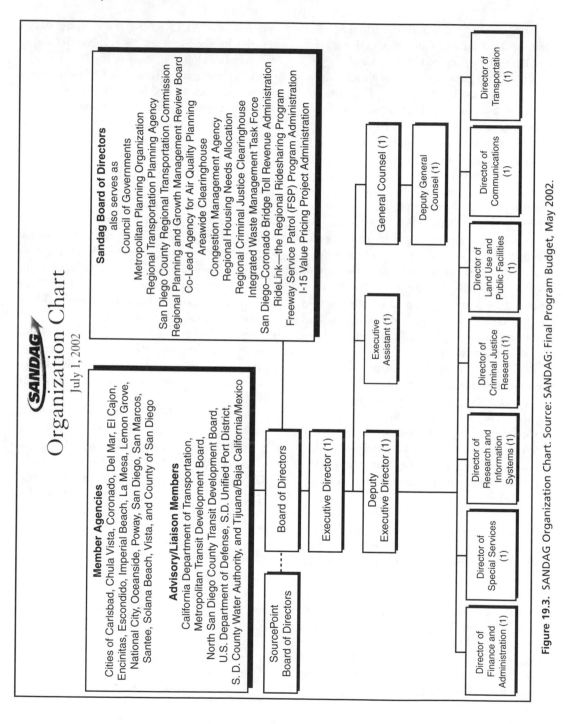

Figure 19.3. SANDAG Organization Chart. Source: SANDAG: Final Program Budget, May 2002.

Growth and the Future of the County

All major urban areas have their own unique set of problems, some more severe in nature than others. San Diego is generally viewed as one of the more desirable urban areas in which to live, one with relatively few major difficulties. While it is true that the problems of San Diego are small compared to those of New York, St. Louis, Detroit, or even Los Angeles, it is also true that San Diego has several characteristics that are less than perfect. The latter are for the most part challenges that can be handled adequately if proper planning is carried out now and in the future. Let's look at a few of the potential pitfalls confronting our region.

The controversial topic of controlling regional growth rates was discussed in Chapter 5. From the standpoint of long-range planning, this is clearly the most important issue facing the county, because all other social and environmental issues are affected by it. Many people would like to leave the Los Angeles area, presumably because that region has become overpopulated, overautomobiled, and overpolluted. There is wide agreement that San Diego cannot allow "Losangelesation" to happen here. The urban form of San Diego County is presently quite different from the urban form found in the Los Angeles Basin, and many local residents would like to preserve that distinction. Those attributes that are distinct and desirable in the San Diego region can be maintained, but only if San Diegans work to achieve this. Chapter 5 outlined the approaches that have been adopted by the city and the county to manage contemporary growth. It was noted that these plans attempt to preserve open space, and to direct growth to areas where it already exists. If they are successful, the region in the year 2020 need not look less attractive than it does today.

But what of the post-2020 period? What will the region be like in 2040, or 2060? Forecasts suggest that the year 2040 population could be twice what it is today. What are the implications of this? Will twice as many cars mean twice as much air pollution? Will we need twice as many freeways, or will there be two hour commutes for everyone driving to work? Will beaches still be enjoyable if twenty people want to spread their blankets where today only ten do? Where will twice as many off-road vehicles, surfers, campers, or joggers go? Will twice as many residents mean higher relative housing costs? How will we treat two times as much wastewater? Will Tijuana's population be 3,000,000 then, and what will that imply? What will be happening in southern Orange and Riverside counties in the year 2040?

Other aspects of San Diego's quality of life are also tied into regional planning, such as the very basic considerations of housing and jobs. How should low income housing be provided? How should it be distributed? Should wealthy communities have the right to zone their land in such a way as to preclude low-income housing? Adequate housing for all thus becomes a topic also requiring a regional planning approach.

To alleviate unemployment, should we entice new industry into the area? But if we do, will the new industry hire local unemployed persons, or will it bring in its own labor force? Will it increase population, and require new services, thereby increasing local taxes? Will new industry serve as a catalyst to develop large areas of surrounding land, such as Otay Mesa, and if so is this desirable? Many of these questions do not have ready answers, and the planners' task to find reasonable answers to them is not an enviable one. It can be seen that all of the above considerations are highly interrelated, and this doesn't make their resolution any easier. They are not unanswerable, but neither are they simple. All this illustrates why comprehensive planning, carried out on a regional basis, is essential in large metropolitan areas. And it goes without saying that the input of an informed public is also essential in the process.

Cross-border Regional Planning with Tijuana

It has been noted that the southern boundary of the San Diego region is a very misleading one. We often draw maps that show "nothing" south of the San Diego County–Mexican border, when in fact well over a million people live within a few miles of it. Whether we think about it or not, we really live in one-half of a binodal region—the greater San Diego–Tijuana metropolitan region. Over 10 million people cross the border locally each month. It is impossible to ignore our neighbors to the south when we consider regional planning, just as it is impossible for them to ignore us.

Cross-border regional planning has been already discussed in Chapter 18, so it will merely be summarized here. Until the creation of CPO in 1966, there was very little formal contact. Today, through the International Boundary and Water Commission, through Baja California's representation on SANDAG, through direct connections between the mayor's offices in the two cities, and through various quasi-official and personal contacts, we are able to jointly address those problems that affect both sides of the border. Examples would include transportation, water supply, air quality, visitation and immigration procedures, flood and waste water control, cultural contacts, and many others. As the two cities increase in size, such cooperative planning will become all the more essential. A 'Committee on Binational Regional Opportunities' (COBRO) has been established to review and make recommendations on SANDAG's binational programs.

One major example of contemporary cross-border planning is Otay Mesa. Located on both sides of the international border, about seven miles inland from the ocean, Otay Mesa (in San Diego) and Mesa de Otay (in Tijuana) are viewed by both countries as a logical focus of cooperative planning. Otay Mesa's chief attraction is its large flat expanse of land now ready for development (Figure 19.4). Other attractions include its highway access to downtown San Diego and Tijuana and to the second border crossing, three airports, and a large potential labor force. The new jobs created would be in communities where they are most needed. The new border crossing conveniently connects Otay Mesa to Tijuana's Mesa de Otay, where over 1000 acres of industrial park are already in operation. Many of these are *"maquiladoras"*, or twin plants (see Chapter 18).

Otay Mesa is a logical candidate for careful joint Mexican-American planning, but it is not the only one. The coastal Border area, the Tijuana River valley, and eventually probably also the Tecate area will also require diligent joint efforts to resolve present or potential problems. There is also consideration being given to building a joint U.S.-Mexican pipeline from the Imperial Valley to convey Colorado River water to the two metropolitan regions, but in 2003 this was only a "study concept". The degree and sophistication of San Diego–Tijuana joint planning efforts must and undoubtedly will increase in the future. Chapter 18, which discusses our "twin" city in more detail, noted that in 2003 a ten-year plan to address health and environmental problems in the cross-border region was released, a good start in this direction.

San Diego is a region of sunshine, ocean beaches, museums, golf courses, zoos, mountains, theaters, resorts, deserts, and opportunities. It is also a region of beach closures, high prices, mushrooming population, inadequate

Figure 19.4. Tijuana's Mesa de Otay. New housing is in the foreground; an industrial area that includes *maquiladoras* plants is in the background. Photo by B. Fredrich.

public transportation, and amenities threatened with being overrun by the overly enthusiastic human response to their bounty and attractiveness. The county can be very accurately described as being at a crossroads, at a time for decision, as to the form it will take in the future. The era of the small city by the bay, surrounded by discrete, quaint, semirural towns, is past. The city has mushroomed, and the suburbs have been fused together by an ever-expanding freeway binder. But the Los Angeles future is not the only possible future. With careful planning there can be a San Diego future, preserving what we cherish most in our region, improving what is yet imperfect, while retaining a healthy blend of the best that both urban and rural landscapes have to offer. The choice is still before us, but only for a little while.

References

Appleyard, D. and K. Lynch. *Temporary Paradise? A Look at the Special Landscape of the San Diego Region.* (Report to the City of San Diego), dated September 1974.

City of San Diego. *General Plan and Progress Guide.* Most recent revision.

City of San Diego. *What is Planning? A guide to Planning in the City of San Diego.* San Diego: City Planning Department, August 2001.

County of San Diego. *San Diego County General Plan.* Most recent revision.

Dibble, Sandra, "10-Year Plan Unveiled to Face Border Issues", *San Diego Union-Tribune,* April 5, 2003, pp. B1 and B7.

Local Agency Formation Commission. *Profiles of Special Districts in San Diego County.* San Diego: LAFCo, 2000.

McDonald Jeff, "Fires Renew Calls to Merge Hodgepodge of Agencies", *San Diego Union-Tribune,* November 30, 2003, pp. A1 and A16.

Michel, Suzanne, ed. *The U.S.-Mexican Border Environment: Binational Water Management Planning.* San Diego: San Diego State University Press, 2003.

Nielsen, D. C. and P. R. Pryde, "Providing for Rural Land in San Diego County", *Urban Land,* Vol. 39, No. 10 (November 1980), pp. 11–17.

San Diego Association of Governments. *At the Crossroads: California—Baja California.* San Diego: SANDAG, 2002.

San Diego Association of Governments. *Fact Sheet: Cross Border Planning in the San Diego-Tijuana Region.* San Diego: SANDAG, 2002.

San Diego Association of Governments. *SANDAG 2020 Regional Transportation Plan.* San Diego: SANDAG, April 2000.

Internet Connections:

City of San Diego: *www.sannet.gov*

County of San Diego: *www.co.san-diego.ca.us/*

SANDAG: *www.sandag.org*

Southwest Center for Environmental Research and Policy: *www.scerp.org*

Unified Port District: *www.portofsandiego.org*

U.S.-Mexico Environmental Program: *www.epa.gov/usmexicoborder*

Epilogue

It occurred to the author, as he reviewed the emerging draft of the new edition, that there seemed to be some element that was missing. Although it contained a wealth of facts, history, data, maps, pictures, interpretations, and conclusions, still it lacked something that its inherent style perhaps precluded. What it seemed to lack was the lyrical soul of the poet.

If we have been successful, the foregoing chapters contain an entertaining and well-crafted historical geography. Yet there is much of the real San Diego region, much of the beauty and charm of the region, that cannot be encompassed in this necessarily descriptive format. There are images of the San Diego region, both timeless ones and temporal ones, that require an artist's touch, but which no regional work on San Diego should close without recalling.

Before closing the cover, rest your eyes for a moment and ask your mind to picture: The winter's first snow crowning Cuyamaca peak. The first time you saw a gray whale spout. An oak leaf filled mortero. The surf cascading along La Jolla's shores. Anza-Borrego Desert in all its April glory. The smell of seafood cooking as you stroll past the waterfront. Horses parading in the infield at Del Mar. The adobe walls of an old mission or homestead. Your first glimpse of a bighorn sheep, or a golden eagle overhead. The ranunculus fields of Carlsbad in full bloom. Gulls following a homeward fishing boat at sunset. Apple pie a la mode in Julian. A child staring at the silent mystery of an anemone. A misty fog around the old Cabrillo lighthouse. Pastel alpenglow on desert hillsides. Giant eucalyptus trees in Balboa Park against a clear blue sky.

These are images of not just the romantic San Diego, but also of the real San Diego, for they are images of the past and present that lend to the region its distinctive appeal. Few people know of these images before they arrive here. The curious, persistent, or lucky find them, and none that find them forget them. Those that do are much the richer, and possess some true measure of the enduring appeal of the San Diego region.

Phil Pryde, May 2003

Index